THE POPE'S ARMADA

THE POPE'S ARMADA

GORDON URQUHART

BANTAM PRESS

LONDON · NEW YORK · TORONTO · SYDNEY · AUCKLAND

To E.F. and S.P.

TRANSWORLD PUBLISHERS LTD
61–63 Uxbridge Road, London W5 5SA

TRANSWORLD PUBLISHERS (AUSTRALIA) PTY LTD
15–25 Helles Avenue, Moorebank, NSW 2170

TRANSWORLD PUBLISHERS (NZ) LTD
3 William Pickering Drive, Albany, Auckland

Published 1995 by Bantam Press
a division of Transworld Publishers Ltd

Neocatechumenate texts quoted from are published by
Centro Neocatecumenale, Servo di Jahve in San Salvatore, Rome

A catalogue record for this book is available from the British Library

0593 033884

Typeset in 11/13pt Bembo by Kestrel Data, Exeter, Devon.
Printed in Great Britain by
Mackays of Chatham plc, Chatham, Kent.

Contents

1

THE SPIRITUAL MARKETPLACE

THE ABBEY CHURCH OF ST BENEDICT, SET AMONG THE LEAFY COMMONS
of Ealing in West London, is the epitome of middle-class respectability and calm. Run by Benedictine monks, the order of England's
primate Cardinal Hume, it is an unlikely flashpoint for a conflict
which is convulsing the Roman Catholic Church worldwide. Yet
this suburban parish has been torn apart by the presence of one
of the powerful new traditionalist movements in the Church
which, in the past ten years, have fanned out globally from southern
Europe and are now established in virtually every country in the
world. Enjoying patronage at the highest levels, principally that of
Pope John Paul II himself, they have also encountered bitter
opposition from cardinals, bishops and laity, and have been branded
fundamentalist sects.

In 1980, at the age of eighteen, Rita was in her first year of a degree
course in biochemistry with a promising career ahead of her.
Attractive and independent, she was one of five children in a closely
knit middle-class family in Ealing Abbey parish. Back home during
the vacations, she became involved with the Neocatechumenate
movement. Hers is the classic story of a recruit to a sect.

As soon as Rita joined Neocatechumenate (NC), her family
noticed a change. Her mother recalls: 'All she talked about at home
was the movement. We had constant arguments about it. Bit by
bit she transferred her affections to Neocatechumenate – they
became her new family.' Eventually, as Rita acquired a new set of

priorities, meaningful communication with her family broke down completely. This was particularly difficult for Rita's father, who is not a Catholic and had enjoyed a close relationship with his daughter.

Now aged thirty, Rita is trapped in an unhappy relationship with a man almost twice her age. She has long since abandoned a successful career with a pharmaceutical company to dedicate herself to the NC ideal of bearing children. Rita has three, including a four-year-old autistic son. The family lives an impoverished existence in a council house, and her husband's job as an unskilled worker is constantly under threat.

After several years in the movement, at the age of twenty-six she had informed her parents that she was to marry a man from her 'community' – one of the subgroups of around forty members into which NC divides its followers in a parish. Rita's mother is convinced that the marriage to an NC leader twice Rita's age was arranged; and reports on NC practices confirm that marriages are indeed arranged – or at least fostered – within NC communities.

Although Rita's parents were paying for the wedding, they had no say in the preparations. They were presented with a guest-list of over 200 names, mostly unknown to them. The majority were NC members from outside the parish.

But there were more surprises in store. Rita's brother Robert recalls: 'I'd never seen anything quite like it. At the start of the ceremony, we were welcomed to our own parish by the Neo-catechumenate leader, who wasn't even a parish member. The guests were separated into two quite distinct groups – the NC and the non-NC. The NC, of course, were much the larger group.' Other members of the parish were bewildered by the nuptial mass, which lasted two and a half hours, and described it as a 'frenzied pop concert', featuring the hypnotic Spanish rhythms of NC songs, all of which are composed by the movement's founder, Kiko Arguello.

For the next few years, relations between Rita and her family were strained. This was aggravated by her attempts to 'evangelize' their neighbours, including a Jewish family who were offended by Rita's aggressive proselytizing – a characteristic of NC. Her mother had begun to resign herself to the situation when, in mid-1993, she visited Rita's home to find that she had gone, taking the children with her. Later she received a phone call from Rita telling her that her marriage was intolerable, and begging to be allowed to come home with the children.

Rita and the children stayed for eight weeks, during which time she had no contact with her husband. But this period ended as mysteriously and abruptly as it had begun, leaving relations between Rita and her family more tense than ever. One evening she disappeared from the house at about 6.30, returning when the rest of the family were asleep. The next day she had been due to take out a court order giving her sole custody of the children, fearing that their father, who is not English, might try to take them out of the country. Instead, she announced at breakfast that she and the children were returning to her husband.

To her parents' amazement and horror, one of the conditions of the reconciliation was that neither Rita nor the children should have any more contact with her family – including Rita's brothers and sisters and their children. This was in spite of the fact that they had played no role in precipitating the split, which had been entirely Rita's decision. Now Rita's mother can only see her grandchildren in secret; and she finds it particularly hard to square the ruthlessness of her son-in-law with his role as an NC leader who spends much time evangelizing in the parish. An exile from her own parish – 'It brings back too many unhappy memories' – she has despaired of a solution to the divisions NC has caused in her family, and carries an air of permanent sadness. 'I don't think Rita will ever leave now.'

Following Rita's wedding, her mother and a group of concerned members of the parish tried to penetrate the secrecy surrounding the organization that had been quietly growing in their midst over the previous ten years. They were amazed by what they found. Far from being a fringe group, NC was headed by the parish priest at that time, Father Michael Hopley, himself a committed member of the movement. Disturbing, too, was the fact that it not only held secret meetings, but also duplicated the most important church services in secret, though celebrated by the parish priest. This suggested a two-tier system within the parish. For ten years, however, these activities had been hidden so successfully that not even the lay members of the Parish in Council, the co-ordinating body within Ealing Abbey parish, had heard of Neocatechumenate. Why all the secrecy? Enquiries were made to the parish priest, the abbot – the ultimate authority at Ealing Abbey – and to Cardinal Hume himself on the structural aspects of NC, its hierarchy and its status as a Catholic organization, but drew no satisfactory response.

In fact, every autumn since it had set up in the parish NC had been holding public introductory courses with the purpose of recruiting new members. These were announced both from the pulpit and in print, but NC was never mentioned by name. A parish bulletin for Sunday, 26 October 1986 lists among activities for the week: 'Who Is God for You? At 8.15 in the parish hall.' No movement or speaker is identified. When parish members attended this course of fifteen evenings spread over an eight-week period they found that, far from having their questions answered, their perplexity increased. The open and positive mood which had transformed the Catholic Church in the early sixties as a result of the reforms of Pope John XXIII and his Second Vatican Council had led to a new emphasis on the love of God. Ealing Abbey parishioners were surprised, therefore, to find in NC teaching, or 'catechesis', an emphasis on sin redolent of the pre-Council era, couched in strikingly harsh terms. But, when it came to gleaning information on the inner workings of the movement, the parishioners drew a blank: in line with standard NC practice, they were told that no questions were allowed at meetings. Attend the fifteen evenings, they were told, and all your queries will be answered.

Frustrated in this line of enquiry, they pressurized the parish priest and the abbot into calling an extraordinary meeting of the Parish in Council to discuss the growing division in their midst. A record turnout of over 200 parishioners indicated the widespread unease over the presence of an élitist and secretive body at the heart of their community. They were concerned that the parish priest now spent most of his time on 'his' community, making the rest of the parish feel like second-class citizens.

The core opposition group had drawn up a list of twenty-five tough questions, reflecting their growing conviction that, though the movement was apparently operating in the parish with the approval of the competent ecclesiastical authorities, its methods were those of a sect. Among the more serious of the charges were: the reported use of 'brainwashing' techniques on members; alleged group confession sessions; sweeping claims made for the movement, which describes itself as 'the Way'; and the wall of secrecy surrounding its hierarchy, its finances and the lengthy training given to recruits. The meeting allowed these misgivings to be aired in group discussions with NC members, but no satisfactory answers were obtained. Indeed, it is unlikely that NC members themselves, at parish level, had answers; in common with many sects, information is strictly graded according to degree of membership.

Although NC members in Ealing declined, or were unable, to enter into discussion on points of detail, they did have a catch-all answer for their critics – the unqualified support for their movement at the highest levels of church authority: from the auxiliary bishop of Westminster diocese responsible for their area, at that time Bishop Mahon; but, more important, from Pope John Paul II himself. To prove it, they had a privately printed book of his many encouraging speeches given to NC communities present in parishes of his own diocese of Rome. His tone in these speeches is uncompromisingly enthusiastic:

> This is how I see the genesis of Neocatechumenate, of its Way: someone wondered . . . where the strength of the early Church came from, and where the weakness of today's numerically much larger Church comes from. I believe that he found the answer in the Catechumenate, in this Way . . . in your communities you can really see how from Baptism grow all the fruits of the Holy Spirit, all the charisms of the Holy Spirit, all the vocations, all the authenticity of Christian life in marriage, in the priesthood, in the various professions, in the world, ultimately in the world.

Faced with the contradiction between the Pope's words and what they themselves had experienced, the Ealing Abbey parishioners who opposed NC concluded that either the Pope did not know what they knew or in some way he had been deceived. The alternative – that he knew and approved – was unthinkable.

'I have been able to recognize', the Pope declared in 1985, 'the great and promising flowering of ecclesial movements and I have singled them out as a cause for a hope in the entire Church and for all mankind.' Neocatechumenate is just one of the strangely named movements which have experienced rapid expansion within the Catholic Church in the past thirty years, boosted by the Pope's enthusiastic support. Two others have also been especially favoured: Communion and Liberation (CL) and Focolare, both Italian in origin. They are three of the largest – and certainly the most wealthy and powerful – in a raft of morally, theologically and politically right-wing organizations claiming a total membership of thirty million Catholics worldwide, all of whom received their greatest boost in the 1980s with the unqualified backing of Pope John Paul. Alarmingly, they look set to outstrip the moderate wing of the Catholic Church in numbers and have long since overtaken it in terms of the power they wield in the Church.

Although they all began in southern Europe and still have their administrative bases in Italy, the movements today are a worldwide force. Focolare was launched in the northern Italian town of Trento in 1943, at the height of the Allied bombardments, by a primary-school teacher, Chiara Lubich, then twenty-five. It now exists in 1,500 dioceses in over 180 countries and has a following of several million 'adherents' with 80,000 core members who have made vows, promises or other forms of commitment. The movement's clarion-call to universal love and the unity of all mankind is expressed in a rigid hierarchy centred around the foundress, now aged seventy-five. Her personality cult is expressed in the blind obedience she commands from members, even though for nearly two years from 1992 to 1994 she lived in seclusion in Switzerland, suffering from a mysterious illness. Needless to say, rumours were rife that she might even be dead. In 1995 she re-emerged in public life.

Communion and Liberation emerged in Italy in the early 1970s as a conservative student backlash to the student unrest of the 1960s, under the leadership of a diminutive Milanese priest, Don Giussani. For the past twenty years the highest-profile Catholic movement in Italy, CL's membership has been variously dubbed 'Wojtyla's lackeys', 'Wojtyla's monks', 'Samurai of Christ' and 'Stalinists of God' for their aggressive and fundamentalist promotion of traditional Catholic values and beliefs, and their devotion to the Pope. The movement has caused havoc within the Italian Church and politics, and has a vast network of secular operations throughout the country, including a number of influential publications and, until recently, its own political wing, the Popular Movement, regarded by many as a distinct Catholic party. CL is now present in eighteen other countries. Although CL's world vision is closest to that of the Pope, and this sympathy was reflected in his enthusiastic support in the early eighties, its transgressive antics in ecclesiastical and political affairs – including the equivocal involvement of a number of its public figures in the Italian bribes scandals of recent years – has led the Vatican to distance itself somewhat in the 1990s.

Neocatechumenate was launched in the shanty town of Palomeras Altas on the outskirts of Madrid in 1964 by a Spanish artist, Kiko Arguello, later joined by Carmen Hernandez, a former nun. Having built a community among gypsies and vagrants in the shanty town, Arguello and Hernandez decided to transfer the tough recruitment techniques they had developed into normal parishes which they believed were equally in need of radical conversion.

In the early Christian church, baptism would be preceded by stages of initiation and teaching known as the catechumenate. Arguello believes that baptized Christians today are pagan in all but name and therefore need to experience a similar initiation process, although, in their case, *after* baptism. Hence the neo-, or new, catechumenate was born. The one major difference is that, whereas the early Christian catechumenate lasted three years, Arguello's version lasts more than twenty. This series of arcane rites, 'passages' and increasing levels of commitment to the movement is only gradually revealed to initiates, who are not permitted to ask questions about what lies ahead and may not reveal details of 'the Way', even to other members at lower levels than themselves.

After making a strategic move to Rome in 1968, just four years after its foundation, the movement rapidly spread throughout the parishes of the Rome diocese and has enjoyed a lightning global expansion. It is now present in 600 dioceses, with 10,000 communities in 3,000 parishes.[1] Current membership is estimated to be around a million. Sinister in its methods, Neocatechumenate is also considered by a number of Catholic theologians to be heretical in its teaching on central Catholic doctrines; yet, paradoxically, it is the closest of the new movements to the theologically traditionalist Pope. NC's founders, Kiko Arguello and Carmen Hernandez, are said to be 'at home' in the papal household, breakfasting and lunching with the Pope, coming and going at will.

With their disparate origins, distinctive jargon and exclusivity, at

---

[1] Figures for 1991, which may be confidently assumed to have increased by at least a third.

7

first sight these movements could appear to have little in common. On closer inspection, they can be seen to share many more traits than their common conservatism. It is characteristic of these movements, for instance – as it was for their forerunner, the secretive Spanish organization Opus Dei – to reject all definitions or descriptions made of them by others, even church authorities. They are more eager to say what they are *not* than what they *are*. Their refusal to be pigeonholed is an expression of their sense of being called to a unique mission. Thus they are not associations nor are they religious orders. Despite the fact that they are all heavily clericalized, they cling adamantly to their lay status. Like many classic protestant sects, each claims to be returning to the authentic faith of the first Christians: at one time, Focolare used of itself the equivocal term 'the first Christians of the twentieth century'. The movements also promote themselves as the authentic expression of the Second Vatican Council.

Pope John Paul has heartily endorsed this view: 'The great flowering of these movements and the manifestations of ecclesial energy and vitality that characterize them can certainly be considered one of the most beautiful fruits of the vast and deep spiritual renewal promoted by the last Council.' He ought to know; as a young bishop and theologian, he had been involved in that momentous turning-point in the life of the Catholic Church. This great gathering of the world's Catholic bishops, called together by the saintly Pope John XXIII, had renounced the static juridical and hierarchical concept of the post-tridentine Catholic Church and replaced it with the dynamic one of the People of God, giving much greater importance to the laity. Its major achievement, however, was to break down the dualism that had characterized Catholicism.

Pope John had hinted at this when he had stated that his intention in calling the Council was to throw open the windows of the Church. The prevailing clerical mentality had opposed Church to World, Sacred to Secular, Soul to Body. The Catholic Church was a fortress of truth, possessing all the answers, which she dispensed with divine authority. She had nothing to learn from the world. The pre-conciliar Church was characterized by triumphalism, expressed in the monarchical pomp and panoply of the papal court. The world and human activity had been seen, if not exactly as evil, at least as morally neutral unless they were given a specifically religious content by the Church or its representatives. Hence, before the Council, specifically religious ceremonies of 'consecration', or blessing, had expressed the need to draw the secular sphere into that of the sacred. The Council Fathers, on the other hand, proclaimed that the World and human activity were good in themselves; they did not need to be 'consecrated'. Catholics could therefore work in harmony with others. Amongst the many upheavals of the post-conciliar period, this change of mentality was probably one of the greatest.

It is interesting that, like Opus Dei, the movements which pre-dated that event – Focolare, and Communion and Liberation – never saw fit to re-examine or adjust themselves in the light of the Council despite the fact that every other mainstream body in the Church felt the need to do so. Far from ascribing value to 'the world', they reject the human sphere as utterly worthless, condemning contemporary society in the most virulent of terms. Members are encouraged to live out every aspect of their lives within the protective confines of the movement, as all external influences are seen as a source of contamination. There can be no dialogue with outsiders on central matters of belief as each of the movements believes itself to be in possession of the fullness of truth and therefore only in a position to teach, not to learn. They have all the answers not only in the spiritual realm, but in the secular sphere as well. Only an explicitly religious presence, their own presence, can give value to secular affairs. But, as the emphasis is on the group rather than on the individual, this 'consecration' of human affairs has to take place within the ambit of the movement.

The result is a withdrawal from the world. Each movement is building totally self-contained societies, even to the extent of setting up businesses and whole villages where they can create uncontaminated environments – examples to the world of how Christianity in a pure and untrammelled form is the only solution to all its ills. Thus they have revived a form of triumphalism more far-reaching than the pre-conciliar Church ever dreamed of: in their private utopias they have already solved the problems of the world. This concept of a religious solution to all issues – 'integrism' as it is known in continental Europe – is frequently attacked by opponents of the movements both within and outside the Church.

Of course, this extreme Church–World dualism is as old as Christianity itself, and many sects who have espoused it have set up 'intentional communities' like those the movements are creating now. Through rigorous indoctrination, members come to see every aspect of their lives and the world through the eyes of the movement. This means that even among Catholics there are ways of interpreting the world, by means of specific 'languages' and cultures, which are totally incompatible with one another.

But one of their most worrying characteristics is the devaluing of reason. Even in the doctrinaire pre-conciliar period, the Church taught that reason and faith were compatible. Faith could not contradict reason. The movements, on the other hand, play down the role of reason. They are militantly anti-intellectual – even CL, which recruits mainly amongst students. Members must entrust themselves wholly to the structures and practices of the movement. The primacy of experience over reason is emphasized. Recruits are encouraged to accept and practise what the movement teaches. Understanding, they are told, will follow.

As each envisages a messianic role for itself, it follows that the greater part of the movements' considerable resources and energies is poured into militant missionary activities. If these proselytizing ambitions were limited to the ecclesiastical field, the new movements would be of little more than curiosity value for those outside the Catholic Church. But they are not. They target not principally Catholics, or even lapsed Catholics, but those 'far from the Church' (lontani), non-believers, even those in some way opposed to religion – and it is among these that the movements have scored their greatest successes. They believe they hold the future not just of the Church but of the whole world in their hands.

Their ambitions, therefore, extend to power in the temporal field as well. With their fanatical zeal and their vast resources of money and personnel, they have achieved startling success in politics, business and the media, seen as steps on the way to creating a new world order. One of their main objects is to impose their extreme right-wing moral views on the majority, and in this they are prepared to use their numerical muscle as a political lever. They have been actively engaged in campaigning against abortion and even divorce laws in nominally Catholic countries like Italy and Ireland.

For all their strangeness, the movements had much to offer Pope John Paul II when he ascended the papal throne in 1978. The whirlwind of change in the years that followed the Council had shaken the Church to its foundations. Thousands of priests left their ministry; male and female religious poured out of their orders; emboldened by the new horizons revealed by the Council, the theologians who had been its architects sought to push the doctrinal barriers still further; the new autonomy of the laity and the emphasis on the role of conscience, rather than on unquestioning obedience to church authority, led married couples to reject the ban on artificial birth control, reaffirmed by the 1968 encyclical *Humanae vitae*; in response to the Council's call for justice and peace, priests and nuns, especially in the Americas, became directly involved in politics, while some made a pact with Marxism, Catholicism's most bitter enemy for over a century.

Wojtyla considered himself a man of the Council, and as Archbishop of Cracow in the early seventies had even written a book, *Sources of Renewal*, on how the Council's vision should be implemented. But it was a vision from a Polish perspective, which involved the laity, but whose impulse came from above, from the hierarchy. His programme as Pope, therefore, was to bring order into the chaos of the post-conciliar Church: to stem the exodus of priests, male religious and nuns; to call unruly theologians to heel; and to reimpose traditional teachings, especially in the area of sexual morality, which he saw as immutable. For those who felt that the Council had not yet been fully implemented, it rapidly became clear that under John Paul II the tide had turned and an era of Restoration had begun.

But, for a man of John Paul's energies, Restoration was not enough. He had an expansionist programme, too. In his first encyclical, *Redemptor hominis*, he spelled out an apocalyptic vision of world peace for the year 2000. By the mid-eighties, he had given a name to this vision: the New Evangelization. This has remained the programme of his pontificate, serving as a shorthand term for the many traditional values which he has fought to restore.

Although John Paul's missionary drive is conceived on a world-wide scale, he has a particular perspective on Europe. Here New Evangelization signifies not only a revival of Christian values but also the restoration of a Christendom not seen since the heyday of the Holy Roman Empire, a Catholic Europe united 'from the Atlantic to the Urals'. For such an ambitious and militant pro-gramme he needed forces, and he was astute enough to realize that

11

the movements had features in common which admirably suited his purposes and which he believed could be harnessed under his charismatic leadership.

Within the Church, the movements appeared to provide solutions to many of the pontiff's problems. They produce huge numbers of vocations to the priesthood, to the religious life and to the new forms of community life created within their own structures, wholeheartedly endorsing the Pope's adherence to priestly celibacy; they are conservative to the point of fundamentalism in the interpretation of Scripture and in theology; they not only reject the moral 'relativism' condemned by John Paul, but also rigorously apply among their members and within their sphere of pastoral influence the absolutist moral values he favours; they place the emphasis on an introspective spiritual programme, taking away the urgency from justice and peace issues which are relegated to a future 'better world' which the movement will create.

The structures of the movements, too, made them the ideal instruments for his project of New Evangelization. They are strongly centralized in Rome (or Milan, in the case of CL), with all directives for local spiritual and practical activities emanating from the centre, usually the founder. The highly sophisticated internal communications system of each movement, coupled with a clear and effective chain of command, makes them instantly responsive on a worldwide basis. They embrace every category of person: children, youth, couples, priests, male and female religious – even bishops. They are miniature churches or slices of church, and therefore self-sufficient.

Most of all, they possessed the unfashionable virtue of fanatical devotion to the Holy See. They cheered and waved their support at John Paul's public appearances all over the world; they rallied to his every appeal and publicly defended even his most unpopular actions. It did not take the Pontiff long to realize that here was the task-force he needed. Disciplined and militant, they could become the Pope's Armada.

Of course, it was a two-way street: the movements stood to gain much from such high-level patronage. Besides, they shared a common problem: the local bishops. CL and NC, in particular, had experienced many conflicts in dioceses around the world.

The Council had emphasized the role of the local churches and hence the authority of the bishops. Collegiality, or the authority of the bishops as a body united with the Pope, had been emphasized as a counterbalance to infallibility. John Paul did not see it quite in these terms. He spent the eighties bringing bishops and their national councils – the bishops' conferences – to heel. Centralization was something the movements knew a lot about. They had no place for democracy in their own structures and were impassioned advocates of the idea that democracy has no place in the Church. The support of the Pope became the calling-card of the movements in the local diocese, especially handy where bishops were hostile. In return, they preached the gospel of the new ultramontanism.

The architect of restoration in the Vatican was the German Cardinal Ratzinger, Prefect of the Congregation for the Doctrine of the Faith, better-known as the Holy Office, or Inquisition. A theologian at the Council, he moved sharply to the right in the 1970s, and in the 1980s, having attained his current position of power, hounded his former colleagues, including some of the world's most distinguished Catholic theologians. He put his name to the Vatican's toughest disciplinary pronouncements. The powerful bishops' conferences became the target of his attacks, in an attempt to claw back the supreme authority of the papacy. It is no wonder, then, that he has been one of the most ardent supporters of the movements. They are probably the only organizations of any weight in the Church which possess all the qualities he admires. He is outspoken in arguing for their authenticity and freedom of action: 'The intense life of faith found in these movements does not imply they are introspective or sheltered but simply a full and integral catholicity . . . Our task – as those charged with a ministry in the Church and as theologians – is to keep the doors open to them and prepare a space for them.'

It comes as no surprise to learn that Ratzinger's, and the Pope's, enthusiasm for the movements is not shared by many in the Church, including a number of influential bishops and cardinals. Cardinal Martini of Milan, a Jesuit and biblical scholar, is the best-known opponent in Europe; while leading figures in the South American Church such as Cardinals Arns and Lorscheider of Brazil have also spoken out against them. The movements are criticized for their fundamentalist approaches and for their presence as parallel churches within the local dioceses. The controversy they have unleashed has caused divisions within parishes, between priests and bishops, between bishops and Pope, and even within the Vatican itself at the very heart of the institutional Church. Although the Pope's backing has forced critics of the movements to keep their counsel, the tensions are increasing in many areas of the Church, and could lead to more serious rifts – even schism.

Nevertheless, even opponents are forced to acknowledge the zeal and effectiveness of these new structures. The moderate Cardinal Danneels of Belgium has pointed out that 'It is a fact that the majority of the "conversions" of our times can be found in these movements, while our classic structures seem to be relegated to a role of servicing and ticking over. Isn't the real missionary work in Europe being done in the movements and groups (small and large) that do not belong to the profound structures of the people of God, in other words to the dioceses and parishes?'[1]

My own interest in the new ecclesial movements was kindled – or, rather, rekindled – towards the end of 1987. A cradle Catholic, I had recently returned to the practice of the faith after a ten-year absence. A synod for the Catholic bishops of the world held in Rome in October of that year had highlighted the new prominence of the ecclesial movements; they were being touted by the Vatican as the models for post-conciliar laity, as the protagonists of John Paul's New Evangelization.

Reports on the new movements at the synod voiced the suspicions felt by many of those present. These organizations were known to be passionate supporters of the new centralization, exalting the authority of the papacy so as effectively to diminish that of the bishops. They were also considered broadly right-wing, favouring the Vatican line on theology and moral teaching. Beyond this, however, it was clear that journalists had failed to penetrate the wall of secrecy that surrounds these organizations. The reaction to the movements, therefore, was one of puzzlement, not of criticism. What is all the fuss about? they seemed to say. I was convinced, on the other hand, that the movements could only be known from within.

It was a conviction born from experience. For nine years, from 1967 to 1976, I had lived within the strange looking-glass world of one of these organizations: Focolare. As far as that movement was

[1] G. Danneels, 'Evangelizzare l'Europa secolarizzata', in *Regno documenti*, no. 30 (1985) 585.

concerned, I had the distinct advantage of inside knowledge; and I believed that this would provide a key to other movements like CL and NC. It would signpost features to look out for: the personality cult of the leader; a hidden but rigid hierarchy; a highly efficient internal communications system; secret teachings revealed in stages; a vast recruitment operation using sect-like techniques; indoctrination of members; and boundless ambitions for influence in church and society. My intimate knowledge of one movement provided a vital key to the others. I soon began to discern startling parallels.

But first I was forced to re-examine one of the most difficult periods of my life: my own membership of Focolare, the traumatic break with its structures, and the long and painful recovery from its influence. From the age of seventeen in 1967, I had been a full-time member, eventually taking vows of poverty, chastity and obedience in 1974. In 1972, together with a more senior member, I had founded a male Focolare community in Liverpool. At the time I left the London men's community in 1976, after following the movement's long and complex exit procedures, I was leading the male youth section of the movement in Great Britain and Ireland (known as the Gen or New Generation Movement), and editing the British edition of the movement's international magazine, *New City*. Neither I nor my superiors realized that within six months the movement would have lost its nine-year hold over me and I would have severed all ties. When I had joined the movement, I had been a devout Catholic and a daily massgoer. By the time I left, I had come to identify the movement so closely with the Church and with God himself that I abandoned the practice of the faith entirely for ten years.

Outsiders do not know what goes on within the movements, and so no-one can offer any help to those trying to readjust to the real world. Some ex-members of Focolare I have met have not fully shaken off its influence, even after a ten- or fifteen-year break. My membership had repercussions for many years.

When I began to view the experience with some degree of detachment and discussed it with close friends, the first questions they would ask were invariably the same: 'Why did you join?', closely followed by 'And why did you leave?' The first question is one I have asked myself a thousand times since. Now, even with hindsight, it is a question that is not easily answered; then it did not seem worth asking.

It is a characteristic of sects to see the individual's first encounter with the group as a crucial turning-point. 'Before and after' stories are carefully honed according to an acknowledged format. Such stories were the lifeblood of Focolare which, like CL and NC, places great emphasis on 'experiences' or testimonies. The 'experience' of meeting the movement held pride of place, and through private and public retellings would be refined into a kind of legend, according to guidelines, not written, but part of the accepted culture as is the case with most of the detailed prescriptions which govern the lives of members within the movements. In this key 'experience', the past would be depicted as wholly negative, as a period of despair and emptiness, possibly of searching, which would culminate in the blinding light of the encounter with the movement, instantly providing all the answers we had been seeking.

In fact, at the time of my first encounter in the summer of 1967, I was not exactly despairing. I had just left school and was about to start a degree course in English and European Literature at the University of Warwick that autumn. I was ambitious and highly motivated. I was set on building a career in a creative field, film-directing being my ultimate goal. Among my achievements at that time were manuscripts of two 80,000-word novels and a number of 8-millimetre fictional films which I had shot and edited featuring family and friends as actors.

Of course, like all adolescents I had problems. I was a devout Catholic, but I was already beginning to question church teachings. Although completely inexperienced sexually, I had long been aware of my homosexual preferences – undoubtedly a problem for a Catholic youth of that era. These issues may have played their part in the eventual grip the movement established over me, but at the time of my first encounter they were very much in the background. My outlook was resolutely optimistic.

In September 1967 I attended a weekend conference in Liverpool held by a Catholic association to which I and my closest school-friends belonged. The guest speaker was a *focolarina*, or full-time member of Focolare, Maria Eggar. She spoke of the movement's idea of world unity and of its model village of Loppiano near Florence which witnessed to a social life based on the practice of the Gospel. I was impressed and, at the end of the speech, handed in my name and address, as requested, so that I could find out more.

Maria herself was fascinating, too – her smile, the feeling of peace she radiated, her aura of selflessness, like a being from another world. Later I was to decide that it was the result of relinquishing mind and personality in total submission to the movement's authority.

I was invited to a residential weekend at Walsingham, the Marian shrine, in October 1967. I was overwhelmed by the warmth of the welcome that awaited me, especially from the *focolarini* men who spent hours talking to me in intervals and at mealtimes. One evening, the superior of the male section of the movement in the United Kingdom listened intently while I held forth on the similarity between the music of China and that of the west coast of Ireland. He appeared to be fascinated. Only later did I realize that he barely spoke any English. He was practising the technique known as 'making yourself one' with others, the Focolare term for making people feel loved and accepted, similar to the 'love-bombing' practised by many sects. I was being seriously 'cultivated'.

Towards the end of my first term at university, I attended another weekend meeting, this time for young men of the movement only. It was held in London. Either by accident or by design, I was the only one who turned up, and so spent my first and very intense period in the men's Focolare community of London, which was to become my new home. I had chosen Italian as the compulsory foreign-language option on my literature course, and could there-fore be started immediately on a crash course of writings and tapes by the Focolare foundress, Chiara Lubich. Jean-Marie, the French *focolarino* who was the head of the London men's community at that time, force-fed me on this spiritual diet at every available moment. Even during mealtimes in Focolare, the conversation is limited to matters spiritual, including anecdotes and lore of the movement.

Rapidly, I was assimilated into the movement's private universe with its own language and culture. At that time, Focolare had made few inroads among young English Catholic men: there was one Irish Catholic *focolarino* and an Anglican *focolarino*, and both were still at the international school for *focolarini* at Loppiano. I was prime candidate to be the first English Catholic *focolarino*.

Even if it had dawned on me at this stage that I was being 'cultivated' for that role, it would not have bothered me unduly. What struck me most about Focolare was the freedom and spon-taneity that were constantly proclaimed. Even living inside the community, I was not aware of any structure at all. It never occurred to me that everything was orchestrated for my benefit. I took descriptions of life in Focolare at face value: one lived in community while continuing with one's job and a normal way of life. So I could be a film-maker and still share in this warm and relaxed communal living.

As the movement began to occupy all my time and influence every aspect of my life, everything that I had valued up to this time lost its charm. We were living on a higher spiritual plane, fed by the illumination which came through Chiara Lubich directly from God. When I was with the *focolarini* I was on a continuous 'high', intoxicated by the 'light'. When I was apart from them, I felt a depression that had not previously been part of my make-up.

This is as it should be, they would reassure me, for nothing can compare to the direct experience of God provided by the movement: the presence they described as 'Jesus in the midst', only available among the members of the movement. The corollary, of course, was that nothing else had any value.

We were enjoined to rid ourselves of all 'attachments', which, according to Chiara Lubich, 'we unavoidably fall into if our hearts are not in God and in His teachings. Attachments can be to things, to persons, to ourselves, to our own ideas, to our health, our time, our rest, our studies, our work, our relatives, our own consolations or gratifications, all things which are not God and which therefore cannot take his place in our hearts which are aiming at perfection.'[1]

A book of Chiara's meditations issued at this time focused on this concept of detachment. It was entitled *Knowing How to Lose*, which became one of the movement's many slogans. Everything outside the movement was worthless and should be jettisoned. Thus I lost interest in the books I was studying on my literature course, previously a passion. 'Literature pales in comparison with the glowing words of Chiara Lubich,' Jean-Marie assured me. I lost my ambitions for any kind of career outside the movement and ceased all my previous creative activities, destroying the two manuscripts I had sweated to produce.

Old affections dried up and, now that the movement had taken over my mind and heart completely, I could no longer communicate even with close friends. Now they were simply prime targets for recruitment, and if they did not respond they would be

---

[1]Conference call of Chiara Lubich with internal members, 14 April 1988.

dropped. I had ceased to think and feel like other people. At one point, I clashed with my mother as I wanted to leave university after my second term and go to Loppiano. She stormed into the London Focolare, and they capitulated. It became painfully obvious that the movement was my new family. What I could not grasp, of course, was that along with everything else that I had held dear I had also 'lost' my self, my personality. This was a loss noticed only by others. Once I became aware of it myself, I would be in far too deep to pull back.

I spent the summer of 1968 at the British Institute in Florence, as part of my university course. At weekends, I was able to visit the Focolare village of Loppiano. It was the year of the student revolts in Paris and elsewhere. Sit-ins had been staged at Warwick, but I had been too absorbed with the movement to notice. To counter this influence amongst the young, Chiara Lubich had launched a 'revolution' with the Gen, or youth of the movement. At the Gen Congress, held in July, she gave impassioned speeches, often blurring her words together in a high-pitched shriek. It was also the height of the cultural revolution in China, and as the movement's answer her 'sayings' were printed in little yellow books. The Gen would wave these in the air, chanting slogans at the end of Chiara's speeches while she waved back, wearing high-collared Chinese-style dresses to make the parallel clear.

I saw her speak several times that summer and was caught up in the euphoria surrounding her. We had a mission to the whole world: it was the secret of universal love which Chiara had received directly from God. Only the movement could bring this revolution about. And it would. World unity, the kingdom of God on earth, would be a reality, and we would be its agents.

While those around us went about their dull, prosaic, everyday lives, we were living on an exalted plane of awareness. Like many messianic sects, we were convinced we were in the vanguard of history.

One of the greatest problems of the Catholic Church today, according to the Holy See, is the proliferation of extreme protestant sects and offbeat cults which are making inroads among the faithful in South and North America, and more recently in the virgin territory of Eastern Europe. John Paul II and the other protectors of the movements in the Vatican have repeatedly pointed out that they are the Church's main bulwark and antidote against the threat from non-Catholic sects. Could this be a case of using a sledge-hammer to crack a nut? The 'Catholic sects' could be said to be even more dangerous than their opponents, coming as they do with the official approval of the Catholic Church and Pope John Paul II, probably the world's most respected moral leader. Catholic critics of the new movements maintain that the Pope cannot know what is going on within the movements, otherwise he would not allow them such a free hand. Perhaps, to some extent, this is true. But could it be that the Vatican's hidden agenda is far more cynical than anyone dares suspect? Have they concluded that their own supreme ends, in the face of overwhelming odds, justify strong-arm techniques more commonly associated with sects? Could the Pope have had this in mind when he conferred special status on lay Catholics who joined the movements, 'which are a privileged channel for the formation and promotion of an active laity that is aware of its role in the Church and in the world'?[1] Is the nightmare vision of Catholic sects John Paul's chosen scenario for the Church of the future?

[1]John Paul II, Loreto, 11 April 1985.

2

ANATOMY OF A CATHOLIC SECT

CANADIAN MARTYRS PARISH IN A SUBURB OF ROME IS THE HOME OF the first Neocatechumenate community in the world – that is, the first to complete the movement's twenty-year course of initiation, the details of which are known only to the top echelon of NC leaders and those who have experienced it for themselves.

I attended a Saturday-evening Eucharist there in November 1993. I had arranged to meet the catechists by the front entrance; but, as I had arrived early, I slipped into the church. A forlorn sprinkling of old ladies formed the tiny congregation before the Exposition of the Sacrament. Outside, a more numerous and varied crowd was assembling and making its way to a side-door leading to the crypt. Like many other NC parishes, Canadian Martyrs not only has parallel services, but also has separate purpose-built facilities beneath the church. With twenty-five communities, each with around forty members, NC here can hardly be described as 'parallel' – the parish has been invaded and occupied. As each NC 'community' has to attend a mass appropriate to its level of initiation, many venues are needed. The vast barn-like church has been abandoned in favour of the halls like the one in which I witnessed the NC Eucharist, decorated in the style prescribed in detail by the founder, Kiko Arguello. What struck me most about the service, apart from its taking two hours, were the comments made after the Gospel, at the stage known to NC members as 'echoes' (*risonanze*) – spontaneous thoughts from the congregation in response to the day's gospel reading. All were personal, and all seemed to hinge on a sense of guilt and dependence on the 'community'. One woman told the congregation that every time she had been tempted to leave the group God had given her a 'beating' to bring her into line.

It is in the exclusive claims of the movements and in the hold they establish over members that they mostly resemble sects. Each believes it is possessed of a unique God-given mission to rebuild or even to save the Church. Demands on members are therefore absolute, because the movements alone can provide the salvation that the Church as it stands cannot. Chiara Lubich uses the word 'totalitarian' to describe this commitment, despite – or perhaps because of – its sinister political overtones (in its early days Focolare was conceived as an anti-communist crusade). Joining the movements is seen as a conversion, which can often be of a sudden and dramatic nature. Even devout Catholics can have the impression that previously they understood nothing and now, thanks to the movement, they understand everything. Experiences like these give rise to fears that the movements are 'churches within the Church'. Such fears are well founded. NC claims to be 'rebuilding the Church from within'. One British ex-member was told by her parish priest: 'The whole Church will be NC in twenty years' time.' The NC catechesis consistently uses the term 'Church' as a synonym for the movement. When I was a member of Focolare, we certainly saw ourselves as the future of the whole Church; the 'spirituality', or doctrine, of the movement was for everyone. Don Giussani, founder of CL, said in an interview: 'Where is the Church? Where are the walls of the parish? The Church is where she is lived . . . I would not want to belong to Communion and Liberation if it were not the life of the Church that I carry within me.'

But the aspirations of the movements go beyond the purely religious. Like many other sects, they believe in a very literal way that their mission is to save the world. This is explicitly stated by Kiko Arguello in the NC Guidelines for catechists when he talks about the effect of the NC communities on society: having defined them as the Church, he then declares, 'The Church saves the World'.

In his analysis of different types of cult, or New Religious Movement,[1] Roy Wallis distinguishes between the world-accommodating, the world-affirming and the world-rejecting. The

[1] *The Elementary Forms of the New Religious Life*, London: Routledge & Kegan Paul, 1983.

new Catholic movements are of the world-rejecting type. According to Wallis: 'The world-rejecting movement expects that the millennium will shortly commence or that the movement will sweep the world, and, when all have become members or when they are in the majority, or when they have become guides and counsellors to kings and presidents, then a new world-order will begin, a simpler, more loving, more humane and more spiritual order in which the old evils and mistakes will be eradicated and utopia will have begun.'[1]

The corollary of the movements' sense of election and uniqueness is that other Catholics and Christians are despised. Chiara Lubich contrasts members of the movement with 'bigots' and people with 'bowed heads', implying hypocrisy. She talks of Sunday Christians who 'take God out of a drawer' one day a week.

CL and NC – using slightly different terms – both claim that they have succeeded, where other Catholics have failed, in bringing together 'faith and life'. In the NC Guidelines, it is taken for granted that even the practising Catholics who join NC have no faith and do not believe in God or Christ in any meaningful sense. Those outside the movement – including Catholics – are termed pagans, because they do not have the total commitment of members. Not surprisingly, many devout Catholics find this offensive.

In order to differentiate themselves from mainstream Catholicism, a movement may coin a word used by members to describe its teachings and philosophy. NC members talk about the 'Way'. Focolare members speak of meeting the 'Ideal'. Internal members will almost always use this more grandiose term in preference to the prosaic 'movement' (NC rejects the term 'movement' out of hand). Interestingly, Jehovah's Witnesses use the phrase 'the Truth' of their organization in precisely the same sense.

Monsignor Joseph Buckley, Vicar General of the Roman Catholic Diocese of Clifton, Bristol, quotes an eminent Catholic psychiatrist's analysis of alleged 'brainwashing techniques' employed by Neocatechumenate. One of these is the use of jargon or 'neologisms – confusing to the uninitiated and laying him open to accept new and unwarranted ideas'.[2] Bruno Secondin, a Carmelite

[1] op. cit., p. 9.
[2] Article in the Catholic monthly *Priest and People,* June 1988.

Professor of Spirituality at Rome's prestigious Gregorian University, defines the new languages of the movements as 'elaborated codes': that is, they evoke a whole gamut of feelings in members – they construct the movement's own 'universe'. These internal languages also furnish trigger-words which can be used to provoke guilt, obedience or a sense of belonging, according to the circumstances. The new terminology may have been developed to give a sense of novelty to the message, avoiding the pious phrases of the past; and yet, ironically, for outsiders, it provokes confusion and mis-understanding, effectively precluding meaningful dialogue.

NC community members are always referred to as 'brothers' and 'sisters'. The various categories of leadership include responsibles, catechists and itinerants. The word 'priest' has been discarded in favour of 'presbyter'. Within the NC teaching, technical terms from biblical criticism like 'kerygma', 'koinonia' and 'kenosis', and philosophical terms like 'ontological' and 'existential', abound without explanation. Other key concepts are 'the glorious cross' and 'the servant of Jahweh'. This last term, like much NC terminology, comes from the Old Testament. The key term 'catechesis' is applied to numerous different contexts. Even the words of the serpent to Eve in the biblical creation-story are described as a 'catechesis'. By the use of its own language NC lays claim to Scripture, the parish and every aspect of the lives of members.

Communion and Liberation, too, has its jargon. Don Giussani's many pseudo-philosophical books such as *The Christian Event, The Religious Sense, Religious Awareness in Modern Man* and *Morality: Memory and Desire* eschew religious terminology for a kind of cultural sincretism, with borrowings from Giussani's preferred authors such as T. S. Eliot, Paul Claudel and Charles Péguy. Like other founders, Don Giussani does not explain or justify; he proclaims his ideas as self-evident truths. The central concept of the CL philosophy is the Christian 'event' or 'fact', a term borrowed by Giussani from another of his heroes, C. S. Lewis. This term signifies both the historicity of Christ and the 'event' which is the movement itself making Christ manifest today: 'You encounter Christianity through coming into contact with people who have already had this encounter and whose lives have in some way been changed by it.' The 'event' also refers to the tangible impact this 'social reality' of the movement must make on society, the key to

CL's militant interventionism in temporal matters, which has made it the highest-profile Catholic pressure group in Italy.

Focolare has developed a vast dictionary of terms for every aspect of members' lives. Love becomes 'seeing Jesus in your neighbour'; 'living the present moment' means concentrating on the job in hand; 'Jesus forsaken' covers the key concept of suffering and the cross. Unity, however, is the over-arching theme of the movement; 'understanding' unity is the key to true membership. Another term for 'unity' is 'Jesus in the midst'.[1] Members talk about 'making unity', which could cover anything from having an intense spiritual conversation to the endless meetings members at every level are obliged to attend. Unity could also mean, as I was to discover after some years in the movement, blind obedience.

But the jargon is not only spiritual; because of its all-embracing nature, Focolare has something to say on every aspect of life. In the early fifties Chiara Lubich developed the image of the spectrum to represent the change the Focolare 'Ideal' brings to every aspect of life: red is the economy, particularly the concept of the communion, or pooling, of all goods; orange is the apostolate or proselytism; yellow is the spiritual life – mass, rosary and meditation on Chiara's writings; green is health; blue is the home and society; indigo is wisdom and knowledge; violet is communications and the media. Each of these has a social application, but they are also used to refer to the minutiae of everyday life. This leads to such bizarre usages as 'Let's do some blue', which means 'Let's do some housework', or 'This is the green day', which would mean a day of relaxation or sport – something that was very rare for full-time members.

When I joined the movement I was already learning Italian as part of my course at university. As it is the official language of Focolare, I got plenty of practice and could speak it in under a year. What I did not realize was that I was learning a very particular kind of Italian. A whole range of words exists, for example, to grade newcomers according to how much they have 'understood', and therefore the level they might attain within the movement's hierarchy. An example is the use of different forms of the word *caro* ('dear'). Plain *caro* in Focolare-speak denotes someone who has

[1]With reference to Christ's words in Matthew's gospel: 'Where two or three meet in my name, I am there among them' (18:20).

'understood' and is considered an 'insider'. *Carino* means a candidate for recruitment with real potential – very different from the common meaning of the word which is 'cute' (looking). *Carissimo* ('dearest' or 'very dear') is used of someone who could become a full-time *focolarino*; another term for such a person would be *popabile* – *popo* and the feminine *popa* ('boy' and 'girl' in Trentino dialect) being the internal words for full-time members, *focolarini* and *focolarine*. So many words were used with altered meanings that a Focolare conversation overheard by Italians could suggest something very different from what was intended!

Certain codes of behaviour also identify members of the movement. *Focolarini* are often recognizable by their fixed grins or seemingly unmotivated laughter. In the words of Chiara Lubich, 'a smile is the uniform of the *focolarino*'. Joy was mandatory, especially at open meetings. It bore no relation to feelings; it was our duty to rejoice. After a while the laughter and grins became automatic. Newcomers would often comment how their face muscles ached with over-use at the end of each day.

There is also an accepted posture for 'making unity' during talks and meetings; this is to perch on the edge of one's seat, leaning forward with arms folded or propped under the chin, staring intently at the speaker and nodding. It was not enough to listen intently; one had to be seen to be doing it. Audiences of internal members will often audibly respond to points in a talk which impress them by cooing or tutting noises. Alternatively they may murmur '*Che bello!*' ('How beautiful!'), another of the movement's stock phrases, an expression of uncritical wonder.

A Focolare member can be *lanciato* ('speeding'), which signifies frantic, enthusiastic missionary activity; or *marian* (like the Virgin Mary): quiet, gentle, moving softly and gracefully, unobtrusively serving. These patterns of behaviour are adopted consciously or unconsciously by members.

Cadences of speech can fall into standard patterns, too. When I recently had cause to phone the movement's Centre in Italy, the mellifluous, carefully articulated tones of the *focolarina* who answered, soothing yet unemotional, struck an immediate chord. After some years, many members in Britain begin to speak English with the same lilt, giving them a slight foreign accent. Such behavioural changes play an important part in providing members with a distinctive 'badge' of membership and have a special appeal for new or fringe members. They are an indicator of the extent to which the movements suffocate individual personalities.

Sociologically, sects are protest groups formed in reaction to existing organizations, such as the established churches. They are characterized by intolerance, elitism and claims of special authority. In English, the term 'cult' has become more widely used to refer to such groups which are also known as NRMs (New Religious Movements). Originally 'cult' denoted a milder version of a sect and is used within the Catholic context to describe devotion to a particular saint or the Virgin Mary. Italian makes exclusive use of the word *setta* (sect) where English would commonly use 'cult'. Thus the Pope and official Catholic pronouncements talk of the threat of sects. Sects or cults can be examined in the light of the criteria formulated by anti-cult organizations such as the British FAIR (Family Action Information and Rescue) which identifies twelve classic 'marks of cults', although it stresses that there are many others. It can be argued that the new Catholic movements possess at least some of these. For example: 'A cult is usually characterized by a leader who claims divinity or a special mission delegated to him/her by a supreme power.' The new movements go as far towards fulfilling this condition as Catholic theology will allow – which is quite a long way – and a little further. They are made in the images of their founders, which is one explanation for their often contradictory and idiosyncratic natures. Like her two fellow-founders, Chiara Lubich is small in stature. A former primary-school teacher, her neat blue-rinsed coiffure and smart bright suits – both much imitated amongst *focolarine* – and her brisk, flat-footed mountain-walker's gait give her the air of a kindly but firm headmistress. This explains why infantile behaviour is encouraged within the movement: members encouraged to run after 'Miss'; use of mnemonics like 'the colours'; constant repetition of simple phrases; childlike speech-patterns, carefully articulated.

With warts on his face and a rasping voice, the diminutive Don Giussani is no-one's idea of an attractive charismatic leader, and yet his convoluted philosophizing has proved inspirational for two generations of Italian youth. His ideology and language underlie every utterance of the movement and have influenced many outside it, including leading figures in the Church like Cardinal Ratzinger and Cardinal Biffi of Bologna. His rigid opinions are reflected in the confrontational stance of the movement in both church and secular affairs.

Kiko Arguello's full beard and sober but casual taste in clothes have set the fashion amongst catechists and seminarians of the Neocatechumenal Way. More sinister, however, is the echo to be found in catechists throughout the world of his harsh and critical style of public speaking and his hectoring aggressive approach to individuals in catechesis.

The day after I attended the NC Eucharist at the Canadian Martyrs parish in Rome, I was invited to visit St Francesca Cabrini parish, less than half a mile away. Renato, the catechist who accompanied me, was anxious that I should see two wonderful 'gifts' that Kiko had made to the parish. Kiko is described by the movement as an artist. Several catechists have pointed out that he was earning a lot of money at the time of his conversion. We are not told what his subject-matter was in pre-NC days; but today his subjects are exclusively religious – pastiche icons, in fact, usually clearly based on well-known works.

The gifts to St Francesca Cabrini turned out to be two large-scale paintings. One can be found in the crypt, in one of several venues used for celebrating the NC Eucharist; it depicts the family of Nazareth, which occupies an important place in the NC scheme of things – Jesus, flanked by Mary and Joseph. The other was a vast mural in rather garish colours behind the high altar of the main church on the subject of the Ascension.

All the images used by Neocatechumenate are painted by Kiko. Many NC churches throughout the world are adorned with his works. St Charles Borromeo Church in Ogle Street in London's West End is one of these. Kiko's artistic ability is highly regarded by members. Liturgical vestments designed by Kiko are exclusively available from a store near St Peter's in Rome and are bought by all NC parishes.

Kiko is described by NC members as an apostle, and he carries himself like one. His circular letters to the NC communities are written in the style of the epistles of St Paul. His teachings are the basis of all NC catechesis – he is the architect of the twenty-year Way, with its secret rites and degrees of membership.

Since the start of Neocatechumenate in 1964, Kiko has been accompanied by an ex-nun, Carmen Hernandez, who has more of a background in liturgical, scriptural and theological matters than he. It is said that she has a powerful influence on him. Nevertheless, it is Kiko and not Carmen who is recognized as the sole founder and focus of the movement. Until the movement acquired its official name after moving to Rome, its communities were known as 'Kiko-families'.

Don Giussani is regarded by CL members as the most important figure in the Church today. Despite his unprepossessing exterior, he exerts a powerful influence over tens of thousands of young people in Italy and in increasing numbers elsewhere. His talks at Italian universities regularly draw crowds of 3,000 and more.

CL claims that the various businesses and secular operations associated with it are quite separate from the movement, even though they may be run solely by CL members. Few who know the movement will doubt that Giussani exerts a powerful influence over this army of works, all of which are expressions of his clearly articulated ideology on culture, education and a Christian presence ('fact') in business and politics. The Popular Movement, CL's political arm, launched in the early 1970s and dissolved with the collapse of the Christian Democrat Party in 1993, claimed to be autonomous. In fact Giussani was a major influence.

CL and its founder have never disguised the fact that the defence of authority and obedience is one of their main platforms. It is also a fact that Giussani heads the two sections of the movement which have been officially recognized by the Church: the 25,000-strong Fraternities, forming the core membership of CL, and the Memores Domini, the movement's communities of celibate members who play a key role in the direction of the movement. Giussani is regarded as the sole fount of spiritual inspiration for CL, providing the key contributions to its large events, which are held in Italy. His writings are vigorously promoted by all CL publications, even those which have been said to be out of step with the movement.

In September 1993 I was sent an invitation for a Focolare event at Wembley Conference Centre entitled 'Many but One . . .' Aimed mainly at the Anglican division of Focolare, which is probably numerically larger than its Catholic following in the United Kingdom, it was, however, open to everyone and was geared to the wider circle of members known as 'adherents', rather than to internal members whose events – at least, in the United Kingdom – are usually on a smaller scale.

Chiara Lubich had been billed to attend, but she had cancelled public appearances owing to unspecified ill-health. Her place was taken by Natalia Dallapiccola, one of her 'first companions', the women who began the movement with her. Natalia played a major role, from the early 1960s, in founding the movement behind the Iron Curtain. Although she and the other 'companions' as well as the first male *focolarini* have done invaluable work in spreading the movement throughout the world, they are mere ciphers in the shadow of the foundress.

Despite my familiarity with this personality cult, I was taken aback by the emphasis placed on Chiara Lubich at Wembley. When I was a member of the movement, the stress on Chiara was frequently questioned in Britain. The change may in part be thanks to the hagiographic efforts of Edwin Robertson, official biographer of Chiara Lubich and Igino Giordani, the first married *focolarino*. Robertson was on hand at Wembley, signing copies of his latest book on Focolare, *Catching Fire*. On first acquaintance with the movement, I did not notice the cult of the foundress at all – I was impressed by the message of the Gospel, the message of love, which I found in all its simplicity in *Meditations*, the first book of Chiara's writings that I read.

By early 1968 I was hitchhiking from university, just outside Coventry, to spend every weekend in the London men's Focolare Centre. The Centres, or Focolares, are ordinary houses or apartments where the full-time members of the movement – those with vows of poverty, chastity and obedience – live together and organize the movement's proselytizing activities. These communities reflect the strict segregation of the sexes in most internal groupings of the movement, even for non-celibates.

At this stage – and for some time to come – I was unaware that a strict hierarchy existed. In fact I was being cultivated by Jean-Marie, the *capofocolare*. After a couple of visits, he suggested I should write to Chiara Lubich. It seemed odd to me to write to someone I had never met. I had no idea what was expected. 'Tell Chiara about how you met the movement,' it was suggested. 'Thank her for the gift of the Ideal – after all, she is your mother.' It was also made clear to me that the letter was to be censored by the *capofocolare* before it was sent. This was standard practice in the movement. I remember a *focolarino* being severely reprimanded because he had not had his letter to Chiara censored before mailing it, a fact which had emerged through negative feedback from Rome. It was clear that information passed to Chiara was screened at both ends. Only the letters that would 'give her joy' would actually be passed on.

Suitable subjects for letters to Chiara were requests to join the movement's various sections, but especially to become full-time *focolarini*. Members who intended to marry would also consult Chiara first. Of course, very few of these letters were actually answered. The real dealings were between the head of your 'zone' and those in charge of the relevant department at the movement's Centre in Rome. When I joined, the movement was already several hundred thousand strong, and in the early seventies a multilingual secretariat was set up in Rome to deal with Chiara Lubich's mail. Today, with membership in the millions, and with faxes pouring in by the minute, there seems to be little chance that Lubich herself ever sees any of them. The point of the exercise is surely more to do with fuelling the members' loyalty to the foundress than with keeping her abreast of what is happening at the grass roots. (The same practice can be found within Opus Dei and Communion and Liberation.)

In the early days, Chiara would occasionally give *focolarini* and other internal members 'new names'. This may have been because her own baptismal name is Silvia; she chose the name Chiara (Clare) in her youth when she joined the Third Order of St Francis, and after the movement began used it permanently. Much play is made of the fact that in Italian her name signifies 'clear' or 'light'. The names given by Chiara were not traditional names, however. Pasquale Foresi, the first *focolarino* to become a priest, was known as Chiaretto, 'Little Chiara' (in the male form); the first married *focolarino*, Igino Giordani (then an MP and a well-known figure in the Catholic opposition to fascism), became Foco, 'Fire'. Around the time I joined, the practice began to get out of hand, and thousands of members wrote to Chiara asking for 'new names'. This led to some increasingly bizarre examples. One *focolarino* of my acquaintance was known as Alleluia. An American was given the unfortunate-sounding Pons ('bridge' in Latin). As the demand grew, the search for different names became more difficult. One young Sicilian I knew ended up as Ignis, which was a make of washing machine in Italy.

Another practice was that of giving members their own phrase of Scripture, or 'Word of Life', to put into practice. When members die their lives tend to be analysed in terms of this phrase as though somehow, in selecting the scriptural verse, the foundress had displayed a unique insight into the soul of that individual, as though her choice had been inspired.

The ability to give 'new names' and 'Words of Life' is strictly limited to Chiara, but it is hard to believe – with the enormous correspondence she receives from members – that she selects them herself.

Six months after meeting Focolare, I went on a trip to the movement's international conference centre, the Mariapolis Centre, then situated near Rocca di Papa in the Roman Hills. Chiara Lubich was scheduled to talk to the group, and I was duly impressed with her powers of oratory. However, Jean-Marie, my guardian angel, decided to leave nothing to chance. 'Don't you feel she is a mother? Don't you feel she is *your* mother?' he whispered in my ear during the talks. I said I did, but at the time I was deeply uncertain. I did not realize that techniques of suggestion were being used – possibly unintentionally – to which I would eventually capitulate. I found it equally strange when he would continually ask me if I was 'happy'; the same mechanism was at work.

The ultimate aim of this careful grooming was that this woman, who was in reality a total stranger, had to become the most important person in our lives, not only as a leader of our minds, but also occupying first place in our affections. The word 'Mamma' was reserved in the movement for Chiara. The natural mothers of the *focolarini* were known by the rather patronizing diminutive *mammine* ('little mothers'). There is more than a whiff of Italian *mammismo* about the mother-cult which surrounds Chiara Lubich. Sentimental songs were sung to her addressing her as 'mamma'. This was all part of the myth of the personal relationship between each member and the foundress. An internal news-bulletin of December 1988 describes an encounter between Chiara and 1,100 *focolarine* (celibate women members): 'Each one felt taken in hand directly by Chiara, led along this road.'

Chiara Lubich's teaching is the one source of spiritual nourishment in Focolare. In the early fifties, one of the first reel-to-reel tape-recorders was purchased to preserve all her utterances. They nicknamed the machine La Nonna, 'The Grandmother'. Since then no expense has been spared to ensure that Chiara's words are brought to the members of the movement as directly as possible. In the early seventies, the very first commercial video-recorders were purchased, and all Chiara's talks preserved in this medium.

Now, of course, video is the norm. It struck me as odd when I first visited the Focolare Centre that, instead of being addressed by the people there, who were presumably experts on the movement, I was played endless tapes of Chiara. For newcomers, this was strange, laborious and boring. Yet it was considered vital that members should hear Chiara Lubich's own voice, even if her words had to be translated. I was still translating those tapes for visitors – sometimes with an audience of one – right up until the eve of my departure from Focolare.

One evening at supper, Father Dimitri Bregant, the superior of the men's branch in the United Kingdom, defined unity in the Focolare sense. It is not some vague feeling, he told us, but something very precise: the movement forms one soul, and Chiara is the centre of that soul. Unity, therefore, means living whatever Chiara is living in her spiritual life at that time. That signifies constantly bearing in mind and trying to put into practice in daily life the thought that currently preoccupies Chiara. This thought is referred to as the 'new reality'. It would be communicated to us by a letter or a phone-call from the movement's Centre in Rome, and would occupy our minds and conversations – even with outsiders – until another idea, the next 'new reality', came along to replace it. It is considered of the utmost importance that this 'new reality' should be communicated to all members and adherents as soon as possible.

At the end of 1980, Chiara launched the 'Holy Journey', which meant that all the internal members of the movement had to become saints. Curiously, this was to be achieved by means of a fortnightly conference call linking some fifty centres of the movement world-wide, during which Chiara herself would give a keynote speech to be 'put into practice' by members until the next call. This network is known in the United Kingdom as the 'link-up', and in America more simply as the 'conference call'. It effectively squeezes out any possibility of a personal spiritual life for the internal members of the movement but confirms the concept of 'unity' described above.

However, the personality cult around the foundress goes further than this. Like Neocatechumenate, Focolare has its secret texts in the unpublished writings of Chiara Lubich which are circulated among the *focolarini*. These had been reserved for private use or had appeared in censored versions because they were considered too 'strong' for public consumption.

I was once shown a text which I did not question until long after I had left the movement. In it Chiara described how she had 'seen' the Virgin Mary as the channel of all graces – a traditionalist Catholic concept. But then she added that next to the Madonna was another, small Mary (herself). 'In me', she said, 'are all the graces for those who wish to join together in unity.' Those graces, in other words, can only pass through Chiara. This is an exaggerated and dangerous claim, but it shows the lengths to which the personality cult can be carried inside the movements. I remember on several occasions being told by *focolarini*: 'It doesn't matter whether you believe in God; it's enough to believe in Chiara.'

Besides such excesses, there is a more orthodox form of 'divinity' the Church can bestow on its members: sanctity. But they have to be dead for that. The movements have found a way of 'sanctifying', or 'deifying', their founders before they die by means of the 'charism of the founder'.

Charism (Greek, 'gift') is a New Testament term for a gift of the Holy Spirit bestowed on the individual for the good of the community. *Lumen gentium*, the Second Vatican Council's Constitution on the Church, is at pains to point out that charisms are distributed to all Christians: '[The] Holy Spirit sanctifies and leads the People of God and enriches it with virtues. Allotting His gifts to "everyone according as He will" (1 Cor. 12:11), He distributes special graces among the faithful of every rank.'

In his book *The Church*, the eminent Catholic theologian Hans Kung reinforces this view: 'The charisms of leadership in the Pauline Churches did not . . . produce a "ruling class", an aristocracy of those endowed with the Spirit who separated themselves from the community . . . Each Christian has his own charism. Each Christian is a charismatic.'

Bruno Secondin, the Carmelite author of *The New Protagonists*, a survey of the new Catholic movements, believes that the idea of the 'charism of the founder' with reference to these movements started around 1985. It was in fact used well before then, however, by Focolare, which, as long ago as 1967 when I first encountered it, was already talking publicly about the 'charism of unity', which was their unique patrimony; sometimes it was simply termed 'the charism of Chiara'.

NC talk of the charism of Kiko. Don Giussani not only speaks of his own charism but has also propounded a general theory of the charisms of the new movements. Bruno Secondin has noted that even Catholic Action, Italy's official association for the Catholic laity, has discovered and talks about its charism, even though for years it had managed without one.

What does 'charism' mean in the context of the movements? It is used to safeguard the supremacy of the founders as the fount of all doctrine and authority within their organizations. It preserves the 'purity' of the message that can only be passed on in the manner the movement deems correct and by the people it authorizes. It is also evoked to ensure non-interference from outsiders – even Church authorities.

Pope John Paul II has played a key part in promoting this concept of the charisms of the movements. Chiara Lubich recalls how, during a vast gathering of the movement in St Peter's Square, the Pope said to her: ' "Be ever an instrument of the Holy Spirit!" Those words are carved inside me and have reinforced in me the fear of God and the courage to have faith in the charism and to persevere on our spiritual path.' NC members are quoted as saying: 'The Pope can be wrong, but Kiko can't be wrong because he has the charism.' 'People object to Kiko's songs,' an NC catechist told me; 'they are like flamenco, they say. But the charism is the package, which includes the songs.' As a result, Kiko's strongly Spanish-flavoured songs are being sung from Africa to Japan.

The 'charism' also allows the founders to proclaim authoritatively on every subject, not just on matters of the soul, and their ideas have the same binding force on members as their spiritual teachings. This omniscient dimension of the charism reinforces the fortress mentality of the movements, isolating them from the rest of society in the belief that they have all the answers to every conceivable subject.

Perhaps the most damaging effect of this new concept of charisms is that the movements are being allowed complete freedom of action under the present regime in the Vatican, with no checks and balances, no accountability. Many people imagine that sects are only for the feeble-minded or the neurotic, and express surprise that intelligent and discerning people could ever become involved; but, as FAIR stresses, 'Established members are often guarded, vague, deceptive, or secretive about beliefs, goals, demands and activities until the recruit is "hooked" '. The potential recruit is even more at risk in the case of Catholic 'sects', because they apparently come with the blessing of the Pope and the bishop. In the case of Neocatechumenate, the support of the parish priest is a prerequisite.

The announcements of the initial fourteen introductory talks which take place on two nights a week over a two-month period, usually in the autumn, often not do not even mention Neo-catechumenate by name. Candidates are deliberately kept in the dark about what lies ahead – and this applies to every stage of the twenty-year Way. On the contrary, they are encouraged to be totally passive and receptive. No questions are allowed during the catechumenate. Even at this early stage, there can be reactions to the predominantly negative message of Neocatechumenate. Many are repelled by the emphasis on sin and man's unredeemed state.

It is at this stage that two further FAIR points begin to take effect: 'Many cults systematically employ sophisticated techniques designed to effect ego-destruction, thought reform and dependence on the cult' and 'The cult may maintain members in a state of heightened suggestibility through lack of sleep, engineered diet, intense spiritual exercises, repetitive indoctrination and controlled group experiences'.

Public confession is a classic technique used by sects to bind members to the organization. This technique is mentioned as one of the more dangerous in Eileen Barker's *New Religious Movements*,[1] which goes out of its way to be even-handed in its treatment of cults (the very title of the book is the politically correct term for cults, usually abbreviated to NRMs). The traditional Catholic form of individual confession is practised by NC, as are Penitential Services in which sins are confessed within the context of a communal service, though always on a one-to-one basis. But members are also required to take part in painful group sessions in which they are encouraged to talk about their worst actions in the most intimate detail. A packed congregation in Trento cathedral, the venerable site of the Council of the Counter-Reformation, was horrified to hear an NC member testify that before he met the movement he used to masturbate up to six times a day. During one of these sessions, an Italian woman was asked by her five-year-old daughter the meaning of the word 'incest'.

The majority of the public confessions take place during the so-called *scrutinies*. Renato, from the Rome parish of St Francesca

---

[1] London: HMSO, 1992.

Cabrini, told me that the purpose of the scrutinies is 'To find out how much of an effect the Way has had on the lives of brothers and sisters. They are asked to describe their attitudes before and after the Way – attitudes to money, work, emotional life.' He volunteered, without being asked, that these are among the most controversial of NC practices but denied that they are enforced public confessions. 'People are free to say what they want. We want them to tell their suffering.'

Yet a woman ex-member from Rome recalls how 'the interviewer plunges his finger ever deeper' demanding to know the most intimate facts. The NC view is that confession is good for the soul, and the worse the sins the better. Kiko Arguello urges members to feel that 'today I am really disgusting, I am a traitor, I am a monster.' One girl in Rome was commanded to admit to being a prostitute. When she protested that this was untrue, her protests were dismissed and she was urged to confess it all the same. A parishioner in his seventies of St Charles Borromeo Parish in London was told by a twenty-five-year-old catechist at a scrutiny that 'He should go out and sin more – he might learn something'. His response was to leave the movement.

The danger pointed out by Eileen Barker – that public confession gives cults a hold over members – is confirmed by those familiar with NC. Sins confessed in NC communities soon become common knowledge in the parish.

The technique of singling out individuals and subjecting them to intense psychological pressure is similar to that used by self-improvement groups like EST at weekend seminars. Neo-catechumenate has its own form of weekends away for communities known as *convivencias* in Spanish, rendered in English by the French *convivences*. Here members are subjected to more intense pressure.

The first *convivence* takes place at the end of the first two months of catechesis, the period known in the NC jargon as the announcement of the Kerygma. It marks the first 'passage' to the stage of the Way known as the Pre-catechumenate. Every moment of the weekend is orchestrated for maximum psychological impact, according to the detailed prescriptions laid down in Kiko Arguello's 'Guidelines'. In the opening ceremony all the doors and windows are sealed to achieve 'absolute darkness'.

Three minutes of silence follow, which one English girl found so frightening that she and her neighbour clung to one another.

After this ceremony, participants are told to go to bed in silence and to get up in silence, 'as a sign that we are listening to the Lord who is passing by in this *convivence*'.

In Kiko's 'Guidelines', the talks for the weekend take up nearly ninety A4 single-spaced typewritten pages. Just one of the talks, scheduled for the Saturday afternoon, is twenty-three pages long and is packed with theological concepts, some of which are of doubtful orthodoxy in Catholic terms.

After the first *convivence* members are asked to make a commitment and begin to experience the insistent demands on their time, fulfilling another of the FAIR points: 'Indoctrinated members put the goals of the cult ahead of individual concerns, interests, education plans, career and health.' Renato told me that top-level catechists like him spent every night of the week working for NC. An Italian former-member talks of 'twice weekly meetings . . . incredibly long, always at night, from which you return with your head beating like a drum, through the ideas that have been chucked into it, that take your breath away, that provoke arguments, mis-understandings, clashes, divisions with your husband and children'.

In fact NC teaches that nothing must come before the commit-ment to the Way. Kiko's 'Guidelines' state uncompromisingly the commitment demanded of members: '. . . there is perfect obedience. Because if there is not obedience to the catechist, there is no catechumenal Way.' This obedience is expected not of monks and nuns with vows but of lay men and women who are required to make their God-given duties, as laid down by the Catholic Church – that is, their duties to one another and to their children – take second place to the needs of the movement. As an English former member observes, 'I hated the constant confusion over what it was we were worshipping – Christ or the Neocatechumenate.'

The catechists even try to exert their power over those who have left. An Italian woman ex-member was invited to what she thought was a private chat with her catechist. She was astonished to find herself facing a kind of kangaroo court, along with other 'defendants'. When she challenged the authority of the catechist, he told her 'You must obey and that's that! Whether you like it or not, we are God!'

The FAIR marks of sects are equally relevant to Focolare; but, unlike the openly aggressive approach of NC, Focolare's iron fist is discreetly clad in a velvet glove of warmth and smiles.

As Focolare is not parish-based, but has its own structures independent of the Church establishment, its main proselytizing methods are open meetings and personal contacts. Convinced that it is the movement's destiny to unite the world, and that it possesses the fullness of truth, everyone is considered a suitable target, not just Catholics or Christians. A recent article in the movement's Italian magazine describes its style of 'evangelization':

> Whoever has received the gift of the charism of unity feels spontaneously in himself the desire to transmit it to others; he feels responsible for all those with whom he comes into contact. He is a little bit like a farmer who first of all ploughs the land for the sowing and then cultivates the shoots in their growth with infinite patience.[1]

The agricultural images are used to suggest the subtle approach which only gradually reveals its true intentions. When I was a member, we considered our immediate work or study environment to be the main field of action where all this ploughing and sowing would be carried out. We were told not to talk about the movement at first. Instead, we were to 'make ourselves one' with those around us. This meant listening to them, interesting ourselves in their affairs, agreeing with them in everything, sharing their tastes, becoming close friends. There was nothing 'spontaneous' about this at all. We were under constant pressure to report back with results and even to deliver converts. Every member of the movement is expected to have his 'bunch' (grappolo, as in 'bunch of grapes') of potential members he or she is cultivating. Most effort would be expended on those we felt had the greatest potential as recruits.

As I know from my nine years' experience in the movement, Focolare's method of showering people with attention closely resembles the 'love-bombing' of the Moonies, especially when practised at the large-scale meetings organized for newcomers. FAIR warns: 'Beware of people who are excessively or inappropriately friendly': such behaviour can be characteristic of sects.

We were urged to 'make ourselves one' with others in everything but sin. We were concerned with saving souls. What did it matter

---

[1] Oreste Paliotti, 'By this you will know them', *Città nuova*, no. 13, 1993, p. 30.

what one said or agreed to in order to achieve this supreme end? The term *sincerity* has no meaning in Focolare and is never used, for it suggests that words and actions should be consonant with feelings. Our behaviour, on the contrary, was to be dictated consciously and consistently by the teachings of the movement, not by feelings which always deceive us and if possible should be stamped out altogether.

The eventual aim of this 'technique' was that, if we 'make ourselves one' with others, they would wonder why we were different and this would be the chance to win them over: 'Sooner or later, it will happen that someone will ask about our life, desiring to enter our world as well.'[1] But behind this discreet method there was a single goal: winning over converts. In addition to our daily contacts, our aspirations for recruitment had to be limitless: 'While this [making ourselves one] happens with the few with whom we are in direct contact, we entrust to God all the others who we come across in our work environment or work in the hope of establishing a direct contact with them.'[2]

It was important to gain the confidence of our missionary targets and only tell them as much as we felt they could handle so that they would not be put off: '[We should not] assume the attitude of teachers, which would be distasteful: then the other person would reject us and all our work would have been in vain.' Although we may be very cautious about mentioning religion or the movement at first, the ultimate objective was quite clear: 'When it seems to be the right moment . . . [the candidate] should be put in touch with others so that he can feel part of a living body and be enriched with other experiences. The goal therefore is the insertion in the community.'[3]

It is vital to realize that we were not being encouraged to 'befriend' in any generally accepted sense. Individuals inside and outside the movement were seen solely in terms of the part they might play in the institution. But there was more to it than that. The movement's goal was to impose its dualistic vision of the world and human nature on every aspect of members' lives and thoughts. Nothing expresses this dualism more powerfully than the fact that the words 'natural' and in particular 'human' have a totally negative

[1] op. cit., p. 30.
[2] op. cit., p. 30.
[3] op. cit., p. 30.

sense for the *focolarini*. 'Human' is virtually synonymous with sin and evil. The worst sin a *focolarino* could commit was to 'fall into the human' ('*cadere nel'umano*'). The opposite state, which is the required one, is to be 'in the supernatural' or 'in the divine'. This means that all our actions must be dictated by the various slogans of the movement such as 'unity', 'Jesus in the midst', 'Jesus forsaken'. We were encouraged to bear these ideas in mind continually, so that ultimately no personal thoughts or feelings would remain. This was particularly true of relationships. To feel love or affection for others was 'human' and bad. The 'supernatural' approach was to 'see Jesus' in others in a very literal sense, almost imposing His image on the target of our attentions: 'to supernaturalize our way of seeing'.[1]

This 'supernatural' love effectively gives an ideological backing to the devaluing of the individual common to all the movements. To love others – including friends, spouses, children – for their own sake is 'human' and therefore wrong. This precept is to be rigidly applied. Feelings of affection have to be consciously suppressed or 'pruned', in the language of Chiara Lubich: 'In order to be "true", love feeds on "knowing how to lose" – in a continuous pruning – affection for everything or everyone that is not the will of God in the present.'[2]

'If in some moment we find something or someone in our hearts which is not God, we should detach ourselves from it immediately,' Chiara adds. Unity as preached by the movement, therefore, is not a *feeling*; it is not, God forbid, a sense of common humanity. It is a conscious collective submission to the ideas of the movement or, more specifically, of Chiara Lubich: 'Unity is the effect of having adhered together to the same shining truth.'[3]

By now it should be evident that the Focolare 'supernatural' approach to recruitment, and indeed to all relationships, is diametrically opposed to what may normally be described as spontaneity. Rather it is one of cold calculation. Potential recruits, particularly the young or those who are seen as having potential for 'understanding', will be doggedly pursued.

Officially, the idea of joining Focolare or enrolling as a member

[1]Chiara Lubich, conference call, 28 April 1988.
[2]Oreste Paliotti, 'By this you shall know them', *Città nuova*, no. 13, 1993, p. 30, quoting Chiara Lubich, *Meditations*.
[3]Chiara Lubich, conference call, 14 April 1988.

is always derided. But in reality detailed files are kept of all those who have been in contact with the movement and are therefore to be 'followed'. These are regularly updated with names, addresses, meetings attended and comments like '*carino*' or '*carissimo*'. Focolare was keeping secret files on its contacts long before they were in vogue. This fact might not seem of great importance, but for one sinister detail which gives an insight into how membership of the movement is viewed. Shortly after I joined, I was working on updating these files after an important open meeting. I noticed that there was a section at the back labelled with a large 'M'. When I asked what this meant I was told it was the section for those who had left the movement. 'M' stood for 'Morti' – the Dead.

The life of Focolare consists principally of meetings, and as soon as contacts betray an interest they are pressurized into taking part in as many of these as possible. Sometimes great effort is required to harvest enough participants for these events, and considerable pressure is put upon members to invite new candidates. These invitations can be vague and even devious. God or religion was not always mentioned, for example. The classic 'line' is 'Come and meet my friends'! I remember how a teenager, a neighbour of ours in the Liverpool Focolare, after attending a number of meetings for young people asked: 'Has this something to do with God?'

The Focolare year revolves around a number of specific events all aimed at winning over new members or deepening the commitment of current ones. In spring or early summer of each year 'Day Meetings' are held in cities where the movement is established. They are aimed at newcomers, as a prelude to inviting them to the Mariapolis (City of Mary). This is a five-day total-immersion experience held during the summer holidays and is the main focus of the movement's calendar. One is held in each of the movement's 'zones', or territories; and in large zones, like the regions of Italy, participants can be in the thousands.

The Mariapolis is designed to create an intense and rarefied atmosphere, and guests are pressurized not only to take part in all the organized events in the packed programme, but also not even to leave the site. For this reason self-contained locations like college campuses are chosen. Some recent Mariapolises in the United Kingdom have been held in remote areas of the Lake District.

However, physical isolation is not enough. Those attending Foco-lare residential courses are encouraged to cut off psychologically from their everyday lives, to 'leave all their worries and concerns outside the door'. Identical suggestions are made to NC community members at their *convivences*.

The Mariapolis, like most Focolare events, is highly structured and offers little chance for participation to those attending – hours and hours of lectures are the order of the day. All the talks are prepared centrally in Rome according to the theme chosen by Chiara Lubich for that year. They are learned by heart by different *focolarini* and other members to suggest a varied input.

Focolare meetings are highly manipulative, and great effort is put into creating an emotionally charged atmosphere for the spiritual items of the Mariapolis programme. This is known as 'creating the mood'. Each talk is preceded by songs, which are soothing, gentle or cheerful according to the requirement, to soften up the audience. Gleeful smiles are exchanged between the singers so that the audience can see their 'unity'. Only the superiors have the ability ('the grace') of knowing when the 'mood' is right to start a talk or the next part of the programme. At the Mariapolis this would usually be the male and female superiors of the 'zone'.

Experiences or testimonies are an important aspect of public meetings like the Mariapolis, usually given after each talk as an illustration of how its main points are 'put into practice'. The word 'experience' is deceptive, because it suggests a random impression whose emotional content could be endlessly varied according to the circumstances; an 'experience' in the Focolare sense is a clearly prescribed formula. The speaker will generally begin by outlining a difficult situation he or she has faced, usually involving a potential clash with others. The subject recalls relevant words of Scripture or of Chiara Lubich, puts them into practice, and the solution emerges – preferably with a hint of the miraculous. Experiences demonstrate the movement's ethos of spiritual success. The happy ending is fundamental and should smack of a 'miracle'.

At the end of the Mariapolis participants will be invited on stage to share an 'impression' of the event, carefully screened beforehand and always positive. These 'impressions' are then circulated throughout the movement, creating a euphoric sense of worldwide conquest and conversion. When practised on a smaller

scale in controlled groups, the telling of experiences is an effective technique. At large occasions like the Mariapolis, however,
experiences are employed to deliver an emotional wallop.

Like Neocatechumenate, Focolare allows very little space for
feedback in its meetings. In the United Kingdom, however, it was
found necessary at least to create the impression of feedback through
group discussions – usually an exchange of experiences as described
above, carefully orchestrated by an experienced group leader.
Diversionary tactics will be used to head off those who ask difficult
questions or who hog the floor in group sessions. No dissent is
allowed in Focolare at any level; and so, although question-and-
answer sessions do take place, questions have to be submitted in
advance in writing so that speakers can choose which they will
answer and prepare their replies. Like other sectarian movements,
Focolare has an answer for everything.

The intense programme allows little free time; and, even during
this, experienced members will circulate to ensure that the conversation is kept to the subject of the Mariapolis or the movement.
The aim is to create an atmosphere of euphoria into which
newcomers will be absorbed. Members are expected to smile and
be joyful at all times – to be 'up', in the jargon. All doubts and
problems must be hidden. Members with difficulties (or those who
actually leave) are described as 'down'.

Late every night, secret meetings are held for the inner circle to
discuss special cases such as those who ask difficult questions
in discussion groups or are spreading dissent. At this conclave,
'guardian angels' are appointed and specific tactics are worked out
to ensure that by the end of the Mariapolis the goal will be achieved
and everyone will be hooked. No-one is aware that they are being
specifically targeted – or, indeed, that there is much of an
organization. In fact, in the United Kingdom, because of meetings
that start late and overrun, there are jokes about 'Italian' time and
a general impression of *lack* of organization. This is far from the
case. In my experience it is striking how efficient the Mariapolis
and other Focolare meetings are in breaking down the resistance
of those who might initially be doubtful.

Within the totally controlled environment created at these
meetings, the main method of indoctrination is by the repetition
of certain basic tenets. There is no reasoned or logical exposition;
the points of the movement's doctrine are simply proclaimed. Ugo

Poletti, then Cardinal Vicar of the Rome diocese, told a Focolare meeting in the city held on 27 May 1990: 'Union, unity, spirituality of unity, mutual love as the construction of a united world: repeated, repeated, repeated, and all this enters your heart . . .' He compares the process to the endless hammer-blows needed to hammer nails into the hard wood of the ancient oaks in his native Piedmont. Coincidentally, Focolare has a similar but more grisly image to represent the way these key ideas and phrases must obsess members: they must be like 'a nail in your head'.

At the beginning of 1971, having finished my degree course and spent three months in the London Focolare Centre, I took the train to Italy where I would spend two years at the school for *focolarini*, based in the movement's model village of Loppiano near Florence. At the end of this period I could be sent anywhere in the world and would take vows of poverty, chastity and obedience, which would eventually bind me to the movement for life. The thought of dedicating my life to God and His work filled me with a sense of exhilaration and adventure. But I had finally been cut loose from my bearings and had lost control of my life. I was not able to understand and analyse what happened to me at Loppiano until much later: it was the annihilation and absorption of the individual personality by the institution. As this fierce and deliberate process of destruction began, I found myself sinking helplessly into the blackest period of my life before or since.

Externally, Loppiano occupies one of the loveliest locations imaginable. Built on land given to the movement in the early sixties by the Italian wine-making Folonari family, several of whom became full-time *focolarini*, it is a veritable Shangri-La. But this site was used, as is the practice of many sects and cults, as a way of isolating us totally from outside influences. It was an exquisite prison.

The isolation was complete. We were nearly a mile from civilization. The local population consisted of old and illiterate peasants. We never saw a newspaper or watched television in the two years we spent there, so we knew practically nothing of what was going on in the outside world, and after a while it did not seem to matter. While I was there, Radio Loppiano was launched, broadcasting each weekday evening for about fifteen minutes to a handful of receivers. Brief headlines of world news would be followed by more detailed news of the movement.

There were no books, apart from the writings of Chiara Lubich and a few other spiritual books published by Città Nuova, the movement's Italian publishing house. Reading was frowned on anyway. It was thought odd for someone to spend time alone in any pursuit – but especially reading. In the time I was there I read just two books. There was one portable record-player generally available in Loppiano and one long-playing record, a well-worn disc inappropriately titled 'La novicia ribelde' ('The Rebellious Novice') – it was the soundtrack of The Sound of Music, which an Argentinian focolarino had been sent by his family. The record-player and this one record were much sought after and would circulate constantly. The only outsiders we met were visitors who would come to look round on Sundays – usually from Italian parishes. Rather than ask them about what was going on in the outside world, our task was to tell them about Loppiano.

Each year there would be an intake of about fifty men and fifty women, strictly segregated, our quarters being separated by a clear mile of open countryside. These future leaders of the movement would come from all over the world. Most of us only had the vaguest idea of what to expect – Loppiano had no prospectus, so we only knew what the focolarini in our respective countries had chosen to tell us, and usually that was very little. When I left England for Loppiano there had been no other candidates for full-time membership on the horizon.

At the beginning of my second year, suddenly four new English recruits turned up. We understood that there had been a 'drive' from the Centre for new focolarini and that the 'zones' had been given numerical targets they had to reach. As these English novices had known the movement for less than a year, I was appointed to be their guardian angel for the first few weeks. I was astonished at how unprepared they were. On the first evening at supper, one, who had been in an Anglican seminary for a time, asked how much pocket money they would receive and when was their day off. He was disappointed to find that the answer to both questions was negative.

Most of us never left the confines of Loppiano at all except in July and August when we would be sent to our 'zone' to help with the Mariapolis, usually followed by two weeks' holiday and a visit to our families. I was lucky in that I was occasionally sent to Rome or elsewhere to translate at various Focolare events. Total isolation was seen as of vital importance. Only towards the very end of our course were we taken for days out – usually to the shrines which abound in Italy – or for a longer visit to Trento where the movement began.

But this isolation was not to avoid distractions to our devotional life. It was to ensure that every aspect of our lives was under the complete control of our superiors. Our minds, attitudes and beliefs were to be radically changed, not through a gradual process of learning and growth of personal conviction but through an intensive barrage which would often be quite openly referred to, jokingly, as brainwashing.

It was at Loppiano that the movement's strong anti-intellectual bias first struck me. Those branded intellectuals would be given the most menial tasks, as practised during China's cultural revolution. An Italian who later qualified as a psychologist and left the movement did hard labour in the fields for the entire two years of his course. But the attack on reason was taken to extremes: a total ban on thought was imposed on us. 'You think too much,' we would be told if we asked questions. 'Don't think,' our leaders would urge us. 'Stop reasoning.' Or, more alarmingly, 'Cut of your head.' Anyone who had problems with the way of life or the ideas with which we were bombarded would be told he was 'closed', 'complicated', 'creating problems for himself' or even suffering from a 'complex'. 'Mentality' was a popular buzzword, and those who disagreed with the movement were said to have an 'old' mentality. We were told not to try to understand but to do as we were bidden, to 'throw ourselves into the life' at Loppiano, and understanding would follow.

Every aspect of our lives was orchestrated to prevent any kind of reflection or personal life and to ensure that we were never alone. We were divided into mixed-nationality groups of about seven or eight people (Italian was the common language) and billeted in small prefabricated chalets or apartments in converted farm houses. Our living-quarters were very cramped, preventing any privacy, although 'modesty' while dressing or washing was strictly observed.

As for personal relations that might have given us some sort of stability and identity, the motto was divide and rule. 'Particular friendships' were strongly discouraged. In view of this injunction, which was conveyed to us in official talks, I found myself avoiding people I liked. A practice aimed at preventing the formation of bonds, or 'attachments' in the movement's jargon, was that of constantly reshuffling the groups. After we had spent a couple of months together, without warning, one evening before supper, a list would be read out announcing the new configurations, and we would all have to pack our few belongings and move in with our new group there and then. The changes were designed so that no-one would still be with a former house-mate.

Each community had a leader, usually an experienced *focolarino* who for some mysterious reason had been sent back to Loppiano from his 'zone'. The hierarchy was as rigid as ever. Each evening the leaders met privately with the superior of the men's section of Loppiano, Alfred Zirondoli, a priest and former anaesthetist known in the movement as Maras (Maria Assunta). This meeting was popularly known as 'Olympus'. Here, the timetables would be decided; and, again, the emphasis was on constant change and uncertainty. The daily or weekly timetable would constantly be altered. Often plans would be changed at a moment's notice. From time to time, we would have to abandon an evening meal halfway through and answer a summons to a general meeting in the main hall.

The timetable was a full one. Generally we would rise at 6.30 or 7 a.m., starting the day's activities at seven-thirty with meditation, which was always a group experience orchestrated by a leader, usually Maras. He would read the gospel for that day's mass and make a brief commentary. Out of the hundred or more present – the first and second years of the course – he would choose at random those who should share an 'experience' inspired by the reading. This was a controlled situation in which the sharing of 'experiences' could be corrected and our past lives redefined in terms of the doctrine of the movement, a recognized method of thought reform. The second in command at Loppiano in the early seventies, an Italian called Umberto Giannettone, was particularly critical of individual contributions. If he felt they were merely ideas, or thoughts, he would insist on a 'proper' experience in Focolare terms. The fear of being picked on in these meetings was part of the continuous feeling of anxiety that was created at Loppiano in many different ways.

After meditation there was half an hour for breakfast and then work from eight-thirty till one o'clock. There would be the traditional long Italian lunch-hour until three o'clock and then work again till seven-thirty or eight o'clock when there was mass. After mass we would have supper and often meet again in the main hall at nine till midnight or later for talks. Very occasionally there would be shows we would put on ourselves, or films. Work was mainly manual. A caravan factory employed about forty of the men. Smaller workshops included one which manufactured carpet tiles, another which repaired meters for the Gas Board, and an 'artisan' centre which produced wooden goods. I spent eighteen months of my time at Loppiano in the last, sandpapering napkin-rings. For the final six months, I was lent out, for reasons unknown to me, to the 'professors' who taught us theology, in order to catalogue their library of books – a task I found rather more congenial.

Two mornings a week we would have lectures with qualified *focolarini* teachers on theology, Scripture, salvation history, and even philosophy and theology. Although these were actually rather good and well prepared, they were taken very lightly by the students as they were considered intellectual and therefore to be despised. Many students, often the favourites of those in authority, would openly sleep during the lectures. This attitude was tacitly approved of by our superiors – though not, of course, by the teachers themselves, who found it frustrating. At the end of the year we would sit ridiculously simple oral exams for which no-one revised and yet everyone passed. The purpose of the lectures, I believe, was to give our course some kind of juridical status in the eyes of the Church.

We would work on Saturday morning, and Saturday afternoon would be free to clean the house or for group activities within our small communities (not to go into town, which would have been unthinkable).

Sundays were the most strenuous days of all. Hundreds, some-times thousands of visitors would arrive and would have to be given the Loppiano treatment. They would come by coach from all over Italy, usually on parish outings, and they would have to be fed, entertained and fêted so that they would leave 'converted'. Half the groups would go to the women's district of Loppiano in the morning and half would come to us. They would each be given a 'show' of songs, talks and 'experiences'. After mass and lunch, the coaches would carry our groups to the women's end and vice versa, for the second performance of the day.

First thing on Sunday mornings after meditation, the duty roster for the day would be read out. Some of us would be on traffic duty; others would be seconded to the kitchens; the members of the resident band and those known to have good 'experiences' to tell would put on the 'show'. The task we dreaded most was accompanying the groups. We would be assigned to meet a particular coach and would spend the entire day with its occupants. However exhausted or depressed we might feel, it was our job to mingle, establishing personal contacts with all of them and, by overflowing with joy and kindness, convince them that this was Utopia. On these occasions, all the 'citizens' of Loppiano were expected to be 'up', *lanciati* ('speeding'). When the visitors had left we would be numb with exhaustion, especially if we had accompanied the groups. But the essential artificiality of the situation never struck us – the fact that we were putting on a large-scale performance, that for one day Loppiano became a spiritual Disneyland.

From September to Christmas, on Sundays some of us would be assigned to perhaps the most dreaded activity of all: the subscriptions campaign. In addition to the other Sunday jobs, a group of us would be condemned to travel by minibus to a nearby town or village and go door-to-door selling subscriptions to the movement's Italian magazine, *Città nuova*. Most of the people we visited looked at us suspiciously and – at least, at first – refused to believe that we were Catholics.

Inevitably, such an isolated, rarefied society developed its own bizarre code of conduct and scale of values. Loppiano was a kind of movement within the movement. While the cult of Chiara was as strong as ever and the whole village went berserk when she visited, our superior, Maras, also had a fanatical following. Success at Loppiano was measured in terms of one's 'unity' with Maras. The instant Maras emerged from his office, he would be surrounded by a swarm of *focolarini,* smiling, cooing 'Ciao, Maras!' and hanging on his every word. Ten people would pack themselves in his Audi to drive a hundred yards with him. When, towards the end of our two years, we went on coach trips, bodies would be piled on top of one another on the seats surrounding Maras, in order to catch his pearls of wisdom. Others would be suspended above him between the luggage-racks. It was the practice to write him letters, often imploring a private audience, which was regarded as the greatest good to which we could aspire. *Focolarini* would hide in his wardrobe or under his bed and leap out in the middle of the night in order to obtain this favour. Others would hang around for days in 'Maras' antechamber' outside his office, a legendary spot for us; they would beg for an interview or simply watch him enter and exit with a hang-dog expression. Maras himself fuelled the insidious belief that if you were 'in unity' he would notice you, otherwise he would not see you. This was another myth which created artificial tensions and anxieties in all of us. As with many of the fictitious mysteries encouraged within the new movements, it was impossible to know what to do in order to be 'noticed'. Stranger still was the court of favourites that Maras assembled around him. This group – known to all, but rarely mentioned, even in private conversations – would eat with him and 'make unity' with him until 2 a.m. We all – very charitably, it seems to me now – assumed that these privileged creatures were *anime belle*, beautiful or privileged souls in the movement's parlance.

Some years later, a surprising but revealing sequel to these events occurred while I was in the Liverpool Focolare. One of Maras' stars, known in the movement as 'Thanks' ('Grazie'), who was never seen at Loppiano without the toothiest of smiles, and who had a patronizing pat on the shoulder for everyone he met, was sent to us to learn English with a view to a plum assignment in Australia. The grin rapidly vanished. In the four or five months he spent in Liverpool, the only routes he ever learned were those to his language school, the supermarket and the church. Apart from these three daily sorties, he never went out of doors. The rest of his time was taken up in a constant barrage of criticism against the British, the British way of life, the stupidities of the language. Needless to say, 'Thanks' said 'No, thanks' to learning English and was sent back to Italy. This incident threw new light on those exalted beings I had so envied and admired.

At the end of the eighties, the school of the *focolarini* moved to another of the movement's villages at Montet in Switzerland. It is curious that, after a short time there, Maras was called back to Rome and given a much lower profile, writing biographies of deceased members of the movement. Could this have been an indication that there was not room for more than one personality cult in the organization?

Within this unreal world with its artificial anxieties, our mental and critical faculties slackened. At the same time, the demands for total, unreasoning obedience increased. One day the leader of my Focolare, a rather humourless German *focolarino* named Heiner, a rigid hard-liner, gave me one of Chiara's unpublished writings to use for meditation. It was on the subject of obedience, and I found it chilling. It quoted St Francis, who spoke of 'planting cabbages upside down' as an example of blind obedience to the point of absurdity. The gist of the piece, however, was that Focolare obedience goes much further than that. Before our superior we had to be empty, nothing, completely unquestioning; we had to fulfil his every whim.

The simplistic concept of unity and community promulgated by Focolare has no place for personal searches or personal interior life of any kind. There can be no search when all the answers have already been provided. The only permitted interior life is internalizing and regurgitating the teachings of Chiara Lubich. The 'unity' required is not only blind obedience at an external level, but also an assent of the mind – so-called 'unity of mind' or 'unity of thought'.

In the course of my time at Loppiano, the true significance of 'unity' in the movement's sense was borne in on me. As it emanated from and returned to the person of Chiara Lubich, in order to be 'in unity' we learned that it was essential to submit totally to our superior who was 'the channel of unity' leading to the summit. This was part of the reason for the cult of Maras. But it also explained the almost nauseating obsequiousness towards those in authority – the kind that under normal circumstances would be given various nasty names. 'Unity' was not at all the egalitarian concept I had imagined but a reinvention of absolute authority and rigid hierarchy.

This theory of unity was particularly frightening in Loppiano because a number of the people in authority had been sent there because they had problems; several I now believe were suffering from severe depression or nervous breakdowns – perhaps others just had difficulties with the movement. For them Loppiano was a kind of open prison where their problems could be contained. Certainly some of them behaved very strangely. Yet these were the people before whom we were expected to 'empty ourselves'.

I had a run-in with one leader, a particularly bitter and uncommunicative man. It was shortly after I had been appointed guardian angel to my four English protégés. One in particular had reached crisis-point, and I was trying to reassure him one evening after work. We were called to supper, but my charge went on talking and I felt that his distress was such that I could not cut him off in mid-sentence. Within a few seconds, the leader of our group came into the room, sent my friend to supper and angrily upbraided me for breaking unity by not coming immediately. He dismissed my explanation as irrelevant. I was experiencing the rigid concept of unity for the first time. Later I discovered that this particular leader was suffering from a severe breakdown. And yet we who were relative neophytes had been placed under his absolute rule. The idea of complaining to a higher authority, which would certainly have been justified, was totally inadmissible within the Focolare frame of reference. After some months with this leader, I fell ill and was moved to another group.

As well as the spiritual blackmail we were subjected to – that if we had problems, then we alone were to blame – a further pressure was that, however unhappy we were, there was no escape. It was impossible to leave. As we simply worked for our keep, we had no access to money. Many of us came from other continents, so we were completely at the mercy of the movement. Our powers of resistance were so depleted that, had we wanted to leave, the prospect of having to persuade our superiors to let us go would have been a daunting one.

At one point I had contemplated running away, hitching to the British consulate in Florence and borrowing my fare home. I had even reached the point of packing my bag and planning the time and route of my escape so that I would not meet with opposition. But that would have meant a complete break with the movement and, in that environment, it was impossible to imagine living outside its embrace. So there was no real alternative but complete surrender.

Today the very concept of brainwashing is challenged by organizations like the Home-Office backed INFORM (Information Network Focus on Religious Movements) which claims to be even-handed in its study of cults. According to INFORM, all groups influence their members; what critics term brainwashing is merely a point on a sliding scale. If brainwashing existed, no-one would ever leave the cults, they argue. But this approach dangerously fudges the issue. The fact that people leave the movements simply proves that brainwashing is not completely effective. If undue pressure is being used to change the way people think, it has to be named for what it is. In this case it is essential to distinguish between the influence the Catholic Church exerts over the common faithful – allowing them a great deal of freedom – and the thought reform practised by the movements. I believe in brainwashing because I have experienced it at first hand.

In *Secret Sect*, an investigation into the School of Economic Science cult, the authors Peter Hounam and Andrew Hogg formulate eight characteristics of a brainwashing environment. These are derived from a standard work on the subject, *Thought Reform and the Psychology of Totalism: A Study of 'Brainwashing' in China* by Dr Robert Jay Lifton.[1] Focolare total-immersion experiences like those I experienced at Loppiano qualify on all eight points. However, even in the mass rallies, or Mariapolis, participants are subjected to strong psychological pressure.

1. *Environment control.* 'Controllers of the environment . . . try to exert power over everything an individual sees, hears, reads, writes, experiences and expresses.' This is reflected in the isolated locations and intense programmes of activity. Individuals are denied the 'chance to stand back and decide personally whether he or she wants to be part of that environment'. Through 'animators', constant pressure is maintained on Mariapolis participants to keep even casual conversations to the 'party line', and they are strongly discouraged from leaving the environment, even for short periods.

2. *Personal manipulation.* 'Controllers set up an environment in which specific patterns of behaviour and feelings are demanded. The behaviour and emotions then create an effect on the individual which appears to arise quite naturally.' Constant smiles, elation, 'joy', the kinds of behaviour tagged with buzzwords like 'marian', 'up' or 'speeding': all these are characteristic of Focolare gatherings and are rewarded by the approval of leaders. Even more bizarre manifestations like running after the leaders at Loppiano seemed natural and spontaneous within that rarefied atmosphere. Members

[1] New York: Gollancz 1961.

not indulging in these forms of behaviour, on the other hand, would be regarded as 'down' or having 'the old man', and would attract the concern or disapproval of peers and leaders. The effort of maintaining the approved behaviour in the enclosed environment over a period of time brings with it feelings of elation which can be perceived as 'unity' or illumination. The authors of *Secret Sect* quote Lifton's observation that the controllers 'By thus becoming the instruments of their own mystique . . . create a mystical aura around the manipulating institutions – the Party, the Government, the Organisation. They are the agents chosen (by history, by God, or by some other supernatural force . . .)'. At Loppiano, it was not enough to give one's total assent to the movement and its doctrines; one had to be seen to be giving it through the accepted modes of behaviour. This in its turn reinforced belief.

3. *The demand for purity.* 'The good, needless to say, is that which is consistent with the brainwashers' ideology. Anything else is said to be bad or impure.' Focolare lays a strong emphasis on the purity of the message, hence the constant recourse to the same formulae repeated over and over, the continuous repetition of the words of Chiara, held to be the pristine source. 'The search for absolute purity is certainly the foundation stone of their beliefs. But, as Lifton points out, no-one can reach a state of perfection, and the guilt and shame which arise with constant failure make members even more vulnerable to their manipulators.' This was felt strongly at Loppiano where indoctrination with the movement's lofty ideals was constant and we were expected to bear them in mind and practise them every moment of the day. Certainly the feelings of worthlessness and self-doubt I experienced there were in part due to these demands.

4. *Confession.* Although we were not expected to confess sins of a sexual nature in group situations, communal meditations at Loppiano, in which we were chosen to speak at random, were designed to achieve self-revelation or 'total exposure of the person confessing'. Most important, these disclosures were 'an act of symbolic self-surrender, an expression of the merging of the individual with his environment'. Favoured 'experiences' were those in which we accused ourselves of not having lived up fully to the 'Ideal' in the past and described how we had understood more deeply our

dependence on the group, that alone we were 'nothing' or that the 'Ideal' is the only answer to all problems.

We also practised the 'moment of truth'. This took the form of what used to be known in religious orders as the 'chapter of faults' or 'fraternal correction'. Once a month, we would meet in our Focolare or house-group at Loppiano, and tell each of our brother-*focolarini* his faults (known as a 'purgatory') and his good points (a 'paradise'). This was an opportunity to reinforce Focolare virtues – like making unity, behaviour like 'speeding' or being 'marian' – and uproot failings like being 'closed' (uncommunicative) or not 'speeding' (lacking in enthusiasm).

It is worth observing that most religious orders have abolished their version of this practice because it is so open to abuses. Focolare, on the other hand, considers 'the moment of truth' of paramount importance. It is recommended not only for the *focolarini* but also for internal members at every level, including teenagers. As Hounam and Hogg point out, 'The underlying assumption here is that the environment and its instigators have total ownership of each individual within it'. Internal members must also undergo compulsory private interviews (*colloqui privati*) at regular intervals with their superiors – sometimes virtual strangers from the Centre in Rome – during which they might be asked specific questions on their sex lives and other intimate topics. Group discussions at Mariapolis are also aimed at eliciting experiences of a self-revelatory or confessional nature. Animators circulate among newcomers, giving them the opportunity to relieve themselves of the burden of their past lives. These personal revelations will then be shared, perhaps in a toned-down version, in the secret meetings for internal members held late each night in the course of the Mariapolis.

5. *The sacred science.* 'This is the aura which the brainwashing environment builds around its basic dogma, "holding it out as the ultimate moral vision for the ordering of human existence".' It would be hard to deny that this is the role Focolare reserves for 'the Ideal'. It is seen not only as a remedy for the spiritual sphere but also as unlocking the secrets of political and economic harmony. According to Lifton, 'In this way, the philosopher-kings of modern ideological totalism reinforce their authority by claiming to share in the rich and respected heritage of natural science'.

6. *Loading of language*. 'The ideological concepts are expressed in words which become shortcuts through the thought processes.' At Loppiano, every conversation was couched in the movement's own jargon. At the Mariapolis, participants vie in their use of Focolare catchphrases, thus to prove their degree of membership. 'By restricting the language used, capacities for thinking and feeling are similarly narrowed.' Over the months and years we spent at Loppiano, this profound conditioning of our mental and emotional lives began to take effect.

7. *Doctrine over person*. 'Once a person enters the new, controlled environment, all his or her previous experiences are re-examined.' Sharing 'experiences' is a fundamental Focolare practice. Its aim is the transformation of behaviour and also the transformation of the subject's image of himself or herself. The encounter with the movement is seen as a fundamental turning-point, no matter how committed a Christian he or she had been previously. The before-and-after effect is emphasized: before, life was all bad; afterwards, the subject is enlightened. The key words 'when I met the movement' or, more subtly, 'then I made some new friends' or 'I met some people who were different' mark the moment of change. Group or one-to-one conversations at Loppiano, which were always expected to relate to the movement and its ideology, gave ample opportunity to discuss our life before meeting the movement and gradually reinvent it, either seeing it as wholly negative or as a desperate search only fulfilled by 'the Ideal'. Current experiences are constantly demanded of members at every level; in this way, their lives and thought processes are constantly subjected to the scrutiny of the community.

8. *The dispensing of existence*. 'In brainwashing environments, in-dividuals who accept the ideology are granted the "right" to live.' At Loppiano existence came to mean being 'recognized' by Maras. It was he who dispensed the right to live, or withheld it, and this is why we longed for a word, a nod, a glance, a smile, any crumb dropped from the table at which he feasted with his court to those of us suspended in the limbo outside. We were constantly seeking what was called a 'confirmation', an acknowledgement that we were 'in unity' with Maras, because only through him could we be 'in unity' with Chiara and the whole movement. If we were not 'in

unity', we did not exist; hence we were not 'recognized', not 'seen'. We were non-persons.

According to FAIR: 'The leaders or founders (usually living) demand absolute and unquestioning obedience and are the sole judges of the member's faith and commitment.'

As with the other movements, the individual in CL only has significance in terms of his membership of the movement. Don Giussani condemns an 'invasion of non-catholic thought in the church', which, according to him, 'arises from an influence which I would call protestant by which christianity [sic] is perceived exclusively in the context of the relationship between the individual and Christ'. The targets of CL attacks are always left vague, but this statement can – at least, in part – be taken to include those who do not belong to movements.

Giussani is at pains to stress the concrete nature of his movement. The individual who encounters it is faced with a 'confrontation'; he is required to react and change: 'The initial factor which constitutes a movement is the "meeting of an individual with a human diversity", with a different human reality.' But how is a potential recruit to react to this 'difference'? Giussani is adamant about one thing – it is crucial that the recruit should show no personal initiative: 'Whoever, therefore, struck by this difference, tries to follow his destiny by "doing" something himself would lose everything.' Just one thing is required: 'He must follow. That different human presence he has encountered is an "otherness" that must be "obeyed". Through this meeting which is constantly renewed, in the process of following and obeying, continuity with the first encounter is established.'

New recruits are required to enrol in the weekly meetings known as the 'School of Community'. Selected passages from the thoughts of Don Giussani are chosen centrally as the texts to be studied at these meetings. 'The work on the text of the School of Community is the most concrete way of maintaining a systematic relationship with the charism of the movement,' its internal magazine, *Litterae communionis,* declares.[1] This text must be the lodestar for every member of the movement – just as the fortnightly conference call with Chiara Lubich must be the sole inspiration for Focolare

[1] *Parola Tra Noi,* year XIX, December 1992.

members: 'It represents the most important content on which we must concentrate and the reference point for judgement and comparison.' The words of the founder must not so much be interpreted as swallowed whole: 'How is the School of Community a point of comparison? First of all, it must be read clarifying together the meaning of the words. Not an interpretation, but following it literally. It is a rediscovery of the scholastic method of the Middle Ages: such a textually literal reading that they used to write their comments in the margin. We must become disciples of the text.'

The consequences of this literal reading must be twofold. First, the words must be internalized by members and 'put into practice' in their daily lives. But, second, this message must not be kept to oneself – it must become a missionary gesture: 'How can the School of Community be valid for me, if I do not feel it full of promise of hope also for the man I meet on the street or for my school or work mate? If it is valid for me, why is it not valid for him? Proposing it to others, human unity clicks between us, the human thirst that binds us together and the anchor or reply that shines for me and the other person.'

Group leaders are under the same obligation of total submission to the words of the founder: 'He should say, "I understand that this particular passage judges me first and foremost". If, on the other hand, the leader passes on his own thoughts to the group, he accustoms each individual to following his own thoughts.' Those who are not convinced about the School of Community are made to feel guilty: 'It is not productive to substitute something else of one's own invention for the School of Community; it would be unconsciously to admit that one is incapable of taking part in the School of Community.'

CL shares with Focolare and NC an emphasis on 'experience' rather than on reason. The follow-up to the study of the School of Community text is the telling of experiences of how it has changed the life of the individual. The primacy of 'experience' over reason is seen in the leap-of-faith approach recommended to those who have difficulties with the movement. Doubting members are encouraged to 'throw themselves into the experience'.

CL is structured so that it becomes 'the convert's new family': 'A welcoming environment is provided for every stage of life, providing new certainties and solidarity . . . In the articulation of the movement, every aspect of the life of the militant must find its place: school, work, family. These stages mark his progress to adulthood, and at each of them the movement must be able to pass on the spiritual and moral values of which it is the bearer. This way a self-regulated and self-protecting circuit is established.'[1]

The application of rigorous methods of recruitment and training common to all the movements effects a gradual undermining of the personality. The goal, to use FAIR's terms, is 'dependence on the cult' through 'ego destruction'. An English ex-member of NC describes how at her last *convivence* she felt 'like a naked person in a long line of naked people with no identities and that they were trying to strip me of my free will'. A former member of CL recalls how 'When I left, I was nothing . . . I had no personal tastes, I had no ideas of my own to enable me to take decisions . . . I had to rebuild myself from scratch.' It is something I experienced most keenly in the 'total immersion' experience of Loppiano. As well as renouncing all 'attachments', 'losing' everything and everyone that was dear to us, we had also been taught to distrust our feelings. Feelings did not matter. They had to be replaced by the many precepts the movement suggested to us, obsessively applied to our daily lives. These included Chiara's frequent exhortations to 'destroy our ego', 'die to ourselves', 'annihilate' or 'nullify' ourselves. Just as all thought had to be rejected, so did the emotions that had guided us up to this point.

Loppiano achieved this most effectively by ripping us out of our former world and creating a new, totally unreal universe of false values. The feeling of disorientation on first arriving at Loppiano was so acute that my first three months there are a complete blank. I remember them simply as blackness. From the activity and motivation of my teenage years I had passed to a young-manhood of pointless and aimless monotony. What brought this home to me was when I realized, to my horror, that I now spent the whole day looking forward to the next meal. And this was not just because food was so sparse. It was mainly because there was nothing else to look forward to. My previous boundless confidence was replaced by self-doubt and a sense of worthlessness. This not only applied to the spiritual dimension but also included a collapse of faith in my intellectual and practical abilities, too.

[1]Ottaviano Franco, *Gli Estremisti Bianchi,* Rome, Datanews 1986.

I have often had my clearest insights into moral dilemmas when waking in the middle of the night. Situations which were confused and murky by day, become crystal-clear. When I woke in the night at Loppiano, the thought and feeling that would overwhelm me was always the same: 'What the hell am I doing here?' This clarity would evaporate in the sunlight of the following morning, and I would return to what I believed was reality. As everything that had previously been important was drained of its value, only one overpowering feeling remained: Nothing matters.

The feeling that nothing, apart from the movement, mattered underlay my life from then on – even when I left Loppiano. The suspicion that something else did matter would later play a part in my departure from Focolare; but, long after I had left, the old sense of hoplessness would come back to haunt me. Having destroyed everything that had meaning for us, our very personalities were uprooted. There was nothing left to us but to depend utterly for everything on the movement and live our life vicariously in its struggles and triumphs. These justified our existence; or, rather, the immense sacrifices we had made – our very selves.

Why are members of the new movements prepared to give up so much? At the core of their message are the 'virtues' which are hammered home as being more important than any others, half-truths which are far more dangerous than lies. In the case of Focolare, for example, there was the idea of 'Jesus forsaken'. This is Focolare's 'answer' to the problem of suffering. Chiara Lubich teaches that, in the moment when he cried out, 'My God, my God, why have you forsaken me?' (Matthew 27:46), Christ experienced not only the height of physical suffering – which had always been emphasized in the past – but also the ultimate in spiritual and mental suffering. He can therefore be 'recognized' and 'loved' in every spiritual and mental suffering we might experience. 'Jesus forsaken' is described as 'the other side of the coin of unity', the difficulties that have to be overcome in order to generate unity.

Perhaps there is a genuine insight enshrined in this idea. The danger comes when this aspect of the spiritual life hardens into doctrine and is advocated with fanaticism – becomes, in Focolare terminology, an obsession or 'nail in the head'. 'So it will be for the years I have left,' the foundress impresses on her followers. 'I will thirst for suffering, anguish, despair, melancholy, separation, abandonment, torment; for all that is He who is suffering.' 'Let us forget everything in life,' she declares: 'office, work, people, responsibility, hunger, thirst, rest, even our own souls . . . so as to possess only Him!'

The mystery of suffering is a central one to Christianity as it is, inevitably, to all religions. It is a concept which preoccupied all Catholic saints, great Christians of other denominations and sages of every faith. Without doubt, this is an area which requires great spiritual maturity and equilibrium. The doctrine of 'Jesus forsaken' is taught, in language of this intensity, even to children. But, like all the precepts of the movement, it is primarily used to bind members ever closer to the institution, justifying almost any mental torment they might undergo within its structures. While at university, I introduced a fellow-student, not a believer, to Focolare. After an initial period of enthusiasm, attending open meetings and visiting the women's Focolare Centre in London, she announced to me one day that her belief had suddenly vanished. I told her that this temptation was 'Jesus forsaken'. She considered my suggestion for a moment and then observed: 'It's a trap, isn't it?'

Indeed, it was. But once you had accepted the formula it worked very well. Any problems or doubts about the movement were 'Jesus forsaken'. Thus we were encouraged not to question the causes of our discomfort. We were convinced that we had discovered the solution to the age-old problem of suffering. This 'solution' would be applied in a simplistic manner to every situation. Because it led to acceptance, this doctrine also encouraged a worrying tendency to fatalism and quietism, an unquestioning submission to adversity. At a Focolare event I attended in Rome in March 1994, I was disturbed by the 'experience' of a mother who described her son's death through drug addiction. She described how she 'saw "Jesus forsaken" in him' and seemed to advocate a passive role where a more interventionist approach might have been required.

Neocatechumenate have an equivalent doctrine – that of the 'servant of Jahweh' or the 'glorious cross'. This is also equated with non-resistance to any harm that is done to you. It becomes a means of ensuring the acquiescence of members and their dependence on the community.

I am convinced that the undermining of the individual sanctioned by this obsessive desire for suffering is linked to the high incidence of depression and other mental and physical disorders which have been noted in both of these movements, bearing out one of the most sinister of FAIR's marks of sects: 'Converts may display symptoms of extreme tension and stress, fear, guilt . . .' An NC catechist in Hamburg reached the verge of suicide and had to be admitted to hospital by his family.

From my limited knowledge while I was in and since I have left Focolare, I am aware of a high incidence of depression among internal members. One Dutch *focolarino* of my acquaintance was transformed, in the space of a couple of years, from an outgoing and dynamic stalwart of the movement in the Netherlands into a shuffling zombie who did not even recognize me when I met him in this state. It is also a matter for concern that the movement tends to send those suffering from depression to approved psychiatrists or preferably to treat them within the movement. A disturbing development is that a clinic has been set up near the movement's Centre in Rome, staffed by Focolare psychiatrists, to deal with the depression and other mental illnesses of internal members. This could be prejudicial to the care of those whose illness might be directly caused by their membership of the movement and for whom the solution might be to leave.

From my own experience and that of others I know, there is also a questionable use of drugs in order to alter the behaviour of individuals to conform to what the movement regards as normal. Homosexuality is still regarded as a disease by Focolare, who have not hesitated in the past to use drugs in an attempt to alter the behaviour of members in this respect.

Perhaps the most dangerous half-truth held in common by all the movements, though couched in their various jargons, is the idea of an 'existential' approach to belief. By this they mean that the individual experiences God *through the community*. The result is the reduction of the individual to a cipher and the deification of the institution.

Focolare expresses this through the concept of 'Jesus in the midst'; CL through the idea of the 'event', which is Christ in history today – that is, in the movement: 'Christ is present according to the method He has created: the company of people He seizes and makes one with Himself. With these people made one with Him and therefore linked between them, He is present in the world and has a face.'

NC – with a debt to Focolare, I suspect – focuses on the concept of mutual love in the community ('By this they will know that you are my disciples'), which Kiko refers to as 'a presence of Jesus Christ for which it is not necessary to have faith'.

All three movements use the idea of 'Come and meet my friends, come and see for yourself and then you will understand'. Hence the evasive 'You can only understand it by experiencing it', also common to these movements.

The methodology of recruitment and training, however, is ample proof that what appears to be an existential approach is in fact deliberately manipulated. The 'existential' slant would appear to exalt the role of the individual's reaction. What happens is the very opposite. Once again, the insight contained in the idea of the community becomes a rigid doctrine with the sole aim of reinforcing the institution. It becomes an obsession.

One of Chiara Lubich's writings on 'Jesus in the midst' says: 'If we are united, Jesus is among us . . . This is worth more than any other treasure that our hearts may possess; more than mother, father, brothers, children. It is worth more than our house, our work, or our property; more than the works of art in a city like Rome; more than our business deals; more than the nature that surrounds us with flowers and fields, more than our own soul.'

Applied to 'unity' with, and within, the movement, this is a very dangerous assertion indeed.

A story I was told by an internal member illustrates the bizarre lengths to which this idea of unity within Focolare can be taken.

Recently a *focolarina* was dying of cancer. Her superior was at her bedside and wished to remain with her to the end. An envoy, one of Chiara Lubich's 'first companions', had been sent from Rome to bring Chiara's unity to the dying woman. The night when the doctors believed the end was obviously very close, the envoy from Rome insisted on taking the superior out to a restaurant for dinner to regale her with stories of Chiara Lubich's latest exploits. This was to teach her that she had to 'lose' her dying spiritual daughter. The payoff of the story as I was told it is that, of course, they got back to the hospital in time for the girl's death. This sort of behaviour bears little resemblance to any definition of love as it might be understood outside the ranks of these movements.

The idea of God present in the institution has many other dangerous consequences. One is the triumphalism possessed by the old-style Catholic Church, the conviction that it cannot err. I was puzzled when, a few years after meeting the movement, I went to my superior in London with a personal problem. His main concern was that I should not blame my problem on the movement – an idea which had never occurred to me. This betrayed the conviction that the institution is infallible.

By emphasizing the presence of God in the community and playing down the importance of the individual, the deep interior spiritual life needed to give inner strength and conviction is lacking. It is almost as though the soul is turned inside out and the spiritual life happens on the outside within the community – hence the need for constant contact and meetings – to 'top up' the communal experience. Those attending the Mariapolis for the first time and experiencing a 'high' would often complain of the terrible 'low' which followed after they had left. They would be reassured that this was normal and be encouraged to come to the next meeting or join a group.

The greatest danger, however, is that the institution becomes totally identified with God. Focolare and the other movements believe they have God in their pockets. God lives within their community; He is theirs to conjure up at will. It is from this conviction that all the other abuses stem: the belief in the omniscience of the movement, the glorification of the institution and the destruction of the individual, the identification of the movement with the Church, the rigid application of its precepts, the assurance that any methods, including deception, which propagate the movement are licit. If the movement or community reveals God, possesses God or in some way *is* God, everything is permissible. These are views which would shock and repel most Catholics, yet they are the fundamental precepts of the movements that were presented by the Vatican in 1987 to the bishops of the world as the definitive model for the laity.

3

World Showcase

'WE ARE WITNESSING A FLOWERING OF NEW MOVEMENTS, AKIN TO the appearance in the thirteenth century of the Franciscans and the Dominicans!' With these ringing words, Bishop Paul-Josef Cordes, of the Pontifical Council of the Laity, affirmed the Vatican's option for the new ecclesial movements before his brother bishops of the world.

The fact that the Synod on the Laity held in October 1987 had been allotted, as its hidden agenda, to showcase these movements took the majority of the Synod Fathers gathered in Rome by surprise. They had been expecting to debate what they considered to be more burning issues such as the role of women in the Church and the greater participation of the laity in its government. Instead they were presented with this vast 'lay' Armada, its centralized structures, ideology and projects all firmly in place and above discussion. It evidently had the Pope's blessing; all the bishops were being asked was to add theirs.

Even Cardinal Martini, as Archbishop of Milan well placed to monitor the mood of the Vatican, had failed to foresee this turn of events. Shortly before his departure for Rome, in an address to Italy's official lay movement, Catholic Action, which is allied to the Italian Bishops' Conference, he had dismissed the issue of new movements as 'a problem which is much discussed in Italy but which does not apply to other countries'. Martini is well known in his native land as an opponent of CL, which has its headquarters in Milan, and also of Neocatechumenate which he has forbidden to spread in the diocese. His predictions for the Synod were proved wrong on two counts: first, because the movements were very much centre-stage at the Synod; and, second, because his brother bishops from all over the world had a lot to say on the subject, both for and against, but mostly against.

The first clue that something was afoot was the fact that the lay representation was 'packed' with members of the new movements. The sixty lay representatives, or *auditores* ('hearers' rather than 'speakers'), included Focolare's foundress Chiara Lubich and Neo-catechumenate's Kiko Arguello. Also present, among thirty 'papal nominees', were the founder of Communion and Liberation, Don Giussani, and the Prelate of Opus Dei, Monsignor Alvaro del Portillo, who, of course, were not laymen, although their movements are deemed to be lay. All of these at some stage in the Synod had the opportunity to extol the virtues of their institution before the assembly.

The sixty *auditores* were representing 700 million Catholics worldwide; yet they were all nominated by the Pope with the assistance of Archbishop Jan Schotte, secretary-general of the Synod. And nobody, not even the bishops, seemed to know according to what criteria they had been chosen. The bishops of England and Wales had certainly not been consulted. The late Cardinal O Fiaich, Archbishop of Armagh, was said not even to have heard of the Irish representative, Patrick Fay, president of the Legion of Mary. The strongest protests came from Brazil's National Council for the Laity. In the forefront of developing base communities, a practical application of liberation theology, the Brazilians had had very clear ideas on who their representatives should be; and yet the nominees were Mr and Mrs Toaldo of the right-wing German Schoenstatt movement, one of the 'pietistic' movements later singled out for attack by South American bishops. In other words, these 'representatives' did not appear to be at all representative of the group this Synod was supposed to be concerned with. It was also clear that the numbers from the movements were out of all proportion to their numerical presence in the Church.

So how had the list of *auditores* been chosen? The previous May, an 'international consultation' had been held at Rocca di Papa, in the Alban Hills just outside Rome. This had been organized by the Pontifical Council for the Laity, the body in the Curia with responsibility for the laity, and the organizers of the Synod. It was presided over by the same Bishop Cordes who was to wax so lyrical over the new movements. About 200 men and women had taken part in the 'consultation', at the Pope's invitation, many of them representing lay associations and movements. About half of the final line-up of *auditores* was chosen from among those present at the Rocca di Papa meeting.

The traditional method for the Roman Curia to point an event like a Synod in their direction is through the *Lineamenta* and *Instrumentum laboris*, discussion documents prepared in advance as a necessary guide to an event which takes place in a limited period of time and where the possible speakers are many. The documents for the Synod on the Laity were prepared by Bishop Cordes. One of the points they stressed, in language that was incongruously vehement, was that 'the laity are to strive to overcome the pernicious separation between professed faith and daily life',[1] a key slogan of the new movements, and a highly ambiguous one.

The discussion document highlighted another theme that was to become a buzzword of the Synod – that of the 'clericalization' of the laity: 'If respect for their secular character is kept in mind, the grave danger of clericalizing the laity will be diminished.'[2] 'Clericalization', in Vatican-speak, means that the laity should not meddle in Church government; in other words, should not expect the Church to be a democracy – a word guaranteed to strike horror into the hearts of every member of the Roman Curia.

The third World Congress for the Apostolate of the Laity, held in 1967 with the authorization of Pope Paul VI and composed of delegates sent by the world's bishops, had sent shockwaves through the Church with its call for a degree of democratization and elected representation for the laity. It was the last gathering of its kind. With the movements, the Vatican was putting its money on a new breed of layperson, tightly controlled by their respective organizations which vowed collective allegiance to the central authority of the Pope. The founders of the new movements have all spoken out vigorously against the idea of democracy in the Church – hardly surprising in view of their own hierarchical structures. Ironically, the word 'clericalization' proved a handy one for the opponents of

[1] *Instrumentum laboris*, para. 28.
[2] *Instrumentum laboris*, para. 31.

the movements in order to highlight their inward-looking and over-spiritualized approach. Soon it was being bandied about on all sides, with a host of different meanings.

The author of the *Lineamenta* and *Instrumentum laboris*, Bishop Paul-Josef Cordes, can be regarded as the architect of the 1987 Synod. He is also the prime advocate and protector of the new movements in the Roman Curia. A former bishop of Paderborn in Germany, he was appointed Vice-President of the Pontifical Council for the Laity by Pope John Paul II in 1980, and since then its prestige within the Vatican has grown steadily. Although his nominal superior is the Argentinian Cardinal Pironio, the Council's President, Cordes is regarded as the key player. In addition to his special responsibility for the vast and sprawling Catholic Charismatic movement, he was appointed by the Pope as his representative *ad personam* to Neocatechumenate – making him John Paul's direct channel to the movement and squeezing out Pironio, who is known to have doubts about NC.

In a recent interview with Bishop Cordes, I had the clear impression that he takes the movements at face value, accepting their own definitions of themselves, and sees them as the most vital spiritual force in the Church today. He has given short shrift in the past to Italian critiques of the new movements that have studied them from a sociological or psychological perspective. Cordes himself is the author of a book, *Charisms and New Evangelisation*,[1] which justifies the movements by comparing their current difficulties (with local bishops) to those of great missionary movements of the past like the Franciscans and the Jesuits. This was written to convince doubters and to 'comfort' members. Cordes also sees the movements as a new justification for the papacy – as their protector – and has developed a theory of *communio*, or Church unity centred on the Pope, expounded in a recent theological tome, published in Italy by *Città Nuova*, Focolare's Italian publishing house. To Neocatechumenate, however, who consider him a fellow-member, Bishop Cordes is simply 'Paul'.

In the light of the thorough preparations in the movements' favour and his close relations with them, the Pope's homily at the opening liturgy of the Synod takes on a new significance:

[1] St Paul Publications, 1991.

> Christ says: 'Whatever you bind on earth shall be bound in heaven, and whatever you loose on earth shall be loosed in heaven' (Mt 18:18). We are confident that the Holy Spirit, who has been given to us in the Church – and for the Church – will help us also to *loose* whatever *needs* to be loosed in this vast sphere of the laity, so that their proper and specific tasks for the ecclesial mission will *spring forth* from their vocation.

For Catholics the authority to bind and loose belongs to the papacy. In this context he appears to be using this authority to grant to the movements the freedom he believes they need to prosper – that is, freedom from the interference of the bishops. Early in the Synod, on 6 October, Cardinal Ratzinger's authoritative voice as Prefect of the Congregation for the Doctrine of the Faith made the Vatican view of the movements very clear: 'Today the many and different spiritualities find particular expression in various spiritual movements, in which the insertion of the laity in the Church is concretely realised.'

As the Vatican's leading theologian – some would wryly comment the *Church's* leading theologian, since, as the Vatican's Grand Inquisitor, he has silenced most of the others – his words bear considerable weight, and here he virtually sanctions membership of the movements as mandatory for all lay Catholics. After the contribution of Bishop Cordes, came Guzman Carriquiry from Uruguay who is considered the highest-placed layman in the Curia and is said to be close to CL. Not surprisingly, his speech on 13 October was a paean of praise to the movements. Besides promoting the myth that they are a sign of pluralism in the Church – a 'sign of the liberty of forms with which the one Church is realised' – his speech consisted of the sort of gobbledegook associated with the movements, CL in particular: '[Their] . . . tonality is more charismatic than "functional" . . . Their "input" [a CL buzzword] is more missionary than "ecclesiastic".'

In the face of these 'big guns' in favour of the movements, on 8 October, Cardinal Aloisio Lorscheider of Brazil, one of the most authoritative figures of the South American Church, had stepped in early to assert the authority of the local bishops and voice the misgivings of many on the dangers of the movements. They must work in 'sincere obedience and communion with the pastor of the local church', he urged. Recourse to the authority of the Pope was not enough: 'Communion with the supreme pastor requires communion with the pastor of the local church who rules the community entrusted to him as the vicar of Christ and does it with his own ordinary and immediate power.' Lorscheider was speaking out on behalf of those who believed a 'parallel pastoral action must be avoided' and were not prepared to cede their power simply because these autonomous groups came with the pontiff's blessing.

In his speech, Bishop Cordes did not mince words but made a direct attack on bishops who oppose the movements 'who show themselves to be openly sceptical or even hostile':

> Some bishops have been irritated by the fact that the epicentre of these movements is outside their diocese and that the orders come from other Churches or nations or cultures . . . In addition, the various post-conciliar diocesan councils feel that the activities of these movements sidestep their authority and do not fit in with the diocesan pastoral plans . . . The occasional bishop has even wondered if he is still 'head of his diocese'.

He appeared to place movements and bishops on the same level and hinted that their difficulties should be resolved by the arbitration of the Holy See. The legitimate complaints he lists are answered with the jibe that 'new wine is bursting the old wineskins'.

Now the movements took the stage. First to speak, on 9 October, was Don Luigi Giussani, founder of Communion and Liberation. He had thrown down the gauntlet to the bishops in an interview which had appeared in CL's magazine just two months previously. In a blunt appraisal of the problems CL had experienced in various dioceses he had declared that 'A movement in the Church is like a child which may not be desired but which cannot be aborted'.[1]

In a direct challenge to Cardinal Lorscheider's intervention the previous day, Giussani made a dramatic appeal to the authority of the Pope in the florid language of the new ultramontanism of the movements: 'The order of the great discipline of the Church, channel of the freedom conferred by the Spirit, flourishes in the living communion with the successor of Peter, place of ultimate peace for every believer.' Having established papal authority as the

[1] *30 giorni*, August 1987.

solution to any clashes at the local level, Giussani conceded that the movements owed 'obedience to the bishop to the point of deep mortification'. The bishops, however, for their part, owed the movements 'the freedom whereby the paternity of the bishop, beyond his personal opinions and expectations, was capable of respecting the identity of the charism so as to accept as a constructive factor, even in the pastoral plan, the practical expressions of the charism in his diocese'. In other words the bishop was not to interfere with the identity and activity of the movement, but simply 'recognize' it. After all, he pointed out, the movements had 'what the institutions often cannot offer in a living' form to the religious needs of mankind today – that is, the 'experience'. The Church 'must always be a presence which moves, that is, movement'. After all, he stated categorically, the movements are 'the historical forms with which the Spirit aids the mission of the Church today'.

Following this bullish entry from Giussani, an equally spirited reply was to be expected from his own local bishop and long-time nemesis, Cardinal Martini of Milan. CL's founder spoke on a Friday evening; and the reply came the following Monday morning, 12 October 1987.

Martini had expressed a belief that the Church was concentrating too much on the élite – 'specialized' Catholics, as he called them. He had come to the Synod rooting for 'the spirituality of the grassroots', the 'ordinary layperson, who lives his daily life, perhaps outside associations, movements, groups'. Earlier in the year, in a pastoral letter entitled 'A Hundred Words of Communion', he had confronted the question of the movements by calling for a united effort for 'the goals of the Church' from *all* members of the diocese. Now he began by roundly praising all those traditional groups which had been eclipsed by the new movements at the Synod – Catholic Action, Scouts, parish youth clubs.

The suggestion that bishops should passively 'recognize' the charisms of the movements was firmly rejected; Martini's stance was a more interventionist one: 'Our principal pastoral duty before these new realities is discernment, which means not only evaluation and judgement, but also accompaniment over time with a view to finding a satisfactory and organic role in the formative and missionary activity of the Church.'

The movements' own belief that the charisms should not brook outside interference – shared by their 'protectors' like Cordes – was also challenged by Martini: 'Such discernment is the responsibility first of all of pastors but also of the group members themselves, who must let themselves be assisted in better understanding the ways of the Lord for the service of the one Church.'

The kind of submission demanded by Martini is of course totally incompatible with the structures and methodology of the movements as they exist today. But he then proceeded to question the catch-all concept of the 'charisms'. 'No appeal to the "charism" ', he warned, 'can legitimise an "exemption" from the authorities whose task it was to guide the common path [of the faithful].' A distinction should be made, he believed, between 'the generous and self-sacrificing' members of the movements, 'the key ideal which sustains the activity', the 'ideology' and 'the concrete practice'.

As far as the last is concerned, Martini felt two questions should be posed: does 'the practice show signs of exclusivity?' and does it 'fulfil . . . the gospel values of poverty and humility, or is it open to temptation by the logic of power?' 'Perhaps,' concluded the Cardinal, 'some of these phenomena need more courage to entrust themselves to the unpredictable ways of the Spirit which also works through the pastors.'

Perhaps emboldened by Martini's forceful and courageous analysis, two Brazilian bishops contributed their observations of the runaway success of the movements in South America.

Archbishop Colling of Porto Alegre limited himself to the comment that 'Autonomous movements or pastoral ministries which do not have a real link with the Church must take responsibility for their own success or lack of success'.

The Jesuit Bishop Mendes de Almeide took a sterner view: 'Christian associations and groups, when they place their gifts and charisms at the service of communion, bring about the growth of the whole people of God; when, instead, they close in upon themselves they can be detrimental to the whole ecclesial body.'

The controversy aroused by the issue was demonstrated by the thirty bishops who wished to have their say, as well as another seventeen who spoke up for the base communities – a South American phenomenon born of liberation theology. The movements are perceived as their direct rivals.

Those in favour of the movements included Cardinal Angel Suquia of Madrid, a protector of Neocatechumenate, who echoed their perennial protest that 'If the Pope – by accepting, defending and promoting them – has recognised the authenticity of a charism . . . it is obviously to be expected that the individual churches should make this recognition their own'. The late Bishop Eugenio Corecco of Lugano, a CL member, pressed the view that the traditional structure of the parish should be given no greater weight than any other grouping and that all communities in the Church should have 'the same ecclesiological and institutional dignity'.

Chiara Lubich's speech to the Synod, made in the presence of the Pope on 13 October, and entitled 'Spirituality and Movements', was so bland and abstract as to provoke little reaction. One lay observer, however, did remark, on reading a copy of the speech (journalists were not allowed into the Synod hall): 'I had to ask myself as often before: Isn't this simply about being a Christian? Why the emphasis on "joining" something?' In reality, as the movements themselves assert with their catchphrase 'experience it and you will understand', joining is what it is all about.

It apparently escaped the attention of observers, however, that in her speech, which was nominally about movements in general, Chiara had seized the opportunity to promote the spirituality of her own movement. Her main points – God is love, living the Gospel, the word of life, the will of God, mutual love and the new commandment, Jesus in the midst, unity, suffering/the cross/Jesus forsaken, the Eucharist, Mary and the Holy Spirit – are the so-called 'points of the spirituality' which can be read in so many words in any Focolare book or pamphlet. Although there might be said to be an overlap in certain points with CL and NC, this speech could hardly claim to represent their spiritualities as well. What it does demonstrate is the rather impudent assumption that Chiara Lubich's is a super-spirituality which somehow embraces the others. It also reveals a total incapacity to think in terms other than Focolare's.

Once all the main speeches had been given, the assembly broke up for group discussion, according to language. It was only then that the bishops' objections to the movements burst forth in their full fury, particularly among the Spanish- and French-speaking delegates.

'Some movements imagine they are going to save the world,' said the report from one Spanish-language group, 'and behave as though they know the only way to be authentically Christian. They tend to self-sufficiency. Sometimes they have a spirituality of a pietistic kind which stresses personal satisfaction, with not the slightest effect on life.'

Another Spanish group accused the movements of rejecting the option for the poor, owing to their wealth: 'One father insisted that if your lifestyle does not proclaim the Gospel, then you have not understood the nature of the Church.'

Other charges included the personality cult of the founder, a tendency to become the self-appointed watchdogs in the local churches, making denouncements and ignoring the pastoral plans of the local diocese. In what could be construed as a crafty move by the Synod organizers, none of these objections made it to the final report, as a synthesis of all three Spanish groups was demanded.

The French bishops also had a number of points to add. 'In the Third World,' one French group commented, 'pastors feel that the movements (international in character and often very rich) stifle nascent home-grown movements which try to develop their own cultural resources.' They condemned the 'biblical or dogmatic fundamentalism' of the movements. Probably with their resistance to Neocatechumenate in mind, the French bishops remarked that 'One should not construe the reservations expressed by a bishop about the arrival of a movement in his diocese as opposition or disobedience to the Holy See'. This was a polite way of saying they had no intention of accepting the movements purely because they came with papal approval. They showed real insight into the workings of the movements and suggested that, in addition to external criteria for evaluating movements such as approval by the hierarchy or 'fidelity to the magisterium', 'internal criteria' should also be used − such as whether members of movements are free to appeal to the bishop against their own superiors, as obedience should never be absolute. Perhaps this was suggested with a touch of Gallic irony as a criterion of this kind could never be enforced in relation to such inscrutable organizations.

Cardinal Hume, with characteristic diplomacy, waited until time and the Pacific Ocean lay between him and the Synod before speaking his mind at a symposium in Australia, in January 1988. He described the movements as 'high-profile and fundamentalist' and took a rather optimistically common-sense view of how they should be handled: 'There is admiration for their energy, zeal and idealism. The bishops, though, were anxious that they should respect episcopal authority and the pastoral plans of local dioceses. When a movement is imported from abroad there is an obvious need to sit down with local bishops to see what modifications are needed to its pastoral methods.' When the controversies surrounding Neocatechumenate broke out in Britain a short time later, the solution was not nearly so simple. So far it has eluded the British bishops.

Those who had championed the movements at the Synod were dismayed at the ferocity with which the bishops had fought back. The rift at the heart of the Church was clear. There was some bitterness in Bishop Cordes' judgement of the bishops' motives: 'Bismarck promulgated the law of the *Kulturkampf* to dissolve the religious orders, following the logic that only a power which is not subject to outside influence is stable.' This was to frame the clash in the starkest possible terms. It may well be that, underlying their many valid objections, what disturbed the bishops most in the affair of the movements was the fundamental undermining of their authority; that the complex issues involved could be reduced to one – a struggle between the the local churches and the centralizing ambitions of John Paul II. Nevertheless, to caricature the problem as a naked power-struggle was an oversimplification and a tactic to avoid facing the worrying accusations that had been levelled.

In their final report – fifty-four *propositiones*, or proposals, voted on by the assembly – the bishops reserved the last word on the movements to the local churches: 'The valid criterion of their authenticity will always be their harmonious integration into the local Church in order to contribute to building it in charity together with its pastors' (no. 5). The parish was specifically named as the principal environment of the local church, within which other activities should be co-ordinated: 'The parish becomes a community of communities, when it is the dynamic epicentre of the ecclesial base communities and the other groups and movements which animate it, and, in their turn, are nourished by it' (no. 10). This is a clear challenge to the movements which, in the case of NC, usurp the parish or, as with CL and Focolare, eschew it altogether.

It might seem that, as a public relations exercise on their behalf, the Synod had been a total failure, but the resistance they had faced cannot have taken them totally by surprise: they had already experienced it in individual dioceses. Far more important was the fact that from relative obscurity they had been catapulted to the forefront of ecclesial life. They had been the centre of attention

– even if not all the attention had been appreciative. For organizations with such an inflated idea of their own importance and
mission, this was already a great deal. Most significant, however,
was the fact that, in the teeth of the opposition, the Vatican had
made a decisive option in their favour. They had another good
reason to be smug. As all concerned were only too well aware, the
Synod is a purely consultative body; however the bishops might
rage and fulminate, in the end they were only advisers to the Pope,
the sole author of the final report. Predictably that document,
Cristifideles laici, published over a year later at the end of 1988 (just
enough time had elapsed for memories to grow dim), contained
none of their objections, but much praise and encouragement for
the new movements.

While the Synod pointed to battles ahead, it was a satisfactory
conclusion to seven years of groundwork and lobbying undertaken
by a curious motley alliance of movements, formed in the early
eighties. Indeed, Communion and Liberation claim that the original
suggestion for the Synod on the Laity, with the express aim of
promoting the movements to the world's bishops, had come from
them. In 1980, the movement's official chronicles recount, a CL
group in Poland met Father Franciszeck Blachnickij, the founder
of the Oasis movement, which was later renamed Zlato-Zwicie
(Light-Life), a group well known to John Paul II as he had been
its protector in Poland while Archbishop of Cracow. In his first
encyclical, *Redemptor hominis*, in 1979, the newly elected Pope had
foreseen a great 'Jubilee' in the year 2000. Blachnickij approached
Don Giussani, CL's founder, with the suggestion that the movements of the world should begin 'preparing for this great rendez-
vous, offering themselves up to the Church as a privileged means
of fulfilling its mission and therefore asking recognition as such'.
They decided to hold an 'International Convention of ecclesial
movements with the aim of bringing them together, of making
them aware of their identity and their mission, and to begin publicly
working out the relationship between charism and institution in
the Church'.
   Don Giussani and Father Blachnickij wrote to the Pope, informing him of the Convention and suggesting a synod of bishops
specifically dedicated to the movements. They were immediately
joined by a third voice – that of Father Tom Forrest, president of

ICCRO, the co-ordinating council of the Catholic Charismatic Renewal.

The first Convention took place in Rome on 23–7 September 1981, attended by 150 leaders of twenty movements, including a number of founders. CL, as the self-appointed ideologue of the movements, had manoeuvred itself into a position of prominence. It should be borne in mind, however, that both Focolare and Neocatechumenate, who are far too triumphalistic and self-absorbed even to care about other movements, are more widespread and faster-growing than CL. Nevertheless both of these organizations attended the Convention. During the event, Pope John Paul gave a private audience to the heads of the movements at his summer palace of Castelgandolfo, celebrated mass and in a brief address of encouragement proclaimed that 'The Church itself is a movement!'

A line-up of prestigious speakers at the Convention spoke on key subjects, with the aim of lending the movements a theological basis. The Belgian theologian G. Chantraine developed the idea of the charism as a 'personal and ecclesial event'. The integration of the charisms was highlighted by the Brazilian bishop Moreira Neves, secretary of the Vatican Congregation for the Bishops, who characterized the movements as 'a reflection of the one church' rather than fragments or splinters or even particular spiritualities. In his talk, Father Blachnickij described the movements as the 'self-fulfilment of the Church', an idea borrowed from a synod held in Cracow under the guidance of its then bishop, Cardinal Wojtyla. The theme of canon lawyer Eugenio Corecco of the University of Fribourg, a member of CL and now bishop of Lugano, was that the laity's right to meet and form movements, which is enshrined in the code of canon law, derives from the 'new nature' conferred on Christians by baptism – it does not require a mandate from the hierarchy. Each of these points strengthened the ideological foundations of the movements in the face of their detractors and eventually found their way into the *Instrumentum laboris* of the Synod and the Pope's official report, *Christifideles laici*.

This first Convention of the new movements created enough of a stir for the Italian bishops' conference, CEI, sworn enemies of CL, to plan a document in which, for the first time, it would lay down guidelines for 'discernment' and 'recognition' of the new movements. The document was never issued.

The second Convention was held in March 1987 at Rocca di

Papa in the Alban Hills, just south of Rome. This time, it found the movements, flushed with their recent successes, in a confident, even aggressive, mood. The formidable assembly claimed to represent 30 million people dedicated to 'total militancy'. Their stated aim was to 'reawaken' the Church and bring about a 'new spring'. Focolare and Neocatechumenate were among the largest of the twenty movements represented, although the event was organized by Communion and Liberation along with the Catholic Charismatic Renewal and Schoenstatt, which claims 2 million members, mainly in South America and Germany, its country of origin. The meeting was clearly envisaged as a dress rehearsal for the Synod. Even the title was almost identical – whereas the theme of the Synod was 'Vocation and Mission of the Laity in the Church and in the World', the Rocca di Papa encounter was to debate 'Vocation and Mission of the Laity in the Church Today'.

Perhaps the chief reason for the elation felt by the movements at their second Convention was the support they now enjoyed from the highest levels of authority in the Church. They had come of age. The proposal that they should form the Pope's shock-troops had been accepted. John Paul II was now their chief supporter and champion. In his official speech to the second Convention, he proclaimed the movements 'indispensable and co-essential [with the hierarchy]'. At the same time, the specific support the movements could give him in return was also becoming clearer. If his backing was crucial in their struggle against interference from local bishops to the 'purity' of their charisms, for their part they could play a key role in his strategy of centralization.

Bishop Cordes' speech to the Convention on the subject of *communio*, or unity, in the Church expounded this theory with inimitable bluntness. He quoted Cardinal Ratzinger's use of the movements to buttress papal authority:

> . . . today we are witnessing the phenomenon of supra-territorial apostolic movements which rise up 'from below', in which new charisms flower and which revive the life of the local church. Even today, these movements, which cannot be derived from the episcopal principle, find their theological and practical support in the primacy [of the Pope].

Cordes employs this argument against what he terms 'the absolutist tendencies of the local churches'. Echoing the movements' fears, he warns against the danger of 'the concept of *communio* thus [being] reduced to empty rhetoric signifying only diocesan uniformity'.

Giussani, in his role as self-appointed spokesman for the movements, revelled in the Pope's recognition, which he claimed to be decisive. 'It represents a point of no return for our future in the Church,' he announced. His hope for the forthcoming Synod was unequivocal: that the bishops would 'recognise this truth and help us to understand it and live it always more'. There was no attempt to hide the sense of triumph which animated this second Convention: 'We hope that the whole Church will burn with the fire of our movements!'

A strong emphasis of the gathering, however, barely touched on at the Synod, was the battle against non-Catholic sects, protestant and otherwise, which seemed to be the main target of this assembly. As Massimo Camisasca, a leading priest member of CL, put it: 'The summer of the sects reveals a kind of winter in the Churches. The movements therefore have to try and bring about a spring, a Pentecost. They are not a reaction to the sects, but if they are an authentic ecclesial phenomenon they will also be able to give an effective answer to a real problem.'

Billed as a crusade against the sects, the Convention pointed out that 'many Christians, including Catholics, had gone over to the sects because they had sought within the Church, without success, a serious understanding of their emotional needs. The movements tend to be an answer to personal needs, realizing a complete expression of the life of the Church.' Perhaps the movements' effectiveness in opposition to sects is that they *are* sects – the means through which the Church can fight fire with fire.

But the bloodiest battles that the movements were to face in the coming years were not with the external enemies, but within the confines of the Catholic Church.

4

WAR IN HEAVEN

IF, AT THE SYNOD ON THE LAITY, BISHOP PAUL-JOSEF CORDES REDUCED the bishops' protests against the movements to a conflict between local autonomy and Rome, an even more extreme polarization is suggested in his *Charisms and New Evangelisation*.[1] The book, whose title in German and French translates as the more explicit *Quench Not the Spirit*, does not directly address the problems raised by the movements' critics – the movements in question are not even named – but aims to show by historical analogy that forces of renewal in the Catholic Church have always been subject to internal persecution. The approach is the circuitous one so beloved of the Vatican; yet, despite the initial impression of blandness, the book is quick to show its teeth.

Cordes states his concerns in the foreword:

> Spiritual movements are not appreciated in the way that the statistical recurrence of the expression would suggest. On the contrary, their impulses are greeted with scepticism; they come into friction with the traditional structures; they frequently fail to clear the hurdles of the post-conciliar consultative bodies; they are often passed over in silence by the Church's media; they are regarded as playgrounds for the outsider.

The bishop goes on to outline the method he will employ in his

---

[1] St Paul Publications, 1991.

study: 'the lesson of history . . . shows how God's salvific initiative is often hindered by human blindness'. He cites a few of the Church's great reformers and founders – Anthony of the desert, Athanasius, Benedict, Francis and Ignatius: during their lifetime they ran up against 'the most obstinate resistance at every level of the ecclesiastical hierarchy'. Cordes' coded attack, therefore, is aimed at those hindering 'God's salvific initiative' today – those members of the local hierarchies who refuse to give the movements the support the Vatican thinks they deserve.

A second aim of the book, I was told by a young Frenchman attending the NC seminary in Berlin, is to encourage the movements themselves, particularly those, like NC, facing difficulties in the dioceses. 'I have written a book that will bring you great comfort,' he had heard from Cordes' own lips. This intention was later confirmed to me by Cordes himself.

For the dissidents, however, the book contains a dire warning, only slightly veiled. In his introduction, Cordes invokes the support of Hans Urs von Balthasar, Pope John Paul's favourite theologian, on whom he conferred the cardinal's hat shortly before Balthasar's death in 1988. Noted for his condemnations of more liberal colleagues such as Karl Rahner and Hans Kung, Balthasar was a respected theologian with a mystical bent, considered, like Cardinal Ratzinger, to have been a liberal before the Council who later moved to the right. He was also a close friend of Don Giussani, founder of CL, whose publishing house, Jaca Book, has issued many of his works in Italian.

Balthasar, we are informed by Cordes, had a 'knowledge of the spiritual currents in our time [that] was really unparalleled'. Having thus proposed him as the 'theologian of the movements', he then goes on to describe the war, in Balthasar's view, that the movements are waging: it is the battle of faith against the rationalism that has invaded modern theology. 'The duel is a superhuman one,' Cordes points out; and then, quoting Balthasar, characterizes the struggle between the new movements and their opponents in this thundering statement:

> It consists not just of a purely human battle about words or ideas, but of involvement in the great theo-dramatic battle that has erupted between God and his Logos on the one hand and the infernal Anti-Logos on the other. Therefore he who takes part

in it must grasp 'the sword of the spirit, i.e. the Word of God'; this means not leading a rearguard action, but facing the adversary eye to eye.

All half-measures are swept aside in Balthasar's – and Cordes' – apocalyptic vision of the movements' struggle. It is a starkly dualistic one in which the forces of light are pitted against the forces of darkness: truly a war in heaven. But, given that the opposing armies both include cardinals, bishops, priests and laity of the Catholic Church, exactly what manner of conflict is Cordes predicting? One thing is certain: he has boldly nailed his colours to the mast, and it does not take much imagination to identify them as the Pope's own yellow and white, for it is inconceivable that one so highly placed within the Vatican, a member of John Paul's inner circle, could state his case so strongly if it were against his master's will. It remains to be seen which side the angels are on.

At the Synod on the Laity, the Fathers identified the local parish as the heartland of Catholicism. It is the visible community of the Church at the local level. The bishops were well aware that the parish needs to be protected from the movements, for it is here that the struggle for the hearts and minds of the faithful will be fought. CL and Focolare have their own distinct and parallel structures, yet they undermine the parish by syphoning off its most committed members. For Neocatechumenate, on the other hand, the parish is its main field of action, and it has sparked off fierce and often very public clashes wherever it has established communities.

Growing controversy surrounding the presence of NC in the diocese of Clifton, Bristol, over the past five years has forced the bishop, Mervyn Alexander, to drastic action. The movement has put down roots in three of the area's parishes: St Nicholas of Tolentino, an inner-city Bristol parish, St Peter's in Gloucester, and Sacred Hearts parish on the outskirts of Cheltenham. This last is a small parish, with 600 members on the books of whom 400 are active and committed. Before NC arrived it was a thriving community. Mary Whyte, a middle-aged widow, is the leader of a small but articulate group in the parish which opposes NC and the division it has brought. 'The first inkling that something was about to happen', she recalls, 'was when Father Tony Trafford was appointed parish priest at the beginning of February seven years ago.'

'We were already running confirmation classes in the parish at the time,' adds Margaret Gilder. She is an official (as opposed to NC) catechist at parish and diocesan levels.

> Father Tony kept telling us, 'In the autumn, something wonderful is going to happen in this parish'. And we kept asking, 'Can you amplify, can you explain?' But he said, 'No, wait till the autumn.' Come autumn, a letter went out to everyone: 'Come and see this most wonderful thing.' So we all did. There were 400 people at the first meeting. This parish has always been very good at responding to the requests of the parish priest.

The first team of catechists was led by Father Carmelo di Giovanni of the Italian Church, Clerkenwell, in London. 'He's a tremendous shouter,' Mary Whyte recalls. 'He's very, very heavy. They're all very heavy and push their own line the whole time.' She found the contribution of a married couple, part of the team of catechists, particularly distressing.

> They insisted on giving us the full details of everything that had ever happened to them, maritally speaking . . . It was so embarrassing . . . We were treated to a full explanation of how she discovered within fourteen days of their wedding that she had married the wrong man and now, five children later, she was still no happier. But they were still together because of something – she didn't say what, because the NC wasn't mentioned at that stage. Then there was a young man who was a solicitor. I think he was English. He went into great detail about the various women he'd had in his life and the drugs he'd sampled.

Mary Whyte is the head of a family affected by an incurable genetic disease which has been diagnosed in seven members so far. Her faith and no-nonsense attitude have supported her through these family tragedies. Not surprisingly, she and other committed parish members did not take too kindly to being told by complete newcomers: 'There is no love in this parish. You've never experienced love in this parish.' The pre-packaged NC message of doom and gloom had a particularly hollow ring in a community of contented and well-adjusted parishioners.

This was the start of the introductory catechesis, although this was never clearly stated, and parishioners were immediately pressurized to attend future sessions. Mary Whyte recalls how the parish priest would almost break down in tears to encourage people to attend, telling them: 'It's so vital for the life of the parish.'

Mary Whyte's group at Sacred Hearts is typical of the vast majority of lay Catholics who welcomed the changes of the Council. One of these was to stress the positive message of the Gospel and play down the elements of fear and guilt which had loomed so large in traditional Catholic teaching. They were surprised and disturbed, therefore, to find that they played such an important part in the NC catechesis.

'I can remember this wonderful drawing of the steps going down,' Mary recalls with a smile. 'Each step was labelled with a sin: "We have *all* committed murder," they told us, "and we have *all* committed adultery, and we have *all* committed incest, and we have *all* committed child abuse and we have *all* committed theft and then we reach rock bottom"; and a dear, very elderly lady in the parish turned to her neighbour and said, "Chance would be a fine thing." '

Parish members began to vote with their feet. 'That catechesis started out with over four hundred and by the last week there were about fifty or sixty,' Margaret Gilder remembers.

Once the new community was formed, following the initial catechesis, the divisions began. It was clear that despite relatively small numbers − around sixty − NC was taking over the parish. From the start, parishioners were upset about the atmosphere of exclusivity surrounding the separate NC Saturday-evening mass, closed to non-members. This exploded into open warfare when the parish's own Saturday-evening mass was permanently cancelled. 'Father Tony stopped it', Mary Whyte says, 'because the curate he'd given a nervous breakdown to had left the parish. He made that an excuse for cutting out the mass on a Saturday night. But in fact he now says *two masses* for the NC − one for each community.'

'What was interesting,' adds Simon Beamish, 'is that when we spoke to the bishop [of Clifton] he had actually been given a different explanation. Father Tony told the bishop that the numbers did not warrant a six o'clock mass − this was reported to us by the bishop himself. He couldn't have used that excuse with us, because the numbers were demonstrably sufficient.'

Although at first they had been completely absorbed in their own activities, after a few years NC began to show an interest in those official parish groups whose function was Christian education.

The pattern of the NC 'takeover' is identical in every parish, although it may appear to be random to local observers. It is dictated by the implacable and unvarying implementation of the NC system enshrined in the twenty-year 'Way'. When the graduates reach a certain stage, they are required to infiltrate and eventually take over all catechetical or teaching activities in the parish so that ultimately the only doctrine available is their own. Target groups include those preparing candidates for the sacraments of holy communion, confirmation and marriage, and parents of those who are to be baptized. It is even envisaged that in these parishes all adults wishing to be received into the Catholic Church should enter the communities rather than receive instruction through the official process known as the RCIA (Rite of Christian Initiation for Adults). NC oppose all parish groups organized by activity or category such as charitable or youth groups. They would hope to see these wither and die, supplanted by their communities.

Perhaps the most disorientating aspect of the arrival of NC in Sacred Hearts parish was the impression that those outside the communities were no longer of any concern to the parish priest. It became clear that his priority was NC.

Opposition to the movement in a parish can often polarize around a non-NC curate, who finds himself at the centre of the conflict and is left to pick up the pieces. This can isolate him, placing an intolerable burden on his shoulders. At Sacred Hearts, the presence of NC drove the curate, Father John Michael, to a nervous breakdown. Mary Whyte explains:

> Father John Michael, our curate, is a Franciscan, a recovered alcoholic. He was here for three years, and everybody loved him. The children followed him from school, like the Pied Piper. Although we didn't realize it, he was having the most dreadful time in the presbytery, because the Neocatechumenate had virtually taken it over. He was driven out of all the rooms downstairs to his own room. They even stole his food from the

fridge. He was under constant pressure from them to join the movement, and everyone who had problems with the NC would bring them to him.

Before Father John Michael went on holiday in the summer of 1992, he was trying to sort out the groups for the confirmation and first communion candidates. He could not get the parish priest to take a decision. 'When he returned from holiday,' says Simon Beamish, 'it had all been arranged and an NC couple had been appointed directors of the confirmation programme. He told them he would have nothing more to do with it, though finally he was persuaded back.'

Just after Christmas 1992, Father John Michael disappeared. 'The weekend he went missing,' Margaret Gilder says,

nothing was said to us. We just realized he was not around . . . It was only when we bombarded him with questions that Father Tony told us what had happened and we discovered that Father John Michael was in hospital in East Anglia. We felt totally betrayed . . . At the same time we were deeply shocked that Father Tony appeared to have done nothing to help Father John Michael. So far as we knew, he had not even said a word to people in the parish, all of whom he knew would have come rushing round to help. We did not even know whether the professional counsellors that Father John Michael had been in contact with in the past had been alerted – before or after the disappearance. This is why we felt that both he and we had been let down. I did not even know whether Father Tony had even visited his own curate in hospital.

This incident brought home to the opponents of NC the profound and worrying changes that had taken place under their very noses. Shortly after this, a group of twelve of them asked for a parish meeting, with their priest, to discuss the general feeling of unease. About two hundred people turned up, indicating how widespread the unhappiness was. Included, of course, was the full complement of sixty NC members in the parish. 'We thought we would be meeting the parish priests,' says Mary Whyte. 'Instead, three catechists gave us the most awful evening. The first hour was a summary of the catechesis.'

Frustrated in their attempts at an internal solution, the parishioners turned to the bishop, taking advantage of a pastoral visit to the parish. 'The bishop would like everyone to cope,' Mary observes. 'He said, "Surely you can find a way to live with it." But it is not our inability: it is fundamental to the nature of this sect that they cannot accommodate anybody but themselves. They cannot, will not accept anything which does not conform to their wishes. It was hopeless because Father Tony just told lies – and the bishop believed him.'

The NC coup in St Nicholas of Tolentino parish in Bristol had reached an even more advanced stage than that of Sacred Hearts, until, in the early nineties, it came up against serious opposition. At the forefront of this counter-move was the impeccably polite but unshakably determined leader of the parish RCIA group, Ronald Haynes, an American computer expert working at Bristol University. His technological capabilities proved invaluable in giving the anti-NC lobby a voice in the parish through the dissemination of information – and so did his degree in theology. Although other opponents of NC flinched at what they regarded as his excessively aggressive approach, Haynes has succeeded in galvanizing the diocesan authorities into decisive action, when they would have preferred to sit on the fence. Nevertheless, his relentless but scrupulously argued attacks on the movement aroused such passion that, in the course of a parish meeting with the NC National Team in February 1993, he was threatened with physical violence by a member of the NC community.

Resistance to NC in St Nicholas parish had begun much earlier, however. Louis and Mary Beasley moved to the area eight years ago with their seven children. Louis was immediately approached by the parish priest, Canon Jeremiah O'Brien, known to parishioners as Father Jerry. 'You're just the person we need to help us with the confirmation classes!' he exclaimed to Louis. 'And there's another group you may be interested in meeting,' he confided, adding, with a touch of Irish humour: 'We call them the Moonies.'

As yet unaware of the many parallel activities going on in the parish alongside the official events, Louis accepted Canon O'Brien's invitation and attended the eight-week introductory catechesis. He now describes the NC catechesis as 'horrific', particularly repelled by constant detailed accounts of past sins in terms he felt to be unnecessarily strong.

Louis and Mary were keen to be actively involved in the life of the parish. Louis played the organ at the parish church and the annexe chapel of St Maximilian Kolbe. Together, they launched a group they named Journey in Faith for adults to deepen their understanding of Catholicism through the study of Scripture and the documents of the Second Vatican Council. Although it was primarily aimed at cradle Catholics, they hoped the group would also be useful to enquirers and those interested in being received into the Catholic Church. As, at that time, there was no official RCIA group in the parish, they felt that this could be another function they could usefully perform. They were slightly puzzled by the fact that no enquirers ever approached them.

The first sign of things to come was when Canon O'Brien decided to take the Journey in Faith name away from the Beasleys and give it to a group he was starting for enquirers into the Catholic faith. This would perform the official function of the RCIA in the parish. The launch of Canon O'Brien's rival body signalled the start of the NC move into parish groups, also experienced at Sacred Hearts. It seemed to Louis and Mary that a deliberate campaign of deception, broken promises and confusion through sudden changes of plan had been launched with the apparent aim of wearing down all active members of the parish outside NC, thus removing potential opposition. The laity had never played a role in governing St Nicholas parish, for there had never been a parish council, as recommended by Vatican II. It seemed therefore that Canon O'Brien was the sole agent of the subterfuge. After a while, however, parishioners began to wonder who was pulling his strings.

At about this time, Ronald Haynes arrived in the parish. He began to attend the canon's new Journey in Faith group, run by the curate. Although he was saying mass for the NC communities, he did not appear to be fully committed to the movement. NC members, however, were 'planted' in the group, according to Louis Beasley, to do the teaching. Although Journey in Faith was the parish's official RCIA group, it had been set up as a means of drawing enquirers into Catholicism towards the NC communities. Members of this group were referred to the NC communities, but very few stayed. At the beginning of 1992, the Journey in Faith group was due to restart after the Christmas break, but there were repeated announcements and cancellations until, suddenly, the NC introductory catechesis was announced. The delay had been engineered to leave the field to NC. As he had no knowledge of NC, Ronald Haynes decided he would attend the catechesis. With his theological background, he soon identified the movement's serious defects and stopped attending.

The Journey in Faith group was started up again, this time with Ronald Haynes, who had the necessary qualifications and had offered his services, assisting the curate. The curate, who had a drink problem, spent less and less time at the group. After the start of each meeting, he would disappear and return at the end, slightly drunk. Haynes became the group leader by default. Later the curate abandoned the parish and the priesthood. Although there were a number of causes behind this, Ronald Haynes believes that, as in the case of Father John Michael, his problem was not helped by the strains of division within the parish.

Easter 1992 was a turning-point which made it clear that any kind of *modus vivendi* with NC was out of the question. Although the communities were in the minority, they wanted nothing less than total domination. Mary Beasley explains:

> The big clash has always been the Easter liturgy because there are two Easter Vigils on the Saturday night: an open ceremony for the parish and a closed one for the NC. Two fires, two paschal candles, two vigils. It came to a head at Easter '92. We had a meeting to which all the parishioners were invited, where it would be decided who would do the readings for the Holy Week services. When we got there, we all felt there was something in the air, although we couldn't quite put our finger on it. We went through the services of the week; then, when we came to the Easter Vigil, there was an awkward silence. 'I think that's all been dealt with,' said the canon. We were stunned to realize that there was indeed to be just one Easter Vigil – the NC ceremony.

It was a masterly move by NC. In one stroke, they had silenced accusations about rival vigils and closed ceremonies. At the same time they knew that none of their opponents in the parish would want to attend the vigil and few others would be willing or able to face an all-night marathon.

Louis Beasley appealed to Bishop Mervyn Alexander. The bishop's reply suggested that, as in the case of Sacred Hearts in Cheltenham, he had been misinformed. The changes had come about, the canon had told him, because of the very much higher attendance the previous year at the NC service! He had been told that only thirty people had attended the parish vigil. In fact it had drawn a congregation of over two hundred. The NC community, on the other hand, totals eighty, many of whom do not even belong to St Nicholas' parish.

But the Easter Vigil was only the start. The following July, Canon O'Brien invited all parish associations to take a summer break. At his request, it was extended until 23 September when there would be a parish meeting. Following this, he announced, all parish activities would be passed into the hands of the laity: 'After that you can do what you like.'

In the period following this meeting, the opponents of NC came to the conclusion that by tinkering with times of services, promising to start groups and then cancelling meetings, an orchestrated attempt was being made by the parish priest to subvert all non-NC activities. On 11 November 1992, members of a recently formed sacramental working party, which included Ronald Haynes, were told that all further meetings in the parish had been cancelled by order of Canon O'Brien.

In early December, with the parish as they knew it disintegrating about their ears, Mary, Louis and Ronald Haynes contacted the Vicars General of the diocese, Monsignors Buckley and Mitchell, whose authority is second only to that of the bishop. Knowing of Monsignor Buckley's personal crusade against NC (he had published damning articles on them in the Catholic press, a few years earlier), they felt it might be better to meet with Monsignor Mitchell, who might be perceived by the NC communities as unbiased. Monsignor Buckley was in full agreement and pointed out that, in any case, Monsignor Mitchell had responsibility for pastoral concerns in the diocese.

'When we set out the situation before Monsignor Mitchell,' Louis remembers, 'he told us: "The first thing you must do is to take back your parish." He counselled drastic action – to the extent of going to the press. We told him that we did not want to cause scandal, that it was a family matter. At that time we were not really aware that the NC was run on a national basis from

London, let alone that it was a worldwide organization.'

On their return to the parish, they announced new meeting dates for all the suspended groups.

At this point, Ronald Haynes was still leading the Journey in Faith/RCIA group, a post to which he had been officially appointed by Canon O'Brien himself. On 10 December 1992, when he came to the presbytery to collect the keys for the parish hall where meetings were held, Haynes was surprised to be invited into the waiting-room by Canon O'Brien.

'He brought in this other guy, whom he didn't introduce, and proceeded to harangue me. "Because of your hatred of the Neocatechumenate, I cannot be trusting you with the RCIA," he told me,' Haynes recalls, 'while I kept asking "Who's he?" "I wanted him here as a witness," said the canon. After the onslaught was over, I turned to the other guy and said, "I'm Ronald Haynes. Who are you?" He told me his name was Jim and that he was "a seminarian". I asked him if he was a member of the NC. "I don't see what that has to do with anything," he replied.'

Following this exchange, Haynes demanded the keys and was given them. As Mary and Louis had their own set of keys, Louis began to accompany Ronald Haynes to all Journey in Faith meetings after this, as his 'bodyguard'. The canon later threatened to change the locks if all the keys were not handed in, but this was never carried out. The presence of the 'witness', however, was the first indication that the canon was not a free agent in the upheavals that had taken place in the parish. It would also explain the U-turns, and joint decisions made at parish meetings which were later inexplicably revoked.

'At the end of the day,' Mary Beasley comments, 'the parish is left thinking: We believed a priest made his vow to the bishop. This one seems to have made his vow who-knows-where.'

Meanwhile, following the discussion with Monsignor Mitchell, Haynes and the Beasleys hit upon a plan that would keep the matter 'in the family' but also bring the problems out into the open. The idea of a parish newsletter had been discussed at the meeting of 23 September and approved in theory, like many other ideas, by the canon. Louis, Mary and Ronald decided to go ahead with the project, using it as a medium to voice their concerns about the divisions in the parish.

'We ran the idea by Father Jerry on four occasions,' Louis remembers,

> but nevertheless, when it hit the streets in January, he went wild. We stated clearly in the newsletter that, according to the Vicar General, we should continue to have meetings regardless of what the parish priest thinks. The morning the newsletter appeared, I was playing the organ at the St Maximilian Kolbe Chapel. Father Jerry stormed in and said he would denounce us from the pulpit. I replied that if he did I would denounce him from the organ loft. During the mass, when I wasn't playing, I stood right up against the rail of the loft where he could see me. At one point during the sermon I could tell he was teetering, but I fixed him with my gaze. I would have denounced him, and he knew it.

A second meeting was scheduled with Monsignor Mitchell; this time, in addition to Louis, Mary and Ronald on behalf of the parish, Canon O'Brien and NC representatives were also present. NC's oft-repeated claim of obedience to the bishop was beginning to wear thin. The parishioners' request for a Parish Council was resisted by Canon O'Brien with the spurious argument that they had been unsuccessful elsewhere and had been stopped. Monsignor Mitchell elegantly exerted some pressure with the words, 'I don't want to *tell* you to do it, although of course I could because the bishop's away'. (As Bishop Alexander was convalescing at this time following an operation, Monsignor Mitchell was acting with his authority.) Despite this gentle nudge, the suggestion was not taken up. Oblivious of the irony, one of the NC members at this very meeting accused NC's opponents of disobedience to the parish priest.

The final showdown between St Nicholas parishioners and NC took place in February 1993. Canon O'Brien had agreed to an open meeting with NC and the parish, adding, however, that he thought it would be appropriate if they brought in some people 'who can explain it better than we can'. Announcing the event, the parish bulletin optimistically proclaimed: 'Come and have all your questions answered.' But the meeting only raised more concerns and intensified antagonisms.

Louis arrived early with Mary and the others, but the NC community had got there first and the seats were arranged classroom-style in rows, with a blackboard at the front – always an important feature of NC catechesis. They rearranged the seats in a more informal semicircle. About seventy parishioners attended, with NC members constituting just over half of the group. The NC National Team arrived from London led by a Spanish priest, José Guzman, who informed his audience that he had a doctorate in pastoral theology from the Gregorian University in Rome. A married man was introduced, in standard NC fashion, by the size of his family – in this case, five children. A third was Jim, the seminarian who had been the 'witness' to Canon O'Brien's firing of Ronald Haynes.

José Guzman followed the pattern of similar encounters and began his presentation with a potted version of the NC introductory catechesis. On the advice of the Vicars General, the parishioners had laid down time-limits for each speaker. In his talk, Father José accused Sunday massgoers of having no faith. He, too, had only had faith for three years, even though he had been a member of NC for over twenty. 'I had no meaning in my life,' he told the assembly. 'Perhaps you are like that.' Ronald Haynes was unimpressed with Guzman's theology. He was also disturbed by Guzman's misleading definition of NC as 'an application of the RCIA', a standard claim of the movement, arrogating to itself an authority that it does not actually possess.

Then Canon O'Brien took the floor. The NC leaders, especially José Guzman, fed him lines throughout his speech. At one point, they even handed him a copy of the *Osservatore romano*, the Vatican daily, and told him to read out a passage in which the Pope appeared to give his blessing to separate Saturday-night services. The parishioners were dismayed to see their priest so blatantly manipulated by this group of complete strangers who had no standing in the diocese. Mary Beasley describes the scene as a 'terrible puppetry'. 'He looked the tragic figure the NC has made him,' her husband adds.

But none of this fulfilled the promise made in the parish bulletin – the answering of questions. Monsignor Buckley had prepared a list, amplified by the parishioners, covering such topics as what approval the movement really had from the British bishops; the internal 'hierarchy'; its relation to the parish; methods of indoctrination and finances. When the list was presented to the canon, he took it, folded it up and put it in his pocket.

Finally, in frustration, Ronald Haynes leaped to his feet.

'This meeting is about the local setting. Let's talk about why there is so much confusion and why the parish feels second-bested all the time.'

Pandemonium broke out, with NC members trying to shout down parishioners. One of them physically accosted Ronald Haynes, and for a moment a fight threatened. It was brought to an abrupt and early end by José Guzman, who, with the demeanour of an Old Testament prophet, hurled accusations at the parishioners: they had disobeyed the parish priest; they were 'faithless'. 'What was really extraordinary,' Louis recalls, 'is that afterwards Father José came up to Ronald and me and told us he was going to report us to the Pope – by name. "I know your names," he shouted at us.'

Ronald and Louis continued their struggle. In May 1993, under pressure from the Vicars General, Bishop Alexander summoned the three NC parish priests of the diocese and told them he would like three points to be observed: they were to suspend the giving of new catechesis for a year until the diocese had had time to study it; any further catechesis should be prepared in line with the New Catechism of the Catholic Church; no separate Easter vigils were to be held. Having said this, to the disappointment of the Vicars General, he immediately added: 'I suppose you will want to go away and think about that before giving me an answer.'

Their backs against the wall, NC resorted to stalling tactics, and a number of meetings were held between the National Team and Bishop Alexander behind closed doors. Nevertheless, on Sunday, 20 March 1994 the three parish priests read from their pulpits, by order of the bishop, a pastoral letter in which he restated his three points and ordered that they were to be observed.

It is rare nowadays for Catholic bishops to resort to such drastic measures. But, in the case of Neocatechumenate, a number of bishops have chosen this option – in France, Italy and South America. But, for matters to reach this stage, an organized resistance is necessary. In parishes where NC assumes power unopposed, the consequences can be far more sinister.

Wherever it can, NC aims for total domination, claiming all rights for the movement and trampling on, or ejecting, all those who stand in its way. The organization's ruthlessness and its sinister manipulation of Church authority can be seen in the confrontation between the NC parish priest of a Catholic church in London, and a young female parishioner.

Laura, now in her thirties, is the British-born daughter of a typical London Italian immigrant family. A cradle Catholic, she had lapsed for several years. Following the death of her mother, she was drawn back to her faith. Laura and her father had recently moved into a council block just round the corner from the church.

'I found a lovely community atmosphere in the neighbourhood,' Laura recalls, 'and, having wanted to come back to the Church, it was perfect to have the parish right on the doorstep. It was beautiful – all the neighbours were there, all the Italians were there. I thought I'd found heaven on earth. But that was when the previous parish priest was there and Father John was only the curate.'

Father John took over as parish priest after his predecessor left. Laura now believes that Neocatechumenate were instrumental in the change. 'They started saying, "Come to these meetings". I'm a very social sort of person . . . So I thought: I'll go and see what it's like. I'd just come back to the Church and thought: If it's Catholic, it must be good. Up to that time I'd got on very well with Father John. I worked in a local hospital as a lab assistant, and he was the Catholic chaplain there – we used to get on great.'

At this time, the early eighties, Neocatechumenate was just starting in the parish; but it rapidly began to replace all the other associations, and Laura attended meetings rather half-heartedly, mainly because her friends were involved and she needed a link with parish life. As well as the NC catechesis, Laura was attending gatherings of the Catholic Charismatic Renewal, at Westminster Cathedral in Victoria. She brought an earthy common sense to her newly rediscovered faith and was disturbed by the contrast between the two groups:

> With the Neocatechumenate, you all had to sit in a circle and do what you were told to do; very different from the charismatics, which are so free. The Renewal told me, 'God does not condemn you, God heals you, God loves you'; and it was coming the other way from the NC, which was saying, 'You cannot be like Jesus Christ'. So what – He came to do what we can't do. Every week you would sit in a circle in a cold church with catechists who

looked very withdrawn and serious, telling us about their past life. I used to think: You sound like you were better before. It was always about the cross and death and the crucifixion and the blood and the gore and the sin. 'I'm in bondage, I'm in chains, I'm a sinner.' I used to say: 'Oh, how awful – I'll pray for you, I'll get my friends to pray for you.' Where was the kindness, the love, helping each other?

Another aspect that struck Laura as odd was the constant expenditure in the parish and appeals that were launched for new artifacts and furnishings for the church.

By this time I belonged to the second community, and they were constantly collecting money from us for new crucifixes, new vestments. Every week they bought new stands, new books, new chalices. A hundred pounds a week was spent on flowers. This isn't simplicity, I thought. The priests especially seemed to have too many possessions. Sometimes I used to clean the presbytery. One day I opened Father John's cupboard, and there was a whole wall of cashmere sweaters, shoes, clothes. I thought: My God, I didn't know priests had all this. 'They're all presents,' he said. But then they told us we had to sell everything and give it to the poor. Later they started making alterations to the church, digging out underneath for new rooms for all the community masses. They bought tiles from Italy for the floors in the basement loos. Then Father John appealed from the pulpit for funds, saying: 'This is the poorest parish in Westminster. We could be closed down any minute through lack of funds.' How could that be true when, at the same time, they were ordering Italian tiles for the basement toilets?

In addition to these growing misgivings, Laura began to find the demands of the meetings too much of a strain on top of her heavy workload at the hospital, particularly the preparation of the liturgy on weekday evenings. Gradually, she stopped attending the NC meetings, although she still had many friends in the communities and remained deeply attached to the parish. Then a series of incidents precipitated her into a downward spiral of depression. They were all directly connected with the parish and Neo-catechumenate.

There are a lot of tramps round here. They caused a lot of trouble to women in particular because they were usually drunk and very aggressive. They used to go into the church during the day, and when we asked for Father John's help he just replied: 'They are the children of God. In my father's house there are many mansions.' I said: 'But we are the children of God, too. You are in control; you should say: "This far and no more, boys – that's it." ' They used to sit at the back of the church, drinking and urinating. The smell was awful, and they would tap women for money, so they were afraid to go in. I thought: This isn't right; this isn't Christianity, because other priests wouldn't allow this. You're out of control. This is my parish as well; and if I can't walk into my church without fear, then it's your responsibility to do something about it.

One guy in particular was really sick. He frightened me . . . He used to go up to the nurses' home and threaten them with an axe – a nurse in the community had experienced this. One day I'd just come out of work and I was very tired. I went to pay a visit to the church as I usually did, and this bloke went for me. He actually chased me all round the church. I ran to the presbytery next door – I was so frightened. This other NC priest opened the door and said: 'What's the matter, Laura?' When I told him, he replied, 'Oh, really,' very casually and closed the door.

Laura went home and called the police, who told her they could do nothing unless actual violence had occurred. Rape Crisis were so infuriated with the priest's response that they wanted to go to the bishop, but Laura felt she could not face the conflicts that would ensue. This incident proved to be the start of her depression.

A further episode proved even more distressing.

I had had a double bereavement in just two weeks – my closest aunt and my best friend died. I was at rock bottom. Prior to this, I had always gone to Father John for help and advice, and he was always nice. But he had started to change as he got sucked into it. 'I can't cope,' I told him. 'I'm really depressed.' We were standing at the bottom of the stairs in the presbytery. He just looked at me and said: 'Laura, you are not a Christian and I don't wish to speak to you.' He turned his back on me and walked up the stairs. I stood there stunned. Then I think he realized what he'd done and he came back, shaking, and he said something like 'Go and believe in the resurrection'. That really clubbed me.

Later that year, as Laura's depression worsened, her father went away and she found herself living on her own for a while. She appealed to Father John, asking if he could send her someone from the NC community to help her with shopping or just to sit with her. His reply was curt: 'Laura, we don't manufacture love here.'

On another occasion, she returned to Father John for counselling; he read out a passage from the Old Testament. 'I can't remember what it was except that it was about God'. 'He told me: "God has sent you this depression because otherwise you would have been an even bigger prostitute than your sister." He was referring to the fact that my sister lives with a man.'

Laura's doctor contacted Father John at this time in an attempt to explain Laura's condition as she felt that his treatment amounted to mental cruelty; she met with a singular lack of enthusiasm.

At the end of 1986, feeling she could no longer frequent the parish under these conditions, but not wanting to leave, Laura wrote to Cardinal Hume, describing some of the incidents that had happened to her and adding: 'It has grieved me for a long time that we parishioners are not getting the pastoral care we need or would like because Father John's time is taken up completely with these communities.'

Cardinal Hume replied promptly and kindly, on 24 December: 'I must thank you very much indeed for your letter. It is an important one and, of course, concerns a very delicate matter. I shall certainly be having a word about your letter with your local area bishop. Perhaps after I have spoken to him we shall be able to decide together what is the best way whereby we could help.'

Some days later, Laura received a letter dated 8 January 1987 from the newly appointed bishop for her area: 'The Cardinal has spoken to me of the correspondence he has had with you. If you would like me to raise the matter with Father John, then I will gladly do so, but I do, of course, need your permission to show him your letter. I will wait to hear from you before taking further action.'

But Laura, and others in the parish, had been upset to discover that the Bishop, shortly after his appointment, had visited the NC communities at their Saturday-night Eucharist behind locked doors and without anyone else in the parish being informed. She had soon realized that the Bishop visited the presbytery often, that he and Father John were close friends. In view of this she felt that her complaints could never get a fair hearing and that her situation in the parish might worsen if Father John knew of her complaints. She decided to let the matter rest; but then problems started to brew again.

Father John launched an appeal from the pulpit for a new main crucifix. Still somewhat under the influence of the NC message and eager to patch things up, Laura decided to give up £300 she had saved to go on holiday to start things off. 'Father John was delighted. He told me I could choose the crucifix myself from a catalogue. The one I chose cost a lot: I think it was £1,600. "You realize that is only the body of Christ," he told me. "The cross is extra," hinting that I should give more. I'd never given that amount of money before to the poor, to the Church, to my own family even. I kept saying to him: "I don't know whether I've done the right thing." "There's no-one poorer than Christ," he told me.'

When the cross arrived, Laura was shocked to find it was not the one she had chosen at all, but a stark modern design which she found very unappealing. When she challenged Father John, at first he assured her that he had been convinced it was the cross of her choice. Later, more bluntly, he said: 'This is my church, and I'll do what I like in it.' Laura felt that she had been cynically used. 'What a dirty trick. I'm a working girl in a hospital on a low wage. When I told my friends, they said: "You're crackers. Go and get your money back." '

Partly because of the way, in her view, she had been misled, but also to see what Father John's reaction would be, she did ask him to return her cheque. 'He went berserk. He started screaming and shouting at me and calling me all sorts of things. He did hand the money over, but that was it: from then on I was ostracized.'

In a second letter to Cardinal Hume in May 1987, Laura wrote how Father John had called her 'sick, crazy, a gossip and a busybody, that I was imagining everything and even having some kind of an evil spirit. I have never known such unkindness from a priest before . . . He never used to be like this and I am actually wondering who is in control of him as I understand he has sworn obedience to certain catechists from the movement.'

Cardinal Hume replied by return of post: 'I am so sorry you are in distress about your relationship with your parish. I promise you that I shall have a further word with the area bishop, but he must be free to discuss the matter with Father John. If he has not got that permission, then we cannot get very far.' Despite her misgivings, as a last resort Laura wrote to the Bishop and visited him in his office in March 1988.

> As soon as I walked in I knew I'd lost. He didn't want to know. I told him that on one of his visits to the church there had only been five parishioners, of which I was one. I'd walked in and the church was packed with Filipinos. It was the NC rent-a-crowd. He just said: 'Yes, yes, yes.' Then I told him: 'Father John doesn't know whether we are Catholic or Protestant, Jew or Christian.' 'Yes, yes, yes.' And then he said: 'The half-hour is up.' I said: 'But I've come here for results; you're my bishop; you've got to help me.' 'Can you leave now, please?' That was it.

The one piece of advice the Bishop did give to Laura was 'for your own healing, stay away from the parish'.

'It was like an amputation for me,' she says now, 'because I did love that parish.'

Reluctantly, Laura began attending mass in neighbouring parishes. Now not only is Laura exiled from the parish she loved, but she cannot even bear to walk past it and takes a roundabout route to avoid it.

'Father John once said to me at the church door: "If you can't beat us, join us; and, if you can't join us, go to another parish," ' Laura remembers.

Although NC causes division in every parish where it takes root, it does not always survive. One of the primary causes of the death of NC communities is the removal of the parish priest and failure to convert the new incumbent. Control over parish priests is essential in order to give NC groups firm authority in the face of often bitter opposition. The changing of parish priests is a sore point with NC, and at every opportunity they push the line that the parish priest should *never* be changed, on principle. Nevertheless, NC communities, like the other new movements, are adaptable and resilient under pressure: where communities die because priests are changed, or opposition is too fierce, members will move to other NC parishes, thus causing more division.

As in the case of all sects, secrecy is the key strategy of the new movements. Corrective action is hindered in NC parishes because outsiders have no way of grasping the bigger picture – or even knowing that there is one. Dialogue is impossible: NC members can only preach, not listen. So those suspicious of the Way and its followers find it exceedingly hard to guess what their next move will be. For all their protests of peaceful coexistence, the Neo-catechumenals have a precise plan of attack. Gianpiero Donnini outlined to me how this has been implemented at Canadian Martyrs, the flagship parish of the Way and blueprint for all the others.

NC has superseded the traditional structure of parish groups, he explained, divided as they are by category – youth, married people – and fields of action – justice and peace, care of the elderly. In the NC view it is essential that all age-groups should be mixed – the young with the old and the middle-aged. At the stage of the Way known as the *Traditio*, when the Creed is received, members embark on the evangelization of the parish, including house-visits. 'We go from house to house *like the Jehovah's Witnesses* [my italics],' Donnini told me. Imelda Bolger, a retired teacher, recounts how this was experienced in Ealing Abbey: 'A primary school head whom I know well was visited by two NC members. They insisted on coming in and reading a passage from the Gospels. Still they wouldn't leave, and when this man – who is the mildest and gentlest of folk – wanted to take a phone call in private they wouldn't budge and he had to insist in the strongest terms.' The visiting couples introduced themselves as representatives of the parish. Neocatechumenate was not mentioned by name. Subsequently, Mrs Bolger was appointed co-ordinator for Catholic households in the area; she was helping with a purely statistical census, which meant visiting homes and asking if family members were attending the parish. She was shocked to discover that the official list she had been given had been used by NC before her and the houses evangelized had been marked up. She felt it was wrong that a list of this kind should have been issued for the use of a group which was highly controversial among the majority of parishioners.

As well as the house-visits, at the *Traditio* stage members are required to move in on certain parish groups and eventually take them over: first communion and confirmation classes, preparation for marriage and infant baptism – all ways of drawing more candidates into the communities. This stage had been reached by communities in both Sacred Hearts, Cheltenham, and St Nicholas, Bristol. Donnini pointed out two recent developments in Rome that are especially worrying. One is the trend for communion and confirmation classes to be run by married couples from the communities: they are expected to become surrogate parents to children in the classes, inviting them into their homes to experience a 'true Christian family'. In line with the bleak NC view of society, these children are all assumed to come from broken or at least unchristian homes. Another new area which is being developed in NC's seminal parishes are groups whose special responsibility is visiting the homes of the recently deceased. Donnini explained to me how in recent years people in Italy have become afraid to have a corpse in the house, and try to get rid of it as soon as possible. The NC shock troops are rushed to these houses before the body can be removed, psalms are said over it and the grieving relatives are evangelized! Such intrusions could prove at best untimely and at worst traumatic, especially in the light of the unwanted housecalls in Ealing. Both of these developments can be seen as unscrupulous methods of recruiting among the vulnerable and unwary.

Intoxicated with its success in the Vatican's own backyard – it claims 80,000 members in Italian parishes – the movement has dispensed with caution or discretion, imposing its will with a total disregard for the rights or sensibilities of those who preceded it. Implicit in its methodology is the old axiom of preconciliar Catholicism: error has no rights. An official parish catechist (that is, appointed by the diocese) in Rome, aged thirty-five and mother of five children, declares that her parish 'doesn't exist any more, because the coming of the Neocatechumenals was like a wave which swept away the people of the district (including catechists) and replaced them with strangers who circulate day and night in the church and its rooms so that the priests next day are tired, on the verge of breakdown, and strange'. She finds much that is disturbing in their teaching and methods:

> Catechists [according to NC] don't need to study theology, teaching methods, psychology – it's sufficient to live the Word

and let the Spirit tell us what to do. I have tackled the NCs and their priests on the subject of confession and sin – confession or not, we are always in sin. It seems that grace does not exist, but it's useless anyway – whoever hopes to take advantage of it is presumptuous and wants to be like God; he's in Satan's hands. God doesn't want us any different, He loves us as we are, so we might as well go on sinning. They sing lauds with our brothers [of the religious community attached to the parish], always getting under their feet (some of them have even left their husbands or wives), their small children sleeping on the pews while their parents dance round the altar.

Florence has become an NC stronghold, with communities dating back to the late sixties. Father Alfredo Nesi is the head of Opera della Divina Provvidenza Madonnina del Grappa, a well-respected Catholic charity based at Scandicci on the outskirts of Florence, specializing in overseas aid, particularly in Brazil. In 1991, Father Nesi wrote an open letter to Don Marco Calamandrei, parish priest of St Bartolo in Tuto, Scandicci, denouncing the 'full occupation' of the parish. In December of the same year, Don Calamandrei was one of several NC parish priests who presented their experience of NC to a group of forty bishops and cardinals present in Rome for the Synod on Europe. 'Twenty-two years ago, the parish was made up of seventy people meeting in a garage,' Calamandrei told them. 'Today, one thousand five hundred people come to mass, we have fourteen communities with a total of six hundred persons, of which fifty per cent are under forty five, while twenty years ago it was only ten per cent.'[1] According to Father Nesi, however, the Neocatechumenate presence at San Bartolo is 'superparochial or extraparochial', because it is not made up of local people – the essential requirement for a parish – but 'at least four-fifths [are] formed by Adepts drawn from other parishes in the area, or from all over Florence and its surroundings'.

He describes the situation as a 'Precedent and a fact which justly alarms and shocks parish priests who see people who are keen and capable of active parish work streaming out to another parish'. The result of this 'occupation', Nesi observes, has been a 'mass exodus of the faithful, including the most active participants in parish life'.

[1] *Avvenire*, Saturday, 7 December 1991.

'The gravity of the situation is brought home by the fact that . . . all the non-Neocatechumenal catechists, some of whom had years and years of commitment and service to the parish behind them, have been ostracized.'

He notes that, out of a healthy total of thirty-two 'people who co-ordinate the various services of the parish', according to the official calendar of events for 1991–2 only four are drawn from the parish. Thirty-one are Neocatechumenals 'of steel'; just one, the leader of the traditional Apostolate of Prayer association, is – for obvious reasons – not a member. 'Therefore a parish of 7,000 parishioners is directed by thirty-one Neocatechumenal organizers, including just three from the parish and one non-Neocatechumenal Co-ordinator.' San Bartolo Church, Nesi underlines, was built on land donated by his own organization 'with money from local people and the support of the diocesan Curia, certainly not through contributions of the Neocatechumenate, even though it disposes of vast sums, like other Modern Ecclesiastical movements'. Nesi's intention is to stress the moral responsibility of the parish to the people it is supposed to serve. Unwittingly, he shows that Calamandrei was somewhat economical with the truth in the impression he gave the bishops that the transformation of the parish from a small group in a garage to its current thriving state had been achieved singlehandedly by Neocatechumenate.

On a visit to Italy in December 1992, I scoured the religious bookshops of Milan for background material to the movements. The shelves were groaning with volumes published by Jaca Book and Città Nuova, the publishing houses of CL and Focolare respectively, but on NC I could find nothing. I had almost given up when I discovered a modest, plain-covered volume with the uncompromising title of *Heresies of the Neocatechumenal Movement*. It made fascinating reading. On my next visit to Rome, I contacted its author, Father Enrico Zoffoli, who invited me to meet him. I took the Metro to St John Lateran, the first Church in Christendom and the erstwhile seat of the papacy. Across the Piazza from the mighty basilica is another ancient place of pilgrimage, the Scala Sancta, or Holy Stairs, reputedly those climbed by Jesus in Pilate's house in Jerusalem; they are worn down by countless pilgrims who have climbed them on their knees. The Stairs are in the care of the Passionist order, who have a monastery next door. It was here, in the visitors' parlour, that I was cordially received by Father Zoffoli.

With his snow-white hair, twinkling eyes and gentle manner, he is an elderly cherub, quaintly sporting a tiny hand-knitted black shawl, drawn over the shoulders of his habit. Yet, behind the sweetness, lurks the steely logic of a Catholic apologist of the old school. Father Zoffoli is unashamedly a traditionalist – proof that somehow the movements have succeeded in alienating both the left *and* the right wings of the Catholic church. Although he deplores NC's methods, it is to their theology that he chiefly objects. In *Heresies* and a second book, *Magisterium of the Pope and Kiko's Catechesis: A Comparison*, he points out theological errors in NC teachings on fundamental Catholic doctrine such as the Redemption, the Sacrifice of Christ on Calvary and the Eucharist. He has repeatedly challenged Kiko Arguello to a public debate – an offer that has not yet been taken up.

NC has tried to discredit Zoffoli in the Catholic press, but it has never defended itself against his charges. Church authorities have made no attempt to silence him – perhaps because, in his isolation, he presents rather a quixotic figure, they have avoided the embarrassment of a public confrontation. Nevertheless, his community see him as a liability. While engaged in conversation with Father Zoffoli, I became aware of an elderly gentleman who would shuffle from one foot to the other outside the door of the parlour, wearing a troubled expression and obviously desperately straining to catch our conversation. Later, while I was studying some papers on my own, he introduced himself to me as Father Marcello, a devotee of the Neocatechumenate, obviously in considerable distress over the work of his *confrère*. After that, he would surreptitiously pass me slips of paper with addresses of NC parishes scrawled on them, or clippings from the *Osservatore Romano* – covered with shaky underlinings and spidery notes – in which the Pope praised NC. One afternoon I was perusing some documents in the parlour when a younger Father entered, wearing the black soutane and emblem of the Passionist order. He introduced himself as the superior of the community. His fear at my presence in the monastery was tangible; although he did not ask that I should leave, he said that he did not want the good name of the Scala Sancta besmirched. Where NC was concerned, he clearly felt the need to look over his shoulder.

This was not mere paranoia. Father Zoffoli has many covert supporters, but few who will give him open backing. The late Father Giovanni Caprile, editor of the authoritative Jesuit monthly

Civiltà cattolica, admired his work, but told him he dared not review *The Heresies of the Neocatechumenal Movement* because, traditionally, the magazine is checked by the Vatican Secretary of State before it goes to press. An internal memo was circulated to all branches of St Paul Bookshops, the largest chain of Catholic bookstores in Italy, ordering them not to stock Zoffoli's titles. When the good Father sent a copy to the Secretary of State, it was acknowledged with the ultimate in Vatican diplomacy: a thank-you note which was not only unsigned but did not mention the gift received. Apart from one or two Italian bishops who have banned Neocatechumenate from their diocese – in the North, with a safe distance and the bulwark of Cardinal Martini between them and Rome – Zoffoli stands alone in his public denouncement of the movement in Italy. He has become the only refuge for many of those who have been damaged by NC. Sadly, more liberal figures who privately oppose the movement have not had his courage.

Priests – and even bishops – in Italy know that NC's influence with the current regime at the Vatican is so great that criticism, even a failure to acquiesce, could lose them their job. Don Paolo, a priest from the Roman suburbs, fears that his parish will be abolished under pressure from Neocatechumenate because he has resisted joining the movement and has therefore halted their planned advance into the territories under his jurisdiction. Until recently, he formed part of a team ministry in which the three priests of small neighbouring parishes lived together in the largest of the presbyteries, conducting a life of community. The aim was to counteract the problems of isolation often experienced by parish priests, and the arrangement had proved a success. Suddenly one of their number was sent elsewhere and his replacement was an NC presbyter. He made it clear from the start that he had no intention of joining their community life and took his meals separately. The presbytery was immediately invaded by NC members, making it difficult for the two other priests to carry out their ministry. The NC priest approached the Vicariate, or governing body of the diocese of Rome and set out his requirements. The team ministry was broken up, and Don Paolo was moved, alone, to another house close to his parish church. The large house which had been the base of the team ministry was now dedicated to the exclusive use of NC. Not content, delegations of NC members continued to persecute Don Paolo, urging him to introduce the movement into his parish, which may, he now fears, eventually be closed down and absorbed into the larger NC parish. He feels powerless to react as the Vicariate itself, he believes, is controlled by NC. Such machinations are not restricted to Italy, however. A prominent critic of NC in a British parish was invited to become a member of the Board of Governors of the local Catholic primary school, a post for which she was eminently qualified. The parish priest (not an NC member – the local community was run by one of his colleagues) laid down as a condition of her appointment that she must make no more attacks on the movement. Resisting this blackmail, she retorted that if her integrity was questioned she could not see why her services were required. In this case, NC lost the war of nerves and the lady now sits on the Board.

When the first NC missionary families arrived in Hamburg from Italy in 1985, they approached the city's Italian mission, run by the avuncular and resourceful Father Quintano Legnan, who carries out his ministry to several thousand migrant workers from a spacious modern villa outside the centre. The mission provides not only masses but catechesis for the children and adults, a course of Italian language and culture for children, and social events. It is well equipped and thriving.

Padre Quintano was not impressed by the missionary families so loudly trumpeted in NC publicity for their dedication and self-sacrifice. The first he met was Gigi Michelon, with his wife and six children, who had come from Italy.

> He needed to find work as soon as possible, as he had six children when he first got here (he now has eleven), so we got him a job in a laundry. Then he complained: 'But I can't work eight hours a day; I came here to catechise. That's what the Pope sent me here for.' So his parish priest, Father Klockner, who is an NC member, asked the bishop if Michelon could have the job of driving the children to and from school so that he could be free to catechise in the evenings. I told him and the others: 'If the Pope has sent you here to catechise, you should give a good example of work, which you don't do.'

A local Italian family, the Racciopis, joined the movement and became unpaid servants to the Michelon family, babysitting for them, doing their ironing and cleaning, so that they could be free to catechise. The Racciopis were the object of another disturbing NC practice. 'They exorcize those who have problems with the catechesis,' Padre Quintano explains. 'The Racciopis have been exorcized on at least three occasions.' Because their children mixed with the children of the Michelons, the Racciopis became aware of how little time Gigi and Maria spent at home owing to their NC commitment. One day, after they had left their son Vito with Gigi's children, they returned to find him crying, because two of the Michelon boys had been taken away by the police for stealing.

The doubts expressed by the French bishops at the 1987 Synod were the result of long years of disputes with Neocatechumenate. The communities were first introduced in the prestigious Saint Germain des Prés parish on Paris's Left Bank, at the heart of French Catholic life. Such were the divisions and controversy unleashed that Cardinal Marty, the then primate, forbade its expansion for many years. Even now, NC is not listed in the French Bishops' Conference directory of approved Catholic associations.

The NC centre for Paris, and France, today is the church of Notre Dame de Bonne Nouvelle in Montmartre. Its parish priest, Antoine de Monicault, admits that the communities have encountered problems in French parishes. When I asked how these were dealt with, his response illustrated the NC inability to take an objective view: 'It is not a problem as long as the parish priest is convinced; if he has doubts, however, it is a problem.' The problems with the Way experienced by dissenting parishioners are not even considered.

Despite these perceived problems, the Neocatechumenal Way now has 100 communities in France, present in 15 dioceses. In addition to Paris, there are NC communities in parishes in Montpelier, Toulon, Meaux, Strasbourg, Nancy and Marseilles.

The Catholic Church in the Netherlands has been riven with conflicts for at least thirty years. Despite the efforts of the Vatican to neutralize the situation, mainly by appointing conservative bishops, it is still strongly polarized between extremes of right and left. In a report, *The Roman Catholic Church in the Netherlands in the Year 1992*, prepared by the country's seven bishops for their January 1993 *ad limina* (literally 'to the threshold') visit to the Pope, the movements are dismissed as having made little impact.

This is not necessarily the view of the movements themselves. Focolare, for example, which works outside the official structures of the Church, has six permanent communities, one each for men and women in Amsterdam, Amersfoort and Eindhoven as well as a Mariapolis Centre, located in the village of Baak near Zutphen. *Nieuwe Stad*, the Dutch edition of the movement's international magazine, is published monthly. A recent youth meeting succeeded in attracting 1,200; and the Dutch *focolarini* estimate that, while the committed membership is two or three thousand, 20,000 have been in contact with the movement through its large events such as the summer Mariapolis and the concerts of the movement's men's and women's international bands, Gen Rosso and Gen Verde. Focolare in the Netherlands has its own band which tours parishes and 'tries to show that there are young people in the Church who are enthusiastic, that there is still life in the Church'.

Despite virtually dismissing them in their report, some of the bishops have acknowledged Focolare: Cardinal Alfrink, the conservative primate of the Netherlands, has visited the Dutch Mariapolis several times, as has Bishop Bluijssen who, according to members, declared himself 'moved' by the atmosphere. Such is the confidence of Focolare in the Netherlands that they are now embarking on their biggest-ever project in the country: the foundation of a 'model town', like Loppiano, for which a site has already been found in the countryside of Zeist, near Utrecht.

Neocatechumenate has found an enthusiastic protector in one of the most conservative members of the Dutch hierarchy, Bishop Bomers of the important diocese of Haarlem, which covers Amsterdam. Although he is considered affable and approachable, he is reluctant to talk about the NC presence in his diocese. The problems, he claims, have been to do with the idea of missionaries coming from abroad to evangelize the Dutch. Formerly the Catholic Church in the Netherlands sent out thousands of missionaries to other parts of the world. The spread of the movement has been hampered by the fact that none of the missionary families that have been sent there speak Dutch yet. Bishop Bomers is helping the movement to establish a seminary in the Netherlands. Unfortunately none of the seminarians speak Dutch, either – they are from Latin America, Italy, Spain, Poland and Egypt. Bishop Bomers claims that NC is not yet present in any parishes. He has accepted invitations to celebrate NC Eucharists with the communities and their priests. He has also been invited 'two or three times to give the Bibles'.

My own attitude is that I know the Pope is behind them. The Neocatechumenate is a service offered to the dioceses and the parishes. I have seen with my own eyes in Rome and Sicily parishes which had been dead, with only a few people, brought to life again. I've seen that the Bible is at the heart of their work. The focus is on living the faith. It strikes me that many of the participants have gone through a profound conversion. It doesn't appeal to many people here yet, but many people don't know it. The lay people sacrifice a lot to follow what they see as their vocation . . . I will give them a fair chance. I am adopting an attitude of wait-and-see.

The Bishop's enthusiasm seems to suggest rather more than that.

It could well be that the bishops' report is short-sighted in dismissing the movements just because they cannot be neatly pigeonholed. While religious practice among Dutch Catholics steadily declines, the movements have the determination and confidence to consolidate and grow. Like all sects they thrive in secularized environments where there is little religious knowledge or tradition. To be sidelined by most of the country's bishops gives them the autonomy that is essential for them to function. By the time the bishops start to take notice, they could well find they have a new problem they had not bargained for.

Nowhere was the Council's core message of justice and peace more enthusiastically adopted than in the churches of South America. The result was liberation theology and base communities, its practical application at the local level, proclaiming the gospel as a means of empowerment for the poor, a way in which they can shake off the yoke of oppression. It is hardly surprising, therefore, that Neocatechumenate, along with the other movements, has experienced considerable resistance from liberal bishops there. In 1993 Mgr Luis Alberto Luna Tobar, bishop of Cuenca in Ecuador, with obvious reluctance, made the following observations on NC:

Many believe there are gaps, doctrinal distortions and intentional absence of theological sources in the presentation of the Neo-catechumenal doctrine . . . [They show] an evident distaste for any theology that is not European in origin. They have no doctrinal link with culture, with our own time and its voices.

> The 'glorious cross' and the 'servant of Jaweh' are not signs and expressions of hope, but of torture. The space given to evil and the devil goes beyond healthy doctrine and leans towards childish fear and abrogation of responsibility. The word justice is never heard among the Neocatechumenals. Faith is closer to karma than grace.

A meeting in Amsterdam in 1980 of European Directors of Catechumenate highlighted the confusion that had arisen in the previous decade between the official Catechumenate of the Catholic Church – that is, the process of reception of adult converts to the Catholic faith – and the Neocatechumenate, which had begun its lightning spread to the parishes of Europe. Needless to say, the confusion had been fostered by NC themselves in their misleading description of the Way as 'an application of the official cate-chumenate', lending a bogus respectability to their own teachings. Any similarities are on a purely superficial level. The catechesis of the RCIA can draw on a unlimited number of sources of official Catholic teaching, from textbooks to documents of the Church, while NC catechesis is rigidly restricted to the teachings of Kiko Arguello that NC catechists learn by rote.

At first sight the NC ceremonies could appear to resemble those of the RCIA, but they could not be more different in intention. RCIA ceremonies are not only public but also have the specific aim of involving the parish at large, whereas the NC rites are held behind locked doors and exclude all parish outside the communities. RCIA rites express the growing conviction of the individual as, by stages, he or she freely enters the faith community of the Church. The NC rites – particularly in the formal scrutinies and other ceremonies celebrated in the presence of the bishop – merely set the seal on the assault that has already taken place on the individual in the secrecy of the communities, coercing him or her to sell their goods and detach themselves from husband or wife and children, demanding unqualified obedience to the catechist and enslavement to the group.

The most obvious difference between the two processes is that the official RCIA takes two or three years while the Way of the Neocatechumenate can last up to twenty years and can be prolonged almost indefinitely. Most important of all is the fact that the RCIA aims to introduce candidates into the freedom of the Catholic community, with its rich heritage and choice of experiences, while Neocatechumenate channels candidates into its own narrow Way. In an address to the European catechists at the 1980 Amsterdam conference, Gerard Reniers, National Director of the Official Catchumenate in France, listed several worries prompted by enquiries received in his office in France: a questioning of the validity of all other forms of pastoral action – such as other Catholic organizations; negation of centuries of Christian heritage in the name of rediscovering the life of the early Christians; a rejection of one's personal history; the tendency to sectarianism.

From experience in NC parishes, it emerges that peaceful existence between the official catechumenate of the Church, the RCIA, and the Way is impossible. Indeed, if the two did exist side by side they would be producing two different kinds of Catholic.

By developing structures independent of, and parallel to, those of the Church, Focolare retains the freedom of action it needs to 'exercise its charism': practically speaking, it is a separate church, with activities independent from the local dioceses, directed from the movement's centre in Rome. However bishops might deplore this fact, there is little they can do about it. Focolare professes obedience to the hierarchy and occasionally will perform a token service for the diocese, such as youth work. Even this is simply seen as another opportunity to fulfil their own purpose – winning new converts to the movement. Public controversy goes against Focolare conditioning; as intellectualism and even thinking are discouraged, the *focolarini* appear vacuous rather than opinionated. Unlike the militants of CL, *focolarini* strike outsiders – including church authorities – as 'harmless' or 'quaint'. In reality, 'cunning' (*furbizia*) is a highly prized virtue among Focolare members, who are encouraged to scheme in order to achieve their ends by stealth and even deception if necessary.

Inevitably, when the movement interfaces with Church structures, conflict ensues. In the case of the New Parishes movement, run by Focolare priests, there are reports of similar situations to those created by NC. In one such parish on the island of Malta, a Catholic stronghold which the movements have carved up between them, parishioners felt that the parish and all its amentities had been taken from them.

Despite their claim to a predominantly 'lay' status, Focolare – and the other movements – capitalized on the crisis of identity that swept the secular clergy and religious orders alike in the years following the Council. Fundamentalism always appeals in periods of uncertainty, and here were formulae for renewal presented in reassuringly absolute terms. Increasingly, however, youthful candidates for the priesthood and the religious life enter communities with their external allegiance – to the movements and their leadership – already firmly in place. Focolare claims that its 'spirituality of unity' helps members of religious orders discover the charism of their own founders. The fact is, however, that the movement's demands on the time and resources of religious are just as heavy as they are on lay adherents – including attendance at local open meetings and specialized national and international meetings for religious. Inevitably, these cause tension with the duties of community life and provoke resentment amongst fellow-religious who have the single commitment to the order. In addition, there is the more insidious requirement of spiritual loyalty to the founder and the adoption of the Focolare 'mentality'. The inevitable result is that the religious become *focolarini* in all but their habit. Through them, the movements are staking out their territory within the powerful and influential institutions of the Catholic Church.

In its early years, CL produced many vocations both to the secular priesthood and the religious orders; the resulting presence of the movement in religious communities throughout Italy has been consistently dogged by rumours of division. Such rumours were confirmed recently when the CL-affiliated Italian Province of the Sisters of the Assumption broke away from the rest of the order owing to irreconcilable differences. The Vatican immediately granted the splinter group official status as a new congregation – an indication of official approval and a worrying precedent for other orders.

But clashes at this level are dwarfed by a power struggle between the movements and the orders on a far larger scale.

In the past, the great religious orders of the Church have been the principal agents of its missionary activity. They are described as its pillars, symbolized by the statues of their founders to be found in the niches of the mighty columns of St Peter's Basilica. For centuries they have been the Church's arms, reaching to the ends of the earth. Many of its most towering and influential personalities, particularly in the field of theology, have been sons and daughters of the religious congregations. Yet increasingly they have appeared to be unruly and recalcitrant children. Almost all the leading theologians who have crossed swords with the Vatican in the past twenty years are members of religious orders: Leonardo Boff, a champion of liberation theology in South America, who has now left the priesthood, a Franciscan, John J. McNeill, in the United States, dismissed from the Jesuit order for his liberal views on homosexuality; two Dominicans – the Dutch Edward Schillebeeckx with his reinterpretation of the divine and human natures of Christ, and Matthew Fox spreading his Creation Theology from California.

Following Vatican II, there has been a seemingly unstoppable flow of defections from the orders coupled with a drop in vocations. Many of those who have remained are activists, demanding fundamental reform within their orders and in the forefront of implementing the Council's call to work for justice and peace. Their radical action has led to friction between the orders and John Paul II himself.

In October 1981, following the disablement by a stroke of the Superior General of the Jesuits, Pedro Arupe, the Pope made an unprecedented intrusion into the life of the 26,000-man order, by appointing the eighty-year-old Paolo Dezza, SJ, as his personal delegate, 'to superintend the government of the Society until the election of a new superior general'. It was the first time in the 500-year history of the order that a Pope had seen fit to override its constitution, which sets out the manner in which a new superior general should be elected. For two years, the order continued in this limbo until, in September 1983, the Pope permitted the general congregation to meet and select a new superior general, the Dutchman Peter-Hans Kolvenbach.

John Paul's intervention was interpreted as a gesture of disapproval for the order's social involvement, which was seen by Rome as too political. At a meeting with the leaders of the order in Rome on 27 February 1982, he stressed the obligation of 'fidelity to the magisterium and the Roman pontiff' and the need of 'genuine priestly spirituality'. In a similar imposition of papal authority, John Paul sent a letter to 200 delegates from 120 countries of the 20,000-strong Franciscan Friars Minor Order, meeting in Assisi in May 1985. He called on them to eliminate certain unspecified 'theories and practices' which were out of keeping with the Franciscan tradition, reminding them that their order was not a 'movement open to new options continually substituted by others in the insistent search for an identity, as if this identity had not been found'. Just to make sure his wishes were observed, he appointed Archbishop Vincenzo Fagilo, secretary of the Sacred Congregation for Religious and Secular Institutes, to oversee the proceedings.

In addition to these disciplinary measures at the institutional level, in the early eighties the Vatican took action against a number of male and female religious for their involvement in politics, including, in the United States, the Jesuit Robert Drinan and Arlène Violet, a Sister of Mercy. Drinan, having served five terms in the House of Representatives, agreed not to stand for office again. Arlene Violet requested dispensation from her vows rather than renounce her political career. Of four priests who held office in the Nicaraguan government when the Sandinistas came to power in 1979, three were members of religious orders. In August 1984, they were given an ultimatum to surrender their posts. They declined, and in 1985 all three were suspended *a divinis*. Fernando Cardenal had already been dismissed from the Jesuit order some months previously.

During the 1984 presidential elections in the United States, a full-page advertisement appeared in the *New York Times* for Sunday, 7 October, stating a controversial Catholic position on the issue of birth control: 'Statements of recent Popes and of the Catholic hierarchy have condemned the direct termination of prenatal life as morally wrong in all instances. There is a mistaken belief in American society that this is the only legitimate Catholic position.'

Twenty-seven religious – twenty-four nuns and three male religious – were included among the ninety-seven signatories. The Vatican's Sacred Congregation for Religious and Secular Institutes demanded retractions, and on 21 July 1986 announced that all but two of the signatories had complied with 'public retractions of adherence to Catholic doctrine on abortion', whereupon eleven of the nuns 'categorically denied' having done any such thing.

A second advertisement appeared in the *New York Times* on Sunday, 2 March declaring solidarity with 'all Catholics whose right to free speech is under attack'. It was endorsed by a thousand signatures including a large number of priests and nuns. This time, there was no response from the Vatican.

But, while the religious orders have proved to be a thorn in the Vatican's side, the movements have assiduously promoted themselves as models of docility and orthodoxy. This has led in recent years to a decisive option in favour of the movements as protagonists in the Vatican's missionary projects, such as the 'new evangelization', with a corresponding side-lining of the orders. This was first noted in the 1991 Extraordinary Synod on Europe in which the movements were given the nod for the building of the Pope's vision of a Europe united 'from the Atlantic to the Urals'. The religious orders barely featured in these plans.

The following year, however, a more serious omission occurred during the Pope's October 1992 visit to the South American Bishops' Conference in Santo Domingo. A respected theologian, a member of one of the Church's oldest and most revered religious orders, who attended from Rome, told me that he and his distinguished theologian colleagues observed a distinct swing towards the movements in the Pope's addresses, while the orders were merely paid lip-service.

A tangible sign of favour was the fact that, as his only appointment outside the official programme, the Pope chose to visit the as yet unfinished Redemptoris Mater seminary of Neocatechumenate.

Many would question the wisdom of giving a free hand to the movements in the volatile South American continent, but the theologian-observer at Santo Domingo feels that the Vatican's option for the movements is also quite simply impractical:

> The new perspective for Latin America depends on everything, including lay people and families, yet the religious have the most prophetic tasks in hand. Not to include them is to have the cart without the horse. Some areas in South America are characterized by the dynamism of the ecclesial base communities and these are in the parishes, often run by religious. Yet the Holy See thinks it can carry out its projects for new evangelization with the new movements rather than religious . . . Even in the Synod for Africa there is little emphasis on the orders who have been the architects of the Church in Africa. It's interesting to have lay people involved, but they cannot make the religious disappear when in actuality they have to carry ninety per cent of the commitments.

> They are not the protagonists by mistake – their involvement is
> real. Sometimes you have the impression that the Vatican is
> dreaming and they imagine their dreams are real.

As he points out, the religious orders may be old, but they are also
more stable, with established activities in the mass media, universities and other educational institutions. Between them, they also
cover far more territory. The problem is that the Vatican accepts
the movements at face value; it believes their publicity. 'The Pope
visits a country and the movements are there waving banners and
cheering while the religious orders, on the other hand, probably
write a letter of protest!'

The seeds of division were present in the Communion and
Liberation movement from its very foundation in 1954. A chance
meeting on a train provided the initial inspiration for the young
Milanese priest Don Giussani, then a teacher at the city's Berchet
High School (Liceo Classico). While on his way to the Adriatic
coast for a short holiday, he was shocked at the lack of Christian
knowledge shown by a group of schoolchildren he encountered.
On his return to Berchet, he set about founding a group which
would be an answer to this problem.

For almost twenty years, his organization would go by the name
of Student Youth (Gioventù Studentesca – GS). At that time, the
official lay organization, Catholic Action (AC), with its various
branches for different age-groups and sectors of society, and the
backing of the hierarchy, dominated life in the Italian dioceses. GS
aimed to be nothing more than a group within GIAC, AC's youth
division.

But there were some fundamental differences. GIAC operated
within the traditional 'oratories', or youth clubs, of the Italian
parishes; while GS was based in the 'environment' – that is, the
school – where youngsters spent most of their time. This was for
a very specific reason, as Don Giussani pointed out: 'To reach
young people where they are most conditioned by society, that is
in the school as the place where their mentality and culture is
formed.' Whereas GIAC members might spend an hour a week
with their group on a Sunday, the members of GS (giessini) could
have daily contact.

A second difference, therefore, was a much deeper commitment and involvement on the part of the *giessini*, expressed by Don Giussani in two further principles: 'To propose Jesus Christ to them as the centre of meaning in their lives and the total explanation of existence (Christocentric formation)' and 'To put them together in the name of Christ in their own school environment as a method of living and experiencing Christ's proposal as the centre of their lives'.

A more evident difference, and a surprisingly liberal one, was the fact that Don Giussani was determined that his movement, unlike Catholic Action, should be co-educational. Besides causing problems at a structural level – GS was after all supposed to be part of AC – this also gave rise to persistent rumours that GS, and subsequently CL, catered for Catholics of easy virtue. GS, therefore, rather than being part of GIAC, was felt to be the opposition. The conflict with Catholic Action was to rage for the next four decades.

GS expanded rapidly in the fifties and early sixties, to the considerable discomfort of the Milanese hierarchy who did not know quite how to cope with this 'shadow diocese' outside the parish structures. On 6 December 1966, the GS leaders sent a letter to Cardinal Giovanni Colombo of Milan, drawing his attention to 'highly relevant facts concerning the role of GS within the diocese'. The letter, which was signed by two GS priests, Don Piero Re and Don Giovanni Padovani, protested against criticisms of the movement within Catholic circles; a priest in one journal had accused GS of 'mass-producing immature enthusiasts'.

In an attempt to end the ten-year dispute within AC, at the beginning of 1966 Cardinal Giovanni Colombo had officially recognized GS as an 'environmental missionary movement in secondary schools. This movement belongs to the two youth branches [male and female] of Catholic Action.' While AC members were satisfied with this solution, Giussani's followers were not too happy about being 'contained' within the larger organization. Besides, another problem was brewing: the original GS members, including most of the leadership, had now left school and were attending university. In Colombo's 'Directives', it was laid down that these *giessini* should join Catholic Action's student body, FUCI (Federazione degli universitari cattolici – Federation of Catholic University Students), which put things back to square one.

The demands of GS were so total that the alternatives of either leaving that way of life or blending in with another organization were equally inconceivable. In addition, many GS leaders now held top posts in AC, particularly GIAC, and found themselves in conflict with the newly liberalized AC leadership whom they regarded as 'catholic intellectuals'. At the same time, the ecclesiastical authorities had turned down Giussani's request that he should extend his leadership to those *giessini* now attending university. GS came up with a unilateral solution with the foundation in 1965–6 in Milan of the Charles Péguy Centre, a meeting-place for university students and graduates, followed by similar centres in other cities.

This was a direct challenge to FUCI, which demanded even more insistently that the *giessini* should renounce their separate identity and join them. Many leading figures in FUCI at that time would eventually form Italy's Catholic left in the 1970s. Giussani criticized the movement for creating a 'dualism' between the spiritual and the temporal, between the world of history and politics and that of faith and hope in eternal life. The dramatic solution of GS was a mass subscription to FUCI to overcome these aberrations by sheer force of numbers.

But the external conflicts were overshadowed by an internal dispute which was to rend GS asunder. The cause was the student revolt of 1968. A crisis of identity had been building in GS since 1965 when Don Giussani had left for America to complete his studies on American protestant theology. Faced with the politicization of the student environment, many members of GS decided to throw in their lot with the student movement, believing that at last they could express their convictions in a practical commitment. This wing polarized around Don Giovanni Padovani, who left the movement in 1968. In this way, GS found itself halved in numbers. The remaining members of GS regrouped under the leadership of Don Giussani. Their war-cry was 'unity and authority' – both within the movement and expressed in their devotion to the papacy. At the same time, the 'integrist' approach was expressed by the concept of the Christian 'fact' or the Church as 'a living experience of the liberation worked by God and already in itself politically relevant'. These two concepts were summed up in the stirring new banner under which the movement was relaunched: Communion and Liberation.

Based in universities rather than in schools, the movement grew dramatically in the early seventies, drawing into its ranks many disillusioned defectors from the extreme left. With the motto 'Tenacity and stubbornness', CL was to become the highest-profile lay association in Italy.

The concept of the Christian 'fact' or 'event' is fundamental to an understanding of the movement's aggressive style. In practice, this means the visible and vigorous defence of a – or, as they see it, *the* – Christian point of view on all matters – theological, moral, social, political and cultural.

CL's militancy is nowhere more in evidence than when it is peddling its extreme ideas, often amounting to bizarre fixations. From the earliest days of GS, the movement's extensive publishing activities have provided a means of bringing its ideas before the widest possible audience. The history of the movement is strewn with leaflets, magazines and pamphlets, distributed by the thousand. In 1972, CL's publishing house, Jaca Book, produced the first Italian edition of the theological magazine *Communio*. It was launched in protest at the prestigious international journal *Concilium* whose theological views were considered too liberal by the Vatican's conservative International Theological Commission. Behind the new publication were two leading theologians: Henri de Lubac and Hans Urs von Balthasar, both very close to CL and actively involved with the movement. The co-director of the magazine was Giuseppe Ruggeri, a theologian who was also a member of CL's arcanely titled Istituto di Studi per la Transizione (Institute of Studies for the Transition), known by the acronym ISTRA.

Among the many Milanese theologians writing for *Communio*, only one, Giacomo Contri, was an official CL member. But things changed when Ruggeri became director in 1974; top CL figures like the philosopher Rocco Buttiglione and the priest-theologian Angelo Scola, both later to play leading roles in the movement and in the Church as advisers to John Paul II, joined the editorial board. CL polemics were immediately in evidence in the journal's regular features: 'Ideologies' examined supposed cultural, political and historical influences on contemporary (liberal) theologians – a chance to trot out the movement's hobbyhorses; 'Praxis' provided a platform from which a constant assault could be mounted on dissenting Catholic opinion.

Perhaps the clearest example of CL's aggressiveness and dog-matism can be seen in the disputes unleashed by the major expansion of its publishing operations in the late eighties. CL claims that the vast business empire run by its members does not actually belong to the movement; but the fact remains that its major Italian publications *Il Sabato* (*Saturday*) – which ceased publication in 1993 – and *30 Giorni* (*30 Days*) have been the mouthpieces of some of the movement's most bitterly fought crusades. *Il Sabato* was a glossy current-affairs weekly, in the mould of *Panorama* or *L'Europeo*, whereas *30 Giorni* is a monthly dealing principally with church affairs. If their contents are surprisingly similar, their ideology is identical. In 1987, the holding company of *Il Sabato* and *30 Giorni* decided to launch foreign-language editions of *30 Giorni*, triggering off a savage confrontation within the international Catholic community.

A quick leaf through an edition of *30 Giorni* ('in the Church and in the world', reads its subtitle) tells a great deal about Communion and Liberation. True, it does deal with current affairs and world events, but from the single perspective of the most conservative backwaters of the Roman Curia. Pictures of the pontiff and curial cardinals cram its pages. If the Council revealed a liberating new vision of the Church as the People of God, *30 Giorni* whisks its readers back in time to the good old days when the Church could be readily identified by a scarlet sash and skullcap. *30 Giorni* falls into the Italian publishing category of a 'magazine of opinion'. Indeed, it is packed with opinions – usually of the most unpopular and reactionary kind, expressed in the strongest and most controversial of terms. It sees as its purpose – or, rather its crusade – to form, or correct, international opinion on all matters pertaining to the Pope, the Vatican and the institution of the Catholic Church. Copies are mailed free to key church figures in Rome, such as members of the Curia and professors of the Roman colleges and universities. International magazines like *Time* and *Newsweek* also receive copies. Articles will appear in advance on major ecclesiastical events such as the Pope's foreign trips, synods of the world's bishops and the latest encyclicals, with the purpose of influencing news coverage. Although even to the vast majority of Catholics *30 Giorni* would appear dry and esoteric, it undoubtedly makes intriguing reading for anyone interested in the inner workings of the Vatican – provided, of course, they can crack the code common to Rome-based Church publications.

While he was in Rome as a papal nominee at the 1987 Synod

on the Laity, the American traditionalist Father Joseph Fessio, SJ, began discussions with CL's Alver Metalli on the feasibility of an English-language edition of CL's flagship magazine. The match seemed an appropriate one: Father Fessio's Ignatius Press, based in San Francisco, had already published in English a number of CL titles and had a reputation as the most prominent right-wing Catholic publisher in the United States. Fessio was impressed by the magazine, which was well written, glossily presented and offered a perspective on Vatican affairs not available elsewhere. Most important, from his point of view, traditionalist Catholics would appreciate its orthodoxy.

The deal was simple: in exchange for a fixed monthly fee, *30 Giorni* in Rome would not only provide all the material for each issue already translated into English, but would furnish it as finished artwork, preserving the house-style of the magazine. After a fruitless search for independent funding in the States, Father Fessio decided to finance the project in-house, making use of his company's extensive mailing-list, and publication began in spring 1988.

So far, dealings between *30 Giorni* and Ignatius Press had been on the basis of a gentleman's agreement; they were, after all, two bodies of some standing within the Catholic Church. But there had been changes in the power structure in Rome. A new holding company for *Il Sabato* and *30 Giorni*, IEI (Istituto Editoriale Internazionale, International Editorial Institute), had been set up. An estimated $1 million, representing a one-third shareholding, was poured into IEI by French millionaire Rémy Montaigne, married to a Michelin heiress. Montaigne's publishing company, GIE 3F MEDIA, with two successful conservative Catholic weeklies to its name – *Famille Chrétienne* and *France-Catholique* – had launched the French edition of *30 Giorni*, *30 Jours*, in 1987.

At this point, CL's most controversial leading figure of recent years stepped into the picture. Marco Bucarelli was director general of IEI. He was also vice-president of the Popular Movement, the political wing of CL. Father Fessio, who describes his dealings with Bucarelli as 'most unfortunate', was astonished when Bucarelli demanded 50 per cent more than the fee that had been agreed with Metalli, plus total editorial control over the English-language magazine. It took two years to negotiate a contract which appeared to resolve the latter issue. Rome retained editorial control, while Ignatius Press reserved a right of veto. In the case of a stalemate, provision was made for inter-company arbitration. This solution seemed to satisfy both sides until it was put to the test. In the course of 1990, Father Fessio and his readers began to detect a disquieting change in the magazine's tone. A letter from Father Andrew Bees of Lewes, England, complained about the magazine's lack of balance:

> Recently . . . it has been all doom and gloom – the Church in ruin and decay on every side, Masonic plots hatching everywhere, not a glimmer of hope to be seen. It seems that the people interviewed are deliberately chosen for their pessimism . . . I am reluctant to expose parishioners to so much despair and desolation – they can get enough of that from the rest of the Catholic press.

In the meantime, *30 Jours*, the French edition of the magazine, had already reached a crisis, with the French publishers refusing to print the November and December 1990 issues. The contentious numbers contained articles attacking Tadeusz Mazowiecki, who stood in the November 1990 Polish presidential elections against Lech Walesa, a good friend of CL, a frequent guest at its vast summer gatherings in Rimini and their candidate for the presidency. Robert Masson, the French editor, did not want his edition to support either man but merely to inform readers on both. Rome took a hard line and insisted that the entire contents of the magazine should go out unaltered. French journalists based at *30 Giorni*'s Rome headquarters who had specifically been brought in at the request of GIE 3F MEDIA to give a French slant to *30 Jours* had noticed a change in policy since Alver Metalli had been replaced by Antonio Socci as editorial director in September 1990. Metalli had taken a flexible attitude, recognizing the need for some 'inculturation' in the style and content of the magazine. Ominously, Socci had told the French journalists in Rome that 'not even a line' was to be changed in the foreign-language editions.

When he discovered that no accommodation could be reached with IEI, Masson sent a letter to subscribers explaining why the issues in question would not be published in France. *30 Giorni* hit back with a violent attack on the French publishers in the editorial of the February 1991 edition, defiantly quoting the French convert Charles Péguy – a hero of CL – in defence of their stand, and accusing the French of refusing to participate in 'free, sincere and open dialogue on cultural and historical perspectives'.

The entire correspondence section was taken up with letters received by the Rome office in support of their position, with the claim that 'Without exception, all the letters from our French readers are in favour of the line that the international editorship of *30 Giorni* adopted. So we cannot publish letters of criticism of the international editorship even if we wanted to. There simply aren't any.'

The editorial and letters also appeared in the English-language edition, although in the American tradition of objective journalism Father Fessio contacted Robert Masson and printed letters that supported the French line. Among these was one from Monsignor Raymond Boucher, the archbishop of Avignon, who approved of the suppression of the offending articles 'out of respect for a country whose difficulties, already burdensome enough, we ought not to increase'. Another letter appeared which had been sent to the Rome office, contradicting their claims of total support.

By February 1991, Fessio was sufficiently concerned over the magazine's content to take the dramatic step of printing a 'Note from the English language publisher' in which he noted five worrying trends in recent numbers:

1. Increased reference to some kind of international Masonic conspiracy – which would at least need some explanation for non-European readers. 'To us,' Father Fessio explains, 'Masonry is like the Rotary Club – one of many charitable associations for businessmen. If there really was something more sinister afoot, we required more documentation rather than assertions. They would point out that Masonic insignia are to be found on dollar bills. There was something about the Masonic conspiracy in every issue.' Conspiracy theories involving Masonry are hardly new in Italy. Masons were the nemesis of Catholicism before they were replaced by the communists. In recent years, the Italian P2 affair gave the subject a new lease of life. However, anti-Masonic feeling is very much the province of the extreme right wing of the Italian Church. It had become an essential part of CL culture – particularly in its Roman chapter; members would attend courses on Masonry at the apartment of a CL university lecturer. *Il Sabato* had a regular 'culture' column entitled 'The Church and the Lodges' in which

it would detect a Masonic influence in the most unlikely current events – always those of which it disapproved – such as the ordination of women priests in the Anglican Church.[1]

2. Emphasis on 'the Power' – 'an ambiguous term for us which also needs explaining. This was a cultic phrase,' Father Fessio comments, 'which they refused to define. When they described world events, they would say "the Power" is behind this.' According to sources close to *30 Giorni*, the CL ideologues conceived of a hidden conspiracy of primarily business interests which was the real, if secret, force behind political events. 'The Power', this source alleges, was considered to be an alliance of Masons and the Mafia.

3. More articles of purely Italian interest – they would at least need extensive rewriting for readers not acquainted with the contents, especially the political contents.

4. A higher incidence of articles implicitly and explicitly promoting Communion and Liberation. 'Every utterance of Giussani had to go into print,' Fessio relates.

5. More intrusion of editorial opinion and moralizing into factual reporting. 'I am not myself fully aware of the reasons for these changes,' Father Fessio admits, but observed that they coincided with 'the replacement of Alver Metalli by Antonio Socci as editorial director and with the departure of Robert Moynihan who did most of the work in Rome on the English-language editions'.

Certainly it appears that, with Metalli gone, there was new insistence that the foreign-language editions should slavishly imitate *30 Giorni*. But had there really been a fundamental shift in the magazine's editorial position, as Fessio believes, or had foreign readers merely been shielded from the worst excesses of CL's bizarre vision of the world? Certainly the magazine's strident views and hectoring tone could hardly be described as out of keeping with the spirit of CL, but were perfectly true to form.

The crunch came with the anti-American position adopted by *30 Giorni* over the outbreak of the Gulf War. A one-page editorial

---

[1] 'Il terzo incomodo', *Il sabato*, 5 December 1992, pp. 99–100.

by Fessio at the end of the March 1991 issue of *30 Days* was a disclaimer and indeed a criticism of articles on the war included in the magazine. 'We are not against criticizing the United States, President Bush or the Gulf War,' Fessio stressed. His objection was that the reasons given for opposing the war were 'intellectually unsupportable'. He highlights one or two of the more outlandish points.

The first is a ludicrous factual error: 'It is claimed that the condition, for a just war, of avoiding unnecessary loss of life is clearly not fulfilled because, according to the *Osservatore Romano*, by day four of the war there had been "100,000 dead in Baghdad". In fact, the Iraqi Foreign Minister claimed only 23 civilian casualties at that time. Even as I write this, on day 21 of the war, the Iraqi Foreign Minister has just announced the number of Iraqi civilian casualties as 458!'

A second point questioned by Fessio was the sweeping claim for papal authority which appeared to lie behind CL's stance on the war: 'It is argued that the third condition for a just war, "reasonable prospect of concluding a just peace", is not verified because "the Pope said 'Problems are not resolved with arms' ". If this were a valid argument, it would prove that no war ever has been or could be a "just war".'

By the April issue, drastic action had been taken. The first page of the magazine carried an editorial boldly headlined 'Notice to our readers' in which Father Fessio explained his decision to print a selection from seventy-five readers' letters received (seventy of complaint) in place of four objectionable articles supplied from Rome for that edition. Fessio gave readers an idea of what they would be deprived of as a result of his 'editorial judgement': '(1) an editorial which begins "The strategy of international Masonic power . . ." and more than implies that the editorial interpretation of the Pope's position on the Gulf War has the same binding force for Catholics as dogmatic definitions of the faith; (2) an interview with a Jewish German philosopher who accused the US of imperialism and – two sentences later – of isolationism; (3) an interview about the "war-mongering chorus of consensus" among the "warlords"; and (4) an introduction to episcopal views on the war accusing Billy Graham of "anti-Roman spite and Yankee ideology", *The Economist* of a "hysterical pro-war campaign", and "the powerful of the world" of "inventing" wars of religion'.

Father Fessio reassured subscribers (30,000 at that time) that the matter would be resolved either by ensuring that 'the editorial staff in Rome will be effectively internationalized so that genuine collaboration becomes possible in determining the subject matter and approval' or else 'Ignatius Press will join with the publishers of other disaffected national editions to produce an international Catholic news magazine that will correspond to the intentions and aspirations of the original *30 Days*'.

Meanwhile, behind the scenes, a grim struggle was being played out between Rome and San Francisco. Father Fessio flatly refused to publish the articles on the Gulf War and cited the clause in the contract which provided for arbitration. But Marco Bucarelli in Rome rejected this agreement and insisted that if the magazine's contents were not printed in full they would simply cease to supply material for future editions. Fessio would not give in and received a summons to appear in court at twenty-four hours' notice. The Italians lost and were ordered to pay Ignatius Press $80,000. Their costs, however, had been $200,000.

The disaffected publishers of *30 Giorni*'s foreign-language editions got together and now produce an independent monthly magazine, *Catholic World Report*, with offices just off Via della Conciliazione, close to the Vatican.

But this was not the end of the story. Father Fessio was surprised to discover, after cutting ties with Rome, that American subscriptions were double those of all the other editions put together. 'I could never understand', he muses, 'why they would never reveal the figures even to their own associates. It turned out that in Italy they only had four or five thousand subscribers. I had never been able to understand why they would never do any promotion. In fact, I discovered that they were financing the operation through their political connections. That's why they had wanted more money from us.'

CL decided to continue publication of the American edition of the magazine, based out of New Jersey. Ignatius Press sells its mailing-list for one-time use. To Father Fessio's astonishment, he discovered that the new *30 Days* had bought the list and were using it on a permanent basis. 'It was like a mafia thriller. I flew to New Jersey and subpoenaed them. They had obtained it under a false name.' *30 Giorni*'s tactics were showing increasing signs of desperation. In fact the whole group was heading for deep trouble.

The entire incident illustrates the impossibility of collaboration between an élitist movement like CL, convinced of the rightness and uniqueness of its own message, and another organization within the Church – even one with approximately similar leanings.

Throughout the eighties, Pope John Paul rewarded CL for their loyalty by coming down on their side in the feud with Catholic Action. But his handling of the opponents of Neocatechumenate has been much more spirited. Far from concurring with the criticisms of his brother bishops in Italy and elsewhere, he has become NC's staunchest protector. Increasingly, therefore, despite often profound misgivings, the bishops, especially the Italians who are on the Vatican's doorstep, have tended to keep their counsel. An attack on Neocatechumenate has come to be seen as a personal attack on Pope John Paul himself.

Nevertheless, some Italian bishops have called the movement to heel. In the diocese of Milan, Cardinal Martini has forbidden further catechesis. The bishops of Umbria advised NC in 1986 to follow the Church's standard pastoral practices. In the same year, Monsignor Bruno Foresti, bishop of Brescia in northern Italy, forbade the movement to start new catecheses in his diocese, informing his priests that ex-members of the movement had discovered within it 'a pessimistic view of man, a climate of psychological subjection, a certain atmosphere of exclusivity, a certain identification of the community with the Church itself and a discredit for the religiosity of others'. The ban was not lifted until 1990, on the condition that the movement came under the direct supervision of the bishop.

Aware of these clashes, and anxious to smooth the path for the Pope's favoured organization, the Vatican has gone to extraordinary lengths to promote NC directly to the bishops of the world. In October 1991, a meeting was held in Rome for 800 NC parish members and their priests from all over Europe, east and west, so that an official presentation of the movement could be made to the bishops assembled in the Vatican for the Extraordinary Synod on Europe. Forty bishops attended the NC event, including Cardinal Glemp, primate of Poland, and Cardinal Lopez Rodriguez, primate of Santo Domingo and president of the South American Bishops' Conference. And, of course, Monsignor Paul-Josef Cordes of the Pontifical Council for the Laity.

Pope John Paul set the tone for the encounter by receiving the NC group in audience and hailing them as 'indefatigable and joyous apostles of the new evangelization'. The event was covered by *Avvenire*, the Italian Catholic daily, once run by CL, now staffed by journalists from all the new movements.

This first attempt to sell the movement directly to the episcopate through semi-official meetings backed by the Vatican proved so successful that it has been repeated on a number of occasions since, on a much larger scale.

At the 1992 meeting of the South American Bishops' Conference in Santo Domingo, at which the Pope had demonstrated his predilection for the movements and had visited the NC seminary, 150 South American bishops attended a presentation of the movement, which, as we have seen, has sparked controversy in the region, in particular for its dismissive attitude to social problems.

True to form, the presentation did not take place by means of debate or discussion but was an NC *convivence* at which the bishops were subjected to catechesis, a service of reconciliation and other aspects of the NC Way.

The meeting of the Bishops' Conference coincided with the celebrations of the 'discovery' of the American continent. Many of those present, mindful of the colonialization and exploitation of the region, felt that the occasion should be one of regret for sins committed in the name of God; indeed, a group of bishops celebrated a service of repentance – a novel gesture in a church which, on principle, never admits to mistakes.

There must have been many present at the NC event, therefore, who bridled at being pointedly told by Señor Kiko Arguello: 'You who ask forgiveness for the sins of Christopher Columbus, shouldn't you be asking forgiveness for your own?' This was a direct snipe at the liberation theology supported by many South American bishops which stresses the sinful structures of society. Arguello is a bitter opponent of liberation theology; for him sin is strictly a personal affair.

From 13 to 17 April 1993 a similar event, this time for the bishops of Europe, was held in a hotel in Vienna – at NC's expense. The location was chosen, it was said, to facilitate the attendance of eastern Europeans. Another reason was that it was more fitting to set such an unprecedented meeting on neutral territory, a discreet distance from Rome and the Vatican. It was unprecedented in the sense that it was a promotional event for a single movement organized with the backing of the highest ecclesiastical authority. Not only was Monsignor Paul-Josef Cordes of the Pontifical Council for the Laity a key figure, but Cardinal Lopez Rodriguez, attended to give an account of the success of the similar meeting in Latin America the previous year.

A total of 120 bishops from eastern and western Europe attended, including Bishop Bomers who represented the Netherlands. 'They told us it was for bishops of Eastern Europe and that it was very important to introduce them to Vatican II,' he told me; then shrugged and laughed. Of course that was not the purpose of the meeting at all – it was a repetition of the Santo Domingo event; the bishops were subjected to an NC *convivence*, conducted by the founders, Kiko Arguello and Carmen Hernandez, together with an Italian priest, Mario Pezzi, who completed their team of itinerant catechists. As in all other NC events, no questions were allowed.

The final seal of authority was set on the event by a letter from the Pope himself. It is now considered by NC to be one of the official documents of papal approval in their regard. 'The Neo-catechumenal Way', he rhapsodized, 'can rise to the challenges of secularism, the spread of sects and the lack of vocations. The reflection on the Word of God and the participation in the Eucharist allow a gradual initiation into the holy mysteries, creating living cells of the Church, renewing the life of the Parish.'

NC journalist Giuseppe Gennarini chronicled the event in the *Osservatore Romano*, official organ of the Vatican. He quotes many approving voices.

Cardinal Sterzinsky of Berlin: 'I hope that these nuclei will form in many of our parishes, giving witness in an integral way to the fullness of the mystery of Christ.'

Mgr O'Brien, auxiliary bishop of Westminster: 'Humanity is at a crossroads: it has found that different systems and ideologies don't work and that the only way ahead is that which leads to God: this is the role of the Neocatechumenate.'

From the Vatican, Mgr Rypar, representing Cardinal Pio Laghi of the Congregation for Catholic Education, waxes lyrical: 'We have realized that something is happening in the Church which is completely beyond us and cannot be evaluated in human terms, but can only be attributed to a direct intervention of the Holy Spirit.'

Not surprisingly, Mgr Cordes goes further, suggesting that NC has had some kind of beneficial effect on the bishops themselves: 'The first fruits of this meeting is to see that Jesus is powerful and He acts.' The implication is that these gatherings are intended not just to win the support of the bishops for the movement's activities, but to make recruits of them.

Confirmation of this impression is given by a group letter from the participants to the Pope, written, according to *Avvenire*, 'to thank him for his paternal and continuous attention': 'Having felt in this *convivence* the powerful breath of the Spirit of God, as at Pentecost, making of all us bishops of the east and west a *koinonia* [communion], we leave Vienna, which has been prophetic in history as the crossroads of East and West, strengthened in Christ's victory over death.'

The formula of the communal letter is a useful means (also frequently employed by Focolare) of presenting a mythical 'unity' and telling those in authority what they would like to hear: references to unity of east and west are guaranteed to be music to the ears of John Paul II.

But this official account is far from the whole story. In reality many bishops who took part were disturbed and disillusioned. A number of them, particularly from Italy, wanted to ask questions but were not permitted to do so. On one infamous occasion, an Italian bishop tried to speak out, but was silenced by Carmen 'in a rude and arrogant manner', 'Because', she affirmed, 'you have not allowed the movement to enter (or to develop) in your diocese'. When he replied that he was about to give the reasons why he felt he could not approve the movement in his diocese, Carmen added: 'You can only know the movement by living it and accepting it. Whoever is on the outside doesn't understand and cannot understand.'

After the meeting, Monsignor Bettazzi, Bishop of Ivrea in northern Italy, wrote to the Pope deploring the fact that the Italian bishops had not been allowed to speak.

From 28 to 31 January 1994, 130 African bishops and cardinals were flown to Rome, all expenses paid (by NC), for a repeat performance of the Santo Domingo and Vienna *convivences* in a city-centre hotel. Bizarrely, Pope John Paul, in an audience with the participants, referred to NC as a 'providential instrument' for inculturation in Africa; it has already been noted how the movement negates the very concept of inculturation, using the idea of the charism to fend off any interference with, or adaptation of, its catechesis, songs, pictures and beards.

An Italian archbishop who has a major role in the Italian Bishops' Conference expresses just how wide the rift between Pope and bishops has grown over the NC affair: 'Many Italian bishops have expressed their criticisms of the NC movement – even in high places. Many of them have spoken about it to the Pope in their *ad limina* visits. But the moment they get on to the subject the Pope brushes it aside and goes on to something else . . . The Pope controls everything and imposes everything! Many bishops, even though they do not approve of what is going on, keep quiet, either through fear for their career or expecting the . . . final solution.'

The archbishop hints at what was stated openly by the late Giovanni Caprile, SJ, editor of the Jesuit monthly *Civilta cattolica*: 'The question of the Neocatechumenals will only be resolved with the death of the Pope.'

5

PARALLEL CHURCHES

'THE LORD HAS HEARD MY CRY AND HE HAS LIFTED ME OUT OF THE pit of death': an ex-Neocatechumenate priest, now based in a North London parish, used this verse from the Psalms to describe his exit from the movement. It was his response to a catechist who was hounding him to restore his NC links.

NC had originally been presented to him with impeccable credentials; Bishop Victor Guazzelli, auxiliary bishop for East London, had invited the priests of his area to a presentation of the movement by an Italian catechist. 'There was a feeling among many priests of being all at sea after Vatican II,' the priest explains. 'I was searching, looking for a religion of love and not fear, a new ideal for the Church, an explosion of the Holy Spirit. Here was the thing that was the answer to all problems.'

He did not hesitate to invite the catechists into his parish to give the introductory catechesis. At the *convivence* which followed, held in the diocesan retreat centre, they 'voted' to form a community. 'From the word go, the movement set up great divisions in the parish. At that time, I thought those who were against it were stuffy and conservative. They were all wrong, weren't they, because they didn't have the sense to join us – join the Neocatechumenate. Now I see they were absolutely right.'

His first misgivings began to surface when he accompanied his community to a large NC gathering in Rome. Although he found Kiko an impressive speaker, he was disturbed by an account the founder gave of a private audience with the Pope. 'He told us how they fixed each other in the eyes and glared at each other. A sort of battle of wills. For the first time I thought: This isn't right; it can't be right.'

Gradually he came to feel that the movement's professed loyalty to the Church hierarchy was suspect. He found himself increasingly under the control of the catechists. 'A priest was just a member of the community. I had the status of parish priest appointed by the bishop, but that didn't seem to count. I was expected to follow their directives . . . They used to say that the lay catechists had to set up the communities. If the priests did it, they got it wrong.'

He began to experience increasingly divided loyalties between the demands of NC and the needs of the rest of the parish. 'I was spending 98 per cent of my time on the community and 2 per cent on everyone else. You had almost two things going in tandem. When you are a parish priest, all the parishioners are important. You have the parish visitation to do – individual house-calls. Whenever a priest gets caught up in the NC it results in neglect of the parishioners in general – that put me off.' The control they were exercising over him undermined established Church discipline: 'They were a law unto themselves. I was subject to the bishop – the bishop is my superior – not to the catechist or the community.'

At the same time that his own authority was being challenged, he was becoming dimly aware of a powerful parallel structure operating within the movement: 'I felt there was a hierarchical structure but I never knew a thing about it, I didn't know how it worked. I knew Kiko was the head of it and that he had started it. I knew that there were catechists but I didn't know anything apart from that.'

Increasingly, the practices of the movement began to trouble him. It was inward-looking: the community was only concerned with its own people, and there was an obsessive concentration on the services. The catechists appeared to consider themselves exempt from the traditional discipline of the Church, but they demanded an extreme degree of loyalty to themselves.'

As his doubts grew, the priest felt trapped.

The solution came when he was transferred from his parish. 'The moment I left, I washed my hands of it. The leader of the community was quite insistent in trying to get me back, but I didn't want to and I never have since.' His advice to bishops or parish priests who are approached by the NC is uncompromising: 'Have nothing to do with it.'

How many others are there for whom the opportunity to extricate themselves from NC's clutches does not come along so easily?

Neocatechumenate reserves a special place for the authority of the local bishop; but the true significance of episcopal authority – and papal authority – to NC, as it is to other movements, is to justify its doubtful practices to members and critics. Often it is a case of approval by default rather than of positive backing. This omission encourages abuses. Until his recent decisive intervention, Bishop Alexander of Clifton, Bristol, had technically given the movement his approval to operate within the diocese, despite a decided lack of enthusiasm; but the truth of the matter is that Bishop Alexander, like the vast majority of bishops in whose dioceses NC has been set up, has never seen the NC catechesis, which is kept secret even from all but the leading catechists, its very existence in written form denied. A claim, therefore, to episcopal approval of specific teachings is a complete falsehood.

Many of the NC ceremonies, such as the scrutinies, require the presence of the bishop as the representative of the Church. Where this is not possible, the parish priest takes on his role. Clearly the movement benefits from the weight the bishop's presence lends to the proceedings. In some cases, bishops are wholeheartedly involved in NC events. Bishop Guazzelli of East London is said to have been a member of an NC community of Guardian Angels parish, Mile End, for a time. Often, however, the bishops are simply wheeled out for effect. The numerous rites, in which they are required to participate and which are given as much weight as the traditional sacraments of the Church, are written in a solemn and authoritative style by Kiko Arguello. Yet an Italian bishop has complained that he was not permitted to read the text of the ceremony in advance – during the ritual, a catechist pointed to the passages he should read as he came to them.

While the movement benefits from the bishops, it does not demonstrate the true spirit of obedience it professes. The true test comes when NC are not permitted to form and grow within a diocese. The NC journalist Giuseppe Gennarini claims that, when a bishop forbids them 'even to catechise, putting the communities in a corner and not allowing them to grow', 'even in these cases, the communities have obeyed, accepting decisions which meant they would die'. He cannot restrain himself from pointing out that such situations only arise when the communities 'clash with those structures or methods which are an obstacle to the conciliar renewal'.

Innumerable examples prove this is simply untrue.

Bishop Hugh Lindsay, now retired, was approached while bishop of Hexham and Newcastle by two catechists – a Spaniard who could not speak English and a Maltese whose English was poor. His request for their teaching credentials was indignantly rejected, and when told he could not give them his mandate they 'refused to shake my hand and ostentatiously shook the dust of my house from their shoes as they left'.

In the NC jargon, parish priests and bishops who do not accept the movement are known as 'Pharaohs'. The late archbishop of Perugia was told by Kiko and Carmen in a 'threatening tone' that he would never be a good archbishop unless he became a Neo-catechumenal and spent years in the Way, which brought that particular meeting to an abrupt close. When the archbishop died of a heart attack, following another altercation with NC catechists, it was said in the movement that his death was the Lord's punishment for his opposition to the Neocatechumate.

The experiences of another Italian archbishop with the movement have convinced him of its total lack of respect for the episcopal office. A deacon in his diocese had had a relationship with a married woman which had threatened to break up her marriage. After a period abroad, he returned to inform the archbishop that he had entered an NC seminary. The archbishop expressed his amazement that he had not been consulted by the superior of the seminary, given that the man was a deacon of his diocese. 'Where do you come into it?' replied the aspiring priest. 'It's our business.'

It is hard to square such evidence with the devotion to ecclesiastical authority professed by Kiko and his catechists.

The authority of, and obedience to, the hierarchy is an important theme within Focolare and Communion and Liberation, too. They have both assiduously courted bishops and cardinals at diocesan and Vatican levels. Like NC, they have their protectors in both spheres. Unlike NC, however, direct conflicts are less frequent because each operates within its own structure parallel to that of the Church.

Ultimately all three movements have the same goal: maximum freedom to exercise their 'charism' and minimum accountability. This therefore is the primary consideration in wooing the Church's rulers.

Obedience to the hierarchy is one of Focolare's 'twelve commandments' – the so-called 'points of the spirituality'. The inspiration is the verse from Luke's Gospel: 'Anyone who listens to you, listens to me' (Luke 10:16). What this amounts to in reality is working extremely hard at the movement's public relations with the hierarchy. Bishops are invited to the Mariapolis in the various 'zones' of the movement. Sometimes they attend, otherwise they send a message of goodwill. Either gesture is interpreted by members and newcomers as a mark of encouragement and approval. Members of the Roman Curia are regularly invited to speak at international gatherings of the movement at their Centre of Castelgandolfo near Rome, or else at Loppiano. It would be hard for any prelate attending a Focolare event to remain aloof, for he is subjected to 'love-bombing' on a grand scale, applauded, sung to and beamed at by a sea of a thousand shining faces.

Focolare has honed its presentational skills over five decades, and its characteristic 'shows' of songs, mimes and experiences with multiracial casts of thousands will often be carefully prepared for, and aimed at, a single VIP. The aim is to win over as many members of the hierarchy as possible – to 'bring them in' (*prenderli dentro*), in the movement's jargon.

But, while it is in the interests of the movement to gain as much episcopal support as possible, bishops are judged by the same criteria as any other potential member. I have often heard the *capizona* (zone chiefs) returning from a meeting with a bishop and commenting that he had not 'understood Chiara' or the 'Ideal'. It was even said of Pope Paul VI that 'he had not understood the Ideal'; he was not a 'popo'. The movement had its own yardstick against which everyone, even the supreme pontiff of the Roman Catholic Church, was measured.

If the attention lavished on the bishops had strings attached, the contempt of the movement for priests was undisguised. Seeing itself as the true Church, Focolare had a strong anticlerical cast. The word *prete* ('priest') was used as a term of contempt. Many diocesan priests had done stalwart work in promoting and spreading the movement, yet despite this they were not considered part of the inner circle. Priests were beyond the pale because they had *una mentalità da prete* ('priestly mentality'), which was clearly a terrible thing to have, although never precisely defined.

I believe it meant that they could not make a total submission to the movement (and a corresponding rejection of everything else) in the same way that those with little previous knowledge of Christianity could. As with NC, priests were regarded as a liability because they might spoil the good work of the *focolarini*.

This bias was particularly noticeable at Loppiano. A number of priests had been released from their dioceses to work full-time for the movement. Three of these were assigned to Loppiano while I was there. They never took advantage of their status, but possessed a quality in short supply among *focolarini* – humility. The trainee-*focolarini* were polite to their faces, but laughed at them behind their backs. When they gave us talks as part of our course, the snores would be especially loud. It was considered bad form to be seen to be too friendly towards them – we might be contaminated by their priestly mentality. They were good for saying mass and hearing confessions, but for little else.

The clerical image of the Church portrayed in *30 giorni* might suggest CL's unqualified devotion to the bishops, but this is far from the case. The movement supports those who back them and condemns those who do not. Don Giussani reserves strong words for bishops who 'refuse' CL, making it quite plain that CL will carry on regardless:

> . . . the faithful who feel enlivened in their faith by their company [that is, their movement] will continue to live it all the same, and will obey the bishop from the disciplinary point of view, but will feel the sorrow of not being recognized . . . [but] that bishop is not a father . . .

Such harsh criticism can hardly be taken for obedience.

As the most powerful opposition to CL came from the Italian Bishops' Conference, the movement has attempted to undermine their very existence. National bishops' conferences are a way of putting into practice the collegiality of the bishops proclaimed by Vatican II – the idea that the Church was governed not by the Pope in isolation but by the college of bishops united with him.

Don Giussani's analysis of the current problems of the Church is expressed in the gloriously abstract terms peculiar to CL. For example:

> In many of its directive methods, whether pastoral or cultural, [the Church] often seems hypnotized by a sort of neo-enlightenment mentality, by the assumption, in the final analysis, of a kind of protestant attitude; a position in which personal interpretation plays a decisive role and morality tends to be reduced to the sphere of social problems, or else of ethical themes most acceptable to the majority.

According to him, this is 'translated into a programme through forms of centralized bureaucracy at the level of the local Church, which in many cases actually achieves the effect of strongly obscuring the primacy of Peter'.

With Don Giussani in this struggle was CL's greatest ally, Cardinal Ratzinger, who has questioned the scriptural and theological basis of the bishops' conference, ignoring the much tougher question of justifying the Roman Curia according to the same criteria. CL sees these bodies as playing a key role in its overwhelmingly negative view of the post-conciliar Church. Inevitably, its constant attacks have won it many enemies among the bishops all over the world; but CL is unperturbed, not least because it also has many powerful allies.

Despite talk of authority and obedience, bishops are seen by the movements as potential recruits – either as protectors or, better still, as simple members. Observers close to the Vatican have noted a policy of infiltration on the part of all the movements both by gaining the support of prelates and by placing their own people in key Vatican posts. From its earliest days, Focolare has aspired to the higher reaches of church government. As well as the seven 'colours' symbolizing aspects of the movement's life, widely talked about within the movement and even mentioned in its publications, there were two 'hidden' colours only known to internal members. One was 'infra red', the other 'ultra violet'. These invisible colours represented the movement's secret progress into 'forbidden' areas. 'Infra red' was the spread of the movement in the communist empire, behind the Iron Curtain. 'Ultra violet' represented another area which had to be approached with stealth: the hierarchy and the Vatican.

One of the many divisions of the movement (twenty-two at the last count) is actually a bishop's branch. In *The Adventure of Unity*, a book-length interview with the Italian journalist Franca Zambonini, Chiara Lubich claims seven hundred bishop 'friends' of Focolare who meet regularly to strengthen the bonds among themselves and with the Pope. She adds that 'they have always been encouraged, first by Pope Paul VI and now by John Paul II. Hardly surprising in view of their stated aims of 'unity' with (=obedience to) the Pope.

The number given for these bishop-members is astonishingly high – around 17 per cent of the total number of bishops in the world (just over 4,000). Something more than a meeting to introduce the movement to the bishops is being described here: these are members with a degree of commitment, in some cases a considerable degree. The movement has always seen a role for itself – and especially for Chiara – as an agent of unity between the Pope and the bishops, especially those it would consider rebellious.

I have heard Chiara Lubich's role among the bishops compared to that of Mary among the Apostles. In the seventies, we were told of a number of bishops whom she allegedly reconciled with Pope Paul VI; one was Cardinal Suenens, then primate of Belgium; another was Helder Camara, at that time archbishop of Recife in Brazil. I recall a meeting at the Mariapolis Centre in Rome at the end of 1972 with an extremely uncomfortable-looking Camara seated on the podium next to Chiara Lubich as she held forth to her rapturous audience of *focolarini*. He looked, for all the world, as though he had been abducted and was present under duress. The scant regard the movement has for its bishop-members is suggested by a behind-the-scenes story reported in an internal news bulletin. One of Focolare's most prominent bishops, the late Klaus Hemmerle of Aachen, had been elected to a key post at the 1987 Synod on the Laity. But the report pounced on the fact that the Pope had remarked to the bishop, in the presence of the foundress, 'It is all to the merit of the *focolarini*'.

NC and CL certainly see the bishops in the same light – as potential members, who need the movement as least as much as it needs them. In the late eighties, three out of four auxiliary bishops in the diocese of Westminster were closely associated with NC.

Thanks to the support of powerful figures in the Vatican as well as local dioceses, NC have been able to mount their assault on the bishops of the world through the meetings for bishops. Without that support, such semi-official events would have been unthinkable.

A letter of 7 December 1990 from Antonio Santucci, bishop of Trivento in southern Italy, to the Italian Passionist theologian Enrico Zoffoli, author of *Heresies of the Neocatechumenate Movement*, reveals the depth of commitment a bishop can have to a movement. Bishop Santucci describes his early experiences of NC while a parish priest on the outskirts of Rome from 1973 to 1985, admitting his initial doubts and the sense of 'walking on a razor's edge with the fear of heresy'. These fears were rapidly overcome, however, and the movement's effects were revelatory:

> It helped me understand better *the true and good spirit of Vatican II, the significance of the new life that baptism brings* (I knew before but the Way helped me to bring the sublime reality of being children of God into my everyday life) . . . the reality of sin, the urgency of evangelization, the Cross of Christ which is the glory of God and our salvation . . . [his emphasis]

He defends Kiko Arguello's *Guidelines*, of which he obtained a copy shortly after he first became involved, as 'the tape-recordings of talks of a convert full of enthusiasm and goodwill'. He maintains that he found 'complete orthodoxy' in the movement and adds that its 'salvation has been that it is linked to the bishop and to the parish priest: in fact a community cannot be born without their agreement'.

But we have seen that groups have been started without the agreement of the bishop, and parish priests are divested of their authority, effectively removing safeguards of authenticity. The voices of member bishops are extremely useful in gaining for the movements the kind of autonomy they desire.

Prominent priest-members of CL have received episcopal appointments. The theologian Angelo Scola is bishop of Grossetto, while canon lawyer Eugenio Corecco is bishop of Lugano. In September 1990, the Vatican daily *Osservatore Romano* published a homily of Corecco in which he defended Wolfgang Haas, the extreme right-wing bishop of Chur in Switzerland, who has been the centre of a bitter controversy in the Swiss Church since his appointment was flatly rejected by his diocese. The Vatican must have been grateful for a helping hand in this highly embarrassing and seemingly intractable situation.

In addition to members who have become bishops, CL has many highly placed friends. Chief among them is Cardinal Ratzinger, the most powerful man in the Church after the Pope. He wholeheartedly shares CL's negative view of the contemporary Church and believes that the new movements are the *only* positive development of the period following the Council.

Another vocal supporter of CL in the Vatican is Cardinal Jerome Hamer. The movement's champion supporter among the great and the good of the Italian Church is Cardinal Giacomo Biffi, archbishop of Bologna, also a right-winger, who recalls GS in Milan as 'a young and courageous group, controversial and debated like all living things, but which could no longer be ignored by the churches of Italy'. Major figures from abroad who are sympathetic to the movement and regular guests at its annual Meeting in Rimini include Cardinal John O'Connor, archbishop of New York, and Cardinal Simonis of Utrecht, primate of the Netherlands.

The movements' belief in a hierarchical Church in which authority is unquestioned and total obedience the pre-eminent virtue is undoubtedly sincere. But, convinced as they are of their own unique role as the future of the Church, it is their own structure that counts above all others. The existing ecclesiastical power structure is valuable to the movements inasmuch as it can facilitate their autonomy, the freedom to 'exercise their charism' without outside interference. Thus the internal structures of the movements, rigid, monolithic, highly efficient, with the charismatic leader at the top of the pyramid, can fulfil their primary purpose of self-propagation. But the key defence against opposition is some form of official recognition of this structure by the appropriate authorities. All the movements have been anxious to achieve this status, guaranteeing independence and freedom from accountability. They have shown great skill and tenacity in doing so.

According to canon law, if a movement or association is only present in one diocese or country, the task of approval falls to the local bishop or bishops' conference. If a movement is international, it comes under the jurisdiction of the Holy See. The Pontifical

Council for the Laity is the Vatican body set up 'to discern the charisms of the movements and lay associations, to discern therefore the ecclesial truth of all creative stirrings among the faithful in the Church'. President of the Council is Cardinal Pironio, but the real driving force is Bishop Paul-Josef Cordes, who has been its vice-president since the early eighties. Focolare, which pre-dates the other movements, received approval the hard way – under the Holy Office of the notorious conservative Cardinal Ottaviani – but CL and NC have received their most substantial recognition through the Council for the Laity. Bishop Cordes has played an important part in both cases.

Bearing in mind the disciplinarian and centralizing tendencies of this papacy, it is notable that the Council for the Laity is anxious to concede the maximum *liberty* to the new movements. This line apparently comes direct from John Paul II himself. Bishop Cordes told me that where the new movements are concerned the Pope has never expressed reservation or caution. His attitude has always been one of encouragement.

Cordes was at pains to point out to me that the relationship of the Council towards movements and associations was one of co-ordination rather than of authority. He stressed that it was not the Council's role to tell the movements what to do, that they must be free to follow their charism. It was only when I pressed him that he agreed that the Council's role in giving movements official status implied jurisdiction over them.

It appears that the many complaints received by Bishop Cordes, from laity and local bishops, regarding the activities of Neo-catechumenate have received only token attention. It is a matter of concern that the movements are accorded so much freedom by the Vatican. Once they have approval from Rome, there is little the local bishops can do to restrain or modify them. The Council for the Laity, which has the power to do so, clearly does not have the will. It would appear, then, that the status of parallel churches has been conferred – wittingly or unwittingly – with the Vatican's connivance.

Under the current repressive regime, why are the movements so favoured? The official view, which has been expressed both by Ratzinger in many public utterances and by Cordes in *Charisms*, is that, because they recognize the Pope and he recognizes them, their existence has given a new relevance to the papal office.

Additionally, unlike the great mass of Catholic laity beyond the reach of the Vatican, they are controllable, which is probably why John Paul recommends membership of movements to all lay people in *Christifideles laici,* the official report of the 1987 Synod.

Opus Dei was the first organization in the Church – at least, for many centuries – to reject every existing category in the Church and indeed every definition others tried to make of it. It was not a movement, although it behaved like one, spreading rapidly amongst the laity at grassroots level. It was not an order, although it had members with vows, many of whom were ordained priests. When the Church created the new category of 'secular institute' – an organization with lay members who took vows but continued in their normal jobs and way of life – Opus Dei was the first organization to be approved under this title, while at the same time insisting that it was not one. It does not call the contract between itself and its *numerary,* or celibate members, 'vows', or its houses where members live together 'communities', because these terms suggest religious orders and it insists that its members are lay.

Surely this is word-play and signifies one thing only: that Opus Dei does not want to be defined in recognizable terms because then it becomes merely another association within the Church. It desires, and always has had, complete autonomy to be a church within the church.

In order to achieve this heretofore unknown status, Opus Dei bred a veritable army of canon lawyers – unlike past religious orders which produced theologians – based in Rome and at its own university of Navarra at Pamplona in Spain. These have dedicated themselves to achieving Opus Dei's unique, self-contained structure, freeing it from the Church's supervision, its checks and balances. The breakthrough came via a document of Vatican II that envisaged a new ecclesiastical structure which it called a *personal prelature,* a kind of floating diocese defined by the *persons* that composed it (*personnel prelature* might be a more accurate translation) rather than by territory. By the time Josémaria Escriva, the founder of Opus Dei, died in 1975, his wish had still not been realized. Opus Dei members say that 'he gave his life' for the fulfilment of this dream – although, as he died of a heart attack, one does not quite see how. In 1982, Pope John Paul II, an admirer of Opus Dei, finally granted their wish, although it has been alleged that it was a reward for the role Opus Dei played in bailing the Vatican out of the Ambrosiano bank scandal.

The head, or prelate, of Opus Dei has the authority of a bishop within Opus Dei; and, indeed, Escriva's successor, Alvaro del Portillo, who died in March 1994, was made a bishop, as was the current prelate Javier Echevarria. This makes the movement completely self-contained. It can carry on its activities with complete autonomy – and in total privacy, although it has recently set up an impressive public relations operation to combat the 'secret society' image. Even the congregations of the Roman Curia have no authority over it. Ultimately it is answerable only to the Pope. This is the model to which the new movements aspire. In practice, it is the model to which they already conform. As each considers it has a God-given charism which priests, bishops and even popes may or may not understand, the only way to preserve its purity – as preserve it they must – is to be completely free of outside interference.

Of all three groups, the only one that seems to be happy with the term 'movement' is CL. At the time of its refoundation, in the early seventies, it did not want to aggravate the bad feeling with Catholic Action by presenting itself as a rival *association. Movement* suggested something more like a pressure group. The reality was quite different, however. After the calamitous experience of the collapse of GS, the new organization wanted to be sure that the same thing could not happen again. A rigid vertical structure was created with a central National Council (renamed International Council in 1985) presided over by Don Giussani and made up of representatives of the regional councils, or *diaconates*, composed in their turn of representatives from the *diaconates* of each town or city. The movement was rapidly articulated into separate branches according to the *environment* of everyday life – schools, universities and the workplace.

CL has spawned innumerable events, groups and activities, including a vast raft of businesses, kindergartens, schools and even a political wing which at its height was virtually a political party in itself. The main branches, however, were CLU (university students), CLL (workers), CLE (educators) and CLS (seminarians), while the old GS banner was retained for schoolchildren. Each of these was represented in the local *diaconates*, except for the university students who had their own separate structure, and were represented on the National Committee.

The movement's leaders are chosen, not democratically, but for their fidelity to the party line. This quality is known within CL as 'centredness' (*centratura*). Don Giussani defines this as 'the conception of, and therefore the fidelity to, the experience; creativity inasmuch as it draws on the fundamental theses of the movement and their expression [which does not seem to leave much scope]; the concrete capacity to be a guide of groups'.[1] Such leaders are acknowledged by the International Council as 'authoritative' and co-opted. This is seen as being 'called to participate in the "ultimate responsibility" of the founder'.[2] CL bishop Eugenio Corecco emphasizes the 'profound difference' between old Catholic associations and the new movements; in the former, the leadership 'has the simple task of executing the wishes of the membership . . . in the movements, however the dynamic of following is promoted'.

All power resides at the top. Local representatives are expected to keep in regular contact with their immediate superiors. Detailed instructions on recruitment, readings, and political and religious activities are conveyed to local leaders through regular circulars. They are also expected to attend frequent courses. Demands on members are equally intense. All members attend group meetings known as *assemblies of recognition*, at which personal and group situations are shared in the light of Giussani's teachings. The *assembly of listening* is an encounter with an authority of the movement, usually a priest, who passes on the current 'line' of the movement.

The *assembly of announcement,* or *the clear word*, is the CL's main missionary activity, when the group brings its message to others by distributing leaflets or some other public form of witness. An important focus for all members is the *school of community*, group study of a text, almost always taken from the works of Don Giussani. Additionally, the various branches have their own particular activities – the *days in common* of CLL (workers) and the *meetings in common* of CLE (educators). Group activities are characterized by traditional Catholic devotions such as a weekly mass celebrated for each branch, psalms said in common by the group at or near the place of work or study each morning. The movement's own hymns will be sung at meetings and liturgical events. Pilgrimages to shrines

---

[1] *Comunione e Liberazione: Interviews with Don Luigi Giussani*, p. 164.
[2] *Comunione e Liberazione, Vitale e Pisoni*, p. 88.

are also organized. Many members will even take their holidays together, and religious functions will play an important part in these.

In recent years, two other institutions have appeared alongside the movement. These are the Fraternities and the Memores Domini.

The Fraternities cater for lay people who wish to make a full commitment to the movement. They are small groups of adults, whose careers are already under way, and may include individuals or couples. Those who belong to a Fraternity of CL do not live in community, but spend a great deal of time together in activities ranging from the devotional to the financial. Each group undertakes a joint activity, usually a small business. CL is dominated by a priestly presence – after all, its founder is a priest of the Milan diocese – and each Fraternity is assigned its priest who says mass for them, hears their confessions and gives counselling.

Fraternities are strongly characterized by a missionary dimension. Their statutes set out as their particular field of influence 'environments of faith that most influence a person's mentality such as family life, school, university, the workplace, one's district, the world of culture'.

Whereas joining the movement is fairly casual, and it is emphasized (as it is in Focolare) that there is no membership card or subscription, joining the Fraternities is highly structured. The candidate has to make a written request to the president, Don Giussani, and the Central Diaconate, made up of about thirty members, who have to give majority approval to an application. The Fraternities have experienced astonishing growth in recent years. From 3,000 in 1982, they had grown to 12,000 in 1988. By 1993 the figure had more than doubled to over 25,000, including 3,000 members outside Italy.

The Fraternities now play a leading role in the overall government of the movement, but their significance is far greater than mere numbers. From the early seventies, CL had been fighting a losing battle to gain official recognition by the Church. As it was a predominantly Italian phenomenon, they came under the jurisdiction of the Italian Bishops' Conference, with which they were almost continually at loggerheads. One of its problems was coming up with a statute that would embody the multifarious aspects of the organization. No statute, no approval, said the bishops.

By the end of the seventies it was clear that the Italian Bishops' Conference had no intention of approving an organization that was a thorn in its side. The Fraternities, which were then beginning to appear in embryonic form, proved to be the answer. In 1980 they were recognized by Martino Matronola, the abbot of Montecassino, and on 11 February 1982 a decree of the Pontifical Council for the Laity, signed by the president, Cardinal Opilio Rossi, and the vice-president, Bishop Paul-Josef Cordes, declared the Fraternities of CL an 'Association of Pontifical Right . . . establishing that it should be recognized by all as such'.

It was the rain after a ten-year drought. CL was now beyond the reach of its enemies; finally there was real clout behind the bravado.

If the Fraternities already have a flavour of the classic religious life, the Memores Domini are a genuine religious order within CL. Members live in separate communities of men and women who make promises of poverty, chastity, obedience and prayer. Although these are not canonically vows, they are observed as such. The Memores consider themselves lay people consecrated to God and go out to work to support themselves, very much like the *focolarini*. The strange name is explained in their 'rule', which describes their aim in typically tortuous, even pretentious terms as 'contemplation understood as Memory continually directed towards Christ . . . and the mission, that is, the passion to bring the proclamation of Christ through their own person transformed by this Memory'.

Each community is assigned by the local bishop a member of a religious order, chosen from a list submitted by the president of the Memores Domini, Don Giussani. They live an intense life of prayer and spiritual reading, observing an hour of silence a day and a half-day a week. Two days of spiritual exercises are held every four months, and there is a four-day meeting of members annually.

Within these communities the movement's stress on authority is even more strongly underlined: 'Reference to authority in terms of obedience is fundamental.'[1]

Aspirants must make a written request to Don Giussani and then undergo a three-year trial period. Fifty aspirants join the order each year, and current membership is around 500. The Memores are rapidly becoming the inspirational force within CL, increasingly taking on roles as leaders within the movement and the Fraternities, making CL's 'lay' character increasingly doubtful.

Focolare, or Work of Mary (Opera di Maria) which is its official

---

[1] *Comunione e Liberazione, Vitali e Pisoni*, Milan: Editrice Ancora, 1988, p. 129.

title, is a canon lawyer's nightmare. Through its fifty years of existence, branches and movements have sprung up within it like weeds – including every category of 'vocation' known to the Church and a few more besides. Yet the foundress claims that she never intended to start a movement – it has all been the work of the Holy Spirit. Newcomers are told that it is impossible to 'join' the movement, that first and foremost it is a spirituality; the structure is merely a vessel to preserve the purity of this spirituality which has been given by God today for the benefit of the whole Church.

In practice, the spirituality and the movement are inextricably mixed; wherever the spirituality takes root, the structures of the movement are never far behind.

Like CL, Focolare has a powerful vertical hierarchy. The movement is divided into sixty-six 'zones' worldwide, each governed by a male and female superior, the *capozona* ('zone head'), both *focolarini*. Each lives and works full-time for the movement in a special Focolare community, the *centro-zona* ('zone centre'), which can often be a substantial property. They govern through centres scattered through the region and report directly to the Centre in Rome.

Until now, everything has emanated from the president and foundress, Chiara Lubich. The term 'the Centre' primarily denotes her presence. She lives at Rocca di Papa in the Alban Hills, just outside Rome, and the administrative centres of the movement are based in the area, in small neighbouring towns such as Grottaferrata and the better-known Frascati. As in most totalitarian, centralized organisations – the Vatican is another – those in positions of authority at the Centre or the periphery are chosen for their pliability and orthodoxy rather than for their talents, personal qualities or even virtue.

Focolare is governed by a Co-ordinating Council made up of the president, Chiara Lubich, and an ecclesiastical assistant, who is a *focolarino*-priest, together with male and female councillors representing the various 'aspects' of the movement – financial, missionary activity, spiritual life, and so on – and representatives of the different branches. As these are segregated, they each have a male and female representative.

The levels of internal membership start with the *focolarine* (women) and *focolarini* (men) with vows of poverty, chastity and obedience, living in community. They are the movement's undisputed leaders. For the members of lower rank, they possess an aura; they are special, set apart, spoken of in hushed and reverential tones.

Next come the married *focolarini,* who make promises of poverty, obedience and chastity 'according to the married state'. The married *focolarini* are attached to a Focolare community (women to the female centre and men to the male) and are expected to spend as much time there as work and family commitments will allow. Theoretically they are equal to the celibate *focolarini,* but within the structure they do not have the same role of authority and leadership. The total of celibate and married *focolarini* and *focolarine* is 5,000.

Next come the men and women *volunteers,* who make commitments to the movement. They are lay people who live in their own homes and meet in *nuclei.* There are approximately 17,000 of these round the world.

The Gen (new generation) form the youth section of the movement. They, too, are divided according to sex. The teenagers and young adults are the Gen 2 (because they are the second generation). The children of the movement are called Gen 3, and toddlers are Gen 4. These internal members all make some kind of financial commitment to the movement, in addition to the constant fund-raising that goes on for the movement's own expansion and building programme, and its charitable activities. These, then, are the internal 'lay' members.

In addition there are several substantial branches of internal 'ecclesiastical' members: 1,400 priests have a deep commitment to the movement – some are released by their bishop to work for it full-time – with an additional 12,000 adherents among the clergy. Their younger generation are called *gen's* (sic), 'gen seminarians'.

The final branches add up to more than all the others put together, giving the movement as a whole a decidedly clerical cast. These are the branches of the male and female religious. The men can claim 19,000 members, while the nuns number 42,000. The *gen-re* are the novices or gen religious. All internal members are expected to attend open meetings of the movement like the summer Mariapolis. They have, besides, an intense programme of their own consisting of regular local meetings, encounters at national Mariapolis centres, courses, summer schools. Now that the main school for celibate *focolarini* has moved to Montet in Switzerland,

Loppiano houses permanent schools for Gen, priests, male and female religious, volunteers and married *focolarini*, all open to members from different nations round the world. Pressure is put on members to take part in all these activities, and many of them will be in contact with the Focolare centre on a daily basis.

Around the main branches the so-called *mass movements* have been developed. The task of these groups is to bring the message of the movement to as vast a public as possible. Their gatherings are usually on a massive scale, with tens of thousands of participants. The married *focolarini* run the New Families Movement; the volunteers run New Humanity; the Gen animate Youth for a United World; while the Gen 3 are the driving force behind Boys and Girls (or Children) for a United World. The secular priests and *gens* are responsible for the Parishes Movement.

The names of these mass movements are designed to entice as many people as possible, playing down the Focolare identity. The meetings tone the message down so that it will be acceptable to as many people as possible, even those without a Christian or even a religious background. All these activities, however, have the purpose of winning over as many new members as possible.

The *focolarini* are the core members and supreme authority in this vast and variegated mass of people. 'The Focolare Centres', according to the foundress, 'are the points of greatest warmth and light: they are, within the movement, the custodians of the flame of love of God and neighbour, which must never go out.'

But the mystique that surrounds these core members reveals little of their true way of life. Their total commitment is essential to preserve the 'purity' of the original message. The selection process has become more rigorous in recent years following large numbers of defections. Candidates must be approved by the local male or female superior and then apply in writing to the foundress. The latter is just a formality, however, with the real central authority vested in the male and female *caporamo* ('branch head'). After a trial period of a year or more in close contact with the local Focolare, most candidates spend two years at one of the schools. Once the candidate graduates, he is assigned to a Focolare community and after another two years will take temporary vows of poverty, chastity and obedience, renewed yearly for five or more years until final vows are taken. These vows can be dissolved in confession with an ordinary priest.

Despite the demands of total obedience made on the *focolarini* and the severity of their training, in the Focolare houses every effort is made to create an illusion of freedom and spontaneity to outsiders – even to other internal members. Nothing could be further from the truth. The life of a *focolarino* is controlled down to the last detail. The *focolarino* hands over his salary at the end of each month, and so the superior has to be consulted on even the tiniest purchases. Although the *focolarino* may stop off on the way to or from work to hear daily mass, he would not make any other stops without prior permission. *Focolarini,* like other internal members, do not have a social life. Every personal contact is seen as a chance to 'cultivate' a potential recruit. Even an encounter of this kind has to have prior approval. The free time of the *focolarino* is completely taken up with frenetic communal activity. Regular meetings are held within the community to share experiences and fix dates for future missionary activities. Each month, the community will have an internal 'retreat' which will consist of more shared experiences and the 'moment of truth', when each member of the community (except for the superior) is required to tell the others his good points and bad points. Tapes of Chiara Lubich's talks will be watched or listened to, along with updates on the activities of the movement round the world. Communal recreation is also included in this weekend, which usually depends on the tastes of the superior – it could consist of watching a carefully selected television programme (the television is always kept in the room of the *capofocolare*, to avoid temptation), a suitable film or sporting activity. The *focolarini* never indulge in recreational activities alone, and in fact have no free time to do so as every available moment is taken up with missionary work.

As the *focolarini* animate the many branches into which the membership is organized, every weekend is taken up with a major event or a trip to another town or city. Every weekday night will be taken up with visitors to the Focolare, outside meetings or paperwork for the movement. This relentless activity allows no time for thought or reflection.

Just like the newcomers who attend the Mariapolis, the *focolarini* need constant 'topping up' with a total-immersion experience at their level of commitment. Those in Europe are whisked off to Rome twice a year for a retreat of four or five days. Most of a *focolarino*'s paid leave is absorbed by these various events that must be attended, not to mention the Mariapolis and other missionary activities.

To ensure that the minutiae of the life of the *focolarino* come under the scrutiny of his superiors the *schemetti* ('little plans') were instituted. These are forms, resembling school registers, which have to be filled in daily by each member and are handed in to the superior at the end of the month to be held on file. They cover every aspect of the life of the *focolarino*, as I recall from my time in Focolare communities. A tick was required for the daily spiritual duties – a tick for daily mass, rosary, meditation, regular confession. But then there were sections to indicate the hours of sleep each night, medicines taken, weekly bath (hopefully the movement's standards of hygiene have improved since I left), exercise or sporting activities; meetings attended; conversations had with potential recruits (give brief particulars, names, addresses, telephone numbers); clothes bought and housework done; courses attended or private study accomplished; letters written and to whom; particulars of our pathetic little expenditures on a bus fare or a Mars bar.

Despite two years of intensive indoctrination, many of us balked at the *schemetti* when we were introduced to them towards the end of our course at Loppiano. The official justification was that, if we had problems, our superiors could check back over these forms for the possible cause of our malaise (the Mars bar is the giveaway).

As in the smallest so in the largest matters, the *focolarino* is at the complete disposal of the movement: he is its jealously guarded possession. *Focolarini* are moved around like pawns, usually without prior consultation, and must leave their jobs often at very short notice, inventing excuses to satisfy bewildered bosses who are generally unaware of their employee's unusual lifestyle. Any concept of partnership or consultation does not exist; for a *focolarino* to resist or question a transfer would be unthinkable. The movement's plans for an individual, which could involve a move to another country or renouncing his profession to work full-time for the movement, are often announced in the most summary fashion.

Despite this iron grip exerted by Focolare over its most committed members, there are defections in large numbers. An Italian *focolarino* was told by his superior towards the end of the seventies that the numbers of apostates equalled the figures for those who were entering communities. The movement does not relinquish its claims to the *focolarini* lightly and clings tenaciously to those who wish to leave, however justifiable their motives. Even long after a *focolarino* has left, the movement will still try to assert its jurisdiction.

As Focolare pre-dates the other movements, it was initially investigated by the notorious Holy Office under Cardinal Ottaviani. Attempts were made to define the movement in the fifties. Pope Pius XII was said to have referred to an early attempt at a Rule for the *focolarini* as 'an immaculate little rule' (*regoletta immacolata*): it dwelt on the spiritual side rather than on the structure, which, quite rightly, was what interested the competent authorities. Towards the end of the fifties, the branch for secular priests, known then as the League (Lega), was ordered by the Vatican to cease contact with the lay *focolarini* for several years. In spite of this they continued to grow and spread the movement.

When the first approval came under Pope John XXIII, in the early sixties, ironically it was for the men's branch, which had been established after the women's. Chiara Lubich insists on the theoretical unity of the movement, even though it is divided by sex. The solution to this problem was found during the pontificate of Pope Paul VI, with the approval of the Co-ordinating Council. The foundress was not satisfied with the various partial approvals and doggedly worked at new statutes and rules until the movement could be recognized in the precise form *she* envisaged for it.

This moment came in June 1990 under Pope John Paul II. Unlike the other movements – but in line with Opus Dei – Focolare now has a fully approved statute governing its overall structure and rules for all its branches. Under the current regime it has full autonomy and authority to pursue its goals. However, it is unlikely to follow Opus Dei down the path of the *personal prelature* – at least, for the present. Chiara Lubich obtained from Pope John Paul II the special concession, now enshrined in the official statutes, that the president should always be a woman. A *prelature* must be headed by a *prelate*, who, under the present ruling, must, of course, be a man.

If Opus Dei rejects the term 'movement' because it suggests a lack of structure, Neocatechumenate refuses it lest it give the impression of too much structure. Like CL and Focolare, however, NC does possess a strong vertical hierarchy, centralized in the founder.

When I met Father José Guzman, the leader of NC in Britain, he not only denied the 'movement' label, but also an NC spirituality. It is very much in the interests of NC to keep its identity as vague as possible. If there is no organization, there is nothing to approve, nothing to be examined. This is its method of achieving autonomy. Thus it describes itself not as a movement, but as a post-baptismal catechesis, a service to the Church, the Way.

Can the Vatican really be unaware of NC's highly co-ordinated worldwide network? Or are they choosing to ignore it? Either way, NC continues to use the methods questioned by so many and remains unaccountable.

The NC structure is still fairly simple. The key figures, carrying the same aura as the *focolarini* and the Memores Domini, are the *catechists*, the majority of whom are not celibate but married. The catechist who evangelizes a community retains authority over it, although he may only visit occasionally; he is its link with the central government of the movement. *Responsibles* are appointed from within each community to lead it on a day-to-day basis. *Itinerant catechists* work in teams, bringing the NC message to missionary territories: 'Each team consists of a couple together with their children, a young man and a presbyter, like a small pilgrim church.'[1]

In each missionary country, the *National Team* is the supreme authority, co-ordinating local activities and liaising directly with the founders, Kiko Arguello and Carmen Hernandez, in Rome. Itinerants attend regular top-up meetings in Italy, travelling from all over the world once a year. As the movement develops and autonomous activities grow up, as they have with Focolare and CL, doubtless this structure will become more complex.

To date, it appears, NC has managed to convince the Vatican that this structure does not exist. Even more mysterious, however, is how the movement has obtained ecclesiastical approval at the highest level for a catechesis which some experts have condemned as heretical, striking at the heart of fundamental Catholic beliefs like transubstantiation and the redemption.

In its early days, the movement came to the attention of Monsignor Casimiro Morcillo, Archbishop of Madrid, who was impressed by the work of Kiko Arguello and Carmen Hernandez among the poor and the gypsies in the shanty town of Palomeras Altas. The two founders called him to their aid when the police

[1]Giuseppe Gennarini, *Avvenire*, Tuesday, 30 December 1986.

threatened to demolish some lean-tos in part of the town where Carmen was living.

When he witnessed the prayer life they had inspired among the people, the archbishop asked the local parish priest to make his church available to them for their weekly Eucharist. Later, he defended them when the NC Easter Vigil was creating problems in some parishes; he believed that their idea of a genuine vigil, rather than the evening mass which the vigil had become in many parishes, was in line with the liturgical reforms the Church was encouraging – a return to ancient practices.

When Arguello and Hernandez went to Rome in 1968 with a priest from Seville who is not named in Arguello's account of the events, the archbishop gave them a letter of introduction for the cardinal-vicar of the Rome diocese, then Cardinal dell'Acqua. The cardinal gave Kiko and Carmen permission to start the catechesis in diocesan parishes with the one condition that the parish priest should be in agreement. After a slow start, a community was set up in Canadian Martyrs parish, and others followed.

The first encounter with the Vatican came in the early seventies when one of the auxiliary bishops of Rome was concerned about the rites of exorcism performed in the first scrutiny. He reported the movement to the Vatican Congregation for Divine Worship and the Sacraments, which has responsibility for liturgical matters. Kiko was summoned to appear before a panel chaired by the Secretary of the Congregation and including experts who had recently been involved in the drawing up of the *Ordo initiationis christianae adultorum* (OICA or RCIA), the Church's official catechesis for adults preparing to be baptized.

The Congregation decided that it was permissible – indeed, to be encouraged – that certain rites from the *Ordo*, which was just about to be published, should be used in the renewal of the baptismal vows by those who had already been baptized. They issued a document entitled 'Reflections on Chapter 4 of the OICA', which noted that 'An excellent model of this is found in the "Neocatechumenal Communities" that started in Madrid'.

The investigation was clearly a superficial one. The official ceremonies held in the presence of the bishop are one thing – and probably the only aspect brought to the attention of the Congregation; but what about the often brutal scrutinies and group confessions held behind closed doors, within the communities?

157

There was no investigation into the methods and techniques of NC as a movement or an organization – no official acknowledgement that one existed in fact.

The next aspect to come under official scrutiny was one of the most delicate – the catechesis itself; and NC were very fortunate in those entrusted with this task by the ecclesiastical authorities. When they had first approached Cardinal dell'Acqua, he had put them in touch with the vicar general (*vice-gerente*) of his diocese, Monsignor Ugo Poletti, who became one of NC's first protectors. It was surely an important factor in their eventual extraordinary success in the Rome diocese that, by the early seventies, Poletti had succeeded dell'Acqua. The newly created cardinal put them in touch with Monsignor Giulio Salimei, who was then the director of the Catechistical Office of the Rome Diocese. He became a vital ally, and today is an auxiliary bishop of Rome and rector of the world's first NC Redemptoris Mater seminary in the outskirts of the city.

Despite the strong official support for the liturgical aspect of NC, there were criticisms within the parishes, and Poletti made the smart move of sending the NC leaders to the Congregation for the Clergy, whose brief includes catechetics. Here, they had another stroke of luck: the official appointed to deal with them was Monsignor Massimino Romero, whom they had known and who had supported them in Spain where he had been bishop of Avila.

Kiko's account, however, shows clearly how nervous he was about handing over the documents containing the catechesis; the leaders desperately tried to play down the importance of these papers: 'We explained that they were only duplicated pages which hadn't even been corrected so that they wouldn't become too formalized: they were outlines, since we didn't want to form catechists who repeated texts written by others.'

In fact, those who have been catechized have later confirmed, contrary to Kiko's protestations, that 'the duplicated pages' were word-for-word what they had heard in the NC meetings. A number of witnesses have independently pointed out that catechists constantly prompt one another to ensure that the catechesis they have received is repeated exactly.

Despite Kiko's protests, the Congregation demanded all the documents; and, according to the official account, though with much trepidation, they were handed over. Again, astonishingly, the official judgement was positive.

Yet again, while the texts were approved, the 'structure' which is explicitly referred to was not questioned nor indeed considered.

In 1986, Neocatechumenate faced its most stringent test when Kiko was summoned before the Congregation for the Doctrine of the Faith, headed by the formidable Cardinal Ratzinger. Kiko was asked to complete a questionnaire covering hermeneutics (interpretation of the scriptural text), pastoral theology and doctrine.

It is significant that on this occasion Carmen, who is more expert in theology, was expressly forbidden to accompany Kiko. Kiko was then called back for a meeting with Cardinal Ratzinger himself, to which he was permitted to bring a theologian.

'At this meeting,' Kiko reports, 'they told us they had studied everything, that they had done some research and that they wanted to help us.'

It should be borne in mind that by this stage the Pope had made several official visits to NC communities in Rome, displaying considerable enthusiasm for the movement. Cardinal Ratzinger and his colleagues in the Congregation must surely have been aware of this even if they were not specifically under orders. Kiko himself was certainly aware of it and took this opportunity to ask for what the movement most needed at this time – some form of official papal approval as a reply to criticism. Kiko suggested a 'Brief' from the Pope, but was told that these were no longer used. Instead, the Pope nominated Mgr Cordes of the Pontifical Council for the Laity as his appointee *ad personam*, in other words his personal representative and NC's direct line to the papacy. But still the NC's organization had not been questioned.

In September 1990, Kiko's desire was finally granted. Neocatechumenate received the written approval of the Pope. But it came in an unprecedented manner – in the form of a personal letter from John Paul to Mgr Cordes in which he states: 'I recognize the Neocatechumenal Way as an internary of Catholic formation, valid for today's society and times.'

Although the letter is addressed to Cordes, its aim is to encourage the reception of NC by local bishops:

> It is my wish, therefore, that my Brothers in Episcopate might appreciate and help – together with their presbyters – this work for the new evangelization, so that it might be carried out according to the indications of the founders, in a spirit of service

to the Ordinary of the place [the bishop], in communion with him and in the context of the unity of the particular Church with the universal Church.

Specific reference is made here to 'the indications [*linee*] of the founders' to discourage any changes to the 'purity' of the NC message. The final phrase seems to be putting the screws on the local bishops by suggesting that rejection of the NC communities would put them out of step with the universal Church, which, in the person of the pontiff, has accepted them.

The Pope is unequivocal in his praise for the movement, singling out their *missionary* drive: 'Such communities make the sign of the missionary Church visible in parishes.' Completely ignoring areas of controversy such as methodology and doctrine, John Paul shows himself interested in results:

. . . the new vitality that animates the parishes, the missionary impulse and the fruits of conversion that flower from the commitment of the itinerants and, recently, from the work of families who evangelize in de-Christianized zones of Europe and the whole world . . . the vocations which have arisen from this Way to the religious life and to the presbyterate [priesthood], and the birth of diocesan Colleges of formation to the presbyterate for the new evangelization, such as the Redemptoris Mater in Rome.

Reference is made to the Way and to the communities, but at no point is any mention made of a movement or association.

This letter has been the calling-card for NC ever since. 'The great novelty of this letter of the Holy Father,' Kiko Arguello enthuses, 'is that it recognizes in the Neocatechumenate a catechumenal form of Christian initiation for adults and thus offers to the Dioceses a concrete form of evangelization without transforming it into a religious order, a particular association or movement.' However, there are a number of factors which suggest that it did not pass through the official channels customary for a document of this nature. According to Cordes, John Paul himself suggested the letter to him at a private audience held on 25 July 1990. That this was in response to a specific request is indicated in the letter by the phrase 'accepting the request that has been addressed to me'. The tenor of the letter would suggest that Cordes had sought a clear gesture of papal approval as an answer to unsympathetic bishops. The letter is dated 30 August 1990. Everyone in the Vatican – like the rest of Italy – is on holiday in August. Cardinal Pironio, president of the Council for the Laity and Bishop Cordes' boss, who, as a courtesy, should at least have had sight of the letter before it was published, only heard about it later and was naturally piqued.

There are three pieces of internal evidence, signs of haste, suggesting that the letter was deliberately rushed out before the end of the holiday period so that its sweeping gesture of recognition could not be questioned. Two basic grammatical errors show that the letter did not pass through the necessary channels which eliminate all mistakes, and that it was written and checked only by non-Italians.[1] The first is a simple error in agreement of gender in the key sentence quoted above, which in the original Italian reads: '. . . *riconosco il Cammino Neocatechumenale come un itinerario di formazione cattolica, valida per la società e per i tempi odierni.*' The word '*valida*' (feminine form) refers to '*itinerario*' and should be '*valido*' (masculine). The second grammatical error comes at the end of the letter where the date is given as '*il 30 Agosto dell' 1990*'. The correct form should be '*dell'anno 1990*'.

But the real gaffe comes near the beginning of the letter where Arguello's celibate co-founder, allegedly a former discalced Carmelite nun, is referred to as Signora (Mrs) Carmen Hernandez. It seems extraordinary that there were no Italians available to read the letter over and correct such simple errors. Could it be that only the Pope and Cordes – and possibly other non-Italians such as the Pope's Polish secretary – saw the letter? And, if so, why the secrecy? Was the intention to push the letter through without interference?

It is curious that the letter was neither published by the *Osservatore Romano* nor given the slightest mention by Vatican Radio, despite the fact that both have NC staff-members. This could indicate resistance within the Vatican. The letter's existence was first announced by the Vatican press office on 19 September 1990. Significantly, when the letter was published in the *Acta,* the official collection of papal documents and speeches, a footnote had

[1]The mistakes are available for all to see in the facsimile of the letter published in *Il cammino Neo-catechumenale*, Rome: Edizioni Paoline, 1993.

mysteriously appeared, qualifying its contents, particularly in relation to the jurisdiction of the local bishops:

> The mind of the Holy Father in recognizing the Neo-catechumenal Way as a valid itinerary of Catholic formation, is not to give binding indications to the Ordinaries of the place, but only to encourage them to give careful consideration to the Neocatechumenal communities, nevertheless leaving it to the judgement of the Ordinaries themselves to act according to the individual pastoral needs of each diocese.

This is a pretty strong disclaimer. Sources close to the Vatican say that the note was added to 'save the Pope's face' from what was seen as an excess of zeal. It also indicates that there is a powerful lobby which does not share his enthusiasm.

At the time of writing, its confidence bolstered by many other gestures of pontifical approval – such as the meetings for bishops – NC still continues to operate as one of the Church's fastest-growing and most fanatical organizations, without needing to give any account of itself such as the appointment of its leadership, its internal structure, or the source of its seemingly unlimited finances.

While all the movements have sought approval of some kind – and always in accordance with their own self-image – in order to gain maximum autonomy, they each have a spirit which virtually defies any attempt at pigeonholing according to the Church's current methods. The new movements have each spawned a culture which extends far beyond any written rule or statute. This culture is not – perhaps could not be – codified. It consists of the new language of each movement, an oral tradition of teachings and anecdotes, stretching back to the origins of the movements and constantly growing. As we have seen, it is even reflected in gestures, modes of behaviour, patterns and inflections of speech. It is this culture, now diffused worldwide, that contains the essence of each movement, its unique character which makes it so different from the others and from the rest of the Church. How can the authorities approve or disapprove of what has not been or cannot be recorded? With all the approvals in the world, the new movements will never be fully accountable.

*   *   *

The new movements make great play of their lay status yet that is highly questionable. None of them can claim to have a truly lay leadership. In the case of CL, the founder and most of the top local leaders are priests. NC's founders are celibates, although they would claim to be lay, and full-time workers for the movement – hardly representative of the average lay man or woman. The foundress and president of Focolare is a woman, again a celibate who has worked full-time for the movement, living in a Focolare community, since her early twenties and has no experience of normal life. Of those who rule the movement with her in the Co-ordinating Council, the vast majority are *focolarini* and therefore vowed to celibacy. Of the male councillors, most are priests.

At lower levels of leadership, too, a genuine lay character seems to be lacking. The *focolarini* are the undisputed leaders of every aspect of Focolare, possessing more authority than secular priests or religious members. But, with their vows and community lifestyle, however strenuously they may deny it, they are crypto-religious.

Among the middle management of CL, there is a similar retreat from a truly lay quality – the Memores Domini, who as celibates living in community also live a form of religious life, are an indication of this. Even the Fraternities have adopted a semi-monastic lifestyle.

NC has both male and female celibates involved in their mission-ary work, alongside married couples. The priests produced by NC seminaries will undoubtedly increasingly occupy the positions of real power in the movement's missionary territories. The manner in which the movements attempt to spiritualize every aspect of the lives of even the most lowly members robs them of that lay quality, that involvement in the world's affairs which forms a bond with their non-Christian neighbours. The members of the movement feel they are different and they want to be seen to be different. This may not fit the definition of 'clericalization' in the Pope's coded sense, but the movement's concept of laity certainly bears little relationship to the laity in the Council's sense of engagement with the world.

The term 'ecclesial' is often substituted for 'lay', acknowledging the fact that all three movements command the loyalty and service of every category within the Catholic Church – the secular clergy, nuns, male religious, even bishops and cardinals. This ecclesiastical component is nurtured and is continually growing in size and commitment, helping to give the movements the consistency of self-contained churches, rather than aspects of the one Church.

Of greater concern, however, is the fact that each of the movements is building a new caste of priests; not men who had their priestly education before meeting the movement but those who have come up through the ranks, often from a very early age, and who have known no other formation but the 'totalitarian' one of an initiate. These candidates for the priesthood can often be singled out for ordination by the movement's leaders in recognition of their orthodoxy rather than for any human or spiritual qualities of leadership they may possess. With their undivided loyalty to the movements, such priests are the alternative hierarchies of the future.

CL has been a source of many vocations to the secular priesthood, while large numbers of its women have joined existing religious orders, particularly the enclosed orders (although the pattern may change with the creation of the movement's own order, the Memores Domini). These candidates for the priesthood entered the diocesan seminaries. At one point, the number of CL seminarians in the diocese of Milan was so great that conflicts were caused within seminaries and candidates were steered towards more CL-friendly dioceses like Bergamo.

In 1985, six CL priests belonging to the Missionary Community of Paradise in the Bergamo diocese, with the agreement of their bishop, became incardinated in the Rome diocese, with the consensus of Cardinal Ugo Poletti, cardinal-vicar of Rome at the time. There they formed the Priestly Fraternity of St Charles Borromeo. Poletti subsequently recognized the Fraternity as a diocesan association, approving their constitution and as their superior, Don Massimo Camisasca, one of Don Giussani's most trusted colleagues, at that time also responsible for relations with the Curia and the Italian Bishops' Conference.

In the same year, the Fraternity announced that it had established its own seminary with Camisasca as rector. It started with fourteen seminarians from four countries – Italy, Argentina, Ireland and the United States. Announcing the formation of the new seminary, Vatican Radio described the Priestly Fraternity's activity as work in countries characterized by 'the dechristianization of modern society and the necessity of a new evangelization' and supporting the work of CL. And yet, paradoxically, it was denied that the new institution could be regarded as 'CL's seminary', although clearly it is.

Since it began in the 1940s, Focolare has had the allegiance of diocesan and religious priests, and yet very early in its history it felt the need for priests drawn directly from the ranks of the *focolarini* men, for only these could fully understand the 'Ideal'. An indication of the gulf the movement feels between itself and ordinary Catholics is the fact that it considers that only *focolarini* priests can minister to members' needs. The first of this new breed of priest was Pasquale Foresi, the son of a Christian Democrat MP, Palmiro Foresi.

Pasquale met the movement in 1949, when he was only twenty. Chiara Lubich, nearly ten years older, felt an immediate empathy with the youth and lost no time in promoting him to head of the male *focolarini* who were already living in community, most of them considerably older and more experienced than he. Chiara 'saw' a special role for young Pasquale in the movement. She gave him the name by which he is known within the movement: Chiaretto, 'Little Chiara' (in the male form). He was to translate the spiritual thoughts of Chiara Lubich into concrete projects and express them in theological language – in the jargon of the movement, he was the 'incarnation'.

The story goes that at one of their daily encounters he said: 'Chiara, I have something to tell you.'

'I have something I would like to say to *you*,' she replied.

Both, it transpired, had decided that he should become a priest who could represent ecclesiastical authority within the movement. The story continues that Chiara told Pasquale that, whatever happened, he had to go ahead with the ordination, even if she changed her mind. And that, of course, is exactly what happened. A black-and-white 16mm film of the event exists in which Chiara Lubich does not appear – only her praying hands are seen.

Don Foresi is one of the movement's most tragic figures. Undoubtedly gifted both as a theologian and as an administrator – it was said that the Vatican sought his help in unravelling their financial affairs – from the late sixties on he has never been able to function in the leading role that was assigned to him in the movement. The few times he would come and talk before the *focolarini* he seemed to waffle less and talk more concrete sense than the others, and yet he was overweight, awkward and painfully shy. We were told that he had been given the wrong medicine for a heart condition, which resulted in depression. Could it be that he was another victim of the intolerable burdens the movement places on its individual members and that he was simply burnt out by his early forties?

Many *focolarini* have followed Don Foresi's example and been ordained. I do not know of a case in which a *focolarino* decided he had a vocation to the priesthood – which is the usual pattern in the Catholic Church. That would indicate a disturbing individualism according to Focolare standards. *Focolarini* of many years' standing in positions of authority are *invited* to study for the priesthood by the Centre of the movement because it is opportune for the particular role to which they have been assigned. Increasingly all the male *capizona* and those men holding important directive roles in the central administration are priests, creating more of a traditional clerical hierarchy, parallel to that of the Church. Candidates for the priesthood become extramural students of a seminary in the diocese of a Focolare bishop. Although they are officially based (incardinated) in his diocese, they are released at the disposition of the movement.

Most of the first *focolarini* have now been ordained priests. If the trend continues, male communities could acquire a heavily clerical bias which would seriously upset the balance with the female side, traditionally seen as more authoritative. To date this style of priest drawn from the ranks of the *focolarini* is far outnumbered by the secular priests who have joined after ordination.

Although NC has thousands of priest members in the parishes, it, too, has begun to ordain those who have already experienced, or are in the course of experiencing, the lengthy process of initiation. This aspect has been dramatically boosted in recent years with the foundation of the NC Redemptoris Mater seminaries, which, as we have seen, are strongly encouraged by the Pope. By 1993, the movement had twenty-four of these seminaries in twenty countries, with 850 seminarians in training. A further 1,500 candidates were at a preparatory stage in NC's national Vocational Centres. Thirty-seven presbyters (priests) and twenty-three deacons have already been ordained within the movement.

The number of priestly vocations within NC is truly phenomenal with literally thousands coming forward at the mass gatherings of the movement. Girls are encouraged to become nuns of enclosed life; and here, too, the statistics are on the grand scale. With vocations one of the Church's most pressing problems, these figures cannot be lost on Pope John Paul II. Nor can the fact that a sizeable proportion of ordinations to the priesthood in the Rome diocese each year are Neocatechumenals. Out of twenty-nine priests ordained by the Pope in a ceremony in St Peter's on 2 May 1993, the World Day of Prayer for Vocations, sixteen were from NC's diocesan college Redemptoris Mater. It was the first ordination conducted by the Pope dedicated exclusively to the Rome diocese.

This 'first' cannot be unconnected with the fact that so many Neocatechumenals were involved. Alongside Cardinal Ruini, vicar of Rome, and his auxiliaries, mostly friends and protectors of NC, the VIPs were a Who's Who of NC personalities: Monsignor Luigi Conti of the Redemptoris Mater seminary, Bishop Salimei, its rector, Bishop Cordes and, of course, Kiko Arguello and Carmen Hernandez. It was significant that only one of the NC priests was from the diocese of Rome, although all sixteen were incardinated in the diocese. Of the remainder, five were from Italian dioceses and the other ten came from Bolivia, Peru, Slovenia, Spain, Germany, Britain, Portugal and Mexico. The missionary philosophy of NC is that you find vocations where you can and put them where you want them.

The NC priests have all completed the twenty-year course of the Way, almost twice as long as the Jesuit training, and many start at the age of thirteen. They are destined for parish work; and it is inevitable that in their parishes the only brand of Catholicism on offer will be that of NC, for it is all they know. At the 1987 Synod on the Laity, the Nicaraguan bishop, Monsignor Abelardo Mata Guevara, who belongs to the Salesian Order, voiced the worries of many bishops who do not share the Pope's enthusiasm for the NC seminaries:

> The bishops are worried by the fact that young priests whose vocation has developed in the context of the spirituality of a particular movement continue to be monopolized by that movement; it is equally worrying that special seminaries are being promoted where all the young people with vocational intentions from the Neocatechumenate groups go to study with the aim of going on to serve their community.

The character of these seminaries is international and missionary, even though the priests are incardinated in the particular diocese; they are 'for all the world, to the ends of the earth'. As vocations decline in most countries of the world, the prospect of wave upon wave of NC priests filling all the vacant parishes is a disturbing one. It could have a profound effect on the entire Catholic Church.

With the ordination of their own totally committed members, the movements are building their own parallel hierarchies which can no longer be dismissed as eccentric lay groups doing their own thing. They are also providing a pool of 'faithful' clergy, at the disposal of the Church, who may well become the bishops, cardinals, even popes, of the next century.

The Pope may not be looking that far into the future. Nevertheless he has ordained bishops from all the movements and has even favoured them with privileged posts such as Vatican advisers. He is undoubtedly impressed, however, by the phenomenon of priestly castes growing up from within the ranks of the movements. Perhaps he is more influenced by this than by any other single factor. To those who believe that the only answer to the shortage of vocations is to relax the celibacy laws, a proposal to which John Paul is bitterly opposed, or even to allow the ordination of women, which for him is anathema, he has another very practical answer: Communion and Liberation, the *focolarini* and, above all, Neo-catechumenate. It is only logical that he should be their most powerful advocate.

6

A Powerful Advocate

CATHOLIC ROME IN THE 1990S IS NO LONGER THE SOBER AND unchanging seat of church government it had been from the austere years of the Counter-Reformation right up to our own times. During the reign of the current pontiff, it has been invaded by wave upon wave of groups and movements of all sizes and shades, many verging on the lunatic. Some have been lured by the recognition and influential ecclesiastical patronage only Rome can offer, and which is readily available under the present incumbent at the Vatican. Others have been imported by enthusiasts studying, teaching or working in the colleges, universities, mother houses or Vatican congregations. Alignment with a movement is *de rigueur* in Rome's ecclesiastical circles these days.

The choice is wide: from the rapidly expanding right-wing Legionnaires of Christ, a 2,500-strong order of priests founded in Mexico, whose members are instantly recognizable as they pass through the city, always in twos, with their hair parted on the same side, to the exotic ravings of the African Archbishop Milengro's services of exorcism and healing. These newcomers are not only taking over the roles of traditional organizations like the religious orders but even occupying the buildings left vacant by their shrinking forces. Today, Rome's venerable basilicas are more likely to echo with the babble of a congregation speaking in tongues than with the clicking of rosary beads; with the thrumming of guitars as priests dance round the altar, rather than with the rustle of a soutane. Not since the mystery religions of Greece and Asia arrived 2,000 years ago has the Eternal City experienced such a motley spiritual invasion. Most prominent and powerful among the newcomers, though by no means the most bizarre, are the new ecclesial movements.

Bishop Paul-Josef Cordes begins his curious book *Charisms and New Evangelization* with a chapter entitled 'Leave Your Country'. Although Monsignor Cordes assures us in his foreword that his subject is the new evangelization and the 'charisms [the Lord of the Church has given] to men and women who are proclaiming the Good News loudly and clearly, who are making its force felt in the world', the book deals only with difficulties experienced by the great religious orders of the past like the Franciscans and the Jesuits. In order to crack its code, a reader would require a fairly detailed knowledge of problems faced by the new movements today.

In 'Leave Your Country', he suggests that a common trait of the great founders was to move away from their home base at the start of their mission. We do indeed find a parallel with movements like Focolare, Neocatechumenate and, earlier, Opus Dei – all of which changed their headquarters shortly after they began. What the author does not make clear is that, unlike their illustrious predecessors, the new founders all moved to Rome; each sensed that only there would they find the necessary launching-pad for the worldwide diffusion they sought.

When Pope John Paul ascended the papal throne in 1978, his in-tray was piled high with problems: an almost universal rejection of Paul VI's birth-control encyclical, *Humanae vitae*, by the Catholic laity, opening the floodgates to moral relativism and the questioning of other prohibitions such as homosexuality, masturbation and pre-marital sex; theologians who, in the wake of Vatican II, were undermining traditional certainties; protestant sects in South America poaching converts from the world's largest Catholic population; in Europe, the increasing secularization of Catholic countries, evident from the waning influence of the Church in politics and the abandonment of Catholic practice on a massive scale; and, finally, the haemorrhage of priests and religious that had begun in the immediate post-conciliar period, far from running its course, was gathering momentum. John Paul's predecessor, Paul VI, had been accused of indecisiveness because he had not sought short-term solutions to these problems. With his incisive intelligence and profound understanding of the Western European mentality, Pope Paul had realized that many of them were symptoms of more profound changes in the Church and in society. Treating the symptoms was not a solution. Committed Catholics must find a way of making their unique contribution to society, but within a pluralist context.

For many of those who thought the first non-Italian Pope in centuries would bring a wind of change, warning bells began to sound almost immediately. Forsaking Paul VI's compassionate approach to disciplinary problems, John Paul's approach was drastic – and harsh. Whereas Paul VI had sanctioned the laicization of 30,000 priests in his thirteen-year reign, allowing them to marry in the Church, John Paul brought the practice of dispensations to an abrupt halt, referring to them as 'administrative solutions'. Now priests would have to marry outside the Church and *then* apply for laicization. The self-confident new pontiff was equally decisive in his treatment of unruly religious orders and theologians. He took the unprecedented step of appointing his own delegate as interim governor of the Jesuits. A new inquisition was launched, disciplining or silencing some of the world's most distinguished theologians. In the next few years he would not hesitate to restrain individual bishops and even national bishops' conferences.

But for a man of John Paul's energies and forceful personality negative measures were not enough. Initiating a new era of strong papal leadership, he launched his plan of action for the Church and the World. In the international political arena, he could capitalize on the prestige built up for the papacy by his three predecessors. Visiting Poland in June 1979, for the first time after his election, he set in motion the events that a decade later would culminate in the fall of communism. But, while this 'foreign policy' met, almost immediately, with spectacular success, things were less simple at home, amongst his own flock.

In his first encyclical, *Redemptor hominis* (*The Redeemer of Man*), he proclaimed his programme for the Church. It was spectacular – indeed, apocalyptic: nothing less than a missionary drive to bring about world unity by the year 2000. By the mid-eighties, he had given his crusade a name: the 'New Evangelization'. But, as he elaborated on this idea in speeches and encyclicals, his dualistic vision of Church versus World began to emerge. Western society was defined – or, rather, caricatured – as the 'civilization (or culture) of death': one which encouraged divorce, birth control, homo-sexuality, abortion and euthanasia, all equally deplorable in his eyes. Coming from the totalitarian regime of Poland, the hard-won social values of postwar Western society such as tolerance, respect for minorities, equality for women, freedom of speech and the press, a sense of social responsibility and a pervading spirit of democracy, counted for little with him, judging by this blanket condemnation. He contrasted this negative picture of reality with a vision of a 'civilization (or culture) of love' in which Christian values were restored to private and public life.

As the decade wore on, and John Paul proclaimed a new Europe united 'from the Atlantic to the Urals', the 'civilization of love' became increasingly identified with a new Christendom, the restoration of a medieval model of the continent.

This goal could not be achieved single-handedly. Where in the contemporary Church was he to find a sufficiently large and zealous mass of people who shared his black-and-white view of Western society? Past Popes had always made use of the religious orders to carry out their plans; but, apart from the fact that the orders were not as compliant as he would have wished, John Paul saw the areas of greatest interest to him, such as politics and the media, as outside their competence.

The necessary forces for the fulfilment of the pontiff's vision, however, were ready, willing and conveniently located on his own doorstep in the form of the new ecclesial movements.

For both sides, there was a lot to be gained from the alliance. The movements were the answer to the Pope's prayers: they were a fertile source of vocations to the priesthood, strictly male and celibate, and both old and new forms of the religious life; in the moral field, they were fervent supporters of the Church's anti-contraception ruling and its traditional teaching in all sexual matters – values which they were willing to uphold in the political arena as well as on a personal level; their zealous and aggressive missionary activity was more than a match for the protestant sects, and they were proving effective in combating the secularization of urbanized Europe; they were prepared to fight the Pope's corner in matters theological; and, though nominally lay, they were a beneficial influence not only on priests and religious, but even on bishops, many of whom were affiliated to one or other of the larger new movements.

But perhaps the most outstanding contrast with other factions of the Church was the total obedience the new movements professed to the successor to Peter's throne: they were prepared to carry out his will to the letter, and they had the resources to do it. They were conveniently centralized in Rome, with a disciplined and effective chain of command headed by charismatic leaders who were owed unquestioning obedience.

Here was the unbounded enthusiasm, the mobility, the grassroots membership, the worldwide diffusion and, above all, the will to fulfil even the most grandiose plans a pope might have.

As bishop of Cracow, Karol Wojtyla had known and encouraged Communion and Liberation, Focolare and Neocatechumenate, all of which were well established in Catholic Poland long before the fall of communism. It did not take him long to realize what an attractive package they offered him in his new role as Pope. But the movements had their plans, too. And they stood to gain even more than the pontiff from this special relationship of which they would soon learn to take full advantage.

Through their Eastern European Study Centre, CL were already acquainted with Cardinal Wojtyla at the time of his election, and he with them. A CL member, Francesco Ricci, head of the Study Centre, prepared the profile of the Pope for the main news-bulletin on Italian television on the night of his election.

Within three months the Pope had received CL's founder, Don Giussani, in private audience. Giussani summed up the meeting in the movement's internal magazine, *Litterae communionis*, with a rallying cry to his followers: 'My friends . . . let us serve this man, let us serve Christ in this great man with all our existence.'

The hard-line, tough-talking traditionalist Giussani had felt an instant sympathy between the language and ideas of the Pope and those of his movement: '. . . it was the encounter in which the message that gave life to the movement was reproposed, became incarnate in the living testimony of the head of the Church himself.'

The meeting of minds lay in the conviction, common to Pope and movement, that Christ is the only answer to every problem. They rejected Vatican II's call for Catholics to work with all men of goodwill for a more just society: '. . . we humbly and ardently call for all men to work along with us in building up a more just and brotherly city in this world.'[1] Always ready with a new term to complicate and confuse the issue, CL coined the term 'presencialism' (*presenzialismo*) for their approach. They asserted that, instead of working alongside others, Christians – that is, the movement – should come up with a clear Christian answer to every problem, providing a visible *alternative*. This belief led them to found their own schools, cultural centres, magazines, businesses – even their own political party, the so-called Popular Movement.

Although CL's do-it-yourself approach had met with rejection from Catholic Action and the Italian Bishops' Conference, it found an immediate response from the newly elected pontiff, who in 1980 declared to CL members: 'Your way of addressing human problems is similar to mine. In fact it's the same.' His address to 10,000 CL university students in March 1979 pinpointed the similarity: 'The liberation the world desires – you have reasoned – is Christ. Christ lives in the Church; the true liberation of man comes about, therefore, in the experience of ecclesial communion; to build this communion, therefore, is the essential contribution Christians can give to the liberation of all.'

This introspective view is a far cry from the Council's vision of 'building up a more just and brotherly city in this world'. It harks back to an older, triumphalistic vision of Christendom as a visible kingdom. It shows a total lack of understanding of today's pluralistic society. Like the other movements, CL had always seen its main message as being the movement itself: in Don Giussani's words, 'the awareness that our unity is the instrument for the rebirth and for the liberation of the world'. Not surprisingly, they found a definitive confirmation of this in the Pope's words to the tens of thousands of CL members gathered in Rimini for their annual Meeting for Friendship between Peoples on 29 August 1982: 'The civilization of love! . . . build this civilization, without ever tiring. It is the task I leave you today, work for this, pray for this, suffer for this.'

Significantly, he added that it is 'faith lived as a certainty and a *claim for Christ's presence* in every situation and occasion of life that makes it possible to create new forms of life for man', reaffirming the CL concept of 'presencialism'.

[1] Message to Humanity at the opening of the Second Vatican Council, *The Documents of Vatican II*, ed. Abbott, Geoffrey Chapman, 1972.

CL responded to John Paul's encouragement with fearless loyalty. The Italian media soon became aware of the special relationship between the new Pope and Italy's noisiest Catholic movement. CL was referred to as a 'johnpaulist' movement and its members dubbed 'Wojtyla's lackeys'. The movement's abrasive style of attacks and denouncements had won it many enemies, especially among the Italian bishops. After two embattled decades, it rapidly reaped the rewards of its high-powered new alliance. The first was the official recognition by the Holy See of the Fraternities as Associations of Pontifical Right. And this came about, as the official decree confirms, through the direct intervention of the Pope. Despite the fact that fifty letters of support from Italian and foreign cardinals and bishops had been submitted with the application, the Pope's personal authority had been necessary to counter the negative pressure from the then president of the Italian Bishops' Conference, Cardinal Ballestrero.

But the greatest triumph for CL, and the high point of its alliance with the Pope, occurred at the Second Convention of the Italian Church which took place at Loreto in April 1985, following a protracted battle between CL and the official Italian lay movement Catholic Action, which is backed by the Italian Bishops' Conference.

CL's glossy weekly current-affairs magazine *Il Sabato* was founded in early 1978 by a group of influential CL journalists, some of whom came from the Catholic daily *Avvenire*. Originally set up to promote CL's view of a visible Catholic presence in Italian politics and society, the magazine declared, after the election of John Paul II in September 1978, that it would take its lead from the Magisterium and the programme of the new pontiff. Thus it threw itself with gusto into the pro-life battle preceding Italy's abortion referendum of 1981.

When the results showed that only a third of the electorate were with the Church on this issue, Catholic Action took a line of 'renunciation', accepting that henceforth the Church would no longer be able to impose its views on the Italian populace but would have to accept pluralism. *Il Sabato*, on the other hand, relaunched its anti-abortion battle with the slogan 'Let's begin again from 32', referring to the percentage of pro-life votes in the referendum. The Pope came out strongly against the idea of pluralism and before a meeting of the Italian Bishops' Conference in Assisi in 1982 stressed that the Church must remain a 'social force'. By now *Il Sabato* was the lone voice backing the papal line which had split the Italian bishops.

In 1983, *Litterae communionis* published a booklet entitled *The Italian Church and Its Choices,* in which it attacked the concept of the 'religious choice' espoused by Catholic Action and the Italian Bishops' Conference in its recent ten-year pastoral plan *Communion and Community.* The 'religious choice' proposed a separation between faith and temporal affairs which then required individuals and groups of committed Christians to make their contribution to society working alongside others, a process known as *mediation.* To this, CL opposed the 'choice of the all-embracing commitment, therefore, in the social and cultural fields, too', which, according to CL, was the Pope's line.

They were right in maintaining that their concept of 'presence', visible Catholic projects in all fields of human activity – politics, education, culture, health – in other words a return to the Catholic ghetto of pre-conciliar times, was diametrically opposed to that of the official Italian Church. CL had no compunction about provoking a highly public split in the Italian Church on this question.

In its booklet *The Italian Church and its Choices,* CL had suggested that the Italian Church's interpretation of the Council necessitated a complete re-examination of the message of that event. To their great glee, the Pope called an extraordinary synod of bishops on this very subject in 1985. CL was riding high.

In April of the same year, the Second Convention of the Italian Church was held in Loreto on the theme 'Christian Reconciliation and the Community of Man'. Here the Pope had the last word on the vexed question of the 'religious choice' and came down heavily on the side of CL. A stunned audience of 2,000 delegates listened for an hour and a half as 'John Paul II said that they must not resign themselves to the dechristianization of the Country'; on the contrary, Catholic movements must give a decisive witness, 'a new united effort of Catholics in the social and political field ranging from the foundation of original activities in the sectors of education, health care (*assistenza*), and social solidarity to unity in the moments of great political choices (in other words elections) that decide the destiny of a Country.'[1]

---

[1]Vitali and Pisoni, *Comunione e Liberazione,* p. 133.

The Pope also pressed home the key role he saw for the movements in achieving his vision, describing them as 'privileged channels for the formation and promotion of an active laity that is conscious of its role in the Church and in the world'.

CL's position had been vindicated, and over the next year they saw off their major enemies as the president and the secretary of the Italian Bishops' Conference, and the lay president and clerical general assistant of Catholic Action were all replaced.

Meanwhile, in an address to priests of CL given by the Pope at his summer residence of Castelgandolfo on 12 September 1985, he confirmed the message of Loreto: 'Participate with dedication in this work of overcoming the division between the Gospel and Culture . . . Feel the greatness and the urgency of a new evangelization of your country! Be the first witnesses of that missionary impetus with which I have charged your movement!'

From the start of his reign, a similar empathy sprang up between John Paul and Focolare. It was the most established of the new movements and the most widely spread internationally – a lead which it still holds today. Focolare had a traditionalist view of the papacy to which Chiara Lubich often referred with Catherine of Siena's phrase, 'sweet Christ on Earth'. Every gathering at the Mariapolis Centre of Rocca di Papa would include a general audience in the Vatican. One of the Gen songs of the late sixties, entitled 'A Leader', addressed to the pontiff, included the lines: 'The world wants a leader,/A man who will take us far,/An Ideal which is not in vain,/That will eradicate hatred, hunger and war./We find that leader in you, Vicar of the Lord, Father of Humanity.'

Chiara Lubich had several private audiences with Paul VI, whom she had already known from the period, in the fifties, when he was in the Vatican Secretariat of State. He had told her that whenever she wanted to see him privately she only need ask and he would grant her an audience immediately.

But with John Paul II there was rapport of a different order. He saw embodied within Focolare his own particular vision of the Council. It was morally and theologically traditionalist but used modern technology and methods to enhance a vigorous missionary activity. Membership was predominantly lay, but also contained the classic vocations to the priesthood and both old and new forms of religious life, held within a strong hierarchical framework, orderly, obedient and under control.

From the start of his pontificate, the gregarious new Pope had responded to Focolare's invitations, attending gatherings of the 'mass movements', where the participants were in the thousands: the Genfest of Focolare youth in 1980, at Rome's Flaminio Stadium, followed by mass in St Peter's Square; the New Families Movement at Palaeur on the outskirts of the eternal city in 1981, and the congress for the secular and religious priests of the movement in 1982 at which the Pope concelebrated mass in the Vatican's Paul VI Hall with the 7,000 participants – an occasion hailed by *Osservatore Romano* as 'historic'.

In December of that year, having witnessed the movement's extraordinary drawing-power, in perhaps the most spectacular gesture of papal approval accorded to any movement, he gave Focolare his vast audience-hall in the papal summer residence at Castelgandolfo for their exclusive use. After extensive conversion, it has functioned since the mid-eighties as a Mariapolis Centre where the movement's principal international meetings are held, with the Pope, when he is in residence, as their next-door neighbour.

Like CL, Focolare was quick to capitalize on the Pope's attentions. Although by the time John Paul came to power they had been talking about the charism of unity for almost two decades – certainly long before any other founder had claimed to possess a charism – the Pope's spontaneous affirmation of this concept was eagerly welcomed: 'Yours is a new charism, a charism for our times; a very simple and attractive charism. Because Charity is the most attractive and simple thing in our religion.'

Recognized by Rome and established throughout the world, Focolare felt no need to theorize about movements and charisms in general, but accepted the Pope's praise as a confirmation of what it already knew to be true.

Internal descriptions of the movement's encounters with the Pope tend to emphasize the aspects which exalt the movement's status rather than the reception of any other message the Pope might have wished to convey. Focolare sets great store by 'confirmations' – that is, when those in authority tell them that they are as wonderful as they already know themselves to be. A report on the pontiff's visit to Germany in 1987, in order to underline the movement's status, mentions that 'There were 700 seats at our disposal in Munster, 200 in Munich at the beatification of Father Meyer'. The subtext of the report is that in some way Focolare is animating the entire proceedings:

> At some of the important gatherings, the *capizona* were also present, as were our Bishops Hemmerle and Stimfle and our priest Wilfred Hagemann. It was a great joy to notice that in the ecumenical meeting at Augsburg the personalities who celebrated the liturgy with the Holy Father were friends of the movement who have a deep and personal rapport with Chiara like the Evangelical Bishops Hanselmann and Kruse. Moreover, the Pope's homily began with the quotation of Matthew 18:20, the basis for the ecumenism of the movement.

A unique rapport between the Pope and the movement's members is implied:

> . . . a wave of white scarves, the customary sign of the movement's presence, accompanied the Pope all over. The signs of greeting, of recognition, the moments of personal contact underlined once again the special love of the Pope for us.

Every encounter is seen as an opportunity to sell the movement to John Paul. The same gift awaits him at each destination: a basket of flowers containing a map marked with the movement's centres.

In recent years, the movement has seized on a theme in John Paul's teachings as a coded means of expressing the unique link between the Pope and Focolare. In *Adventure of Unity*, Chiara Lubich, highlighting the aspect of John Paul's doctrine which has 'most impressed and inspired' her, quotes from a speech he made to the Roman Curia in December 1987 where he declares that the 'Marian aspect of the Church precedes the Petrine, although they are strictly united and complementary'.

Chiara describes her excitement at hearing these words. The movement has always described itself as a Marian presence in the Church; it has even used of itself the questionable term 'the mystical body of Mary', just as the whole Church is described by the apostle Paul as the body of Christ. Chiara Lubich has pointed out that John Paul 'does not see the Marian profile of the Church only as a spiritual or mystical reality, but also as a historical reality, and he witnesses this with facts. He knows, for example, that our movement has been defined as the Work of Mary, and he never hesitates to highlight its Marian presence in the Church.'

Before an audience of 700 *focolarini* at Castelgandolfo in 1986, John Paul referred to the house of Nazareth as the first Mariapolis:

> . . . in this house the main mystery is certainly Christ, but transmitted to us through her, the woman: this woman of whom Genesis and the Apocalypse speak, the woman who became a historical person in the Virgin Mary. And I think that belongs to the very nature of what you call Mariapolis: to make Mary present, put her presence into relief as God himself did in the night of Bethlehem and then as he did for thirty years in Nazareth.

A *focolarino* who was present told me that he and the other members of the movement who made up the audience had the clear impression that the pontiff was drawing a parallel between Chiara and Mary.

Can this be written off as Focolare hysteria? Is a privileged description of the movement's place in the Church being read into the Pope's words? On the other hand, the Pope's devotion to the Virgin is well known, and so is his penchant for the mystical. An additional factor which must not be ignored is the female dimension in Focolare. It fits well with John Paul's romantic view of women as 'the heart of humanity', but who do not share the priesthood or the power of the hierarchy. At the Angelus of Sunday, 6 March 1994 in St Peter's Square, before a crowd of 5,000 members of the New Families Movement, he referred to the Focolare communities as families invented by the 'female genius of Chiara'.

Beyond doubt is the fact that the Marian-Petrine theory has become Focolare's touchstone for its relations with the papacy. When Chiara Lubich was among 'seventeen distinguished ecclesial and cultural personalities worldwide' invited to contribute a chapter to *John Paul II, Pilgrim of the World*, a commemorative volume published in 1988 to mark the tenth anniversary of the pontificate, she chose to write on 'The Petrine Dimension and the Marian Dimension'.

*　　*　　*

The fact that Neocatechumenate is the movement which is currently closest to John Paul II could well indicate a shift in mood from the combative but optimistic early days of his pontificate, symbolized by the aggressive CL and the fervid *focolarini*, to a darker, more dualistic view of the world.

We have seen how Kiko Arguello and Carmen Hernandez made the strategic move to Rome in 1968, only four years after the first stirrings of the Way in Spain. The NC doctrine as it stands today took shape only after their arrival in Rome; and, though some Spanish communities pre-dated those in Italy, it was seen as very significant within the movement that the Roman communities should be the first to complete the catechumenate – after twenty years – with the baptismal vows.

When John Paul acceded to the papal throne in 1978, he announced that, as bishop of Rome, he would make it his business to visit personally the parishes of his own diocese, which was notoriously de-christianized. This was a godsend for NC, fully justifying the move to the Eternal City.

By 1980, Rome was the NC showcase, with many parishes boasting several communities – some of them twelve years old. Having been prepared for the worst, the Pope was astonished to find these distinctive and enthusiastic communities in parish after parish, with their instantly recognizable songs, liturgy and décor. In every parish, the Pope would meet separately with the NC communities; he became convinced that they were the animators of every parish. Because of the Roman connection he saw more of NC than of any other group, and got to know their songs and liturgy very well. A strong rapport developed. Where another man might have felt ill at ease or wondered exactly where these *ad hoc* celebrations fitted into the wider pattern of Church practice, Pope John Paul rose to the occasion.

On 7 January 1982, Kiko introduced a group of 300 catechists from over seventy-two countries to John Paul II, following their annual meeting. He explained to the Pope how he had exacted an oath of fealty from the group, asking them, 'Do you recognize that the Bishop of Rome, Peter, is the stone on which Christ has built his Church?', and 'Do you promise obedience and fealty to Peter and all the bishops of the Church who are in communion with him?' All, he assured the pontiff, had vowed their assent.

Moreover, he continued, they had all agreed to offer their lives in the service of the Church, 'helping to continue the renewal of Vatican Council II through this Neocatechumenal Way that renews the Baptism of Christians'. In solemn confirmation of this oath, he declared: 'Therefore, Father, I would like in the name of all of them – if you permit me – to kneel before you, and all these brothers with me, as a small gesture of total fidelity to Peter.'

The significance of such a gesture from a burgeoning lay movement such as NC was certainly not lost on the Pope at a time when he was attempting to stem the growing tide of dissent against traditional teaching, especially from members of religious orders, including some of the world's most prominent theologians.

During the catechumenate, each community visits Rome to pledge its loyalty to the successor of Peter before his tomb. To a group from Madrid which he received in audience in March 1984, Pope John Paul said: 'I am grateful for this visit to the tomb of the first Apostle which is an act of submission (adhesion) to the Successor of Peter, as a guarantee of ecclesial fidelity.' On another occasion, the Pope referred to this visit as the 'central pilgrimage of twentieth-century Christianity'! Later in the decade, in fact, the Vatican was to take the unprecedented and highly controversial step of imposing a mandatory oath of loyalty to the magisterium on the clergy.

Another aspect of the Neocatechumenal movement of vital interest to the Pope was portrayed in a similarly flamboyant manner in a ceremony on Palm Sunday, 27 March 1988. The thousands of NC young people attending the third World Youth Day, which had just taken place, were received by the pontiff in the Vatican's cavernous Paul VI audience-hall. Seminarians from the NC Redemptoris Mater seminary in Rome entered in procession, carrying a life-size statue of Christ Crucified, carved in wood, the gift of the community of Ecuador.

Once this image, a favourite of Kiko's, had been set up before the assembly, Kiko proceeded to proclaim the NC message of the 'glorious cross', ending with the words: 'What else is there to do but bring this water into the desert of the world?'

At this point, he launched NC's characteristic method of recruiting vocations to the priesthood and the religious life. All those young men who felt a vocation to the priesthood and all the young women called to the cloistered religious life were invited to step forward and kneel before the Pope. Sixty-five responded to his appeal.

While many Catholics would question the suitability of this method, considering it more suited to an evangelical rally than to the serious question of a lifelong vocation, the Pope in his speech which followed justified the unusual procedure, declaring that: 'If in fact a boy, a girl can present themselves before all and say before all and to Christ crucified, "Behold, I am yours", this means that God loves you, that He is calling you.'

The urgency with which he feels the question of vocations is confirmed by his words: 'Priestly and religious vocations are proof of the authentic Catholicity of local churches and parishes . . . I have spoken from the heart.'

A report on the event, by the NC journalist Giuseppe Gennarini, which appeared in the Catholic daily *Avvenire* two days later, appropriately summed up the grand gesture: '65 say: "Here I am."'

One of the novelties of NC is the *missionary families* which have been sent out to various parts of the world since the early eighties in teams of itinerant catechists. The *focolarini* also have their Focolare families, and CL have also launched their missionary couples; but the phenomenon is found on the largest scale within NC.

Astutely, they invited the Pope to 'send out' the first batch of twelve families on 28 December 1986. A mass was celebrated by the Pope at Castelgandolfo, in the course of which the Pope presented the families with 'missionary crosses'. This first event launched a tradition. Now the Pope sends out new NC families every year on the feast of the Holy Family, or thereabouts.

On 30 December 1988, the Feast of the Holy Family, the Pope visited the movement's international centre at Porto San Giorgio at Ascoli Piceno, close to Italy's Adriatic coast. Here, in a mass concelebrated with numerous bearded NC priests and a dozen bishops, under the geodesic dome of the NC centre, the Pope consigned the missionary cross to no less than seventy-two families and strongly condemned what he saw as attacks on the family: 'Today much is being done to normalize these destructions, to legalize these destructions; profound destructions, deep destructions of mankind.' One can safely assume that the Pope was referring to the legal moves which have been most hotly contested by the Vatican – in favour of divorce, abortion and the legalization of homosexuality. He singled out this cause as 'the most fundamental and important in the mission of the Church; for the spiritual renewal of the family, of human and Christian families in every people, in every nation, especially perhaps in our western world, more advanced, more marked by the signs and the benefits of progress but also by the defects of this unilateral progress'.

The importance the Pope ascribes to the NC missionary families is confirmed by a reference to them in the official report he wrote following the 1987 Synod on the Laity, *Christifideles laici*: 'Even Christian married couples, in imitation of Aquila and Priscilla (cf. Acts 18; Rom 16:3 ff), are offering a comforting testimony of impassioned love for Christ and the Church through their valuable presence in mission lands.'

Perhaps it is mere coincidence that this long-awaited document was finally published on 30 December 1988, the Feast of the Holy Family, the very day that Pope John Paul was officiating at the NC ceremonies of Porto San Giorgio?

These carefully stage-managed events, giving special attention to John Paul's personal causes, have had the desired effect, building the movement's prestige in his eyes. And he has proved their best defence in the many struggles they are engaged in throughout the length and breadth of the Church. They have exploited his backing shamelessly, but they are only stretching the truth slightly when they claim to laity and bishops alike that they have been 'sent by the Pope'. The Pope is always seen in relation to them, his words used as endorsements. A certain possessiveness is evident: they have his special favour, and therefore he is 'theirs'.

This was most impudently expressed in a meeting I had in 1989 with Father José Guzman, head of Neocatechumenate in Britain. He showed me a copy of the Pope's report on the 1987 Synod on the Laity, *Christifideles laici*, in which he had highlighted the passages he claimed had been suggested to the Holy Father by Kiko Arguello! Even more revealing is an incident which occurred during the Pope's visit to Canadian Martyrs parish on 2 November 1980. Following an address by Kiko Arguello on his spiritual journey and the foundation of the NC Way, the Pope responded with a speech to the NC communities of the parish in which he referred to Arguello's 'enthusiasm for the movement'.

At this point, to the consternation of the accompanying police and bodyguards, a woman's voice called out: 'Father, it's not a movement, it's a Way.'

Again the word 'movement' cropped up, again the same cry.

After this voice had risen in protest for the third time, the Pope, irritated, said: 'It moves, doesn't it, so it's a movement!'

The heckler was none other than the redoubtable Carmen. If she would correct the Pope himself on such a small point, one wonders to what lengths the founders would go to defend other more crucial aspects of their beliefs.

From a series of talks given by Pope John Paul to CL members in the early eighties, Monsignor Giussani developed a fully fledged ideology of the place of the ecclesial movements in the Church, an approach which has been dubbed 'Movementism'. He describes movements as 'essential' to the life of the individual Christian, 'a sure way in which the relationship between God and man, which is Christ, comes about in the present. It is the way in which the fact of Christ and His mystery in history, in the Church, have met your life in a manner that is evocative, persuasive, facilitating, educative, revealing itself as existentially true.'

These words are inspired by the Pope's own declaration to the priests of CL in September 1985: 'Sacramental grace finds its expressive form, its concrete historical influence through the diverse charisms that characterize a personal temperament and history.'

Giussani expands on the Pope's words, commenting that: 'Christ reaches the person in a persuasive, operative and effective way in history through the encounter of His grace with a personal temperament [i.e. the founder of a particular movement: Giussani himself, for example] that proposes His reality in a persuasive and interesting manner.'

The implication in the Pope's words, spelled out clearly by Monsignor Giussani, that the movements are for everyone is an alarming one, suggesting that Catholics who do not belong to movements are second-class citizens. It also effectively deprives the bishops of any sort of pastoral role in their dioceses, given that the movements receive their directives from elsewhere.

If John Paul gave the movements a decisive impetus, convinced, unlike many bishops, that they 'have and will have great relevance in the future of the Church', the movements returned the favour by supplying a new significance to the papacy. 'Movements', Monsignor Giussani declares, '. . . have been most fully understood and valued by the papal magisterium.'

Cardinal Joseph Ratzinger has also recognized the value of

portraying the papacy as the champion of the new movements. Suddenly, according to Ratzinger, the Catholic Church has embraced pluralism – in the form of the movements. Only the fuddy-duddy bishops are too conservative to accept it. 'Even today', says Ratzinger, 'we see certain kinds of movements which cannot be reduced to the episcopal principle, but rather draw support, both theologically and practically, from the primacy of the Pope.'

Ratzinger and Bishop Cordes have gone on to develop a theory of greater centralization in the papacy using the movements as an argument. This finds clear expression in *The 'Communio' in the Church*, a talk given by Cordes at the Second International Conference of Ecclesial Movements in March 1987.

Cordes sees the papacy as saving the Church from 'the absolutist tendencies of the local churches'. What we are witnessing in the case of the current pontiff is the defence of pluralism. This is, of course, used in Ratzinger's sense; not with the commonly understood meaning of a diversity of ideas, but the varied structures represented by the movements.

Cordes calls on the historical parallels of the papacy of Gregory VII (1073–85) and the rise of the mendicant movements, Franciscans and Dominicans, in the thirteenth century – periods which, according to Cordes, have 'extreme relevance' for today's situation. He quotes an article of Cardinal Ratzinger's on *Pluralism as a Question for the Church and for Theology* in which he asserts that 'the two major impulses which produced the full flowering of the doctrine of the primacy – that is to say, the struggle for the Western freedom of Church from State under Gregory VII (d.1085) and the controversy over the mendicant orders in the thirteenth century – are not derived from a desire to unite but from the dynamic of pluralistic needs'.

He explains how the mendicant orders of monks who were no longer confined to monasteries, but roamed freely from one diocese to another, no longer depended on the bishops but received their orders from general ministers who owed allegiance directly to the Pope. 'This centralism, thus provoked by the monks, naturally had its repercussions on the conception of the Church of the faithful in general: the Petrine ministry emerged with greater clarity.'

Thus the argument of the importance of the papacy to the movements is used to justify a model of papal power that returns to the excesses of the Middle Ages.

The historical parallels used by these advocates of the new ultramontanism to sustain their arguments are quite extraordinary. Gregory VII and Innocent III (1198–1216), who approved the Franciscan order, were guilty of the greatest abuses of papal power that the Catholic Church has ever known. It is curious that Gregory VII is bracketed with the events surrounding the mendicants in the thirteenth century, still more strange that he should be held up by Cordes as an example of 'extreme relevance' for today. His main claim to fame was to have asserted the jurisdiction of the papacy not only over spiritual matters but over temporal, too, in his excommunication and humiliation of the Holy Roman Emperor Henry IV. Powers claimed by Gregory for the papacy included 'That the Pope is the only one whose feet are to be kissed by all princes . . . That he may depose emperors . . . That the Pope may absolve the subjects of unjust men from their fealty . . . That he himself may be judged by no-one . . . That the Roman Church has never erred, nor never, by the witness of Scripture, shall err to all eternity'.[1] Not satisfied with the title 'Vicar of Christ', Innocent III styled himself 'Vicar of God'.

Does this view of the papacy tie in with the Pope's mandate to the new movements: the 'New Evangelization'; the creation of a united Europe 'from the Atlantic to the Urals'; the new Christendom, not only in the spiritual but also the temporal realm? Can Cordes and Ratzinger seriously be suggesting a return to this model of the papacy?

But, in addition to the ideological boost they have given to the primacy, the movements demonstrate their devotion to the Pope in many tangible ways – at the same time, of course, chalking up points in their favour. The magazines and publications of CL and Focolare roundly defend John Paul's most unpopular teachings. They have also responded to his concern for Eastern Europe by reinforcing their presence there since the fall of communism. Together they fulfil the Pope's wishes for a crusade against sects – of the non-Catholic kind. Focolare organizes huge media jamborees which always feature the Pontiff as a guest star. NC are churning out vocations almost as fast as they are producing children, and they are contributing to the Pope's vision for a new Christendom by

[1] *The Limits of the Papacy*, Patrick Granfield, The Crossroads Publishing Company, 1987, New York.

evangelizing the 'de-christianized' areas of Europe and the world. CL, having fought the Catholic corner in the political arena before running into the storms of the Italian bribes scandal, is still the Vatican's traditionalist think-tank. Rocco Buttiglione, CL's erstwhile resident philosopher, who learned Polish so that he could study John Paul's early writings in the original, is a papal adviser and leader of the Partito Poplare Italiano (PPI), the successor to Italy's Christian Democrats. He, along with CL bishop Angelo Scola, was an adviser on John Paul's controversial morals encyclical *Veritatis splendor* (1993), although it is said that the leaked original version was so harsh that it had to be toned down before publication. But perhaps the greatest impact the movements have made on the style of this pontificate has been their role in creating a new form of aggressive papal outreach – the World Youth Days – as a direct answer to the mass-evangelizing techniques of the protestant sects.

The movements have become the enthusiastic sounding-board for John Paul's most reactionary statements. They form a vast and growing body of apparently submissive lay men and women, with a significant following of priests and religious. But what about the millions of Catholics who do not belong to the movements and who do not respond to the message of the current pontiff? And then there are the bishops with their particular knowledge of local needs, bypassed by the movements who follow the directives from their centres in Italy. What is emerging, in contrast to the Council's vision of flourishing local churches in unity with each other and the See of Peter, is a monster: a kind of Octopus Church – all head and arms. And there is every sign that it is growing while crisis paralyses the rest of the Catholic diaspora. Even now the visible strength of this triumphalistic new model of the Church is formidable.

7

CHURCH TRIUMPHANT

'THE WHOLE CITY IS CHOKED WITH CATHOLICS,' THE CAB DRIVER explained when I arrived in Denver, Colorado, on the night of 12 August 1993. Indeed, such was the strain on the city's transport resources that his was the only cab in sight outside the airport. As long as I did not mind travelling with four others, he agreed to deliver me to my guest-house for a flat fee.

A few blocks towards the city, hordes of youngsters loomed out of the darkness, flooding the pavements and spilling onto the streets. They were returning to their improvised quarters in schools and church halls from Denver's Mile High Stadium where Pope John Paul II had opened the Sixth World Youth Day. I had come to experience for myself this massive biennial event which draws hundreds of thousands of young people from all over the world. The quintessence of the pastoral style of this pontificate, the Youth Days are hi-tech, commercial, show-bizzy and, above all, *big*. They are the 'New Evangelization' in action. And they are the brainchild of the new Catholic movements.

In 1983, the youth sections of the new movements were invited by the Pontifical Council for the Laity to set up and staff the San Lorenzo Youth Centre, just off St Peter's Square in Rome, in order to give an enthusiastic Christian welcome to the Eternal City's younger visitors. Some of the animators of the centre approached the Council with the idea of staging a large-scale youth event in

1984 to mark the Extraordinary Jubilee Year which had been announced by John Paul II.

This first World Youth Day, organized by the movements, took place in Rome on Palm Sunday, 15 April 1984. It was so successful, and appealed so much to the pontiff, that he adopted it as one of the hallmarks of his reign. Although the World Youth Day title was not adopted until 1987, the event was held again in Rome in 1985, then in Buenos Aires, Argentina (1987), Santiago da Compostela, Spain (1989), and Czestochowa, Poland (1991). Estimates for attendance at the 1984 Youth Day veered wildly from 50,000 to 300,000. The final papal mass at Czestochowa in 1991 drew an estimated 1.5 million people.

Today the Youth Days are one of the most important events in the life of the Catholic Church. Half the Roman Curia was present in Denver together with a good many bishops and cardinals from around the world in addition to the entire United States episcopate, 350-strong. Although the event is seen as the most novel and personal expression of John Paul's pontificate, it still boasts a formidable participation from the new movements. More important, it bears their unmistakable stamp, inspired as it was by the mass international youth gatherings they had been holding in Italy for more than a decade.

The format is closest to the Genfests of Focolare. It is part of the lore of the *focolarini* that nothing is ever planned – it all just happens spontaneously. In the case of the Genfests, to some extent, this was the case. It all started at Loppiano on 1 May 1971, and I was there. As the audience of over a thousand visitors was too great to be crammed into our two largest venues, we decided to stage an al-fresco performance in a natural amphitheatre in the men's district of Campogiallo. The show was composed of songs, dances, and quotations from Chiara and the Pope. The germ of the current World Youth Days can already be discerned in that formula.

The following year, a much more ambitious event, by now christened Genfest, was held in the same location before an expanded audience of three thousand. The idea and the name caught on, and soon Genfests were being held all over the world.

In June 1975, the first truly international Genfest was held in the Palaeur, a 60,000-seater covered sports stadium at EUR, Mussolini's model village on the outskirts of Rome. It was an all-day event at which the movement's star bands, Gen Rosso and Gen Verde,

1111

111

111111

played, groups from around the world sang, danced and mimed, 'experiences' were told, and Chiara Lubich gave the keynote speech.

At the 1980 Genfest, Pope John Paul himself was present and addressed the crowd. He was back again in 1985.

The international Genfests were established as the five-yearly rallying-point for the youth of Focolare.[1] What was most significant about these manifestations was that Focolare proved to themselves, to the Pope and to the world that they had the muscle to draw vast forces. For it was not enough to announce these events; pulling in crowds on this scale required a single-minded drive by the entire movement worldwide. The scale of these events served only to confirm Focolare's conviction that they were ushering in the millennium.

Communion and Liberation, on the other hand, had already been flexing its political muscle for more than two decades when it launched its own mass event. The first Meeting for Friendship between Peoples was staged in August 1980, and has been held annually ever since in Rimini, attracting tens of thousands of participants. The Meetings offer a mixture of performances, exhibitions, and musical and sporting events, but tend to grab the headlines in Italy with the speakers they attract – one of whom, in 1982, was the Pope. The intention was to provide a Catholic challenge to the huge Unity Festivals (Feste dell'Unità), the cultural manifestations of the Italian Communist Party held in various cities throughout the country.

The Meeting became one of the established highlights of the Italian political calendar and did just what CL hoped it would – got the movement talked about. It provided a platform from which CL could launch its latest ideological onslaught on Italian or world politics. Even the bizarre titles the organizers dreamed up for the Meetings were deliberately designed to provoke, and they did. 'Men, Apes and Robots' was the title for 1983; while the 1985 banner, 'The Beast, Parsifal and Superman', puzzled even the Pope.

---

[1] In 1987, there were 44 Genfests around the world, involving 130,000 people, including four in Brazil with a total audience of 28,000, one in Peru (3,000), Argentina (9,000), Germany (2,000), the Netherlands (1,000), France (2,500), Austria (1,000), Switzerland (3,500), Spain (2,700), Portugal (3,700), South Korea (1,000), the Philippines (5,000) and the Lebanon (1,100), and nine separate Genfests in Italy with a combined attendance of nearly 40,000.

Neocatechumenate may not yet have launched a mass youth event of their own, but they have gone one better and appropriated the World Youth Days, mobilizing young members to attend in tens of thousands. In 1991, 50,000 NC members from Italy alone attended the Youth Day in Poland. With the Denver event, they were posed a tougher challenge; as they would need to fly in the bulk of their forces from other continents, the costs would be colossal. Undaunted, at a meeting held on 28 March 1993 in the Vatican before a crowd of 8,000 young Italian members, Kiko Arguello promised the Pope that their numbers in Denver would not be less than 50,000. Delighted as he must have been at the news, even the pontiff raised an eyebrow, starting his speech with the query, 'But where will these Neocatechumenals find enough money?' By the end of the speech, however, he had talked himself round: 'I wish that you might all come to Denver. Even if you do not have great riches, you will find a way. I don't know how, but you will.'

I was curious to see whether that promise could be fulfilled.

Denver was the first World Youth Day not to be held in a Catholic country, so there was a certain risk involved. Would people come?

At least the movements could be relied on. Then there was the fact that the Church's publicity machine is a formidable one, and publicity is the air America breathes. Celebrity is one degree below divinity in the United States, and Denver was soon caught up in Pope fever. After all, even the President himself had turned up to pay his respects and bask in the reflected glory.

And he was not the only one to jump on the papal bandwagon. The local radio station, who were covering the visit, had launched a massive poster campaign, featuring their stars arm-in-arm with the Pope, under the headline 'Father Knows Best'. The Colorado Trading Post in the City's main shopping street featured one window crammed with *Jurassic Park* souvenirs juxtaposed with another jammed with Pope memorabilia. A papal beer – Ale Mary – was on sale. McDonalds, who had won the exclusive catering franchise for the event, were giving away cardboard mitres. T-shirts proclaimed: 'I brake for Catholics.' A dry-cleaner's had a papal message blazoned across its canopy: 'Welcome Pope – We cleanse too.' Even the local gay rag ran a cover story headlined 'The Cat in the Hat Strikes Denver'. On a higher cultural plane, the Colorado

Museum of History took up the theme with an exhibition of Vatican treasures.

World Youth Day is a misnomer; it actually lasts four very long and intense days. The first two would be based in Denver City Centre. Then the caravan to Cherry Creek State Park, fifteen miles outside the city, would begin. It was the only location large enough to take the 189,000 registered participants and the thousands more casual visitors expected for the final mass on Sunday, 15 August, the Feast of the Assumption. Twenty thousand would be permitted to make the fifteen-mile 'pilgrimage' on foot. The rest would be condemned to travel in luxury. The hub of the festivities in Denver itself was the Civic Centre Park where a non-stop programme of gospel songs and homilies was unfolding the morning after I arrived. Alongside this was a market. A few stallholders were selling souvenirs; most were simply selling themselves. The *focolarini* had a stall and so did Opus Dei, in a rare public gesture. Most of the others represented the older, traditional Catholic associations. It was a colourful image of the cut-throat spiritual marketplace which now operates within the Church.

At the press centre, based in the cavernous ballroom of the Radisson Hotel in downtown Denver, among the wagonloads of publicity material available I was taken aback to find nothing whatever on the movements. After all, they were the ones who had started it all. I questioned a press officer from the United States Bishops' Conference who were running this part of the event. He had never even heard of the movements. Later that morning, in the city centre, a leaflet was thrust into my hands advertising the 'Youthfest'. That sounded familiar. Indeed, it was an event to be presented that afternoon by Youth for a United World – the Focolare 'mass movement' for young people. Although the leaflet gave nothing away, I already had a pretty fair idea what the Youthfest performance would consist of.

It was not hard to find the way to the Youthfest later that day. It was enough to go with the flow. Focolare had rightly predicted a large crowd and booked the vast hangar-like Currigan Hall, part of Denver's exhibition complex. The habitual smiles of the *focolarini* handing out programmes at the door were eerily familiar; I even recognized one or two of them, and noted the premature ageing I have observed in many full-time members of my generation.

The programme did not differ substantially from that first improvised Genfest in Loppiano over twenty years before. Making no concessions to its audience or the World Youth Day umbrella, it simply, shamelessly did the only thing Focolare knows how to do: sell itself. Talks and experiences were buoyed up by plenty of rousing songs and some rudimentary dancing. It has to be said, however, that the formula works – especially the first time round. As a procession of smiling young people in national costume poured across the stage to the stirring beat of a rock band and the announcer called off the countries represented, the audience responded with enthusiastic cheers and sustained applause. It was impressive and emotive.

A few more songs were needed to 'create the mood' for the crux of the presentation. First came the life of Chiara Lubich presented in mime and dance performed to music and extracts from letters she had written in the early days of the movement. Then the inevitable 'Story of the Ideal', basically the identical narrative told straight by the female *capozona* (representing the spiritual side) and a talk on the movement's towns by the male *capozona* (the practical side or 'works'). I calculated that there were 7,000 in the packed auditorium, and crowds continued to pour in well after the show had started.

Although attention flagged during the lengthy talks and experiences – the audience was multinational, while the language of the event was English – by the end, as the full cast filled the stage and unfurled huge flags of their various nationalities to a rousing pop anthem, the audience was dancing in the aisles. This was the formula – songs, testimonies, talks, even the flags – that the World Youth Day has made its own and which preceded the Pope's first appearance at Cherry Creek State Park the next day. Yet it was interesting to observe how much more effective the Youthfest was in grabbing and holding its young audience. It is a manipulative formula, but a skilful one, honed by years of practice. At the same time it demonstrates the tendency to fossilization within the movement. Such presentations, they reason, have not been developed by human means but conceived by Jesus in the midst – therefore they are canonized, fixed, unchangeable. How will they hold up twenty-five or even fifty years from now?

★   ★   ★

But there was still no sign of Neocatechumenate. Was it possible that Kiko's promise to the Pope had come to nothing? What a terrible loss of face that would represent for NC. The whole town was awash with Catholic youth from all over the world: wandering in the streets, chatting in the cafés, inspecting shops, congregating before the stage in Civic Centre Park or milling around the stalls in the 'market'. Lacking information from the press centre, it was impossible to locate a specific group. It would be easier to track them down the next day, I decided, when they would be assembled, by group, in Cherry Creek State Park.

Very early on the morning of Saturday, 14 August 1994, the Long March from Denver City Centre to Cherry Creek State Park began. I arrived, via the press shuttle-bus, in the early afternoon, well before the start of the scheduled warm-up programme due to begin at four, allowing for three hours of preparation before the Pope arrived at seven. He was to lead a Vigil that would go on until eleven. After that, the majority of the pilgrims would pass the night on site, in sleeping-bags, ready for the Pope's return and mass the next morning. The discomfort was part of the pilgrimage aspect of the event. Besides, it would be physically impossible to transport nearly 200,000 people from the site and return them for the next day; it had taken the best part of a day to get them out there.

As I arrived, the pilgrims were already pouring through the designated entrances into the vast prepared site delineated by rows of McDonalds catering trucks. In fact, it was impossible to take in the full extent of the enclosure owing to the undulations of the terrain. I wandered among the crowds. As I passed in front of the stage, the largest ever built in the United States, the land rose. Looking back from this incline, I could see, beyond an artificial lake, an endless stream of tiny figures moving along the ridge that curved around it, like the lip of a volcano.

As I walked on through an area that was already quite full, I began to spot familiar motifs among the crowds – icons of the Madonna painted on banners, and strange brass crosses with a medieval figure of Christ and angels' wings around the base. Suddenly, there were banners everywhere: small ones at first, identifying the Neocatechumenal community of a certain parish and city. Then larger ones: 'The Neocatechumenal Communities of Australia greet the Pope'; 'The Neocatechumenal

Communities of St Thomas More Church, Washington, DC';
Neocatechumenal communities of Chicago, San Diego, Phoenix;
'Santa Caterina Parish, Alicante, Spain'. Banners proclaimed the
presence of Italian NC communities; others addressed a message of
support directly to the pontiff: 'Upon this Rock, I will build my
Church' or 'In Camino con Pietro' ('On the Way with Peter'),
illustrated by a stark picture of a bare cross implanted upon a crag.

This image and the icon of Mary were repeated on thousands of
T-shirts. I had now crossed the vast enclosure, and every group I
passed was from Neocatechumenate: they had massed together, as
close as possible to the stage. The flamenco chords of Kiko's songs
rang out on all sides. 'We are the Way, the Truth and the Life,'
chorused one group.

Striking up a conversation with a group from Rome, I discovered
that 10,000 NC members were present from Italy alone. The total
figure, they had been informed, was 35,000. At the close of the
main event, they told me eagerly, NC's own gathering would be
held in the nearby Fort Collins Stadium with Kiko Arguello. The
following day, in a brief conversation with an English NC priest,
I learned that the official NC figure for their presence at the Youth
Day was 40,000, well over a fifth of the total registered participants.
The Pope would not be disappointed at the loyal showing from his
most faithful followers.

NC regard the World Youth Day as, in some way, theirs. But,
even though it is the creation of the movements and reflects their
characteristics, officially participation is open to all Catholic youth.
I later learned, however, that – at least, in Britain – attendance from
NC parishes was strictly limited to NC members. The first mention
of the event in St Nicholas parish, Bristol, was an item in the Parish
Bulletin announcing that the participants – all from prominent NC
families – had already left. In Cheltenham, no announcement was
ever made; the news was leaked to non-NC parishioners, the way
of other NC happenings in the parish.

In France, where NC is not even acknowledged as a Catholic
association approved by the Bishops' Conference, the press office
admitted to me that a large proportion of the 3,000 youngsters who
journeyed to Denver from France were from NC parishes.

At the first sighting of the Pope's helicopter, the vast crowd went
wild. I was witnessing a phenomenon I knew well. When Chiara
Lubich visited Loppiano or a congress in Rome's Mariapolis Centre,

the expectancy before her arrival would build to fever pitch. Temperatures would rise at false alarms, and the tension mount higher. Then, suddenly, a sense of her presence swept through the auditorium, there would be a sudden flurry at the entrance, and there she was, always surrounded by a phalanx of attendants. Even those who could not discern her diminutive figure would be caught up in the wave of emotion that engulfed the crowd, and every pulse beat faster. People leaped to their seats to see over heads; there was wild applause and waving.

This same phenomenon of manipulated mass hysteria animates the World Youth Day – it was, after all, manufactured by the movements as a showcase for the Pope, and they know a thing or two about personality cults.

The helicopter made low circles over the whole of the vast crowd as nervous security men scanned the skies. After a few minutes of this, there was pandemonium. And yet no-one could even see him as he flew overhead. Knowing there was such a liberal sprinkling of Neocatechumenals, as well as members of other movements, it is hardly surprising that the rest of the assembly would be swept along on the tide of enthusiasm.

On that first evening the Pontiff delivered his address as evening fell. From where I stood in front of the stage I could look back on the whole crowd, stretching away to the horizon on all sides. As the Pope's exhortation rang out in the stillness of the purple dusk, out of the silent crowds, one by one, Neocatechumenate banners rose in an orchestrated gesture: in a wall along one edge of the enclosure; festooned from a bank of speakers in the centre of the crowd; dotted through the area in front of the stage. They were a private message to the pontiff, pledging allegiance, but they also said: 'We are here and we are thousands.' It was a chilling display of strength.

The presence of the movements at that gathering was out of all proportion to their numbers in the wider ecclesiastical community; yet the effects of their influence were evident. And the image the World Youth Day gave of the Church was a badly distorted one. The real message of the Day was not in the Pope's interminable rambling speeches inveighing against the moral corruption of the Western World and especially an America 'in danger of losing its soul'. It is doubtful whether many of the young people could begin to identify with the Pope's world view. What did come across loud and clear, however, was that the role of the participants was passive. This was not the active and committed laity of the Council. CL proposes the 'dynamic of following'; Focolare and NC allow no feedback at their meetings and demand total conformity to their 'charisms'. The World Youth Day took the same approach. The 189,000 registered participants were there to listen, to learn. The only voice given to the young people themselves was that of a remote and mysterious body known as the International Youth Forum; but that conclave had completed its deliberations, under conditions of the strictest secrecy, before the others had even arrived. The Forum's membership of 270 young adults from around the world had been carefully selected by the authorities. Their final 600-word 'pronouncement' was hardly worth holding one's breath for. It contained not a whisper of controversy, rebellion or questioning:

> From our Christian experience, we want to share with all the world's youth our desire to build a new society, a society of love. . . . We thank Pope John Paul II, Peter's successor, for his encouragement and we pledge to him to be the new evangelizers and the living stones of the Church. But we are convinced of one thing: in Christ we can change the world. But before we can change the world each one of us has to change his heart through humility.

The line chosen by the delegates is a spiritual one, which speaks of a new society but in vague and utopian terms. There is no engagement with the problems of the world; in fact, the document clearly states its unwillingness to dwell on these problems. It prefers to be upbeat, vague, safe.

But the key message of the World Youth Day is surely a powerful and tangible image of centralization. Its sole thrust was to showcase not a person but a media personality magnified out of all reality. The Church was presented as an across-the-footlights rapport with this faraway figure brought close by massive banks of speakers and videowalls. The illusion of the Pope's *personal* contact with each Youth Day participant was fostered; this was Chiara Lubich speaking directly to the heart of each of her thousands of followers. But it was also the rock-star communing with his fans. The term which best captured the essence of the event was 'Popestock'.

★   ★   ★

The new movements delight in statistics. This is especially evident in the accounts of their missionary expansion, especially those of NC and the *focolarini* who are present worldwide. The implication seems to be that the rate of expansion is proof in itself that the movements are right.

Don Gino Conti is an elderly Roman priest who has studied the theological shortcomings of NC. When told by his nieces, who are devout members, that the movement must be right because they have 80,000 members in Italy, he replied: 'In that case the Jehovah's Witnesses, who have 800,000 members, must be ten times more right than you.' (The figures may not be accurate, but the principle is clear.)

The movements, however, fail to grasp this argument. Statistics, they believe, speak louder than reason. They serve the dual purpose of infusing members with a triumphalistic sense of being on the winning side and offer a 'proof' to outsiders that the message of the movement is answering a need and achieving results. The results take on special significance, especially for Catholics, against the background of a Church in retreat – at least in western Europe.

The missionary urge is implicit in the unique sense of destiny each of the movements possesses. Hence their phenomenal expansion. By the end of the forties, in a matter of about five years, Focolare had spread throughout Italy. In the fifties they had reached most countries in Europe, at the same time sowing the seeds of an even vaster diffusion through the many members of missionary orders who were already carrying the Focolare gospel across the oceans. In the sixties, these seeds sprouted, and Focolare communities were opened throughout the world. By the mid-sixties, just twenty years after its foundation, the movement was firmly established in Asia, Africa and both North and South America, with a particularly strong presence in the last. All these new territories, or 'zones', produced 'vocations' to the different branches of the movement, including the full-time *focolarini*. One by one, even the most obscure countries were reached, and now the estimates of the number of countries with active communities of the movement vary between 180 and 200 – virtually the entire world; 245 permanent women's Focolare centres and 202 men's centres now exist in 143 nations.

The progress of NC, which started twenty years after Focolare, has been, if anything, even more extraordinary. Launched in Madrid in 1964, it transferred its headquarters to Rome just four years later. By the early eighties, it had put down roots in all major European countries and was present on the five continents.

The international diffusion of CL, on the other hand, has been slower. Its achievement in Italy, particularly in the field of politics, demanded such a concentration of forces that serious expansion was halted in the seventies and eighties. Nevertheless, the thrust has always been present. As early as 1961, CL saw missionary work overseas as a natural extension of an everyday preoccupation: 'The mission is first and foremost here, where one lives one's everyday life.'

Although the movement at that time consisted mainly of secondary-school students, with just a handful who had reached university, it launched its first missionary project at Belo Horizonte in Brazil. A group of the movement's finest came from Italy; but, faced with poverty and injustice on a scale they had not seen before, they felt that CL lacked the political dimension needed to deal with Brazil's social problems. Of this first group all but one abandoned the movement in the mid-sixties for more radical approaches to the country's social problems. That one, Pigi Bernareggi, who had been president of GS in Italy, kept the faith and became a priest of the Belo Horizonte diocese. He provided the continuity the movement needed, and today it has a strong presence in Brazil with thousands of followers.

In 1969 the movement established an African foothold when three members left as volunteers for Uganda. As a result of their work, an offshoot of CL, known as CCL (Christ is Communion and Life), was established, fully acknowledging the charism, central authority and teachings of the movement in Italy. The political overtones of the parent-movement's name were considered too inflammatory for the country's delicate political situation.

In Europe, CL had already reached Switzerland in the sixties, and today is present in Fribourg, Zurich, Berne and Geneva. By the mid-seventies, CL was established in Spain where it now has groups of workers and, in the educational field, secondary-school and university students.

But the real impetus for expansion came with John Paul II's exhortation to the movement to mark its thirtieth-anniversary celebrations in 1984: 'Go out into all the world and bring the truth,

the beauty and the peace which are found in Christ the Redeemer
. . . This is the charge I leave with you today.' Taking this to heart,
in the eighties CL entered a phase of expansion. Today it has a
presence in more than thirty countries; and, now that – probably
temporarily – CL's Italian political activity has lessened, the nineties
should see its biggest expansion yet. As Don Giussani has remarked
of his cohorts, we can expect to see results 'disproportionate to the
smallness of its numbers'.

While CL does not yet have figures sufficiently impressive to
conjure with – at least, not outside Italy – NC has and does. The
obsession with numbers is taken to bizarre lengths in the only book
yet published by Neocatechumenate to contain information on the
movement's structure and spread, *Il camino Neocatechumenale*.[1] A
chapter entitled 'Some Fruits of the Neocatechumenal Way' uses
the results of detailed surveys to prove the movement's efficacy.

We are presented with graphs, pie-charts and lists, lending a
veneer of pseudo-science to the proceedings. Some of the diagrams
do give an insight into the movement's strengths. There are
eighty-two NC parishes in the Rome diocese, one pie-chart tells
us, giving NC a 25.5 per cent market share. A list breaks this down
further into 349 communities and 11,846 'brothers' (and sisters –
the movements have no truck with inclusive language). The stages
of the Way attained to date by the various communities are revealed
in a graph. We learn that, while only ten communities have finished
the complete twenty-year course with the renewal of the baptismal
promises, 185 have reached the stage known as the Shema, usually
achieved in the first three years, suggesting a rapid expansion in the
nineties. Over 5,000 NC members are in influential (and well-paid)
professions, including 1,887 civil servants, 907 businessmen, 557
teachers, 193 doctors and forty-six in university teaching posts with
another forty-one in research at university level. We learn that the
diocese has provided thirty-two missionary families distributed in
Norway, France, Germany, Austria, Holland, Russia, Serbia, the
United States, Salvador, China, Japan, Ivory Coast and Australia.
In addition eighty-six itinerant catechists have been sent out to
various parts of Italy and twenty-five countries, including Turkey,
Egypt, India, Korea, Zaïre and Uganda. In a breakdown of 'vocations' provided by NC in Rome, tucked away at the bottom of the

[1] Milan: Edizioni Paoline, 1993.

list are thirty 'sisters in support', women 'who help and sustain [mi ;ionary] families'. Men are not expected to perform this menial chore.

The movement's bias against social responsibility is shown by the figure of 3,500 members involved in some kind of ministry such as adult catechesis (1,550), catechesis for the various sacraments – baptism, communion, confirmation, engaged couples – and extraordinary ministers of the Eucharist, against only 479 involved in any kind of community care, such as work with the poor and the sick. The majority of members in the Rome diocese (6,009) are between the ages of twenty-six and fifty, the age-group most poorly represented in official statistics of the Catholic Church in Italy.

One of the statistics of which NC is clearly most proud is the birth rate, which at 3.11 per cent is almost three times Italy's national average. This translates as 8,040 children born to 2,585 couples. Of these, virtually all enter a community at the age of fourteen. It is probably too early to say whether this trend will last or even whether these youngsters who have never been offered an alternative will remain faithful to the movement. For the present, however, they constitute its best hope and are described in the report as its 'first source of vocational riches'.

If NC use statistics as pseudo-scientific 'proof' of the movement's worth, Focolare use them in the context of a delirious language that has more in common with modern public relations than with science. It is a language of success in which not only are negative facts ignored, but also the positive facts are reported in gushing emotive terms. This goes not only for news bulletins aimed at outsiders in publications like the various editions of the *New City* magazine round the world, or at open meetings like the Mariapolis, but also internally. News reports take on a hyperbolic tone, smacking more of wishful thinking than of factual reporting. As in all totalitarian organizations, it is essential that the institution is perceived by both outsiders and members as perfect and successful in every way.

Circulation of news among internal members, or *aggiornamento* as this practice was known in the movement, long before the term became a buzzword for modernization in the Church in the reign of Pope John XXIII, is an activity of fundamental importance. As new means of communication have appeared they have been eagerly snapped up in order to make the internal communications system of the movement, or the 'violet' as it is known internally, ever more efficient, so that each individual member can 'live' what the movement is undergoing throughout the world, sharing its joys and sorrows, although the emphasis is overwhelmingly on the joys or triumphs. News is communicated on a daily basis to the *focolarini* through faxes and phone calls. This is one of the most successful methods of subordinating the individual to the institution. Members are avid for these *aggiornamenti*, identifying more strongly with them than they would with a letter from a friend. Their own lives, emotions and problems pale into insignificance in comparison with this white-hot frenzy of successful activity worldwide.

In the early eighties Chiara Lubich's fortnightly conference call to fifty Focolare Centres round the world was launched, mainly as a vehicle for the foundress to communicate a keynote spiritual thought to internal members. It also served as a medium for *aggiornamento*, with a special emphasis on the doings of Chiara Lubich. This news round-up, collated and read by Eli Folonari, for many years Chiara Lubich's private secretary, is indicative of the *aggiornamento* style.

But the *aggiornamenti* do not limit themselves to citing figures. They also give them a precise interpretation. In the conference call of 14 May 1987, for instance, Eli Folonari uses characteristically extravagant terms to describe the 'explosion of fruits brought about by the Genfests held all over the world'. With a concision suggesting divine guidance, she manages to sum up the intimate feelings of hundreds, or even thousands, of participants in a single phrase:

> In the zone of São Paolo, Brazil, the 3,000 young people involved in the preparation of their Genfest, gathered together 9,000 friends in the Sports Arena of the University of Cantina for a day, filled with joy and of celebration which instilled in the hearts of this multitude the desire to transform the world into the kingdom of God. At Caserta near Naples, 6,000 declared that they were with us, the same went for the 5,000 of Turin who expressed their commitment with their lives to Chiara's message . . . In Bogotá there were 1,500 of them, all very happy and inflamed by the festive atmosphere each one felt to have personally built. In Jerusalem, 250 Christians of different churches and Moslems experienced the beauty and the richness

of this life. In Walsingham, England, after two days of workshops and the Genfest, the 500 youth left really changed . . . In Lisbon, the 3,700 participants departed with the certainty that a united world was not a utopia.

'Joy', 'celebration', 'commitment with their lives', 'inflamed': all these are standard phrases used in news bulletins such as this. Usually this technique of summing up collective emotions in a phrase is based on nothing more scientific or democratic than slips of paper distributed at the end of a meeting for participants to write their 'impressions'. Of course only favourable remarks are quoted. Positive comments made to members will generally go into the reports submitted by the 'zones' to the Centre in Rome. Often these will pick up on one or two positive 'impressions' to sum up the views of the majority. No doubt Eli Folonari lifted the finest of these phrases in preparing her overview.

In the news round-up of 23 February 1989, she is even more pithy in her description of Gen congresses round the world:

> In the Azores, there was a day for girls with 500 participants, *all very much conquered*. The school for Gen 2 boys in Hong Kong was *deep*. The Gen 2 girls of Mexico were *on fire*, wanting to be *Gen at the level of the Work of Mary*. The Gen 2 boys from Austria were *happy*. With their *souls open to the vast horizons* to which they are also called, the Gen girls from Peru, Ecuador and Colombia left from their school.

If these descriptions arouse suspicions of oversimplification, the summary given in the conference call of 8 June 1989 of the annual Mariapolis meetings of that year is still more sweeping:

> For many of the participants, who numbered more than 23,000, the Way of Mary was a strikingly new reality. They felt the certainty of having found a way that could lead them to sanctity. Every event of every person's life was seen in a new light and given value.

It would be hard to make this claim with accuracy for one participant, let alone 23,000.

Focolare events cannot merely be successful; they must be

epoch-making, and the language of hyperbole often shows the strain. Can we really believe that a congregation of a hundred members of the Church of England, having been addressed by the *focolarini* at a Sunday-morning communion service, were 'inflamed' by their encounter with the Focolare Ideal?

The claims made for the movement's unique contribution to the Church and to the World are still more exaggerated. At the various congresses for religious held in Italy in June 1988, a video of a talk given by Chiara Lubich to superiors general of religious orders 'appeared as the answer the Church today needs for religious life'. On a tour of Focolare's centres in Asia, Don Silvano Cola, head of the priests' section, declared that faced with the continent's social problems, the movement 'appears as an oasis of pure spring water . . . the only remedy capable of healing the social, political and religious contrasts that exist'.

The 1988 annual conference for the leaders of the 'zones' in Rome is described in these terms:

> This year has the special characteristic of an overwhelming light. Chiara on 17 October, in an hour which she herself called an hour of foundation, showed us the Work [Work of Mary – the official name for Focolare] in a whole new beauty – the inner part as a whole interweaving of vocations and supporting structures and outside simply as a renewed Christianity, a spirit that can renew the world. The Work of Mary is in a more concrete way the presence of Mary in the Church and in the world of today.

The movement's most extravagant claims for itself are summed up in this paragraph.

In an interview which she gave in 1991, when asked about her alleged low profile, Chiara Lubich replied: 'If I think of Mary, of her who conserved all things in her heart, I wonder whether she would have considered the limelight and the excessive care of one's image to be appropriate.' Despite this rather whimsical appeal to modesty, the foundress hardly needs to waste time grooming her image when she has millions doing it so efficiently on her behalf.

Focolare meetings at every level – international congresses in Rome for the various 'branches', corresponding national meetings, local gatherings of nuclei and groups – feature *aggiornamenti*, always expressed in the characteristic language of hyperbole. For the full-time *focolarini* living in the centres, these take place on a daily basis. Much of this circulation of news is verbal, face-to-face or by phone. But modern means of communication have been employed to increase the effective circulation of news.

As the movement's *New City* magazine in its various language editions became more orientated towards spreading the movement to a more general audience, its role of passing on news of the movement's activities was delegated to internal newsletters. A communications centre, Centro Santa Chiara, was set up as early as the fifties to distribute tapes of news along with recordings of Chiara's talks. Later slide-shows were produced, covering both spiritual themes and events such as Chiara's trips to other continents or the movement's ecumenical activities. Even in the fifties some events were captured on 16mm film, despite the cost of the medium at that time.

Now many events in the life of the movement – especially Chiara's activities – are recorded on videotape for programmes to be screened at Focolare gatherings worldwide, and so that future generations will have direct experience of the foundress.

The obsession with singing the movement's praises is a direct result of the exaltation of the institution at the expense of the individual. Members are taught to devalue their own feelings and concerns, gradually replacing them with the concerns of the movement. When the *focolarini* have conversations with outsiders or fringe members, they will feign interest in the mundane facts of these people's lives – their families, their jobs, their problems – but when it is their turn to recount the latest news of the movement they come alive and their enthusiasm is palpable. They truly come to *feel* more for institutional than for personal matters. The para-doxical result of this 'impersonality' is a kind of mass megalomania in which each individual member shares. While they have truly re-nounced their own lives and are totally lacking in self-interest, they participate in the incredibly inflated mass-ego of the movement.

With its unlimited ambitions for conquest, it is not surprising that Focolare takes a keen interest in using the media as a rapid means of putting its message across. When Franca Zambonini suggests in *The Adventure of Unity* that Focolare receives much less press and media coverage than, say, Communion and Liberation, Chiara Lubich replies that:

It's out of choice. Historically, it goes back to the origins of the movement and it has never been revoked, despite the advent of the era of the mass media. I remember being very struck by the words of a holy priest, Don Giovanni Calabria, now raised to the honour of the altars, who used to say in his Veronese vernacular *'Taneta e buseta'*, which in basic terms means humility and concealment, not showing off, not making a fuss.

But this attitude of the shrinking violet is not borne out by the many reports of press and media contacts listed in the conference calls, often directly involving Chiara Lubich herself, who appears to have developed quite a flair for handling the media.

After being awarded the first prize for the Festival of Peace by the city of Augsburg, we find Lubich very much at her ease with the press:

In the afternoon at 4.00 Chiara met with 23 journalists in the hall of the Mariapolis Centre of Ottmaring for a press conference. They represented 23 news services (7 belonged to the Movement). Chiara answered their questions very spontaneously and a very special atmosphere was created, so much so that the conference finished with a general applause.

The news round-ups in the conference calls are peppered with references to newspaper, radio and television interviews given by Chiara Lubich and members of the movement throughout the world. The media are exploited in every way possible as vehicles of the movement's message. The Word of Life is the most successful example: it is a phrase chosen from the gospel each month and printed in various languages with suggestions by Chiara on how to put it into practice. This interpretation is invariably in terms of the movement's standard slogans. In addition to more than 3 million printed copies distributed by members of the movement each month, it is broadcast by sixteen television stations and 217 radio stations throughout the world. Chiara Lubich is anxious that the movement should infiltrate the secular media. In a conference call of December 1988, it is reported that 'She underlined the positive value of educating people in the use of images. She is encouraging our people who work in the media to develop programmes conveying the spirit of the Ideal.'

Focolare's media breakthrough came with the Genfest of 1990, which was broadcast worldwide over the Olympus satellite courtesy of RAI, the Italian state television company, who took the opportunity to put the new technology through its paces.

The myth that Focolare courts obscurity was laid to rest once and for all on Saturday, 5 June 1993, when it staged its largest media jamboree to date – the Familyfest. An audience of 14,000 filled the Palaeur; but, in what was claimed to be one of the largest satellite link-ups ever attempted, the show reached an estimated international television audience of nearly 700 million viewers.[1] Once more, the technology was provided by RAI and did not cost the movement a penny. The operation was launched under the auspices of the New Families mass movement, but drew on the combined forces of the worldwide Focolare empire. It was an impressive demonstration of what these highly efficient organizations can achieve internationally with the formidable resources of finance and manpower at their disposal.

Unlike Focolare's major media events of the past, the Familyfest did not just speak with its own authority, or even with that of the Pope; it was billed as an official 'preparatory event' of the United Nations Year of the Family, 1994, and one of the illustrious 'stars' of the show was Henry J. Sokalski, UN co-ordinator for the Year of the Family. The imposing line-up of participating luminaries also included the President of the Italian Republic, Oscar Luigi Scalfaro, Egon Klepsch, President of the European Parliament, and Bartholomew I, the Ecumenical Patriarch of Constantinople. Cory Aquino, the former President of the Philippines, sent a recorded message; while top of the bill was Pope John Paul II, who gave his address in a carefully staged live relay from his office in the papal apartments.

In order to give this a family flavour, children were seen at play on the mosaic floor of the pontiff's bachelor pad – not, one would imagine, an everyday occurrence; this added a surreal note to the proceedings, though no doubt it struck the organizers as a fitting reminder of family values.

---

[1] The breakdown of the worldwide audience of 686 million people included an average of 1 million spectators during the four-hour transmission on RAI 1 in Italy, part of which was seen by a total audience of 7 million; an additional 100 million in the rest of Europe; 148 million in North America; 50 million in South America; 380 million in Asia; 2 million in Oceania and 5 million in Africa.

Needless to say, the occasion gave rise to a veritable orgy of statistics. Thirteen satellites were used to achieve what the *focolarini* dubbed 'worldvision', covering 150 countries from Tierra del Fuego to Siberia. More than 200 stations picked up the broadcast. In addition the New Families movement organized 500 local gatherings in fifty-three countries at which the satellite relay was received.

The logistics for the Rome operation were also on the grand scale. The 14,000 delegates represented eighty-eight countries. The four world religions – Christianity, Judaism, Buddhism and Islam – were represented and eight Christian denominations. Simultaneous translation into twenty-four languages was provided in Rome, while the broadcast went out in five languages. The delegates were accommodated in 165 Roman hotels.

The broadcast did not begin until the afternoon, but the morning programme for the benefit of the live audience at Palaeur was opened by the leaders of the New Families movement, Annamaria and Danilo Zanzucchi. They set the emotive tone of the event with a gesture characteristic of the movement: 'Today we would like to experience here among us what mankind could be if it was one family. This morning therefore we would like to reconfirm before you all the unity between the two of us.'

The programme continued in the same vein with the familiar mix of 'experiences', specially reduced to soundbites to suit an international television audience, mimes and songs from the Familyfest Band, made up of a hundred members of other bands, including Gen Verde and Gen Rosso.

The broadcast section of the programme, which began in the afternoon, also included segments beamed live from all five continents via two-way link-ups with Melbourne, Hong Kong, Yaounde (Cameroun), Brussels, São Paolo, Buenos Aires and New York. (A technical hitch scuppered the broadcast from Africa.)

The Brussels segment, in addition to a piece of choreography on the theme of the countries of the European Union performed by a group of seventeen children, featured the official speech of Egon Klepsch in the presence of Prince Albert and Princess Paola of Belgium, who have since become king and queen.

In order to boost audience appeal, internationally known artists were booked to perform at the Familyfest, including the Israeli pop singer Ofra Haza, who is at least as well known for her skimpy costumes as for her vocal talents. (Perhaps someone slipped up on their research here.)

With sixty journalists present, four press conferences held and forty New Families press centres set up on all five continents, the rest of the media were well catered for. The Focolare philosophy of 'making yourself one' with others in order to win them over makes its members natural publicists. Although official Focolare reports of the event were predictably rhapsodic, writer David Willey, the BBC's correspondent in Rome, was not impressed. The participants struck him as being brainwashed, and he noted a self-congratulatory tone he described as 'preaching to the converted'. Willey was surprised at the absence of Chiara Lubich, who by this time had been mysteriously indisposed in Switzerland for almost a year. A particularly odd note was struck, he reports, by the playing of a sound-only message from the foundress, a 'disembodied voice' echoing through the cavernous stadium.

The Familyfest provided Focolare with an opportunity to reach in just four hours an audience which exceeded the total number of people they had evangelized in the previous fifty years of its existence. They were not going to let the opportunity pass without capitalizing on the resulting interest. Freephone numbers were made available to viewers in countries who were part of the link-up. Sixteen lines were manned by thirty-two telephonists speaking a total of twenty languages. Viewers were invited to phone in with their 'impressions' of the programme, or to ask for contact numbers for the New Families and Focolare in their countries. They could also make a commitment to two appeals that were launched during the Familyfest – one for a New Families project supporting women and children in Bosnia and another to sponsor orphans.

Predictably, according to the official reports, out of over a thousand calls received, half declared themselves 'Very strongly impressed and moved as much by the fact of experiencing a live event like this as by the actual content'. There were only ten negative calls and no hoax calls.

With the Familyfest, Focolare achieved a coup in Catholic televangelism. Use of the media on this scale fits in well with the concept of the 'mass movements' like Youth for a United World, New Humanity and New Families. It is disturbing, however, that a sect-like religious movement is concealing – or, at least, playing down – its identity behind vague and innocuous-sounding labels.

At the time when I was living there, the movement's model village of Loppiano had different names and letterheads to suit different purposes. One was 'Istituto Internazionale Mistici Corporis' ('The "Mystical Body" International Institute'), used when the religious dimension could be of benefit, and the other was 'Centro Internazionale di Cultura e di Esperienze Sociali' ('International Centre of Culture and Social Experiences'), adopted on occasions when a secular image was preferable. The most dangerous consequences of these 'disguises' can be seen in the case of the Familyfest. By presenting itself in an almost secular key, it obtained the endorsement of two of the world's most authoritative secular organizations – the United Nations and the European Union.

The United Nations World Forum for non-governmental organizations working in the field of the family met in Malta from 28 November to 2 December 1993 to launch the Year of the Family. One of the items on its agenda was to bestow an official UN award on the New Families movement recognizing the contribution it had made to the preparation and launch of the event of which it was named a 'benefactor'. And yet organizations like the UN and EU clearly do not subscribe to the moral crusade which is the subtext of the Familyfest. Focolare espouses the most extreme right-wing 'family values' from a complete ban on birth-control to the promotion of 'cures' for homosexuality, from the condemnation of sterilization even when the mother's life is at risk to a total opposition to divorce and abortion.

On the other hand, Pope John Paul's hearty endorsement of the Familyfest was entirely predictable. Not only did he make his own live contribution to the television broadcast, but he also celebrated mass the next day, 6 June, in St Peter's Square, not only for the 14,000 who had attended the Palaeur but for a crowd that had swelled to a massive 100,000. The Pope took advantage of the occasion to announce the Catholic Church's own Year of the Family to run concurrently with the UN celebration, giving Focolare still more to crow about. He brought out the true significance of the Familyfest – its underlying moral message – when he pointed out in a long speech to the New Families movement that 'Something extra is required of Christians, which derives from the faith and the dignity of the sacrament conferred by Christ on this natural institution. It is a question of witnessing to the truth and fidelity to love in matrimony and the sincere openness to the gift of life.' In other words 'No' to divorce and birth control.

Long before its recent gargantuan media exploits, Focolare was anxious to use the means of communication at its disposal. By the end of the fifties, its Italian magazine *Città Nuova* (*New City*) was already a substantial publication. Today it is a glossy magazine which has spawned thirty foreign-language editions of varying levels of sophistication. In 1992, Citta Nuova Editrice, the movement's Italian publishing house, was hailed by the glossy current-affairs magazine *Panorama* as being 'of great prestige'. A vehicle for spreading the works of Chiara Lubich, which are produced relatively cheaply and inevitably sell in the tens of thousands, it has gained credibility by issuing scholarly editions of the works of the Fathers of the Church, many of which had been previously unobtainable.

Recently, it has exploited this reputation for scholarship on behalf of the movement's cause, publishing a number of theological studies on the doctrine of Chiara Lubich. Focolare's ambitions beyond the realm of the sacred are reflected in a list which also includes a series of works on psychology, science, politics, sociology, children's books, a book on 'natural' birth control, even a volume on Christian make-up tips. As in the case of the magazine, parallel publishing houses have been set up in all the countries where the movement is well developed. They have pursued a similar policy of publishing popular works in order to build a reputation which then reflects on the works of Chiara Lubich and the movement. *New City* in Britain has taken a leaf out of the book of its parent company and has recently published several volumes of the works of the Church Fathers. The foreign-language publishing houses are often given first refusal on the rights to top titles published by Città Nuova in Italy. An important advantage of this network of publishing houses is that it enables the movement to do 'favours' to important protectors and friends. Città Nuova publishes the works of Vatican prelates that probably would not find another outlet; the foreign houses do the same.

CL's publishing house Jaca Book is also one of the major religious publishing houses in Italy. Its rather odd list reflects the tastes of CL founder Don Giussani – works by C. S. Lewis, Charles Péguy, Paul Claudel and, of course, Hans Urs von Balthasar, the Pope's favourite theologian. Powerful friends like Cardinal Jozef Ratzinger and Cardinal Inos Biffi of Bologna are also published by Jaca Book. In Italy, at least, CL is a formidable media power. It has members in key positions on newspapers, magazines and in television companies. The movement has used the Meetings at Rimini to forge links with leading figures in all disciplines and professions, including the media.

But CL has built up its own powerful and high-profile magazine-publishing empire. Most important of its publications is the glossy *30 Giorni*, with its four foreign-language editions. The internal magazine of the movement, *Litterae communionis*, has recently exchanged its Latin title for the more approachable Italian *Tracce* (*Tracks* – the kind that one follows), also handsomely produced with colour on every page. Rather confusingly, CL also publishes each month the complete speeches of the Pope in a magazine with the almost identical title *Traccia* (*Sign*).

From the early eighties, CL also produced *Il Sabato*, a glossy weekly, well printed with plenty of colour, quality typography and a high standard of journalism. In terms of appearance, it could hold its own on the shelves alongside Italian periodicals such as *Panorama*, *Epoca* or *Europeo*. Ostensibly a current-affairs magazine, *Il Sabato*'s articles were well written and well researched. True, they did reflect some of CL's stranger obsessions such as the conspiracy theories which usually involved CL's *bête noire*: Freemasonry.

To date, NC has made least inroads into the media. In its key territory of Rome, it claims only twenty-four journalists and sixteen television professionals out of a total membership of 11,000. Perhaps the movement's uncompromising style of world-rejection, which regards members' careers as 'idols', will mean that they distance themselves from such a profane profession. In the religious media in Italy, however, they have the ubiquitous Giuseppe Gennarini, who writes regularly on the movement for *Avvenire*, the Catholic daily, or else for the Vatican's *Osservatore Romano*. It is said that several of the staff of Vatican Radio are NC members. The Italian Catholic Radio station Radio Maria (Radio Mary) is closely affiliated to NC. It features regular programmes of the songs of Kiko Arguello and has launched fierce campaigns against the movement's detractors like Father Enrico Zoffoli. With the resources the movement has at its disposal in terms of finance and personnel, and aware of the Pope's fondness for the media, it surely will not be long before their media empire begins to take shape.

As an ex-actor John Paul II is the first media pontiff, not only at home with journalists and the cameras, but positively relishing their presence. The development of a worldwide Catholic media empire – and especially television – has been one of the goals of his reign. Unfortunately, he has not chosen to foster artists who happened to be Catholic and who might therefore have something of real value to offer. Rather, he has encouraged a populist approach; what he has in mind is a media war on non-Catholic sects, and therefore the projects he has supported have shown the same crass simplistic style as their opponents. The Familyfest falls squarely into this mould.

In line with the Pope's wishes, one of the key media drives of recent years has been eastwards – towards Russia and the former communist countries. In this he has been aided by the Dutch-based Catholic media multi-national, Lumen 2000. A million Bibles have been distributed in Russian. They have launched an edition of their American youth magazine YOU in Lithuania. A school of evangelization has been opened in Siberia. A 1½-hour television special from the Marian Shrine of Fatima was broadcast to Russia. In 1988 a joint initiative with Father Werenfried van Straaten's Aid to the Church in Need began broadcasts to the Soviet Union. This operation has since become the Catholic Radio and Television Network. But even this ambitious programme was modest compared to what Focolare, CL and NC were achieving in the same territory – in person.

The common enemy of the movements was the Church's own Nemesis at the time they were founded: communism. Focolare was initially envisaged as an anti-communist crusade. For many years the destruction of communism was the 'specific objective' of the movement.

I have already described how Chiara Lubich identified two of the movement's 'secret' areas of missionary activity: one, represented by the 'invisible' colour of ultra-violet, was within the top echelons of the Church itself; the other, coded 'infra-red', was the

'Church of Silence', the persecuted Church behind the Iron Curtain. In the sixties and seventies, while I was a member of the movement, this was probably the only area of missionary activity that was kept strictly secret, except from the top echelons of the hierarchy such as the authorities at the Centre and the 'zone' leaders. The leader of the movement in these territories was Natalia Dallapiccola, the first of Chiara Lubich's 'companions'. We were told at Loppiano of how Natalia would pretend to be a harmless religious nut, waving her rosary beads and prayerbooks at the officials when she passed back and forth between East and West Germany several times a year. Even more thrilling were the stories of Liliana Cosi, a ballerina at La Scala who was, secretly, a full-time *focolarina*. When she danced at the Bolshoi, we heard, the Russian critics used a word that had all but vanished from the language – 'Soul'. Vale Ronchetti, one of Chiara Lubich's 'first companions', would accompany Liliana Cosi on her trips to Moscow, and we laughed to hear how she wore full make-up and painted her nails (usually the women with vows do no more than pluck their eyebrows, although rare exceptions are made for those who work in the media). In Rome, the movement had a kind of undercover operation called Roman Encounters (*Incontri Romani*) whose specific task was to make contact with groups of visitors from Eastern Europe. How this interfaced with the clandestine movement in Eastern Europe was, of course, shrouded in the utmost secrecy.

With the fall of the Berlin Wall and the collapse of communism, Focolare was finally able to reveal the story of its spread in Eastern Europe. The first contact had been through an East German theologian, Hans Lubscyk, who had met the movement in Munster in West Germany in 1957. Two of the first *focolarini*, Aldo Stedile, and, once again, Vale Ronchetti visited him the following year in Leipzig. Khrushchev was visiting the city in the spring of that year to open an important fair. The *focolarini* took advantage of this diversion to hold meetings with the groups Lubscyk wanted them to meet. As doctors were escaping to the West, foreign doctors could easily find work in East Germany at that time. In 1961, two *focolarini* men, both doctors, opened the first men's Focolare in Leipzig. The women's Focolare followed in 1962, composed of a doctor and a nurse. Natalia Dallapiccola, the superior of the movement in the forbidden 'zone', went along as their housekeeper.

Chiara Lubich herself made an early sortie into the region, visiting distant relatives in Budapest in 1961 (Lubich is a name of Hungarian origin). In 1969, she visited East Berlin as the guest of the city's Archbishop, Cardinal Bengsch. With East Germany as its base, Focolare spread throughout the communist empire just as it was invading the free world. Its cellular structure, outwardly secular appearance, talent for blending in and skills in secrecy made it ideally suited to the territory.

At the time communism fell, NC and CL had made less progress in these areas, but they both had a strong presence in Poland. Since the late 1970s, CL had worked closely with Father Franciszeck Blachnickij's Light-Life movement, whose protector among the Polish episcopate was none other than Karol Wojtyla, archbishop of Cracow. The movements, therefore, were already known to the Polish Pope when he acceded to the throne but, more than that, they were his soulmates; they were fighting the battle that had been, and still was, closest to his heart.

When communism collapsed, the structures the movements had built up in secret suddenly had complete freedom of action. The world's most coveted missionary territory lay at their feet. Every crackpot sect in the world, plus a few new ones specially invented for the occasion, leaped into the ideological void left by communism. But the movements felt in a special way that this was their territory. They had worked for it – and, indeed, it has yielded results. NC is well-established in Poland, with 500 communities – some parishes have thirteen to fourteen communities each with forty to fifty members – thousands of local catechists and twelve itinerant teams. Before the fall of communism, it had already made in-roads in Hungary, Czechoslovakia, Croatia, Slovenia, Serbia, Lithuania, Georgia, Romania, Bielorussia and the Ukraine. In the Catholic parishes of Moscow, the introductory catechesis is not held annually, as it is elsewhere, but once every two months with attendances of 100 each time. Three seminaries – in Berlin, Yugoslavia and Poland – have been established with the aim of evangelizing Eastern Europe.

The ecumenical situation in Eastern Europe is extremely delicate. Catholic-Orthodox relations are strained, despite Vatican protests that they are concerned only for the care of Catholics in these countries and do not regard them from a missionary perspective. Yet the movements are expansionist by nature. A cartoon which appeared in a Moscow newspaper in 1992 shows just how high-profile these three movements are in Russia today and how their intentions are perceived. A row of men is shown fishing in a river labelled 'the Russian People'. In the background is an anonymous group identified as 'religious orders'. In the foreground, however, are caricatures of Opus Dei, Neocatechumenate, the *focolarini*, and Communion and Liberation. Each of these fishermen is dressed in characteristic style and has a box beside him bearing the name of his founder. The CL representative looks around him aggressively, teeth bared. At the end of the row, the Patriarch of Moscow is fishing, too – with a broken rod. His box bears the one word 'Help'. Above, on a cloud, Christ, with just the gospel baiting his hook asks: 'What about me?'

If John Paul II was instrumental in bringing about the downfall of the totalitarian regimes of Eastern Europe, the movements are his agents in a vital follow-up operation, bringing Catholicism at a grass-roots level. Dancing on the grave of communism, they are celebrating one of the Catholic Church's greatest triumphs this century. At a time when the Church is in retreat on all sides, the bullish response of the movements is, as always, to present themselves as the solution. By means of public relations, statistics, vast gatherings and manipulation of the media they pose as the Church of success, the Church expanding, constantly growing in numbers and in fervour: the Church Triumphant.

It might well be asked whether, in a world of 'images' and illusions, it is not the Church's role rather to indicate a different approach, seeking for a deeper authenticity and commitment, even to the extent of adopting a lower profile. Without doubt, the public 'images' of the movements have achieved the desired response from many top church figures including the Pope himself as well as from the public at large. Problems begin, however, when celebrities and organizations begin to believe their own publicity – and the movements certainly do, fervently. They, and the clerics who admire them and see them as the arks that will carry the authentic remnant of the Church into the future, run the risk of living in a world of make-believe, choosing to ignore the real problems of the Church and the contribution it must make to the problems of the world.

As the Carmelite theologian Bruno Secondin has said, 'A church . . . which fabricates, by self-hypnosis, an image of itself which does not in fact exist serves little purpose today'.[1] And yet, illusion or not, it is this boundless self-confidence that allows the movements to pursue what they see as today's burning questions: the condemnation of a depraved world and the creation of an uncontaminated society.

[1]P. 224, *I Nuovi Protagonisti*, Edizioni Paoline, Milan, 1991.

8

SEX, MARRIAGE AND THE FAMILY

FUNDAMENTALIST CHRISTIANITY HAS ALWAYS RESERVED ITS BITTEREST condemnations for the sins of the flesh. Until the Second Vatican Council, this was also the traditional line of the Catholic Church. The dualistic view of the goodness of the spirit and the evil of the body, externalized as Church versus World, has always resulted in the condemnation of man's sexuality.

Pope John Paul has pursued a traditionalist line on sexual morality throughout his reign in a series of documents which culminated in *Veritatis splendor* in 1993. This is probably the area of church teaching which has cost the pontiff most dearly in terms of popularity among the vast majority of Catholics. His gratitude to the movements in this case must be particularly profound, for they have supported him vigorously.

In *Veritatis splendor*, John Paul denounces 'the rise of a depraved moral relativism'.[1] He is attacking a tendency among moral theologians to question traditional teachings by overemphasizing, in his view, the rights of the individual such as freedom and conscience. In a quotation from one of his own speeches, John Paul hammers home his key message that 'the Church teaches that "there exist acts which *per se* and in themselves, independently of circumstances, are always seriously wrong by reason of their object" '.[2]

These acts are 'intrinsically evil', the Pope insists.

[1] Footnote 131.
[2] Para 80.

The document plays down the fact that its main target is sexual morality. Other kinds of 'intrinsically evil' sins are listed to throw us off the scent:

> . . . whatever violates the integrity of the human person such as mutilation, physical and mental torture and attempts to coerce the spirit; whatever is offensive to human dignity, such as subhuman living conditions, arbitrary imprisonment, deportation, slavery, prostitution and trafficking in women and children.[1]

John Paul passes effortlessly from these horrors, which no decent human being would condone, to the subject of birth control, also identified as an 'intrinsically evil act'. Other matters of a sexual nature, casually dropped into the text as examples of transgressions that some moral theologians would like to justify include 'direct sterilization, auto-eroticism, pre-marital sexual relations, homosexual relations and artificial insemination'.[2]

The Vatican, concerned with its public image, and certainly not wanting to appear lacking in compassion, is at pains in *Veritatis splendor* to cushion its attack. The movements do not share the Vatican's scruples. Their charism comes directly from God and it gives them full jurisdiction over everyone who falls under their influence. Just as the spiritual ideas must be preserved in their purity, so moral imperatives must be applied without mitigation and without exception. In fact, with absolute conviction of their own infallibility, the movements are prepared to go much further than the Vatican in the demands they make on members and to impose their will on those under their sway with a ruthlessness worthy of any totalitarian power.

Chiara Lubich, whose writings are normally spiritualized to the point of banality, reserves a rare outburst of spleen for a description of the immorality of modern society in a 1972 speech to Gen leaders in Rome:

> As in the blackest periods of history, a tempest has been unleashed in the moral field which, under all sorts of pretexts, uproots every

[1]Para 80.
[2]Para 47.

law, smashes every barrier, spreading a vomiting eroticism, coming up with every possible motive to justify the most deviant experiences so as to stress in man not the spirit which makes him like the angels, but the flesh which he shares with animals.

The dualism spirit/flesh, angels/animals is bluntly stated. It is, of course, fatuous, because man is evidently not a chimera composed of incompatible parts: while he may not be an animal, he is certainly no angel, either. The remark comes from a lecture on Mary, the gist of which is that devotion to the Virgin Mary has declined because she represents the unpopular virtue of virginity.

Chiara Lubich does not argue; she asserts. This is an understandable approach in an organization which condemns the use of reason. Nevertheless, it could be countered to this particular declaration that devotion to the Virgin has declined simply because in the past it was overemphasized. But we get the point. Just in case we do not, in the unpublished version of this lecture – Focolare does a great deal of judicious editing of Lubich's works – she used, for her, an uncommonly harsh turn of phrase to express disgust for acts of a sexual nature – and to arouse the same feelings in her listeners: 'Whoever has tasted the dregs always desires something more piquant.'

Many, including Catholics, would find this language exaggerated and even dangerous, particularly when addressed to the young. It could be mitigated if it came in the context of a balanced view of human sexuality and sex education. But it did not. It was one of maybe half a dozen times I *ever* heard the subject of sex touched on in the nine years I spent in Focolare. If it was absolutely necessary to allude to it, then the most elliptical of euphemisms would be used. Far preferable, however, was to ignore the subject completely. Certainly, at the time the words were uttered, no sex education of any kind was given to the young members of the movement. I know this because from 1973 until I left the movement in 1976 I was responsible for the male section of the Gen movement in Britain. The only message they received from the movement – in the strongest possible terms – was that sex was evil.

Following the Second Vatican Council, the Catholic Church opened up to contemporary ideas in the field of psychology. One of the fundamental concepts that has been taken on board by moral theologians and committed Catholics working in psychology and psychiatry is that sexuality is a basic part of the human make-up. Even celibate priests, nuns and monks have to come to terms with this aspect of their personality. Not in Focolare, though. Its angelistic view of human nature can at best be comical and at worst – as in the pastoral care of members – do damage that is possibly criminal.

Focolare's attitude to sex, as with every other aspect of the movement, mirrors that of Chiara Lubich. She took a vow of celibacy before the movement even started. That event, on 7 December 1943, is considered to be so fundamental that it is regarded as the date of the movement's foundation: the fiftieth anniversary was celebrated in 1993. Chiara Lubich has made quite clear that for her anything other than lifelong celibacy was un-thinkable, repellent even. This is illustrated by an incident in her early twenties when she went to visit her brother Gino, a doctor, in the hospital where he worked. Another young doctor looked at Silvia (as she was then) 'with interest' and, the story goes, she literally 'ran a mile', never returning to the hospital.

Like all aspects of the movement, this was celibacy taken to an extreme. Chiara's doctrine is an idiosyncratic amalgam of ultra-traditionalist Catholicism mixed with a few ideas of her own. One of the most traditional of these is the supremacy of virginity. 'We understood,' she says, 'because we had a background of Catholic culture, that the state of virginity is superior to that of marriage.'

The very structure of the movement embodies the concept of virginity. Strict segregation of the sexes is enforced at every level – not just in the celibate communities, but among all full members of the movement. Although the segregation within the movement is often criticized by outsiders, it is regarded as of supreme importance by the foundress because it is a reflection of the celibate leadership. Among the new movements, this aspect is peculiar to Focolare. The *focolarini* refer to their single-sex structure with the euphemistic term 'the distinction'.

With characteristic cunning, public meetings of the movement are mixed, designed to give an appearance of normality. Visitors to Loppiano, when the male and female 'schools' for *focolarini* were based there, received an entirely different, and much more accurate, impression of the internal structure. The male and female 'districts' were located at opposite ends of the large site, with over a mile of open countryside between them; the women's 'district' was

Loppiano proper, while the men lived in an area known as Campogiallo. Both living-quarters and workplaces were separate. Visitors, who would be ferried backwards and forwards between the male and female districts, were puzzled by the set-up.

The 'college', a modern building where the women lived, had the air of a convent about it. The main entrance led to a huge bare reception-area with one woman seated at a desk in the middle of it. Stairs rose to the living-quarters where no men were allowed. We jokingly referred to this as 'the cloister'. During my second year at Loppiano, my sister, Ann, came to visit accompanied by the sister of another Englishman who was at the school. They were to stay at the college and would be ferried over daily by car so that we could spend time with them outside working hours.

After a couple of days, without explanation, they did not appear. We decided to go over to the 'college' and find out what had happened. We crossed the echoing hall to reception, and the girls were duly summoned from 'the cloister'. They could not explain why they had not been to see us; all they knew was that no-one had been prepared to give them a lift. Suddenly one of the *focolarine* leaders drew us to one side. 'We could not allow them to go over to the boys' side undressed like that,' she explained with a grimace. Indeed, the fashionable miniskirts sported by the two girls had reached the apogee of skimpiness that year. Unilaterally, without informing anyone, the hidden hierarchy at the 'college' had decided that the men's district of Campogiallo should not be exposed to such temptation.

The thorny issues of sex and sexuality were never mentioned in the entire two-year course at Loppiano. I became convinced that I was the only one there with sexual stirrings, which served to aggravate my feelings of self-loathing and alienation. Perhaps we all felt that way.

Then, at last, it seemed that the questions on matters sexual which teemed in my brain could be answered. A course was announced entitled 'Hygiene'. This rather clinical term was to cover two subjects with two different teachers. The talks were welcomed because the teachers would be Fiore ('Flower'), one of the earliest female members of the movement, and Maras, our revered superior. Fiore's talks interpreted 'hygiene' in a narrower sense, and the raciest of them told us how to remove unmentionable stains from our 'personal linen'. As Maras was a doctor his talks were to be on the subject of 'the body'. At our first, eagerly awaited lesson, he suggested that each week we could take a vote on which organ would be discussed. Immediately a hand shot up: 'The heart!' Mine sank. A chorus of 'Si!' went up. Next time: 'The stomach!' The following week: 'The liver!' 'The brain!' 'The lungs!' 'The feet!' Somehow we never got round to the subject I was secretly hoping for. Perhaps none of us dared suggest it. Obviously the authorities did not feel it was a subject that needed airing.

For the *focolarini* celibacy was a kind of miraculous spiritual castration. After all, we were not beings of flesh and blood; we were angels. We were taught to distrust and ignore all emotions – to 'lose' them, in Focolare-speak – and this, apparently, applied to sexual feelings as well. It seemed that the preferred stage of emotional development for the *focolarini* is that of pre-adolescence. We referred to one another as *popi* and *pope*, 'boys' and 'girls' in the Trentino dialect. Indeed, in Britain the *focolarini* are always referred to as 'the boys' and 'the girls', even though most of them are in their forties and fifties. The gospel injunction to become like little children is given a fundamentalist interpretation. Childish behaviour is encouraged: running after Chiara Lubich and the other leaders; sitting on the floor, listening to them speak, like children round a storyteller; reciting the 'rule' by heart. The complexity and force of adult emotions is feared and rejected. In this state of arrested development, sex plays no part and therefore need never be mentioned.

Not surprisingly, the result of this neglect is a dangerous ignorance and naïvety. Once I received a passionate 'fan letter' at Loppiano from a Sunday visitor, a young boy of fifteen, telling me that he had not been able to get me out of his mind since his trip to the village and thought about me every night in bed before he went to sleep. I knew there was something odd about the letter, and I thought it best to throw it away unanswered. The ignorance of sexual matters was so profound that I believe that to some extent it encouraged the behaviour it was designed to prevent.

When I revisited Loppiano a few months after I had left for England, a *focolarino* of my year who had stayed on as a leader in one of the small communities told me of problems they had had with a young man who had arrived at Loppiano out of the blue and had been given permission to stay on. Normally applicants to the school had been vetted by the 'zones' before they arrived. This particular newcomer had fooled everyone so well that only after six months was it discovered that he had been systematically seducing the youthful (male) innocents attending the school. Such was their naïvety, they probably imagined he was teaching them a new way of 'making unity'.

In June 1971, during my first year at Loppiano, I went to the Mariapolis Centre at Rocca di Papa to translate for an ecumenical meeting between the Catholic *focolarini* and members of the Orthodox Church. The subject was the Virgin Mary. On the first morning I was given a particularly tough assignment. An Orthodox theologian was to give a talk in Greek, and I was to translate into English from an Italian transcript. Hopefully we would finish together. One of the organizers of the conference was one of the first *focolarine*, Gabriella Fallacara.

'If you can't translate something, just skip it – it doesn't matter,' she told me.

It was an odd suggestion, because usually at these meetings everything was considered to be of life-and-death importance. I got into my booth and began to translate. I soon realized what she meant. The subject of the lecture was the virginity of Mary, and, according to Orthodox tradition, included long and graphic descriptions of the female genitalia and reproductive system. Out of courtesy to the Orthodox guests, the address had to be endured.

Throughout the session, an agitated Gabriella paced up and down behind the row of translation-booths, which were open-backed, hissing to the translators: 'Skip it! Skip it!' She need not have bothered: most of us were totally out of our depth. The content of the lecture was never referred to directly, of course.

In July of the same year, I was sent to Rome to interpret for a convention of married *focolarini*. Even though the location was Villa Mondragone in the hills above Frascati, where Michelangelo's patron Pope Julius II once enjoyed the summer breezes, the weather in 1971 was sweltering. But things were due to get hotter still. There was a male and female team of interpreters, and the men used to work mornings while the women did afternoons. One morning, however, Don Gino Rocca, a theology professor at Loppiano, asked the men to stay on to interpret his talk, even though it was the women's turn. We were given no indication as to what the subject of the talk was to be, even though when technical terms are used, as in this case, it would be customary to alert the interpreters so that they can prepare. To my horror, I suddenly found myself translating a talk on birth control with explicit descriptions of sexual acts. I was so disturbed by, and unused to, the words I heard issuing from my lips that my heart began to race and I came close to blacking out.

This was one of the very rare occasions when explicit language was used, but only in order to push the movement's anti-contraception line. It is an interesting reflection on the role of women in Focolare, incidentally, that it was not considered proper that they should translate a lecture of this kind.

In the early seventies a defection took place which sent shock-waves through the movement. The male and female superiors of the German 'zone' left and married. Although we were never officially told anything about this matter – it was not the uplifting stuff of newletters and *aggiornamenti* – rumours ran riot. One was that they had claimed they were fulfilling a spiritual unity as the personification of Jesus and Mary. Another was that they used to tap messages to one another through the walls of their adjacent bedrooms while attending conferences at the Mariapolis Centre in Rome. Chiara Lubich was not present at the marriage ceremony but sent one of her 'first companions'.

The Focolare leadership learned no lessons from this incident. Instead of taking a positive approach and confronting the issue of the emotional needs of members with open discussion, there was a crackdown on contacts between male and female members with the 'distinction' even more rigidly enforced. The new rules stipulated that the *focolarini* men and women should not visit each other's Focolare Centres and that they should never travel by car together even *en route* to a joint meeting.

Such attitudes revealed the dualistic thinking of the movement. At about this time Chiara Lubich gave a pair of bizarre lectures on the subject of modesty – one to the women and another to the men *focolarini*. Ours contained suggestions like keeping our knees together when we were seated in the presence of female members. It resembled the talks given in convent schools of pre-conciliar days on how girls should behave in the presence of priests.

The official interface between the male and female branches of Focolare is at the summit, between the respective superiors in each zone. Reports of tension at this level often filtered down to us; these differences of outlook must, at least in part, be due to the fact that the male and female members occupied entirely different worlds. Nevertheless, I once heard the theory outlined by a top official of the movement that these superiors of ours were struggling on the frontiers of male-female relationships, precisely because there was no emotional connection between them, and would (God alone knows how!) bring about a new harmony between the sexes. But this was typical of the movement's disincarnate approach. While imposing rigid segregation, it talked of the importance of the unity of the movement as a whole – the 'One Work' (Work of Mary – Opera di Maria – being the movement's official name according to the statutes). But this was purely a spiritual unity.

Unlike the other new movements, Focolare was founded by a woman; and Chiara, along with the female companions who were with her from the start, was acknowledged as pre-eminent. Sadly, this status does not translate into a radical revision of the role of woman in the Church. When questioned in 1991 on her achievements as a woman in the Church, she replied: 'I've never thought of myself as a woman.' Nevertheless, Chiara requested, and obtained, from the Pope the unique concession that the president of Focolare – who has authority over all the branches, including priests – will always be a woman.

While this could seem to be a blow struck for feminism, I believe it is not a tribute to the equality of womankind but the best guarantee of orthodoxy in the future, an attempt by Chiara Lubich to ensure that there will be no changes to the monolithic structure she has created and that, especially, her doctrine will never be, to use a favourite phrase, 'watered down'. Women members and especially Chiara's 'first companions' are, after all, regarded as the most authentic exponents of the 'pure' Ideal.

On the subject of women priests Chiara Lubich comes down firmly on the side of Pope John Paul: 'They are not called to the priesthood . . . the teaching of the Church is absolutely clear on this.' She believes that the Christian woman has to imitate Mary and therefore has 'a different task in the Church, though very important and indispensable: she must affirm, in the way only she can, the value, the primacy of love above all other treasures, above all the other realities that make up our religion'.

Surely there is some confusion here. Love is the virtue demanded of all Christians. It is the very substance of Christianity; take it away and there is nothing left. To say that women are called to love sidesteps the real issue, which is one of power, and plays straight into the hands of those who would like to keep women in the Church in their traditional submissive role.

According to Lubich, 'woman [is] already filled with natural love which leads to every sacrifice'. Surely women have something more positive to offer apart from self-sacrifice. She quotes Hans Urs von Balthasar: 'Mary is Queen of the Apostles without claiming apostolic powers for herself. She has something else and more.' What this 'something else' might be is left to conjecture. Certainly the virtues considered 'Marian' within the movement are submissiveness, silence, unobtrusive service – the traditional 'female virtues' of anti-feminists.

This attitude is confirmed in a speech entitled 'Mary – Humanity Fulfilled', in which Chiara rails against 'unisex fashion'.

> This fashion wants to demonstrate equality between the sexes, and that's fine. But there is an undercurrent in this fashion which is not acceptable: there is an attempt to mix up the sexes, a confusion that could mean something absolutely negative. We must go against this. Our Lady was really the female sex: she was the woman . . . In her all the characteristics of femininity emerge: she is the woman who serves God with her specific gifts, not wanting to take someone else's [di un altro – the masculine] role, but fulfilling her own completely.

It is a sexist view of 'roles' that is being so resolutely defended here.

Although Focolare insists that it has no uniform – a smile is the uniform of the focolarini – it encourages a quaint and many would feel exaggerated modesty in dress for women. This is the so-called moda Mariana, or Mary-like fashion, which means covering up about as much of the body as would be respectable for a woman in a fundamentalist Muslim state. A neckline lower than collar height is out, as are bare arms and hemlines above the knee.

At Loppiano we were told a story – one of the triumphalistic anecdotes that abound within Focolare – about the period when Chiara and the first focolarine arrived in Rome. It was summer, and in the late forties sleeveless dresses were fashionable – a boon in the Eternal City, which becomes a fiery anvil for several months of the year. The focolarine contested this immodest fashion by wearing long sleeves. But they had become so numerous (we were told) that they changed the tide of summer fashion in Rome and long sleeves became the norm.

Some of the styles of the late sixties and early seventies – not miniskirts! – were welcomed by the *focolarine*. When I was at Loppiano the 'look' among the women was smocks over flares, but some sported trouser-suits. (Could this be shades of unisex?) The maxi was welcomed, of course, and then came the breakthrough which has influenced fashion for female members of the movement ever since – the midi. It was embraced wholeheartedly. The *focolarine* are invariably dressed in well-cut, expensive clothes. The style is sober and matronly, and bright colours are favoured. (Needless to say, as in everything else, Chiara Lubich is their model in fashion.) But the midi reigns supreme. At all Focolare gatherings, the full-time female members can be identified by it, as can the degree of commitment of women from other branches.

Most of the *focolarine* women go out to work, as do the men. They are employed in many different professions, and some occupy important posts. Within the movement, however, the 'distinction' has definite sexist consequences. The role of Chiara and the women is considered to be a spiritual one; whereas the practical side, or the 'incarnation', is considered to be that of men. Thus, at the Mariapolis, the woman superior of the 'zone' will tell 'the story of the Ideal', or how the movement began; while her male equivalent will deliver talks on the 'works' of the movement, such as the small towns. Tasks are similarly apportioned between the sexes. The women run the Mariapolis Centres, carrying out the domestic tasks of catering and cleaning, while the men are in charge of the various editions of the *New City* magazine and the publishing houses. Businesses created internally demonstrate similar stereotyping. At Loppiano, the women specialized in handicrafts like batik and pottery, while the men concentrated on light industrial work. The work environments were, of course, strictly segregated.

While I was translating at the 1971 convention for married *focolarini*, I stayed at a luxurious and fragrant flower-covered villa near Frascati, which was then the world headquarters of the male *focolarini*. One evening, a married *focolarino* dropped me off there at the end of the day. Just before he left, he blurted out a thought which he obviously felt impelled to communicate: 'Stay faithful to your vows,' he said. 'I was a *focolarino* like you, but I didn't stay faithful. It's not worth it – just for those thirty seconds.' He drove off and left me shocked and repelled. Was this all that marriage was about?

Focolare claims to have given a new Christian dignity to marriage with the invention of the married *focolarini*. What they have really done is to confirm the traditional pre-conciliar concept of marriage as poor second-best to 'a vocation' – that is, to the celibate priesthood or the religious life. The movement rates celibacy more highly than marriage. The vocation of the married *focolarini* is a kind of hybrid of marriage and the religious life invented by Chiara Lubich for the Christian Democrat MP Igino Giordani. He had been a prominent Catholic layman in Italy for the best part of three decades when he met Chiara in 1948, yet still felt that, as a married man, he was a Catholic of second rank. He and Chiara were so convinced of this, in fact, that they felt a 'new vocation' was called for, something different from ordinary Christian marriage.

'I think it must have been Our Lady who invented this way,' said Chiara in 1963, '. . . since this people of ours is so deconsecrated, so desecrated, she must have thought of a way for married people and this is it.'

The corollary of this notion is the confirmation that marriage as such is an inferior state. Chiara makes no bones about it: '. . . the third branch [i.e. married *focolarini*], I see as a way (the third branch, that is, I'm not talking about married people) to become saints.'

Married people in general are therefore excluded from Christian perfection – unless they become *focolarini*, of course. Heavy demands are made on the married *focolarini*, who are regarded as individuals rather than as a couple. The men belong to the male Focolare community and the women to the female community. Although they live at home, they are expected to spend as much time as possible in the Focolare, including all the community meetings. They are expected to make a financial commitment to Focolare and to observe its rulings on sexual morality such as the ban on birth control. But most strange of all are the demands made on the emotions of the married *focolarini*.

'This is what the third branch is,' says Chiara: 'to have renounced or severed (because if we do not sever we are not followers of Christ) all natural affections, including that of one's wife, at least to have understood that God must take the place of one's wife and to love her . . . (even while still engaged) for God.' God must be taken to include one's commitment to the movement. If this sounds drastic, it is probably because Chiara Lubich has little time for romantic love: 'If it's Prince Charming you're after, just see where you'll end up,' she tells a group of women aspirants. With great delight, she describes the fate of celibate *focolarini* who run away to get married: 'After seven days of marriage (those who do it secretly, "popi" of the movement), they write me a little note: "Dearest Chiara, I am desperate, because, because . . ." And they usually write to me at night when she [!] is asleep. It always happens that way, I assure you. There was one just recently, after only twenty days. He's desperate.'

Her advice to these black sheep is: 'Now take up your cross on your shoulders.'

This new style of marriage appears to consist in reducing its value as much as possible, rather than in emphasizing the benefits of what is, after all, held by Catholics to be a sacrament. Chiara tells how her sister, the night before she was due to marry, came to see her, pleading on her knees to be allowed to become a celibate *focolarina*, while her fiancé was waiting outside, distraught. Chiara did not feel the girl had a celibate vocation and therefore advised her to go ahead with the marriage: 'I remember clearly telling her: "Don't say 'yes' to Paolo [the fiancé] – I actually denied it – but say 'yes' to the will of God."'

As Catholicism teaches that a couple administer the Sacrament of marriage to one another by their mutual agreement, years later Chiara Lubich had scruples over this incident of youthful zeal, wondering whether the marriage had even been a valid one. But the expectations of the married *focolarini* are not much different: God must replace emotions. Married *focolarini* are expected to enter the Focolare community permanently if their spouse dies. Despite the official line that the married *focolarini* are equal to the celibates, it is simply not the case. The unmarried *focolarini* hold the positions of real power and possess a mystique among other members that the married people do not. Among celibate members, there is a firm conviction that their state is superior. Visiting the London men's community, shortly after I had moved out, though before the definitive break, I remember the *capofocolare*, or leader, of the men's community ridiculing marriage and referring to those who marry as 'mad'. This was, to say the least, untactful as at that time I had actually been told to marry by my superiors in the movement.

In view of the scant importance given by Focolare to the emotional involvement of a married couple, it will come as no shock to learn that marriages were arranged between members. Of course, it is not unusual for people within social groups to marry, and many marriages that take place between Focolare members may well be spontaneous and loving. But I was aware of situations in which there was an element of coercion and – as far as the partners known to me are concerned – where those involved were going against their true feelings.

But the movement demanded more than mere spiritual martyrdom from its married *focolarini*. In addition to the ban on birth-control, sterilization, which goes against official Catholic teaching, is outlawed, too. At a New Families meeting in Rome in March 1994, I heard a husband and wife recount their distressing experience of how the wife has undergone four pregnancies and four caesarian sections, endangering her life each time. They described their fear and pain when they discovered each new pregnancy, and yet they have resisted medical advice and refused a sterilization. The husband, who is a doctor, described the last caesarian, for their fourth child, at which he was present. The surgeon suggested performing the sterilization right there and then, and the husband relented. But moments before it was about to be performed he changed his mind and withdrew his permission. While rejoicing in the children they have, the couple clearly live in dread of another pregnancy. Their distress was palpable. It might well be asked what kind of love the movement practises that it can demand this of its married members. Perhaps if it were not so dominated by celibates it would give more evidence of compassion.

A glaring omission from our syllabus at Loppiano was any kind of guidance on counselling or pastoral care. In fact, when I did a year's postgraduate teacher training, shortly after leaving Loppiano, I came across the word 'pastoral' for the first time and did not even know what it meant. Yet, as *focolarini*, we were constantly being approached for advice on a whole range of personal problems, many of them sexual. Not only did we know nothing of counselling techniques, but we were also totally ignorant of the subjects on which we were being questioned.

I remember being deeply disturbed and confused when a troubled young man, on his first encounter with the movement, told me of his traumatic homosexual experiences, which included a barbaric course of 'aversion therapy'. Worse still, we could not even discuss these matters with other members of the community or our superiors because one simply did not talk about such things. As far as the leaders of the movement were concerned, we needed no training in this area. The ostrich method was greatly favoured: if we did not know about problematic areas of human experience, hopefully we might never experience them for ourselves. But more important was the absolute conviction that in every situation, if we 'emptied ourselves' (that is, let our minds go blank), the Holy Spirit would inspire the perfect response.

A young Brazilian Gen in his mid-teens visited the English Mariapolis while I was responsible for the Gen in the United Kingdom and Ireland. He approached me before mass one morning in a state of extreme agitation. He told me he had masturbated the night before. Could he go to communion, or should he find a priest and confess? I found his admission deeply disturbing and I had no idea at all what advice to give. The only time I had ever heard masturbation mentioned in the movement was in the case of a *focolarino* who, constantly assailed by temptation to abuse himself, asked his companions in community to tie his hands behind his back. This did not seem a very practical solution in the public circumstances of the Mariapolis, so I mumbled a few platitudes instead.

Answers we were never short of. At Loppiano, for example, we were convinced that whoever stepped across the town's borders would magically find the solution to all his problems. That failure was out of the question is illustrated by a bizarre incident from my first year there. One afternoon, while I was sandpapering napkin-rings, one of our leaders ushered an Italian youth into our workshop. He was introduced to me as Bianco and must have been in his early twenties; he was from a nearby town and would be spending a few days with us. I was to be his 'guardian angel'.

There was something odd about the boy. Apart from the fact that he seemed reserved, he experienced great difficulty in getting the hang of the work, which was mindlessly simple. He plied me with endless questions on the techniques of sandpapering napkin-rings, and seemed to need constant reassurance. But I knew I must not judge, and spent the afternoon patiently demonstrating and correcting. After work we went to mass during which Bianco was devoutly attentive. At that time, my community lived in a chalet some distance away from the main men's district of Campogiallo. We would collect our food from the communal kitchens and drive in a minibus through the dark, unlit country roads to our chalet. Bianco was to dine with us.

The mass seemed to have roused him from his semi-comatose state, and during the journey he grew increasingly more agitated. He began to talk about a spiritual book that was popular at that time, *The God Who Comes* by Carlo Carretto. 'He is coming,' he whispered to me. 'God is coming.' He turned to the driver. 'Stop the bus!' he called. In a flash, he was out on the road and could be seen in the glare of the headlights, running away from us, gesticulating wildly. It began to dawn on me that there was something seriously wrong. I leaped out and caught up with him.

'God is coming,' he cried to me. 'Let's go and meet Him.'

He grabbed my hand, in which I was clutching the keys of our house. Snatching them, he threw the keys into the shadowy vineyards. 'Leave the others. Come with me. I am going to meet God, God who is coming.' He held my wrist in a vice-like grasp and took off again with me in tow. After about half a mile, he let me go and disappeared into the darkness. 'He is coming! I am going to meet him! The God who comes!' His cries echoed among the hills and slowly grew fainter.

By this time his parents, who must have been still in Loppiano, had been alerted. They managed to find him, and he was hauled off in a straitjacket. No-one had thought to mention to those of us who were looking after him that Bianco was suffering from an extreme form of religious mania. It was taken for granted that his problems would magically disappear. Loppiano was probably the last place on earth they should have brought him.

Needless to say, this incident was quickly forgotten. We revelled in success, but ignored failure. It never occurred to us that we should refer anyone to experts such as counsellors or doctors. We would certainly never refer anyone to a priest outside the movement. The 'Ideal' was the answer.

The trouble was, as I was to discover only too painfully later, the great and the good of the movement were no better prepared than we were, although far more ready with sweeping and misguided solutions.

That Focolare's irresponsible and misguided 'pastoral care' can seriously damage and almost destroy the lives of those who are completely at its mercy was demonstrated by the case of Valentin. He left his country in South America for Loppiano in the mid-sixties, when he was eighteen. At that time, he did not intend to be a full-time *focolarino*, but a volunteer who makes a lesser commitment, lives in his own home and is free to marry. The euphoria of Loppiano, then in the first flush of foundation, and the pressure of being one in a group of young men all of whom intended to become *focolarini* – the training was orientated exclusively in that direction – led him to believe that perhaps he was called to be one, too. At twenty-one, he left Loppiano for a community in a European city. Away from that rarefied atmosphere, plunged into a high-pressure lifestyle of daily work and missionary activity, and exposed to the influences of a modern city, feelings began to re-emerge which he thought had disappeared or at least been overpowered by his new way of life.

From his early teens, he had experienced homosexual urges, but he had never acted on them. When he decided to choose a life of celibacy, he believed that chapter of his life to be closed. It was not. He felt strongly drawn to meet others like himself. But, living in an environment where the subject of sex and sexuality was taboo, and now having taken temporary vows of chastity, he was torn and confused. He outlined this situation to his superiors, who advised him to 'love Jesus forsaken'.

On a visit to his 'zone', Chiara Lubich met privately with each *focolarino* to talk of their spiritual progress. Valentin, convinced that the foundress would have the solution to his problem, decided to unburden himself with her. She appeared to be understanding. She even spoke of her own spiritual trials. He could not help his feelings, she told him. She decided, however, that he should leave the zone, where he had now been for three years, and return for a period to Loppiano. Here he should have psychiatric help. She made one other remark that was to remain fixed in his mind for the next twenty years. She also gave strict instructions that he was not to discuss his 'problem' with anyone else in the movement (this was standard practice) and urged him to write to her at any time. Bearing in mind the semi-divine status of the foundress within the movement, Valentin was understandably encouraged and reassured. Perhaps his problems were at an end.

Valentin found Loppiano a changed place: several courses had come and gone since his time, so he knew no-one there. The village was used as a kind of open prison for *focolarini* with 'difficulties': those who could not be assimilated into the small Focolare communities could be dumped there and forgotten. They would find it harder to run away from such a remote spot, had they a mind to. Not that that was a possibility for Valentin, who was penniless and an ocean away from home. With its school for *focolarini*, Loppiano was principally for new blood, not for failures.

Valentin felt even more isolated and depressed here than he had in the Focolare community. He was sent to a psychiatrist trusted by the movement. The bad news was that Valentin was sick; the good news was that he could be cured. The doctor traced his 'problem' to having been 'interfered with' as an adolescent. The recommended treatment was drastic: a 'sleep cure'. Over a period of several months, he was to take sleeping pills at night, rise in the morning, have breakfast and then take another dose of pills and sleep all day. The theory was that sleep would blot out the childhood memories and with them the homosexual 'tendencies'.

Thus began a painful – and expensive – twenty-year pilgrimage from one psychiatrist to another, searching for a cure.

When the 'sleep cure' did not work, Valentin was sent to other psychiatrists, including one who had treated Chiara Lubich herself. The problems were only aggravated. He began to suffer from depression. Overcome by irrational fears, he even believed that he was possessed. The superior of the *focolarini* men at that time, Giorgio Marchetti, known as Fede ('Faith') in the movement, decided that as Valentin was making no progress he should be sent back to his home 'zone' in South America. Valentin was stunned by Fede's smug and patronizing parting comment: 'Well, we've done all we could for you.'

He did not return to his own city, but to another one nearby. Here, Valentin did not live in the Focolare community but as an 'extern' *focolarino*. Accommodation was provided for him by Focolare in a flat-share with another 'extern'. Focolare continued to pay for psychiatric help aimed at 'curing' his homosexuality. Now that he was no longer living full-time in an environment of the movement, he had his first sexual encounters. The *focolarino* priest who headed the 'zone' advised that casual encounters could be forgiven but he must not on any account become involved in a relationship as this would put his sin on a permanent basis.

One evening on his way home, Valentin visited the Focolare. He was taken aside by the leader, who told him that there had been a problem in his flat. With characteristic secrecy, they had hidden from him the fact that his room-mate was a schizophrenic; it was essential for his equilibrium that he take regular medication. If Valentin had known this, he could have kept a check on him. As it was, the room-mate had gone berserk, smashed up the flat and destroyed the few possessions Valentin had managed to accumulate since he left Focolare, including the one he treasured most – a typewriter. The incident symbolized the clean break with the past that was long overdue. Gradually, Valentin began to take control of his life. He had experience in translating and took a degree in languages. His ties with Focolare were attenuated. Perhaps it was also time to take a fresh look at his homosexuality as, after years of psychotherapy, the famous cure was a long time in coming.

An opportunity for a new beginning presented itself when, in the mid-eighties, he was offered a post in the United States. It was a chance of financial freedom at a time when his country was going through a severe depression. Finally the day-to-day contact with Focolare which had held him in thrall for so long was severed. Maybe the distance from family and old friends would allow the freedom to find a relationship. However, although he began to see a more understanding psychologist in the United States, he could not shake off the influence of the movement. In particular, he still felt tied to Chiara and continued to write to her, receiving an occasional reply. This dependence, suggested by her – 'do not speak to anyone else' – was paradoxical in view of the fact that, as we have seen, she was virtually inaccessible in person or by post because of the tight coterie surrounding her. Above all, he was haunted by a remark she had made to him in that conversation almost fifteen years before, when, having assured him that he should not blame himself for his feelings, that he could not be held responsible for his orientation as such, Chiara had added: 'However, I would prefer you to be knocked down by a car than ever to commit a homosexual act.'

Try as he might, and despite the help of a therapist, Valentin could not shake off his obsession with these words, nor the command that he should not form a relationship. The only alternative was promiscuity. In 1986 Valentin discovered himself to be HIV-positive.

Eight years later, Valentin is still healthy and living in a long-term relationship. His HIV status helped him to escape from the pervading influence of Focolare. In 1992 he spoke again with the *focolarino* priest who heads the movement in his country. When told of Valentin's HIV status and his relationship, the priest took a much milder line than before, encouraging him to go to confession with a sympathetic priest, and urging him not to avoid receiving the Sacrament. But this pastoral concern was pathetically little and far too late.

Focolare's crude approach to the question of homosexuality can still be seen in a recent book of questions and answers on moral questions written by the same Don Gino Rocca who asked me to translate his talk on birth control to the married *focolarini* in 1971.[1] There is still talk of 'curing' homosexuality, a concept relinquished by most psychiatrists over twenty-five years ago. Rocca distinguishes between two types of homosexual. There are ' "occasional homosexuals", whose behaviour, as the word suggests, derives from a mistaken education, from habits picked up, from bad example, from ideological influence, or else from the external environment (boarding school, barracks, prisons etc.). As it is linked to external conditions, it can be cured quite easily.' Then, according to Rocca, there are 'exclusive homosexuals' who are victims of a 'pathological constitution': 'Being linked to deep internal conditionings, [this type] is judged by the specialists "incurable", in the sense that the cure is much more difficult, but not impossible.'

Even the Vatican in its recent homophobic documents has not gone so far as to suggest 'cures' for gays. This could well be because it is better-informed and knows that few psychiatrists today still give credence to this idea. The eminent Catholic psychiatrist Jack Dominian observed in his 1987 book *Sexual Integrity*: 'Vogues of treatment come and go but there is no generally acknowledged way of reversing homosexual trends.' He adds a comment that Rocca might do well to ponder: 'Indeed, when the social, legal and moral pressures recede, most exclusive homosexuals have no wish to change their orientation.'[2]

---

[1] Don Gino Rocca, *Conscience, Freedom and Morality*, Rome: Città Nuova, 1992.
[2] London: Darton, Longman & Todd, 1987.

Rocca's analysis of homosexuality reveals the movement's dualistic view of human nature, which they divide into natural and supernatural. Focolare would claim that 'unity' – that is, 'supernatural love' – even between the same sex, is on a higher plane than 'human' love, such as that between husband and wife. We have seen how romantic love in marriage is played down. Yet now we are told that marriage 'between man and woman [is] the fullest and deepest communion that exists, on the natural level'.

That 'on the natural level' is the essential proviso. Clearly, in the Focolare perspective, human nature can be compartmentalized to allow for different levels of 'fullest and deepest communion'. Rocca goes on to point out the lack of the essential – in the Catholic view – procreative aspect in homosexuality. Thus, 'The homosexual relationship is radically deprived of, or rather it contradicts, these two essential components of the love-dialogue intended by God'. Just to underline this point, Rocca adds: 'In fact, this is confirmed by the serious limitations that, according to the observations of experts, characterize homosexual friendships.'

Completely contradicting the Focolare line, Jack Dominian believes that: 'For many male homosexuals the effort to form and sustain a stable relationship can be the most vigorous effort towards maturity, wholeness and holiness . . . I would like to switch the major pastoral effort towards stable relationships.'[1]

Incidentally, it seems that for Don Gino Rocca, like Queen Victoria, lesbians do not exist, as they are never specifically mentioned in his book.

One of the principal aims of Neocatechumenate is to bring the lives of married members into line with its own vision of marriage. This vision was put to me very succinctly by an Italian catechist, part of a missionary family based in Washington, DC: 'For us marriage means two enemies living together.'

This may sound a harsh, even cynical, view; but it is the conviction of all the married members I have met. Each has made the identical comment: 'This Way saved my marriage.' Is it possible that these men and women, most of them practising Catholics when they met NC, were all in such an acute state of marital disarray?

In the first scrutiny, NC members are taught that marriage, wife,

[1]op. cit.

family, along with job and possessions, are idols. Kiko Arguello says: 'I'm telling you this: Look here – *the first myth Christianity destroys is the family*, which is a tremendous myth, when the family is a religion.'[1] In practice, as we have seen, this means putting NC first, even when children have to be neglected.

The aspect of the NC message that puts the greatest strain on families is the total condemnation of birth control and the encouragement to have as many children as the Lord sends. Contrary to the teaching of the Catholic Church, the movement forbids even 'natural' methods of birth control using the so-called 'safe period'. Kiko's writings are filled with vigorous condemnations of contemporary married couples who use birth control so that they can give themselves up to the unbridled pursuit of selfish pleasure. 'It amazed me when I was living in Paris', Arguello relates, 'that you don't see children at all. I didn't see any children in the district. Having children is a disaster. They all use the Pill.'[2]

Elsewhere in the catechesis, he cites a horrific suicide pact of an elderly Roman couple which he had read about in a newspaper. Not one to miss a lurid illustration, he gives the grisly details of how the husband had first slashed his wife's wrists as she lay on the bed and then, having covered himself with the blood-sodden blanket, had jumped from the top floor of their apartment-block. They left a brief note of explanation, saying they were 'Alone, old and sick'. Arguello then proceeds to give what appears to be his own gloss on these events, blaming the tragedy on the fact that in their youth the couple had decided not to have children but to have fun instead, frequenting nudist camps in Yugoslavia.

Catechists are always introduced with a reference to the size of their family. But, for many married couples in the NC Way, the decision to be 'open to life' was their biggest hurdle.

Renato, one of the first catechists of the movement, based at St Francesca Cabrini parish in Rome, had two children when he and his wife realized they had to stop using birth control. The moment of truth for him was when he heard Kiko declare that 'You cannot say "Our Father, who art in heaven" if you do not believe he is a Father to your children. Of all the children he may wish you to bear.' After this the couple had two more surviving children. 'It is

[1] *Primo scrutinio battesimale*, p. 179.
[2] op. cit., p. 181.

not easy having all these children,' Renato admits. 'My wife and I both work, but it is still very difficult. One woman in our community has eleven.'

Offspring born to members after the decision to be 'open to life' are known as 'the children of the community'. As in the case of the *focolarini*, the ban on birth control extends to sterilizations even in cases where the mother's life is in danger.

One of the most extraordinary examples of the lengths to which this teaching is taken occurred in Sacred Hearts parish in Cheltenham. Before entering the NC community, one couple, who already had two children, had decided that the husband should have a vasectomy as for health reasons his wife had been advised not to risk another pregnancy. Great pressure was put on this man to have his vasectomy reversed. His eight-year-old son was even prompted to ask his father at the community Eucharist why he was disobeying God in this matter. Eventually, the man capitulated, and the community collected the £800 necessary for the operation. It was successful, and his wife was delivered of a third child by caesarian section. Other members of the parish were taken aback at the interference in what had obviously been a carefully considered choice and one which is ultimately the responsibility of the couple concerned.

Husbands and wives who join the community separately are strongly pressurized to recruit their spouse. If a husband or wife has not been joined by his or her partner at the stage of the NC Way known as the *Traditio*, instead of their being sent out to evangelize two by two in the houses of the parish the lone husband or wife is sent home to evangelize his or her spouse and is debarred from any more NC meetings except on special occasions. If they succeed in converting their spouse by their intensive efforts, which apparently many do, they are allowed to return. If not, they are permanently exiled from the community. As this occurs after eight years of membership, the effect on those who are ejected is devastating.

All community members who do not become priests or nuns are pressured into marriage. It is alleged that arranged marriages take place in NC, as they do in Focolare. Young men of the communities are told to 'seek among the daughters of Israel'. Marriages must take place within the same community, not even between members of different NC communities within the one parish.

NC claims to have launched a new development for the Catholic Church: the missionary families. Married ministers of other Christian denominations do, of course, take their wives and families with them to missionary territories; but the way the NC families are selected is unusual – and questionable. At a large annual meeting which takes place at the movement's international centre of Porto San Giorgio in Italy, in September every year, families who have reached the necessary stage of the Way are asked to stand up and volunteer for missionary service. The volunteer families are then invited to a second gathering on 29 December, the Feast of the Holy Family. Here, their names are put into a basket and drawn at random in a kind of raffle. Out of 300 names, between fifty and a hundred families are chosen each year. There are scenes of hysterical joy as the candidates' lucky numbers come up. Since 1986, the Pope himself has presented each of these families with their 'missionary cross' at a special ceremony before an audience of up to 10,000 NC members. It is the proud boast of these families, to bishops and laity alike, that they have been 'sent by the Pope'.

The randomness of this method of selection is troubling, as it offers little or no consideration of the suitability of the step for the numerous children involved. The choice of location for the missionary work is also worrying from the children's point of view – areas chosen are 'de-christianized urban areas' like the suburbs of Amsterdam, the South Bronx district of New York, the South of Washington, DC, a shanty town in Yokohama, near Tokyo. An example often quoted by NC is the fact that a number of families have been sent to the Russian towns of Boibruisk and Gomel, where, as they tell you, no-one wants to go because they are so close to Chernobyl. It could well be asked what sort of parents would possibly want to expose their children to the potentially fatal dangers of those places.

Most of the missionary families face enormous problems. Work must be found – although they do receive financial help from their communities back home. They have the additional problem of the language – families are not chosen for their skills in this area. In territories like China and Japan, where mastering the language is particularly hard for Westerners, it may be years before they can begin to exercise any sort of useful ministry. Although they are hushed up, there are reports of a number of missionary families who have returned to Italy, having undergone traumatic experiences, especially with their children.

According to the public statements of the movement, NC families are 'called by the bishop' of the place to which they are sent, but this does not always appear to be the case. An Italian archbishop counters that 'the majority of the bishops in the dioceses where the Neocatechumenals go don't want them, because their presence, despite their protestations to the contrary, serves no purpose – in fact it's counter-productive. But they make the Pope believe who knows what!'

Not surprisingly, NC's meddling in the private lives of members has led to disaster in a number of instances. In at least two cases in Britain 'community' marriages have been annulled by the Catholic Church only two years after they were contracted. The effect of the movement on existing marriages can be catastrophic. Officially, NC promotes marriage and is fanatically opposed to divorce. In reality, when it suits its interests, it will actively encourage marriage break-up – a form of 'NC divorce'. Two cases of families in Rome are particularly bizarre, and are worth looking at in some detail.

Giorgio Finazzi–Agro and his wife Fidalma were married in 1966 when he was thirty. They have four children: the eldest, Lorenzo, born in 1967, who has psychological problems; the second, Maria-Angela, two years younger; and, after a gap of seven years, twin boys, Antonio and Francesco. They live in Rome. Although they had the small ups and downs of every couple – mainly caused by the problems of the eldest son – it was a happy marriage and, when Giorgio returned from short periods away from home for work purposes, his wife and children would give him a warm welcome.

Giorgio's work as a geologist was interrupted by a period of unemployment in the early eighties. His wife was supportive; and, if anything, this period brought them closer together. She was also active in the local parish of San Clemente and had enrolled in a course for catechists in the hope of being able to teach religion at middle-school level. In 1983 Giorgio finally found work with the Italian oil company AGIP, which required a move to Milan. His wife was reluctant to do this because it would interfere with the treatment Lorenzo was receiving at that time. She accepted that Giorgio should take the job, however, and they agreed that he would spend the week in Milan, commuting to Rome at weekends.

Despite these drawbacks, Giorgio settled happily into his new job and, although he was now approaching fifty, his career prospects had never looked better.

About this time the former parish priest, whom Giorgio had much admired, went into retirement, and was replaced by Don Carlo Quieti. Giorgio was not as impressed by the new priest: in his frequent visits to their house Don Quieti was often angry and aggressive. Then he brought in Neocatechumenate. Giorgio only learned this when Fidalma told him she would like to join the first community that was about to be formed. Knowing nothing about the movement, her husband had no objections; but he made some enquiries among his Catholic colleagues in Milan, who informed him that the movement was not highly thought of in Cardinal Martini's diocese of Lombardy.

One evening, at about 11 o'clock, he rang home from Milan. He was taken aback when the children told him that his wife was still out at the parish. As the twins were only seven at the time and Lorenzo needed constant supervision because of his illness, Giorgio was understandably alarmed. He rang the parish priest and demanded to speak with his wife. Don Quieti informed him that this would not be possible because she was in prayer. Giorgio told him that if he did not fetch her immediately he would return home the following day. Eventually Fidalma came to the phone, and he asked her to return home to take charge of the children. She angrily refused, and Giorgio decided that indeed he would return to Rome.

He went to see Monsignor Appignanesi, then vicar general of the diocese of Rome, who reprimanded Giorgio for his impulsiveness and warned him that, knowing NC, his family problems would be common knowledge by now. Giorgio returned to see him a second time – bringing Fidalma with him; and, after a private conversation with Monsignor Appignanesi, she consented to leave the community for a while on the understanding that, if Giorgio moved back to Rome, they could enter a community together. He applied for and obtained a transfer to Rome with a subsidary of AGIP, for whom he still works today.

Meanwhile, Lorenzo's behaviour was becoming more disturbed; and so, on the advice of a doctor relation of Fidalma, they decided to permit a course of electro-shock therapy which was the only treatment they had not yet tried. The clinic where this was to take place suggested to Fidalma that she should stay there with her son during the therapy, to give him support. During this very difficult period for her, Neocatechumenals, including a number of catechists, paid frequent visits to the clinic.

When Lorenzo was discharged, Fidalma decided not to return home but moved in with her mother instead, taking the children with her. Giorgio began to fear for his marriage. He contacted a priest from another parish to act as a mediator. A meeting with Don Quieti, his wife's parish priest, turned into a slanging match. To Giorgio's astonishment, Quieti accused him of subjecting his son to the barbarism of electro-shock therapy and of trying to nave his wife committed as well. While Giorgio was still reeling from this, Quieti also informed him that his wife had the right to a separation on the grounds of the doctrine of St Paul regarding the pagan husband who will not allow the wife to practise her faith – a regular recourse of Neocatechumenate in the case of a reluctant spouse.

With his back to the wall, Giorgio agreed to join the NC community, seeing no other way to save his marriage. He began to attend the meetings, and within a couple of weeks his wife returned home. Giorgio was allowed to attend the *convivence* of the first 'passage', which was the stage his wife's community had reached, on condition that he join an earlier community at a later date.

> The memory of that stay is still painful for me . . . the catechists imposed readings, "echoes" and catechesis for twelve hours a day . . . long periods of silence followed by group meetings of four or five people in which each of us had to tell the others his temporal and spiritual problems . . . promises to give possessions away to the poor . . . the lack of attention to the children (ours were twelve then) who were left alone all day and when they disturbed us were told off and sent away.

His chief objection was the emphasis on group sharing: there was no respect for 'the intimacy of the soul – everything was brought into the public domain' with, he felt, 'a strong encouragement towards hypocrisy'. He was bothered, too, by the insistence on secrecy: they were not to tell anything of what they had heard to others – even those in the more junior communities. He also felt pressurized by the constant enquiries as to 'how he felt – almost like an invitation to autosuggestion; that I should feel different from the way I always had'.

Giorgio decided to withdraw from NC; and within a few days his wife left him again, accusing him of harassment.

In an attempt to resolve what he felt was a hopeless situation, Giorgio decided to appeal to the highest authorities: the Pope and the Vatican. Surely at that level he would find concern for the sacrosanct institution of Catholic marriage.

To the Pope, he wrote on 11 November 1987:

> I love my wife and I believe in the indissolubility of marriage, but it has been indicated by the parish priest of the . . . [Neocatechumenal] community that my wife has the right of separation because living with me disturbs her to the point of making her offend God . . . I have sought help within the structures of the Church but everyone has advised, for reasons of prudence and good sense, that I should just pray and accept the will of God . . . That is right: but I want to implore the help of God's Vicar on earth because, though I accept the Will of the Most High [God], my spiritual situation is still one of uncertainty.

The letter received no acknowledgement. Apparently it is easier to issue glib condemnations of the Evil of Divorce than to help save a single real-life Catholic marriage.

At the same time Giorgio wrote to Bishop Paul-Josef Cordes, the Pope's own appointee *ad personam* to NC, asking him to intervene directly with the NC founder, Kiko Arguello, because, he points out:

> I am really discouraged because, after virtually five months of separation from my wife and my children (who, because they are young, have followed their mother), no-one has interested themselves in our case and everyone is nervous about seriously taking the matter up with the Community. For my part, I am ready to respect my wife and her ideas; but, while having forgiven the rashness of the people involved, I don't feel like going back into the San Clemente Community.

Bishop Cordes replied on 30 November 1987 expressing concern and promising action:

> I thank you for your letter. It is superfluous to express my compassion for the painful circumstances you are living through . . . I have contacted the responsibles of the NC movement to highlight the problem, which I also intend to bring up with Kiko Arguello. This should be possible before Christmas.

Although no immediate solution was forthcoming, wheels were set in motion. Giorgio remained in telephone contact with the bishop's office. On 29 February 1988, however, he wrote to Cordes strongly denying the claim relayed to him by Signorina Federici, the bishop's secretary, that his wife's parish priest, Don Quieti, had contacted him during the period of separation in an attempt to work out a reconciliation. 'If you require confirmation of this,' Giorgio writes, 'I am prepared to meet the parish priest in question in front of witnesses of your choice.' Quieti did not take up the challenge.

Giorgio wrote to Cordes yet again on 16 April 1988, requesting a personal meeting with Kiko Arguello: 'I would like Signor Arguello to confirm that it is not the desire of the Community to alienate its members from the obligations connected with the Sacrament of Matrimony and the serious commitment of the movement to a catechesis of the family . . .' He pointed out that his concern was not only prompted by his own marital experiences but also by what he witnessed in the meetings of the first community of San Clemente: 'In those gatherings I was able to observe how the obedience and formal submission to the Presbyter and the leaders were given priority over the obligations linked to the choice of marriage (care and love for children and spouse).' He added that an NC catechist, Eugenio Frediani, had telephoned him the day before his legal separation and assured him that everything possible would be done to arrange the desired meeting with Arguello. The purpose of this call seems to have been to silence Giorgio's appeals to Cordes. The promised encounter never materialized.

In May 1988, Signorina Federici from Bishop Cordes' office advised Giorgio in a telephone conversation to contact a certain Don Dino Rossi. As he was given no contact number or address and was unable to trace the priest, he sent a telegram supplying his own details to be forwarded to Don Dino. There was no reply to this telegram. In fact there was a total silence from the NC camp until early 1989.

By this time, as the legal separation had taken place and Fidalma had been awarded the matrimonial home, Giorgio had rented a furnished room. He was experiencing a period of calm and had succeeded in adjusting to his new situation. Then Eugenio Frediani contacted Giorgio once again – apparently through the intervention of Cordes – with the assurance that he wanted to restore the unity of his family.

Giorgio was suspicious, but at the request of his children he agreed to return home. He was attending another Rome parish where the agreeable atmosphere had been of great help to Lorenzo, and his wife began to go there with them. But, although she had agreed not to attend NC meetings, she continued to do so, and his daughter Maria-Angela also joined one of the NC communities.

Now one of his younger sons, Antonio, refused to do any homework in an attempt to force his father to allow him to attend the junior seminary and begin studying for the priesthood – this, too, at the instigation of NC. Eventually Giorgio gave in, 'to the rejoicing of his mother and sister – and of course the Neo-catechumenals'. One by one, the whole family was being drawn more deeply into the movement. In a desperate attempt to prevent Antonio's twin, Francesco, from becoming involved with NC, he wrote to the auxiliary bishop of North Rome, Monsignor Boccaccio. Knowing that in NC parishes the sacrament of confirmation is regarded as the moment in which young people enter a community on their own behalf, following a preparatory course given by an NC catechist, Giorgio requested that his son should not be confirmed at San Clemente's. The bishop did not reply.

The atmosphere at home was strained. Giorgio became aware of frantic whispered conversations at night between his wife and daughter, who knew about his letter to the bishop and his determination that Francesco should not enter the community. A few days later it exploded. When Lorenzo tried to attack his mother, Giorgio stepped in and vigorously defended her.

'Call the police,' Fidalma screamed to Maria-Angela. But it was her husband and not her son that she wanted them to restrain. The incident blew up into a full-scale row as Giorgio tried to snatch the phone from his daughter's hand. At this point he realized that, under the circumstances, any attempt at reconciliation was doomed to fail. His position in the family had become untenable. He packed his bags once more and left. A few days later, his sister received a telegram from Fidalma's lawyer forbidding him to return home.

Since this final break-up in 1990, Giorgio's relationship with his children has declined, although he sees them occasionally. His wife only telephones when she has a request. Lorenzo's condition has worsened, although it had stabilized during the period when Giorgio returned home. He is now convinced that his only hope is to find a way, with the help of the Church, to convince his family that Neocatechumenate is not orthodox Catholicism.

'All this mess', Giorgio believes, 'has been caused, or at least accentuated by, the influence of the Neocatechumenals who have taught my family, not the true Christian faith, characterized by an intimate relationship with God, but a fanatical and superstitious form of religion in which the public aspect and therefore hypocrisy dominates.'

There are some remarkable similarities in the case of Augusto Faustini, also from Rome. Over Christmas 1989, he staged a hunger strike outside the NC parish church of San Tito to protest against his wife's allegiance to NC. He believed that NC was systematically destroying his marriage and family life.

In early 1984, Augusto, then aged thirty-nine, and his wife Rosina had entered a Neocatechumenate community at San Tito parish on the advice of their local bishop Monsignor Bona, who was a close friend. They were hoping the experience would help their marriage which, after twenty years and with three boys in their late teens, was passing through a difficult period. The couple were both devout Catholics, and Augusto had belonged to a number of mainstream church groups including Catholic Action and, as an expression of his religious convictions, held office in the church-backed Christian Democrat Party.

Augusto was initially well disposed to the new group: 'We went to their first lectures (because that is the only way to describe meetings in which the only one who speaks is the person who is giving the explanations). I was relaxed about it, because the parish had welcomed them and therefore was a guarantee that they were genuine.'

But Augusto rapidly changed his mind, coming to the conclusion that NC was a sect. Like Giorgio Finazzi-Agro, he later wrote to the Pope, describing his disillusionment:

We did not know, and none of those invited knew, that by taking part in those meetings we would have to commit, for about twenty years, our evenings, our nights, from two to four a week, and often Sundays and weekends! We did not know, and no-one knew, that once we had entered that group there would be a sort of brainwashing process, psychological pressures which would make flight from that strange association difficult if not impossible.

Augusto went on to describe how, despite its protests that it is not a 'group or association', in fact NC is a ' "Secret sect", since they are manipulated from above, through a pyramidal hierarchy that is rigorously kept secret, and that reaches up to "him": Kiko Arguello! He has established how you are, how you sit, how you sing, how and what you play, how you pray, how you confess, how you take communion, how you read the sacred Scriptures. Making clear that anyone who does not do all that is lost in error.'

Augusto was increasingly repelled by all this, but his wife's reaction was quite different. He was horrified to find his marriage falling apart as Rosina increasingly fell under the influence of the movement. He later wrote to Monsignor Giuseppe Mani, auxiliary bishop of Rome East:

As you are the bishop of the family, you should look into the devastating effects that one of the concepts hammered home by the Neocatechumenals has on marriages: 'Woman, you must love God alone, you must love your husband like any other brother in Christ. If you are in love with your husband, he becomes an idol for you! The woman who is in love is not a true Christian – in this case she must learn to hate her husband.'

Rosina spent long hours outside the home, several evenings a week and also at weekends. She also refused to take part in any other Catholic services, apart from those of the Neocatechumenals. She refused to enter a church that was not theirs and would no longer take part in family prayers. Although their three sons were initially opposed to the movement, her insistence gradually wore them down and one by one they joined the communities and found partners there.

'Can a boy not yet twenty-two', Augusto says of his second son, 'resist if he is thrown into the arms of a Neocatechumenal woman much older and more experienced than himself and is driven by the "free love" of the Neocatechumenals? Because that's what happened.'

When, at one stage, owing to arguments over the movement, the two eldest boys beat their father, his wife excused them, saying that parents are always in the wrong and forced Augusto to apologize to them.

Although they continued living together, the marriage of Augusto and Rosina had completely broken down. They slept and even ate apart. His hunger strike produced a brief reaction. Rosina stopped attending NC meetings for some weeks until, without warning or explanation, she disappeared from home for three days. Even their sons had no idea where she had gone. 'I managed to trace one of those who call themselves catechists (Dr Piermarini). After I pleaded with him, and he could see I was desperate, his conscience pricked him and he took me to Santa Marinella where I found my wife who, only after much insistence, agreed to come home.'

After this she demanded that Augusto should move out of the matrimonial home, but he refused. On one occasion, however, it seemed that Rosina had had a change of heart. Augusto described this bizarre incident in his letter to the Pope:

> Allow me, Holy Father, to share an intimate detail; it is necessary in order to understand to what extent this sect conditions its initiates. One Christmas my wife came to me – she wanted to be with her husband. I was happy because it seemed that our family unity had been restored. Hardly! Afterwards my wife confessed that it had happened during her most fertile period. She had only done it so that she could conceive and have another child (number four) and make a good impression on the prolific Neocatechumenals.

To Augusto's relief, this ruse was unsuccessful.

Besides his letter to the Pope, Augusto also sent detailed accounts of his case to Cardinal Ratzinger, the cardinal-vicars of Rome (first Ugo Poletti and later Camillo Ruini), the five auxiliary bishops of Rome, the relevant NC catechists and the parish priest of San

Leonardo Murialdo, Padre Paiusco. When he visited the last to ask for his help in reuniting the family, Augusto was told: 'Your family is fine the way it is. First come the Neocatechumenals, then the family. Be satisfied the way things are. That poor priest has invented "Catholic divorce"!'

Bishop Bona, who had introduced the family to the movement in the first place, gave his authoritative confirmation of this view: 'My dear Augusto, either you join the Neocatechumenals or you will have to separate! But you are the one who must choose; she is Neocatechumenal.'

The fact that the Catholic Church's authority reaches into the bedrooms of the faithful is one of the principal sources of its immense power. Or was. Today, its teachings on sex are a main cause of mass defections, especially among the young who find it impossible to reconcile their experience with what appear to be outdated and unyielding moral strictures. Others who remain in the Church ignore or bend the rules. The hierarchy can no longer use sexual guilt to manipulate the laity.

But in the movements this power is still a living force. Every aspect of CL members' lives has to be submitted to the competent authorities. Unlike Catholic Action and most other Catholic associations in Italy, CL has always been mixed – a fact which gave it a doubtful reputation among its opponents. There is very little reference to sexual morality in the movement's official writings. It professes itself opposed to 'moralism', but this certainly does not betoken broadmindedness. In fact it is said that the original version of Pope John Paul's encyclical on morality, *Veritatis splendor*, on which he was advised by CL members Rocco Buttiglione and Monsignor Angelo Scola, was so Draconian that it had to be toned down before publication.

Like all CL terminology, 'moralism' has a coded sense. It refers to a secular morality which, by its very nature, is relative. The only true morality for CL is that dictated by the encounter with the Christian Event; that is, with Christ in history; that is, with Christ in the movement. Even the emotional life of members has to be submitted to the authority figures who dominate CL. If a young member is attracted to another, or a couple are drawn together, this burgeoning feeling has to be revealed to a priest so that it can be interpreted, directed and recognized. The crucial factor is that the relationship should be integrated into the group, 'offered to the community', rather than being a motive for distraction or withdrawal, for this would lessen the power of the community over the individual.

An ex-member tells of an occasion when, during a CL 'summer camp' it was discovered that some couples had had sexual relations and a kind of public witch-hunt ensued:

> When a priest, during a famous sermon, declared that we should behave towards one another as brothers, that even a kiss was to be avoided because it was a stimulation of the senses, for some of us it made no difference: we had already known for ages about those couples and we continued to discuss them without inhibition. For others it was a real trauma. There was one guy who certainly had not gone beyond the petting stage with his girlfriend who began to confess and repent saying he had committed a grave sin.[1]

Clear public moralistic pronouncements or denouncements are not CL's style. Their rigid moral views can be interpreted, however, in the tortuous and obscure condemnations to be found in their publications, following the dictum: 'Never use one word when a thousand will do.'

In the February 1994 edition of *Tracce*, the movement's internal magazine in Italy, a leading article attacks what it calls 'the age of feeling' (*l'epoca del feeling*). Our times, it states,

> are times in which the only theoretical and practical criterion in the lives of the majority seems to be *satisfaction*, the attainment of a 'pleasure in living' much sought though grasped only fleetingly and in an illusory manner. In the name of such satisfaction, relationships are entered into or ended, preferences are established, small refuges (or large ones for those who are able) are built against stress and the turbulence of daily life.

In their writings, CL members take perverse delight in being arcane and provocative. This article accomplishes both when it borrows a term from the right-wing Catholic philosopher Augusto

---

[1] Piera Sera, *L'adoloscente sublimato*, Florence: Guaraldi, 1978.

del Noce, one of CL's favourites, who in a letter written in 1984 referred to 'gay nihilism in the two senses that it is carefree . . . and that it has its symbol in homosexuality'. Thus, in the *Tracce* article, the 'age of feeling' is dubbed 'the gay nothingness'. Only CL could couch its narrow-minded moralizing in terms of high-flown ideologizing.

After proselytizing, the second most effective way of building a religion or sect is by physical propagation – something at which the movements are highly skilled, given their ban on birth control and their penchant for large families. The founders see in the offspring of members the future of the organization – *their* future. This message is hammered home to their followers: if everyone they meet is fair game for evangelization, this is especially true for those over whom they have absolute power – their children. Not one must be lost. They ensure this in two ways: by shielding them from the evil influence of the world and by starting the process of indoctrination as young as possible.

In 1967, Chiara Lubich launched the Gen, or New Generation movement, the second generation of Focolare. Many of the initial members were the children of married *focolarini*, volunteers and adherents of the movement. Certainly most of the leaders in the early years came from Focolare families. Since founding the Gen, Chiara has taken a keen interest in passing her doctrine on to them directly, frequently attending their international congresses in Rome and meeting with them on her trips round the world. She has attended all the international Genfests in Rome, some of the largest events Focolare has organized. 'You . . . are and represent the dearest, most delicate and precious element that the Lord has kept for himself in the great One Work [of Mary],' she told a group of Gen leaders in February 1971. 'You are the new generation and therefore represent the future of the Work. What would be the point of a movement, flourishing and spread throughout the world, if it was to end in a few years' time?' Receptivity was a quality which Chiara discovered and prized in the Gen: 'One sees that you are like a sponge which absorbs, and this is very beautiful.' The Gen are internal members of the movement, despite their youth, and strong demands are made on them.

I was closely involved with the Gen movement in Britain from 1973 to 1976, at first responsible for the north of England when I was stationed in Liverpool, and later for the whole country. When the Gen movement was launched in Liverpool young men in their late teens and early twenties were forcefully recruited, often by daily phone calls and constant invitations to meetings. Once a group was formed, activities were on an almost daily basis; two members, I recall – one already working in a responsible job and the other at sixth-form college – were expected to travel from Manchester to Liverpool every evening, arriving home well after midnight, following gruelling sessions of exchanging experiences, listening to tapes of Chiara Lubich or work on current projects. Most weekends would also be taken up with Gen activities. A band was started which would spend days rehearsing and staging concerts round the north of England.

The result was that the young people would have no time for any other social life. Besides, the sort of entertainment that their contemporaries enjoyed, such as going out to pubs and clubs, was considered strictly off-limits. The Gen group was expected to be their world. Directives for activities came directly from Rome; and, in addition to spiritual teaching, much time was taken up with fund-raising activities. Gen were also required to pool their money and give as much as they could to the movement. Every aspect of their lives and thinking had to be filtered through the ideology of the movement. They were given no space to develop ideas or identities of their own, which would have been appropriate for their age-group. The commitment expected of them, despite their lack of years, was very similar to that of the *focolarini*. Naturally, given that they were unmarried, they were expected to observe total celibacy.

Chiara's diatribe against the 'vomiting eroticism' of our times goes on to remind the Gen that

> through their work the youth of today [must] reacquire a sense of purity, sing to purity, raise hymns to virginity, fight to the point of shedding blood so as not to fall on this front . . . Are you pure? Stay that way, even at the cost of throwing yourselves into the snow as Saint Francis of Assisi did when he was tempted. Have you fallen? Come back to God through Mary . . . with the idea of bringing many more to her.

The Gen groups or units are single-sex, although some activities are mixed. There was little chance to mingle with members of the opposite sex in a relaxed way at mixed events, however, and even less chance for friendships to develop.

I remember once my *capofocolare* in Liverpool, Marcelo Claria, an Argentinian psychiatrist, who now runs the movement's psychiatric surgery near Rome, commenting how important it was for us to get young people by the age of seventeen or eighteen as later they were much less impressionable. If this sounds worrying, it is mild compared to Chiara Lubich's own view. Having founded the Gen movement as the second generation, she went on to launch Gen 3 for younger children, and in 1971 she founded Gen 4, or the fourth generation – that is, the under-sixes. In 1988, she decided that the Gen 4 should have their own catechism, 'adapted to their age. It will cover two or three years and be part of their regular meetings.' This has since been published.

CL is equally anxious that its beliefs and practices should be passed on intact to its next generation. This is the duty of each family, but the children of CL families are seen as very much the responsibility of the whole group. The movement's line, in this as in other fields, is isolationist: it runs its own educational establishments, which ensures that its children are untrammelled by the evil influences of the outside world. This begins at the kindergarten stage:

> We realized that, if we had sent our children to any old kindergarten, its structure would not have permitted the continuity of the experience that we are living with our children. And therefore we created a kindergarten that we have promoted with the families of our relations and our district. Since there are some children who have left the kindergarten and started school, we have begun to think about the question of primary schools and we are working on that.'[1]

CL now has primary and secondary schools throughout Italy. Some of these were offered to the movement by religious orders, who lacked the vocations to staff them. CL would supply the bulk of the teachers. This was the case of the Sacred Heart Institute in Milan, which has over a thousand pupils. It was entrusted by an

[1] *Litterae communionis*, no. 11-12, 1972.

order of nuns to a foundation made up mainly of members of CL Fraternities. By dint of energetic fund-raising the foundation subsequently succeeded in purchasing the school building. CL turned this ideological commitment to its own schools into a political policy and has campaigned tirelessly through its various political organizations for schools free of state interference.

'We will also teach you to pass the faith on to your children,' Kiko tells his followers in the course of the *convivence* known as the Shema, 'because this is an absolute commandment that you have, which does not only belong to the Israel of the flesh.'

The many offspring of NC members are educated in the Way and protected from outside influences within the communities. They remain in the same community as their parents until they are thirteen and then they can choose to start the Way on their own behalf, from the beginning. NC claim a success rate of 'around 100 per cent' for entry of their children into later communities.

NC parents are put under extraordinary pressure to relinquish their children to the movement. Kiko Arguello is at his most rabid when, at the stage of the scrutinies, he launches a violent attack on the parent-child bond. Children are 'idols' and must be renounced. 'It is difficult for these people whose whole life has been based on their family, on their career, to find out that these things will not save them and they will be destroyed by fire.' He returns to one of his constant themes: that human love kills and that children are damaged by the love of their parents, which in his view is invariably 'neurotic', a favourite word:

> We see so many parents who are in anguish – and so are the children – because they are not loved, they are neurotic, probably because they did not want them in the first place, because they get on their nerves, because they are expensive, because they upset their lives.

Amongst his many bizarre theories, Kiko's view of parents' love for their children ranks among the most outrageous and shocking:

> Since we have a super-ego which does not permit us to be murderers, this brings about a deep internal conflict that we do everything to assuage, to put things right, because at this deep level we did not want this child, therefore we do the opposite –

we mollycoddle it, we become anxious towards it. Why? I'll tell you why. We are anxious about our children because we are constantly thinking of death. I would ask this question: why are we thinking of our child's death? I would say: BECAUSE IN YOUR SUBCONSCIOUS YOU DESIRE IT.

If the Neocatechumenals are prepared to accept that they are indeed harbouring murderous thoughts towards the children they thought they loved, doubtless they will be anxious to reform. The main way they can do this is to stop 'mollycoddling' them by spending more time out of the house at NC meetings. Most importantly, however, they can ensure that their children join NC.

In the education of their children, the movements demonstrate definite sectarian tendencies. These young people are raised in a puritanical, sheltered environment, protected from harmful influences but also deprived of the beneficial effects of friendship, simple enjoyment, freedom and the exploration of contemporary thought and culture. Above all, they are deprived of the chance to reason and choose for themselves. A new generation is being created, with little understanding of the outside world, to people the new and separate worlds, complete in every detail, which the movements have begun to build.

9

CULTURAL REVOLUTION

'MAY A HUNDRED FLOWERS BLOOM!' WITH THESE WORDS, THE Undersecretary of the Pontifical Council for the Laity, Mr Guzman Carriquiry of Uruguay, said to be the highest-placed layman in the Curia and close to Communion and Liberation, hailed the new movements in the Church at the 1987 Synod, before going on to praise their attributes in more detail in his keynote speech. Although these words were originally spoken by Chairman Mao Tse-tung, it is unlikely that Carriquiry wished to imply a parallel between Mao's savage reform of a regime and a nation and the role of the movements in today's Church. Nevertheless, there are some striking similarities.

The new movements, too, are a grass-roots phenomenon, with the implicit backing of the highest authority, aiming to restore orthodoxy in the middle ranks. Indeed, many of their main characteristics reflect those of Mao's Red Guards – the fanaticism, the blind obedience, the sloganeering, the personality cult around the Pope, manipulation of the media, anti-intellectualism, denunciations, the formulation of rigid ideology, a younger generation mobilized in the struggle against their elders.

But what makes Carriquiry's choice of quote particularly apt is that the New Evangelization proposed by the Pope is not limited to the spiritual sphere. 'Participate with dedication in this work of overcoming the division between the Gospel and

Culture,' he urges the priests of CL.[1]

His concern is with culture in the broadest possible sense – the common 'mentality and customs' in all their possible expressions through the world of ideas, the arts, education and the mass media. By influencing culture, the Church can play a leading role in society and politics. 'Only from within and through culture does the Christian faith become part of history and the creator of history,' says John Paul in *Christifideles laici,* his official report on the 1987 Synod on the Laity. Given the advanced stage secularization has reached in today's world and the Church's current resources, the pontiff's hopes of altering the course of history could seem nothing more than a harmless pipe-dream. But the movements certainly take it seriously. They, too, plan to change not just the Church but the world. Like all fundamentalist groups, they wish to be a visible force with clear social and political as well as spiritual goals. John Paul II has recognized in them the principal means of fulfilling his vision: 'In the new lay charisms [lies] the key for the vital insertion of the Church in the historical situation of today.'

In *Cristifideles laici,* a section is devoted to the new movements. Here John Paul specifies the quality in the movements which he finds of special appeal: it is their 'effectiveness' as agents of *cultural* change: 'In fact, their formation itself expresses the social nature of the person and for this reason leads to a more extensive and incisive effectiveness in work. In reality, a "cultural" effect can be accomplished through work done not so much by an individual alone but by an individual as "a social being", that is, as a member of a group, of a community, of an association, or of a movement.'[2]

The concept of manipulating or engineering a culture is in itself a sinister one. The twentieth century has seen the horrific effects of such manufactured cultures, almost always motivated by what appeared to be the loftiest of intentions. In the Western world, culture is an expression and a safeguard of freedom. The trend over the past few decades, in spite of the homogenizing effects of the mass media, has been away from monolithic cultural expressions and towards the sort of cultural pluralism which many would consider healthy.

But this view is not shared by the Pope and the movements.

---

[1] Speech to priests participating in a course of Spiritual Exercises promoted by Communion and Liberation, Castelgandolfo, 12 September 1985.
[2] *Cristifideles laici,* para. 29.

Their view of society and its cultural expression is essentially dualistic. They believe they are the embodiment of a perfect society. Outside is the world, which is evil. John Paul confided his stark personal vision of contemporary society to an NC audience in 1980:

> We . . . live in a period in which one feels, one experiences a radical confrontation – and I say this because it is also my experience of many years . . . faith and anti-faith, Gospel and anti-gospel, Church and anti-church, God and anti-god, so to speak.

This dualism has become the dominant message of John Paul's pontificate. Alongside his clarion-call of New Evangelization, he has developed another, more grandiose theme of a new culture, a new civilization, which has become the *leitmotiv* of his encyclicals and addresses. This 'culture of love' or 'civilization of love' is John Paul's antidote to contemporary Western culture, which he perceives as a 'culture of death' or 'civilization of death'. This is sweeping pontifical shorthand for the Pope's moral hobbyhorses of 'contraception, direct sterilization, autoeroticism, pre-marital sexual relations, homosexual relations . . . artificial insemination',[1] abortion and euthanasia, in no particular order. These issues are not graded according to a hierarchy of values. Masturbation and contraception are, like euthanasia and abortion, 'intrinsic moral evils'.[2]

But what is even more curious about the Pope's *Weltanschauung* is that, for him, these issues are the hallmarks of Western culture; they characterize it absolutely. Values it champions such as pluralism, feminism and minority rights count for nothing in his eyes; in fact, they are just as likely to come under attack. The movements are John Paul's answer to this society in decay, this perceived 'civilization of death'. In them we must find his blueprint for the 'civilization of love'.

Like the Pope, they also take a grim and apocalyptic view of Western society, perceived as teetering on the brink of a moral abyss. When the world's press failed to show enthusiasm for the United Nations 'World Forum of Non-governmental

[1] *Veritatis splendor*, para. 47.
[2] *Veritatis splendor*, para. 80.

Organizations' on the Family, held in Malta from 28 November to 2 December 1993 (in which the New Families movement was a participant), Focolare's *Città nuova* magazine read into this oversight the imminent collapse of civilization:

> The fundamental cause of the silence is certainly the absence at a world level of a 'culture of the family', an ignorance of the quality and scale of the human problems it faces, very similar to the widespread recklessness that can often be found in periods preceding the great disasters of history.[1]

In an editorial in another edition of the same magazine, at least in part provoked by an article criticizing the Familyfest, a more concerted attack is made on today's 'culture of individualism'. 'There is a tendency', rails Guglielmo Boselli, one of the first *focolarini* and long-standing editor of *Città nuova*,

> to present as 'progressive' only that which corresponds to the culture of individualism, and which is therefore strongly polluted with the selfishness and hedonism endemic to the affluent and pragmatic West. There is a tendency to present as positive everything which is exaggerated, permissive, transgressive, experience for its own sake, as though these were the foundations of a new society.

It is vital, Boselli thunders, in order to oppose these ills, that we should recognize them for what they are: 'the sign of the decadence of a people. That from many points of view we are sliding towards a low level of human degradation. That in no way can this be considered "progress".'

This doom-laden view of contemporary society is nothing new for the *focolarini*. When I was living in the London men's Focolare centre, Dimitri Bregant, the priest who leads the men's branch of the movement in the United Kingdom, was reading the works of the French palaeontologist and theologian Pierre Teilhard de Chardin. Writing before the Council, Teilhard broke with tradition by advocating an optimistic view of creation. Expanding St Paul's image of creation 'groaning in labour', he contemplated a universe

[2]Antonio Maria Baggio, 'Chi ha paura della famiglia', *Città nuova*, no. 24, 1993.

which was evolving both spiritually and physically towards the Omega Point, or ultimate meeting with Christ. In direct opposition to the dualistic view of the movements, human endeavour was seen as having intrinsic value inasmuch as it was a contribution to the ultimate evolution of creation.

This seemed like highly subversive stuff in the early fifties, and Teilhard was silenced by the Church, only to be rediscovered after his death. Not surprisingly, Dimitri Bregant took an equally dim view of Teilhard's concept of an improving world. 'I don't think the world is getting better,' Bregant declared. 'It's getting worse!' Such judgements are inevitable given the world view at the heart of the Focolare doctrine.

Chiara Lubich says: 'The Crucifix we must follow today is Jesus in His greatest suffering . . . It is He whom we must strive to see in poor humanity, confused, mad, immoral, secularized, without God.' It is significant that mankind's temporal sufferings such as poverty, disease and war are ignored in favour of its moral depravity. But Lubich's world-rejection is not merely directed at what she perceives to be 'sin'. At the heart of her philosophy is a deep-seated sense of despair even in regard to the good things of life.

Among the first words of the standard introduction to the movement, known as 'the Story of the Ideal' is a quotation from the bleakest book of the Old Testament, Ecclesiastes. Its most famous line, 'Vanity of vanities . . . all is vanity' – more accurately translated as 'Sheer futility . . . sheer futility, everything is futile' (Ecclesiastes 1:2) – is invoked to describe the experience of the first *focolarine* whose dreams were shattered in war-torn Trento. Deciding that 'everything passes away except God', they concluded that therefore everything else – marriage, home, career, learning – was worthless.

This sense of the emptiness and purposelessness of all human activity remains fundamental to the Focolare message. This is why, in Chiara Lubich's vocabulary, only spiritual values denoted by words like 'paradise', 'supernatural' and 'divine' are considered good; while terms like 'world', 'natural' and 'human' are all used in a negative sense. The Focolare view of a new society, therefore, begins with a rejection not just of society but even of the most wholesome human motives like love of family and friends, or the creative impulse. To be inspired by any of these is 'to lapse into a human attitude' ('cadere nell'umano') which is to be avoided by members of the movement.

They should avoid newspapers or magazines, and exercise great caution in selecting books, films and television programmes: 'Television transmissions . . . bring the world into the soul and leave the heart empty – and so a lot of prudence is needed to use this medium.'[1]

Variations on this theme of detachment are a constantly repeated refrain in Lubich's messages to her followers:

> The world is saturated with materialism, with consumerism, hedonism, vanity, violence, and we must be ready to give up some programme on the television which, although perhaps not totally bad, may be ambiguous and useless . . . to avoid curiosity or the desire of looking at everything indiscriminately . . . to renounce the slavery of fashion, useless possessions, vain or worthless readings.

In order to shut 'the world' out, we were encouraged to develop the practice known as 'custody of the eyes' – that is, to keep our eyes fixed on the pavement in front of us when walking along the street in order to avoid the distractions and temptations that assailed us from all sides.

Neocatechumenate rejects the world, if anything, even more vehemently than Focolare. Kiko Arguello takes up the theme of the futility of all human activity and values:

> Bear in mind these words of a Father of the desert that I have often quoted to you: 'There is no happiness in this world or the next other than to love God.' Everything else is vanity. Marriage – vanity. Your children – vanity. Your wife – vanity. Your husband – vanity of vanities . . . My paintings, art – vanity.

Human feelings are devalued in Arguello's catechesis, just as they are in the doctrines of Focolare. Those preparing for the second scrutiny are told:

> The man of flesh does not love his children; on the contrary, he

[1]Chiara Lubich, conference call, 22 January 1987.

kills them – he always loves them selfishly. Nor can he love his wife or she her husband; they cannot love each other in the deepest sense, perhaps with a human love but that does not satisfy man completely, but rather exploits him and kills him.

In an interview with Don Giussani, the founder of Communion and Liberation describes 'the dominating culture of today' thus:

It is the attitude summed up by the Latin *carpe diem*: to extract the greatest pleasure possible from a world which is seen as made up of matter, nothing else. There is a contradiction, however, which is dramatically manifest in the solitude, the unhappiness, and the suicide which characterize the life of so many people today.

According to Giussani, modern man is 'condemned to choose between two alternatives, presumption or cynicism: either he presumes that he has within him an absolute and total principle of salvation or he lets himself be persuaded that he is totally determined by the omnipotence of matter, he is like a piece of dust in the whirlwind.'

The mass media play a decisive and, in Giussani's opinion, sinister role in shaping society and the individual:

In this way at a certain point, the very physiognomy of the way in which society and the individual moves can be completely explained by the images and parameters laid down by the media. But how terrifying it is to see an individual whose judgement and way of acting are totally determined by the common mentality.

But worse still is the schizophrenia inflicted on the individual by Western culture:

The culture of today's society produces an image and sense of the ego as a collection of fragments. Every segment, every fragment – relationships, work, religion, rest, entertainment etc. – has its laws, its fixed and inescapable pattern.

The result is the destruction of the personality: 'As in the aftermath of a violent earthquake, the house, the country no longer exist; just piles of stones, bits of wall, the "great destruction" of which Dante speaks.'

Don Giussani's rhetoric might be more high-flown than his fellow founders', but the substance is the same: today's world has nothing to offer.

Yet this dualistic view of Church versus World, which held sway in the Church before Vatican II, contrasts starkly with the Council's proposition. This was much more in tune with the optimistic world-view of Teilhard de Chardin and the younger theologians who had been vilified in the fifties but were vindicated by that momentous event in the history of the Catholic Church. 'God's plan for the world is that men should work together to restore the temporal sphere of things and to develop it unceasingly,' the Council Fathers proclaimed in the Decree on the Laity. The value of human activity is strongly affirmed:

> Many elements make up the temporal order: namely, the good things of life and the prosperity of the family, culture, economic affairs, the arts and professions, political institutions, international relations, and other matters of this kind as well as their development and progress. All of these not only aid in the attainment of man's ultimate goal but also possess their own intrinsic value. This value has been implanted in them by God, whether they are considered in themselves or as parts of the whole temporal order. 'God saw all that he had made, and it was very good' (Gen. 1:31).

The laity are encouraged not to cut themselves off from contemporary culture, but to be a part of it: 'Well informed about the modern world, the lay person should be an active member of his own society and adjusted to its culture.' The 'lay person will throw himself wholly and energetically into the reality of the temporal order and effectively assume his role in conducting its affairs'. His task is not to represent the Church but simply to be a Christian who then acts with total freedom: 'Led by the light of the gospel and the mind of the Church, let them act directly and definitively in the temporal sphere. As citizens they must co-operate with other citizens, using their own particular skills and acting on their own responsibility.'

★   ★   ★

The movements see no need to be 'well informed about the modern world' nor 'adjusted to its culture'. Why should they, when they have the answers to every problem – secular as well as sacred? The openness of Catholics to learn from others is roundly condemned by CL and NC as a secularizing influence which has corrupted the Church. Much of CL's time is spent attacking fellow-Catholics, often distinguished and highly respected ones, for importing alien ideas into the Church.

The movements reject all outside influences on principle. They share the fundamentalist conviction, known within the Catholic context as integrism, that their religious beliefs will provide an answer to every possible question.

In a speech to CL members at the Meeting for Friendship among Peoples in Rimini in 1982, Pope John Paul said: 'The faith lived as a certainty and a claim for Christ's presence in every situation and occasion of life makes it possible to create new forms of life for man.'

The movements, naturally, take a more extreme view.

As Don Giussani has said: 'My only hope is that, through the true freedom of the lay person, the Spirit will communicate His energy which springs from the sacraments to all the possible and imaginable areas of modern-day life.' For CL's founder, hope for the secular order can only spring from a radical religious conviction and a rejection of 'common values'. The Council's idea that Christians might share these values with men of goodwill does not enter his scheme of things: 'I . . . [invite] Christians to rethink the hope they place in progress, evolution and in common values, and to found it instead on the promise of the final resurrection which can render their actions capable of the "one hundredfold here below" of which the Gospel speaks.'

An extreme integrism underlies Focolare's anti-intellectualism – indeed, its opposition to thought of any kind in its members. This attitude dates from the very beginnings of the movement.

Chiara Lubich describes how God told her to give up her philosophy studies: 'It was when, in order that He could become our Teacher and instruct us in the truth, God asked us to sacrifice all the truth that men could give us. It was when, so as to reveal Himself to us, God gave us the strength to put all the books of other teachers in the attic.'

The symbolic act of 'putting one's books in the attic' came to signify, in the lore of the movement, the rejection of human learning. It remains one of its most powerful slogans. Chiara Lubich emphazises that this radical rejection of outside knowledge is a fundamental step to be taken by all recruits: 'This act of our life is the basis of all the doctrine of the "Ideal". It has to be the basis for anyone who wishes to follow Jesus in His Work [the movement].'

Having sacrificed the use of reason, Chiara believes that she received an illumination directly from God:

> Jesus made us see very clearly that it was absurd to seek for the truth when it was contained wholly in him, the Word, Truth made flesh. When He told us in practice: leave all other teachers and follow Me, and you will learn everything. When, following His first illuminations, it became clear to us that there was a light that was not so much the fruit of reasoning, but that descended from above.

Not only were these 'illuminations' given priority over orthodox forms of knowledge, but they were also considered the one source of information on all subjects.

Chiara states categorically that 'One thing was certain: He who lived among us was God and therefore he was able to reply to *all the questions that all men of all times might pose.*' And the condition for this 'illumination' is also made quite clear: 'But it is not enough to take this step once and for all . . . Yes, Jesus wants *the complete void of our minds* so that he can illuminate us, to teach us the truth.'

This emptying of the mind could easily be confused with the interior experience of the mystics, who emptied themselves so as to experience the fullness of the God. It must be borne in mind, however, that the spiritual experiences of the new movements take place within the context of the community. 'Jesus the Teacher', the fount of all knowledge, is an aspect of Focolare's core concept of 'Jesus in the midst', or unity. This unity is always expressed by the 'pivot' or authority figure within the group. Members may be required to provide 'the complete void of . . . [their] minds', but it is the task of the authorities of the movement, culminating in Chiara Lubich, to fill or 'illuminate' that void.

From this integrist approach of the new movements, each has

generated a complete, self-contained culture covering the entire gamut of human existence. Though the religious experience is the starting-point and is present more or less explicitly in every facet of these cultures, it is expressed in ideological, political, social, economic and artistic forms. In this respect, these Catholic movements are close to classic forms of fundamentalism such as contemporary evangelical movements in the United States: they affirm their identities as a visible religious and social community of believers. It this 'visibility' or 'cultural' effect of the movements that appeals most to John Paul II.

Because they see themselves as the repository of all truth, the cultures of the movements are *messianic* in character. Focolare believes that its role is to renew every aspect of society from science to the arts, from politics to medicine. This process of renewal is rather sinisterly termed *clarification*. The New Humanity 'mass movement' is assigned the task of infiltrating existing social structures. While from its earliest days Focolare has always aspired to a political presence, this dimension became so strong within CL that at times it threatened to swamp the spiritual dimension of the organization.

As early as 1975, CL was preaching a political millennium of which they were to be the architects. Roberto Formigoni, the first leader of CL's political wing, the Popular Movement, expressed these far-reaching political ambitions: 'To live an experience of communion that involves every dimension of human life, that realizes an experience of concrete liberation, including the social possession of the means of production.'

This is no airy-fairy spiritual goal, but a hard-nosed political one. He speaks of the 'real reconstruction of the life of a people' and states unambiguously that 'Despite the crisis of the Church and the ambiguity of Christians, we can say that this work will either be guided by Christians or it will not happen'.

While denying that the movement aspires to a confessional state, Don Giussani comes perilously close to it when he envisages 'a state guided by religious people, who may even be non-Christians': 'such an ideal becomes historically feasible if its coming about is not entrusted to one individual, however exceptional, but rather to a fellowship of religious persons, a true company of Jesus'.

CL's militancy in the political field derives partly from its millenarian sense of mission: Christians cannot collaborate with existing parties, therefore they must carve out their own space.

> The Christian finds he has to fight first and foremost to gain once again his right to existence and to affirm the historical 'usefulness' of his presence in the world which considers his claims as absolutely irrelevant and insignificant.

Giussani is prepared for a bitter struggle: 'The Christian . . . [is] confronted with a state which is no less an enemy to him than the Roman Empire of the first centuries . . . Today's state is more radically hostile to him.'

The Council was not dealing in utopias, but in the practicalities and even the benefits of a pluralistic society. Messianic Christian sects of the past have tended to express their vision of a perfect society by isolating themselves from the evil influence of the outside world in self-contained social experiments or 'intentional communities'. The movements are no exception. In this they comply with one of FAIR's marks of cults: 'Cults encourage exclusivity and isolation, some of them using the excuse that all outside the cult is evil or Satanic.' Indeed, given the grim vision of today's world the movements possess, it is only logical that each should opt for a society of its own: it is a concrete expression of their ideological dualism.

The Focolare politician Tommaso Sorgi maintains that 'Utopia is one of the greatest forces in history'.[1] Yet it has rarely been a force for good. It is sufficient to think of the horrific price in human suffering that has been paid for the political utopias of this century alone.

Neocatechumenate takes the most extreme position. Although it sees its mission as 'saving the world', and describes its members as 'leaven' and 'salt of the earth', in fact its world-rejecting stance is so extreme that little interaction with the wider society is possible. The emphasis is on the spiritual life and detachment from all worldly cares, which are considered 'idols'. All attempts to change or influence society are actively discouraged as presumptuous.

---

[1] Tommaso Sorgi, 'La politica un amore più grande', Città nuova, no. 24, 1993, p. 29.

Social reform is looked on as God's work, not Man's. The parish communities are the utopia of Neocatechumenate, although in the future larger and more permanent communities could well evolve within the movement. Already, in Italy, the first NC businesses are springing up – mainly concerned with supplying specialized products needed for the distinctive liturgical celebrations.

CL's extreme anti-state position, partly fuelled by its original anti-communist views, has led to the development of its own schools and crèches, but also a whole range of businesses and social services, including manufacturing companies, going some way to fulfil Roberto Formigoni's dream of 'social possession of the means of production'. Five thousand companies run by CL members in Italy are now gathered under an umbrella organization known as the Company of Works (Compagnia delle Opere). It is possible for CL members to bank, shop, educate their children, receive health care and take their holidays within the structures provided by the movement.

Focolare have gone one step further and founded their own towns, permanent versions of the summer Mariapolis meetings, complete societies in miniature. The first was Loppiano near Florence, which began in the early sixties. Others were started in the succeeding decades, usually when suitable land or property was donated to the movement. In recent years, however, there has been a decisive drive to expand this operation inspired by a speech Chiara Lubich gave in the Focolare village known as the Araceli Mariapolis near São Paolo in Brazil in 1991. Here, the foundress launched the movement's own economic policy, tagged the 'Economy of Communion'. She encouraged the growth of businesses run by members of the movement, on similar lines to that of CL's Company of Works.

The profits of these companies are split three ways – one third is reinvested in the company, another goes to the financing of the movement's own projects and the final share goes towards helping the needy – though only within the ambit of the movement. The profits, therefore, stay within the organization.

Given Focolare's considerable diffusion and the fact that many internal businesses already existed, this economy of the movement was rapidly established on a wide scale. At the heart of it are the 'towns', of which there are already twenty, with more in construction. A large-scale expansion of these settlements is envisaged.

'Every "zone" ', Chiara Lubich has declared, 'should have its own town eventually. This in fact will be our witness. Because, if there is Christ among those who live there, with the centuries a thousand towns should result.'

The Second Vatican Council placed the issue of social justice at the top of the Catholic agenda. This message was taken to heart by many of the faithful, especially in parts of the world where injustice and inequality were most in evidence. Theologians in South America responded to the Council's call with liberation theology. This was inspired by, and in its turn helped to inspire, base communities at the grassroots level in which the poor and oppressed discovered how the gospel could be a means of liberation, enabling them to take charge of their destiny. Liberation theology was embraced by the South American Bishops' Conference, who declared their 'preferential option for the poor'. This option was shared by religious orders in the affluent West, some of whom renounced their schools catering for the children of wealthy Catholics and chose to work in the poorest of missionary areas instead. The blurring of the lines dividing the religious sphere from left-wing politics set alarm bells ringing in the Vatican, especially during this pontificate.

The movements, however, with their strong spiritual emphasis, have clearly set themselves apart from the current within the Church characterized by its commitment to issues of social justice. This marked difference of approach has been particularly obvious in South America, where the movements act in parallel to, rather than in concert with, the local Church.

NC and CL are bitter and vociferous opponents of liberation theology. It is rumoured that CL's insensitivity to local concerns was such that plans for a holiday camp in Amazonia were only cancelled after vigorous protests from conservationists. Even in a country like Italy, there is a marked difference in the approach of the movements. No fewer than 4 million Catholics are committed to the 'volunteership', or regular voluntary work with the poor; yet the main thrust in the movements, which are predominantly middle-class, is missionary work and the spiritual 'formation' of its members. Social work takes place within the ambit of the movement or aids its expansion.

None of these three movements has actually achieved anything of note in the field of justice and peace outside its own structures.

Furthermore, social issues tend to be robbed of their urgency by being viewed in a spiritual light. They are just one aspect of a much larger programme of cultural change. Some commentators regard the movements' nod in this direction as pure tokenism, to show that they are 'at least doing something'.[1] The emphasis the movements place on the right spiritual motivation and the religious significance of the 'works of mercy', rather than being motivated by a sense of outrage and desperate need, appeals to the Vatican – it is a safe and orthodox approach. There is no chance of the movements' members taking to the barricades.

Even while I was still a hardline member of Focolare, I found it difficult to come to terms with its attitude to society's problems. All that mattered, we were told, was to build the movement. Once it had been built up into a vast international organization, *then* it would provide a solution to the world's ills.

In July 1968, when we were seeing off the last guests of the summer Mariapolis which was held that year at St Mary's Catholic Training College in Twickenham, a vagrant wandered through the gates and asked for help. I was asked by the *focolarini* to do what I could for this man. Just eighteen and fired with the enthusiasm of the Focolare ideal of mutal love, which at that time I took at face value, I felt privileged to be able to help someone who was genuinely in need. This was surely Jesus asking to be loved.

The man, who was probably in his forties, told me a terrifying story of alcoholism and attempted suicide. He had to leave the hostel where he was staying and needed help in finding accommodation. After being turned away from innumerable hostels and seedy boarding-houses, feeling completely out of my depth, I rang the Focolare Centre, where I was living during the summer vacation, and asked for assistance. Obviously, those in authority felt I needed to learn a sharp lesson. 'This is not what the Focolare is here for,' I was told. 'You will have to sort this problem out yourself.' I was shaken – after all, it was they who had entrusted me with this task. I learned my lesson; but for many years, until I was thoroughly indoctrinated, I struggled inwardly. Could it be right to postpone these vital questions? Direct social action was merely an afterthought. Local action or fund-raising on an international level also served some kind of missionary or expansionist

[1]Bruno Secondin, *I nuovi protagonisti*, Milan: Edizioni Paoline, Milan, 1991, p. 222.

purpose – such as building a hospital for the movement's settlement in the Camerouns, for example. Social action was one element in the spiritual education of members.

In 1987, Focolare founded AMU (Azione per un mondo unito – Action for a United World), 'a non-governmental organization promoted by Focolare to give life to projects of development in the Third World'.[1] This was a vehicle to show that the movement was making a contribution to the improvement of social conditions, but it also provided yet another innocently named front organization to aid the development of the movement.

The same could be said of CL's practice of *la caritativa*, or charity work, which from the earliest days of GS was one of the activities undertaken by members. As always with CL, 'charity work' was given an ideological justification, in a pamphlet published in 1961 entitled *The Meaning of Charity Work*. It is, of course, a spiritual meaning, as we discover in the impersonal description of

> the discovery of the fact that, precisely because we love them, we are not the ones who make them happy; and that not even the most perfect society, the legally most solid and astute organization, the most enormous wealth, the most robust health, the most peerless beauty, the finest breeding will ever make them happy. Only Another can make them happy, the Reason for everything, God.

The social projects that are undertaken by the movements tend to be inflated because good works are expected of Christian organizations and they are a good way of answering the oft-repeated query, 'But what do you *do*?'

Unlike CL, Focolare has not tried to combat liberation theology. Instead – as in every other field – it has come up with its own alternative. Chiara Lubich proposes the 'Economy of Communion' as 'the movement's contribution to the struggle to eradicate poverty'; in the eyes of the movements, it is in the utopias, or 'pieces of new society', that they have created that they are making their most important contribution to society.

Sadly, however, I believe that it is precisely here that they are at their most irrelevant. Focolare's 'towns' are seen as experiments in

[1]Oreste Palioti, 'Pace attraverso l'unità', *Città Nuova*, no. 3, 1994, p. 31.

which solutions to the world's problems are being worked out in microcosm; they are considered to be 'crucibles' of a better world. But such parallels are fallacious.[1] Far from providing solutions for world problems, the 'social experiments' of the movements prove nothing more than that they work for their participants; and it also has to be borne in mind that these experiments are being carried out under very unusual, highly controlled circumstances. It was our proud boast that we had no need of a police force at Loppiano; but that must be seen in the context of the other strict controls we were subject to: constant personal indoctrination, blind obedience to authorities, and the fact that we were effectively policing one another. These conditions would be impossible to reproduce on a wide scale, mainly because they do not take personal freedom into account.

But Focolare insists that its utopias are of vital importance to the future of the world, 'a witness that it is possible to create a united world here on this earth: an "earthly city" which seeks to fulfil the "heavenly city" '.[2] Unfortunately, this heavenly city may just be a fool's paradise.

Kiko Arguello makes no attempt to appease those who believe that it is a Christian's duty to alleviate human suffering. NC's utopia is wholly spiritual; evangelization is all that matters. Those who believe otherwise are condemned:

> Human promotion, the true development of peoples, is found in Jesus Christ who is made present in the Holy Spirit. This is a totally different approach from the social action which is so fashionable, that wants to develop man before talking to him about Jesus Christ and the Gospel.

Christians who work for social justice are neglecting what is essential in Christianity:

> What holds these Catholic groups for social action together is social action, revolutionary action, changing the structures, the fact of recognizing that man is oppressed by unjust structures etc. Each group conceives this in their own way, because there are

[1]Bruno Secondin, *I nuovi protagonisti*, Milan: Edizioni Paoline, Milan, 1991.
[2]Mario Dal Bello, 'One city is not enough', *Città Nuova*, no. 21, 1993, p. 29.

extremist groups and others that are less extreme. But all are united by action and they substitute Jesus Christ Risen . . . with social action. The Christianity of these groups is just a varnish.

In the course of the penitential service which forms part of the introductory catechesis, Kiko Arguello describes three different attitudes to the world. The first two are mistaken, the third is correct.

First, there is the man who will not accept that, with the Fall, God 'cursed' the world. He sees that 'the world is hostile to him, that life and work become hell'. Escapism is the solution he chooses, 'taking refuge in sport, football', even drugs and alcohol.

The second kind of person 'Does not accept a world with sin, with wars with vices'. Those who struggle to build a more just society, including 'all the political movements you like', fall into this category. They are compared to Hitler, who 'wanted to build his world: a perfect world. But it is always a world in which the police rule with a rod of iron.'

The third attitude is one of acceptance, passivity, waiting:

> They accept that what God has said is true: that we are sinners, that the world is cursed because of the sins of men. And accepting this reality they continue to listen to this Word and wait for God to come and *bless the earth*: God. We are here because we are waiting for God to send the Messiah truly into our midst to transform us, to establish his Kingdom, a kingdom in which all men can be happy for ever. But only God can set up this kingdom in Truth.

Paradoxically, despite their right-wing position in church politics and their middle-class membership – at least in the western world – all three new movements have had considerable success in attracting recruits from the political far left. In fact, these two extremes have a great deal in common: the promise of a new world in the dim and distant future; the need for a tough, centralized, totalitarian but efficient structure in order to achieve the ambitious goals; the total obedience of individual members with no room for dissent.

Chiara Lubich recalls how two Marxists were impressed with the work of the original group of the movement among the poor of Trento. 'What you are doing, we want to do throughout the world,' they told her. Lubich realized that her project was also a global one, and decided that her movement would be a direct challenge to Marxism.

Before the fall of communism, Lubich saw Focolare as a mirror image of the socialist world. 'We are made for them,' she would say. 'They have the right structures; all they need is our spirit to animate those structures.'

Indeed, both Focolare and CL borrowed from socialism the concept of operating through cells within the 'environment' – that is, the workplace – rather than through the more traditional medium of the parish. Focolare's idea of 'mass movements' came from the communist world; CL, too, has always described itself as a 'mass movement'.

But, above all, the movements share the socialist view of the individual's role in society: he or she has meaning only in terms of the collective, in the context of the 'history of the party' or 'history of the movement'.

Focolare is constantly attacking 'individualism' in its publications. There is no revolution without violence, but the violence of the new movements is spiritual, directed against the individual. Focolare and NC both reserve some of their strongest words for subjugation of the individual to the community. 'We know that the more we annihilate ourselves,' says Chiara Lubich, 'with Jesus forsaken as the model who brought Himself to nothing, the more we shout out with our life that God is everything . . . let's live dead to ourselves and alive to God's will, to love for neighbours.'

Kiko Arguello has much the same message for those in the Way:

> Obviously, for this new life to be born inside, you must first detest that old life of yours. If basically what you want is just a reason for your life and you are looking in the Gospel for a law to improve yourself and so, while you are listening, you are thinking, 'How can I change a bit to change this little life of mine?' This is the problem, isn't it? The person who enters the community to build himself up. No my friends, it's to destroy yourself.

For CL, the role of the individual within the community is simply to 'follow'. 'Obedience constitutes, therefore,' Don Giussani instructs, 'the characteristic virtue of following and it is put to the test when one has to follow a particular man, a particular group.'

The culture of conformity, of following, is characteristic of the movements. Added to this, in the case of Focolare and Neo-catechumenate, is a tendency to passivity, acceptance, quietism, even fatalism. Both movements teach resignation to suffering and difficulties, Focolare through its doctrine of 'Jesus forsaken' and NC with its catechesis of 'the glorious cross' and 'the servant of Yahweh'.

NC's fatalism is taken to extremes in Kiko Arguello's catechesis for the *convivence* known as the Shema. At first we find him in rare good spirits:

> Because it is true that everything comes from God. Because life is a marvel, because everything is stupendous: to go out into the country, to have children, to be married, to be unmarried. Everything is wonderful because everything is grace and everything is love.

Suddenly the euphoria takes a strange and unexpected turn, offering a fatalistic vision of the world that many, including the majority of Catholics, would find repellent and unacceptable:

> Even the suffering of others is an absolute grace for them, even conflicts, even wars, everything is grace. Because God, says Scripture, guides the peoples with wisdom. He guides the nations. He guides the world; he knows what he is doing. Everything that he does contributes to a much greater mission.

Is Arguello seriously suggesting, as he appears to be, that God *causes* conflicts and wars?

The dependence the movements require from recruits fosters passivity. This lack of an independent spirit has resulted in a failure to produce figures of stature. Within thirty years of the foundation of the Franciscan and Dominican Orders, to which the new movements are often compared by their supporters in the Vatican, the two organizations had produced theological giants of the stature of Duns Scotus and Thomas Aquinas respectively, both of whom were teaching in Paris, the cultural centre of Europe, in the mid-thirteenth century. Fifty years after its foundation, Focolare has not produced a figure remotely comparable. Instead a think-tank of 'tame' theologian members of the movement (the same group who taught us at Loppiano over twenty years ago) produce endless theological studies on a conveyor belt, attempting to tease out theological conclusions from the thought and works of Chiara Lubich. This process consists principally of combing existing theological works, Scriptures, the tradition of the Church and the documents of the magisterium for quotations which prove or, to use the movement's term, 'confirm' Chiara Lubich's assertions. Inevitably, these attempts are derivative and uninspired.

For its part, Neocatecumenate has come up with Ricardo Blasquez, auxiliary bishop of Salamanca, author of a treatise entitled *Neocatechumenal Communities: A Theological Discernment* which purports to defend the charism of the movement by means of self-authenticating declarations such as 'The Way is always accompanied by signs given by God and interpretable by those who are open to the Spirit'.

The theology of CL is, of course, propounded by the founder himself, Don Giussani. Unfortunately for outsiders, barring a small circle of ecclesiastical admirers, his works are all but impenetrable. Ignatius Press in the United States discontinued their project to publish Giussani's works in English because readers found them incomprehensible.

The priest has constantly stressed that the movement has no need of leaders or inspirational figures (apart from himself, of course). Earlier, it was noted how his ideal government was a 'fellowship of religious persons, a true company of Jesus', rather than 'one individual, however exceptional'.[1] He has further specified that the movement has no need for the special gifts that individuals might have to offer, but simply their compliance:

> The chance our group has of doing good to the world and society is not dependent on what each individual manages to do according to his special gifts but on his readiness to do the 'Work' of the Spirit. To obey the Spirit in the final analysis means to obey a man, a human reality – fragile, incoherent, whatever you

[1] 'Laity i.e. Christians, An interview with Luigi Giussani'.

like – which has been chosen by God to be the terminal of the Incarnation, as a charism that exists for the good of the whole Church.

The same inability – or deliberate refusal – to produce major creative figures can be seen in the important field of the arts. However, another major factor comes into play here. For the movements interpret the world through the filter of a fixed ideology. They do not approach reality with curiosity or with an attitude of discovery. Indeed, the empirical approach which is at the basis of modern methods of enquiry and research in all disciplines is anathema to the movements. Instead, they seek reflections of their canon of revealed truths in the ideas of others. This approach is applied to theology, science or the arts. Reason and intelligence are drained of all intrinsic value and regarded only as instruments to be harnessed to the service of ideology.

In her speech on 'Jesus the Teacher', in which Chiara Lubich urged her followers to 'put their books in the attic' and offer Jesus 'the complete void of their minds', she went on to describe what their attitude should be when it is 'the will of God actually to have to handle books'. She is referring, of course, to those occasions when the members of the movement might be obliged to read for study or professional purposes – the implication is that no other motives for reading would be justified. She instructs the members of the movement not to look for something new but to seek out a reflection or 'confirmation' of what they already know, to look for 'whatever part of the truth there might be in those people, such as the famous thinkers for example, who are remembered by history because they have managed to grasp some fragment of light in the light of Truth'. That 'Truth' is of course already possessed in its entirety by the movement.

Focolare, with its anti-intellectualism and condemnation of emotions, is basically antithetical to the arts. Indeed, they have not produced an artistic tradition worthy of serious consideration. Yet Chiara Lubich is firmly convinced that Focolare not only has a spiritual but also a unique *aesthetic* message for the world.

At a meeting in Rome in December 1988 between the foundress and leaders of the movement responsible for its properties round the world, 'it was noted that the movement presents, in a certain way, Christianity in a new dimension – that of harmony and beauty which penetrates all its members and its buildings'.

An article in Focolare's Italian magazine *Città nuova* on the movement's 'towns' says it is 'logical . . . that the permanent Mariapolis wants to express ["life"] even in architectural terms, in the modern lines of its environments'.[1] The Focolare 'look', is intended to be modern, in order to make the movement accessible and 'normal'. But Chiara Lubich's aesthetics also contains a mystical dimension. In an article she wrote on the centres or headquarters of the Gen youth groups, she decreed that 'All the Gen must be committed to keep [the centre] . . . clean, tidy and decorated in such a way that whoever enters by chance, even if they find it empty, would say with surprise: "This is the home of someone who is not of this world." Yes, because Jesus, for it is He who lives among us, has a style of his own which is unmistakable, and He "consecrates", so to speak, the walls and the few things that have welcomed Him, so that the walls and the things speak by themselves.'[2]

Members of the movement share this profound conviction that even its interior design has a metaphysical purpose. This 'style', therefore, has nothing to do with the personalities of the flesh-and-blood inhabitants of the properties.

The Gospel, of course, tells us nothing whatever about the Virgin Mary's ideas on décor, yet Focolare is convinced that, as the spiritual presence of the Virgin Mary in the world today, it has a special insight even into such arcane details. On meeting the movement, I was actually instructed on how to do the washing-up the way the Virgin Mary did it – this meant cleaning each utensil immediately after it was used in the course of preparing a meal. At Loppiano the urge to achieve the Virgin Mary's own standards of housekeeping was so strong that one enthusiastic newcomer spent a whole Saturday afternoon cleaning a single shelf in a kitchen cupboard.

The aesthetic strand of the movement's ideology has been carefully elaborated. It has also been embodied in the practices and the culture of the movement, strongly influenced by the tastes of the foundress herself. An internal newsletter breathlessly tells us

[1]Mario Dal Bello, 'One city is not enough', Città Nuova, no. 21, 1993, p. 29.
[2]Chiara Lubich, 'Sede Gen', *Colloqui con i Gen*, Rome: Città Nuova Editrice, 1974, p. 74.

how, when the former Mariapolis Centre at Rocca di Papa was reopened as the administrative centre of the movement, the foundress personally chose the pictures that would adorn it and where they would go.

Like many religious movements in the past, Focolare has appropriated a contemporary architectural style with which it feels in sympathy. As the movement began to build its own properties in the early sixties, they were in the plain and unadorned modernism of that period, slightly tempered by stylistic references to the Tyrolean chalets of the movement's origins.

This severity and impersonality was an apt vehicle to express the spirit of the movement, which exalts simple spiritual ideas and plays down the individual or particular. The qualities of detachment and rejection of 'the world' were embodied in its very buildings. Focolare's architecture has never gone beyond this stage. Indeed, it would be unthinkable that it should adopt the playful stylistic references of post-modernism, for that would be to give value to cultures external to its own.

Emptiness, complete lack of clutter and sparse decoration are the essentials of Focolare interior design. Such simplicity helps show off the virtues of cleanliness and neatness encouraged by the foundress. The obsession with tidiness is taken to such an extreme that Focolare dwellings often give the impression of being un-inhabited. The 'college' building which housed the school of the women *focolarine* at Loppiano while I was there had a tiled lobby so vast, echoing and devoid of furnishings that the building appeared deserted. When tourists visited the village on Sundays, they would be escorted in groups round the small prefabricated chalets where the groups of men lived. These would be vacated and scrubbed to perfection. One English visitor who did not speak a word of Italian, having completed this tour, was convinced that he was visiting some kind of Ideal Home exhibition as the chalets gave no sign of ever having been lived in.

Visiting a Focolare centre in Grottaferrata near Rome in 1993, I noted how the movement's style of interior design has fossilized. The starkness of sixties décor, now that it is no longer fashionable, appears bare and cold. But what I found unnerving was the lack of any expression of the personalities of those who lived there.

Whenever art is recruited to the service of ideology, it is expected to follow standard guidelines: it must be populist and low-brow;

relentlessly upbeat, expressing joy and optimism; content must dominate over form, and the main purpose must be didactic.

When I was at Loppiano, the artefacts we produced were either specifically religious or glorifying Loppiano itself. Their hallmark was a lack of personality. Statues of the Virgin, or of the Holy Family, for example, would have a blank featureless mask instead of a face. An outline of the figure of Christ was cut out from a crucifix, creating a void where the body should be. Portraiture, which exalts the individual, is the antithesis of the Focolare form of representation. Like the movement's interior design, even its simplest artefacts were deemed to 'speak by themselves'.

With its emphasis on the collective at the expense of the individual, it was inevitable that Focolare would formulate an ideology of a group art, expression not of the individual but of 'Jesus in the midst'. One Sunday afternoon, I spent a considerable time trying to explain to a sympathetic but puzzled English visitor how a ceramic tea-set could 'express' unity because it had been made by the women's workshop with 'Jesus in the midst'. For us the ideological standpoint was so strong that it transcended the physical facts.

The songs of the Gen Rosso and Gen Verde bands were also seen as products of the collective, even though, in fact, certain creative individuals were ultimately responsible for them. (Later I was to discover just how fiercely this orthodoxy was upheld.) Gen Rosso's songs were always copyrighted in the same two names of *focolarini* who had nothing to do with their creation.

In addition to her spiritual supremacy, Chiara Lubich is also regarded as – and apparently believes herself to be – an authority on artistic matters. In one of her books of meditations, she dismisses Simone Martini's stylized portrait of St Clare in the Basilica of St Francis in Assisi as having 'little to say to Christians'. Yet, in another 'meditation', she waxes lyrical over a Michelangelo Pietà. It is, of course, the strongly figurative one which stands in St Peter's; representational art is always favoured by ideologies because of its didactic possibilities.

Within the movement, there is an ideological bias against fiction. Inevitably, this can be traced back to Chiara Lubich herself, who declares that as a child 'I did not like dolls, maybe because they were pretend. I did not like fairy tales: I wanted the truth.' The characteristic 'literary' form of Focolare is the 'experience'. The collections of 'experiences' issued in book form by its various publishing houses resemble treasuries of very simple short stories. Although they follow the rigid formula of Problem – Application of Movement's Ideas – Happy Ending, Focolare is not usually mentioned by name, giving them a universal quality, like modern parables. For the members of the movement, 'experiences' are 'true' and fiction is 'false'. Such literalism, typical of the encounter between the arts and ideology, shows the narrowness of its cultural outlook as well as its woolly thinking. Are the parables of Christ and the myths of the Old Testament, such as the Creation story, which are fictional forms, to be regarded as untrue?

The subject-matter of most literary works past and present is also unacceptable from the moral point of view. Giorgio Marchetti, one of the first *focolarini*, known as 'Faith' ('*Fede*') within the movement, once dismissed the works of Shakespeare with the comment, 'He was very well acquainted with the "old man" ' (the Pauline phrase 'the old man' was adopted by the movement to refer to the evil side of human nature). Many of the fundamental themes of world literature clash with the ideology of Focolare. The concept of tragedy was meaningless in Stalinist Russia with its 'cult of optimism'; the masses were under strict orders to be joyful. The same is true for the *focolarini*. Once again, 'experiences' provide the matrix of the obligatory happy ending. Under the influence of this thought process, I wrote an essay at university in which I set out to prove that *Hamlet* was not a tragedy; the personal sacrifice of the unhappy prince would lead to the construction of a new social order. My professor remained unconvinced, preferring to believe that I had completely misunderstood the concept of tragedy.

Chiara Lubich played an important part in the censorship which was to be found at all levels of the movement. All the songs written by Gen Verde and Gen Rosso had to be submitted to her; and, if she did not like the words or the tunes, they were rejected. Indeed, in the early days of the movement, Lubich used to pen the lyrics of Focolare songs herself – to folk or popular tunes of the day. The films we were shown at Loppiano – almost always cartoons, lives of the saints or family films – were viewed beforehand by the authorities and sent back if deemed to be unsuitable. Even in the 'zones', permission had to be sought before going to the cinema – not that we would ever have dreamed of going alone. At Loppiano, we often staged improvised shows. We soon learned the virtues of self-censorship – in particular any hint of 'protest' or criticism had to be excised. Once a French-speaking group of European whites and African blacks put on a satirical sketch about missionaries arriving in Africa and converting the 'natives' with the aid of beads and trinkets. The performance was halted halfway through, in front of an audience of 100 of us, by the deputy leader of the men's section, Umberto Giannettone. He deemed it 'uncharitable' (to the missionaries, I presume).

Although censorship was constantly present, I never questioned it until I took over the editorship of Focolare's English-language magazine *New City* in 1975. Within a matter of a few months, two complaints were received directly from Italy.

In autumn 1975, the women's band from Loppiano, Gen Verde, visited Britain. We decided to produce a special Gen Verde edition of the magazine which could go on sale at concerts as a souvenir, and hopefully boost the circulation of the magazine. I decided that we would produce our own articles rather than translate them from the Italian *Città Nuova* as was customary. One of the original members of Gen Verde was then living in the London women's Focolare house, and so I interviewed her on the origins of the band. I wanted the article to be factual and entertaining, avoiding the usual stress on ideology and semi-mysticism, and produced an interview enlivened by firsthand descriptions and anecdotes. A number of readers commented on how informative and amusing the article had been.

I was taken aback, therefore, when, within minutes of Gen Verde's arrival in Britain, I was buttonholed by its leader, a formidable German *focolarina* named Saba, who was outraged that I had published an interview with an individual member of the group; Gen Verde was not the creation of individuals but of 'Jesus in the midst'. She claimed – and only the *focolarini* could have drawn this conclusion – that I had given the impression that my interviewee had dreamed up Gen Verde singlehandedly. Furthermore, she declaimed, no new material on Gen Verde should have been produced without their authorization.

The second time I attracted the wrath of Rome was in connection with an article I wrote on modern dance. I was informed by Dimitri Bregant that the article had been brought to the attention of Chiara herself by Liliana Cosi, then a ballerina at La Scala, Milan, and a full-time, though undercover, *focolarina*. My innocuous little piece reviewed a number of modern dance groups which had recently performed in London. The ideological slant of the article – there had to be one – was that dance is the most truthful art-form because the body cannot lie. Harmless stuff. And yet the article had been translated into Italian so that Chiara and her circle could scrutinize it more carefully. Although a formal charge was never made, I later learned that the objection was to the fact that I had praised the French choreographer Maurice Béjart and his Brussels-based company, Ballets of the Twentieth Century. The objection was not to the subject-matter of the article but to Béjart's lifestyle.

But the movement's censorship has now begun to spread beyond its own confines. Margaret Coen, a full-time *focolarina*, is an English television producer who played a key role in the creative team that produced the Genfest in 1990 and the Familyfest in 1993. Taking to heart Chiara Lubich's decree that members of the movement working in the media should find ways of promoting its spirit through their programmes, she set up an independent production company in Britain, rather cheekily named Link-up Productions ('link-up' is the English term for Chiara Lubich's fortnightly conference calls). She then set about winning commissions from television stations for religious programmes. Not surprisingly, one of these was a half-hour biography of Chiara Lubich, 'Woman with a Dream', which was commissioned and financed by Central Television to the tune of £30,000 for their 'Encounter' series. It was a shameless piece of propaganda for Focolare – paid for by Central Television. The programme did not contain a single dissenting view. It is a matter for concern that Margaret Coen a full-time member of the movement with a vow of obedience was constrained to submit the programme for the editorial approval of Chiara Lubich in Rome.

Banality was the keynote of all the movement's 'artistic' expressions. The triter the better. A childish simplicity of expression was encouraged. Postcards and paintings of Loppiano adopted a style inspired by children's drawings. Any show of sophistication or intelligence was out: it would have been viewed as suspect, élitist and affected (*ricercato*).

In 1992, Chiara Lubich visited Africa where she gave a speech on the theme of inculturation entitled 'Typhoon of Love'. A film of the same name, covering this event, was produced by the movement's media arm, the Saint Clare Centre. In the title sequence, sound effects of a roaring wind accompanied stock shots of a storm. This example of heavy-handed literalism was greeted with rapturous applause when it was screened before the women *focolarine* gathered in Rome.

When I was at Loppiano in the seventies, the movement's most popular song was a rousing hand-clapper by Gen Rosso unsubtly titled 'I Am So Joyful'. One of the band's earliest 'hits' proclaimed the deathless lyrics: 'Gen, gen, gen/Coming soon/Gen, gen, gen/ What will happen?/Gen, gen, gen/will bring/Gen, gen, gen/unity!'

Lowering standards as much as possible was inclusive. A collective art form to which everyone could contribute had more value than the efforts of individual artists because it was an expression of 'Jesus in the midst' – that is, of God himself.

The artistic heritage of Neocatechumenate consists wholly of the works – songs and paintings – of the founder, Kiko Arguello. As they form part of the 'charism' package, they come with a divine blessing.

CL's range of cultural references is wider and richer than that of Focolare or Neocatechumenate, but nevertheless it serves an ideo-logical function. Its canon of inspirational writers, poets and thinkers was established by Don Giussani in the early days of GS, and it reflects both his tastes and his ideas. Many of these favourites are prominent pre-conciliar Catholic writers like Paul Claudel, Georges Bernanos and especially Charles Péguy. C. S. Lewis is a seminal figure for Giussani and his followers, but their chief theologians are De Lubac, Romano Guardini and, of course, Hans Urs von Balthasar. Both Balthasar and Lubac were close to CL. Although the Christian significance of these figures is evident, others have been accorded an idiosyncratic ideological significance by Giussani. Take the poet Leopardi, for example, Italy's answer to Keats or Shelley; the founder claims that only after reading one of the poet's love lyrics, 'Leopardi's Song to His Woman ('*Canto alla sua donna di Leopardi*'), did he fully understand the opening of the Gospel of St John.

Although his message is a traditionalist one, Giussani specializes in surprising, even shocking, his listeners. The use of unexpected references is part of this approach. The most surprising of the figures that CL has steadfastly championed is the writer-poet-film director Pier Paolo Pasolini, who was brutally murdered by a male prostitute in 1975. The movement made their own Pasolini's analysis of Italian society in the seventies when he acknowledged 'the end of two worlds' – the Catholic and the communist worlds – and discerned the emergence of a new and amorphous technocratic and financial 'power'. According to the Catholic philosopher Augusto del Noce, who was adopted as CL's in-house philosopher in the eighties, 'Pasolini (who was close to the Italian Communist Party) has proved to be an interpreter of today's trends. He was more "Catholic" and better able to grasp the value of the philosophy of Catholic history than many who are the authorized leaders of Catholic political thinking.' In order to promote its pantheon of cultural icons, CL has over a hundred Cultural Centres in cities and towns throughout Italy, often run with financial assistance from local councils, offering a programme of lectures, films and performances featuring major guest speakers.

CL members have always seen themselves as militants, a visible and uncompromising Christian presence in a secularized society, willing to stand up and be counted. Whereas Focolare holds its truth to be self-evident, CL's stance has always been a combative one: distorted and dangerous ideas in society and in the Church have to be countered with the truth.

Following the 1974 Italian referendum on divorce which saw the defeat of the Catholic anti-divorce camp, CL issued a pamphlet entitled *After the Referendum*, which asserted that 'The Christian life has not generated an adequate cultural expression and therefore was not able to resist the attack of worldly power'. They saw as their task to demonstrate concretely and unequivocally that 'the Church was an effective historical force'.

From the earliest days of GS, Giussani's followers have unleashed a blizzard of pamphlets, leaflets, statements and declarations. Thus a distinctive and elaborated ideology has been developed over the years. Despite the intransigence of its ideological position, CL has shown a remarkable adaptability to the changing circumstances of Italian life and politics. Its opinions have always been allied to action as a large and effective pressure group. The high and controversial profile GS carved out for itself in the Italian school life of the fifties and sixties was later to blossom into a national presence in big-league politics in the seventies and eighties. The ideological stance that underpinned this action was expressed on an increasingly wide scale through publications like *30 Days* (*30 Giorni*) and *Saturday* (*Il Sabato*).

CL's own think-tank, the cryptically styled ISTRA (Istituto di studi per la transizione – Institute of Studies for the Transition), was founded in 1972. Its *Theological Yearbook* for 1974 indicated the methodology the movement has followed in formulating its ideology: 'The originality of the CL movement . . . is linked to the unique doctrinal synthesis of which Don Giussani – and now his numerous friends [followers] – is the author, and its evolution in contact with the religious, social and political context in which the movement has been called to express itself.'

The 'working units', or departments, into which ISTRA was divided give an indication of the wide range of subjects on which CL felt confident to pronounce: Philosophy, History, Architecture and Town Planning, Political Theory, Economics, History of the Catholic Movement, not forgetting Theology. As well as the movement's own thinkers like Rocco Buttiglione and Angelo Scola, sympathetic outsiders were also recruited.

The work of ISTRA has produced concrete results. In 1992, the psychoanalyst Giacomo Contri founded the Practical School of Psychology and Psychopathology as a direct challenge to the accepted beliefs and even the history of psychology. The school's approach demonstrates the methodology of CL's ideology, which is to retrieve what is seen to be a lost Catholic inheritance. 'Catholics at the beginning of the twentieth century', Contri maintains, 'sold out a vast patrimony of psychological enquiry and knowledge of man, espousing uncritically the working methods of the Anglo-Saxon philosophy of science on the protestant model. Now, I as a Catholic, even though this might appear immodest, am going to recuperate that patrimony.'

In line with CL's ideology, Contri identifies a vague and sinister 'power' which has manipulated psychology in order to destroy man's religious dimension; it is this he intends to oppose. 'If I were to sum up this situation in a phrase it would be that we've sold our souls. To whom? Naturally to the power that wanted them out of the way so that people could be more easily manipulated. We on the other hand want our souls back.'

This new school of psychiatry, therefore, takes a specifically religious approach, couching psychology in terms of man's 'religious question', and aiming to restore his soul. Contri has taken his inspiration from Don Giussani's teaching that only in man's relationship with God can he find his true self, his ego: 'Starting from the relationship between man and God it is possible to affirm the ego and to understand that we are not machines enslaved by a greater mechanism, but co-authors of ourselves.'

The school, which is subsidized by the Council of Milan and the Region of Lombardy and is based at Milan's University of the Sacred Heart, has succeeded in drawing a number of distinguished lecturers into its ranks.

The teachings of Don Giussani are couched in philosophical rather than spiritual language, and his ideas form the basis of the movement's ideology as it is expressed in its publications. The homogeneity of the movement's thinking shows that its development has not been haphazard but guided mainly by the founder, with some input from a very select group of thinkers within the movement. Ex-journalists of *30 Giorni* recall how Don Giacomo Tantardini, the *éminence grise* of CL's Roman Chapter, would stand behind the editor of the magazine, making changes to the copy. This was during the period when the editorial board in Rome clamped down on changes in the foreign-language editions.

The thrust of CL's ideology is twofold: first, it is anti-modern and finds its inspiration in Catholic thinkers of the past – sometimes the remote past; second, its aim is not so much to formulate solutions as to denounce errors.

In the early years of this century, under Pope Pius X, a witch-hunt was carried out against Catholic theologians who were dubbed 'modernists'; because they rejected a fundamentalist interpretation of Scripture and adopted a historical and critical approach, one which is now fully accepted by the Catholic Church, these 'modernists' were believed to be protestant quislings undermining the Church from within. At the time, they appeared to be questioning the supernatural origins of Scripture and the Church's own authority and making a fatal pact with the World.

The 'modernists' of today, according to CL, are those who are once again undermining the Church's (and therefore their own) claim to a monopoly on God. CL is campaigning for a retreat from the conciliar view that grace is present throughout the world; instead, it promotes a return to the fortress mentality in which the Church is the repository of all truth and goodness, and all outside is error. To suggest that the Church is not the sole channel of God's grace is to detract from its unique role and, more important, from the charism of CL. It also reduces the urgency of the missionary activity which is the lifeblood of the movements.

Thus the great German theologian Karl Rahner, one of the most distinguished figures of the post-Conciliar period, is regarded by Giussani as a crypto-protestant for his belief that 'God and the grace of Christ are in all things' and his concept of 'anonymous Christians', non-believers who unknowingly live out the Gospel. Thus the label 'rahnerian' which Giussani applies to Cardinal Martini represents strong criticism. For CL, the suggestion that Man can achieve anything outside the institutional Church is 'a horrendous and hidden poison' (Henri de Lubac). When the Swiss theologian Hans Kung suggested that the bloodless revolution of Eastern Europe has a religious dimension, he was accused in *30 Giorni* of 'merely expressing the dominant gnosticism of the day'.

Yet in fact CL's position is an impoverishment of Christianity. CL accuses others of minimizing the action of grace, the importance of revelation and the dimension of mystery, while on its part demonstrating a singular lack of faith – and this is shared with the other movements – in an approach which sees God as a prisoner or puppet of the Church, even of a particular movement, and denies to the Holy Spirit the freedom to 'blow where he wills'.

Although the movements appear to be modern because they accept the trappings of modern life – such as technology – they are deeply inimical to modern culture; they are anti-modern. CL looks back to a golden age of Christendom, before the Enlightenment denied the possibility of revelation, before the Reformation with its heretical schisms, to the Middle Ages. CL's main structural unit – the Fraternity – is consciously based on a medieval model; and, while the medievalism openly embraced by CL is not an evident feature of Focolare, it is curious to note that the idea of that movement's little towns first occurred to Chiara Lubich while she was holidaying in Switzerland and looked down upon the Benedictine settlement at Einsiedeln. The abbey is, of course, the quintessential religious/social unit of medieval times. The fascination that particular era holds for the movements is that it was the last age of a unanimously Christian society. The aspect of modernity that the movements cannot cope with is pluralism.

★ ★ ★

Dialogue is another modern concept which is outside the range of the new movements. Those holding immutable positions cannot engage in dialogue, yet 'dialogue' has been adopted as one of the buzzwords of Focolare.

According to Chiara Lubich, the movement sustains four types of dialogue: within the Catholic world, with Christians of other denominations, with members of other religions and 'in the world of secularization, collaborating with men of goodwill to enkindle, or consolidate and extend, universal brotherhood'. The theory sounds fine. But the movement's concept of dialogue is based on the idea of 'making yourself one' with others, which, as has been noted, is a subtle recruiting technique. Chiara Lubich herself explains how the aim of the 'four dialogues' is to reach the point of 'talking about our religion, dialogue which becomes evangelization'.[1]

The expansionist activities of the movements are regarded by members as missionary activity on behalf of the Church. This is hardly surprising in view of the fact that each of the movements considers itself to be the Church in a special sense. The Vatican seems to be guilty of the same confusion. But the distinctive, exclusive nature of each of the movements must be borne in mind: each has a language, a mindset, a raft of beliefs and values which would be virtually unrecognizable to the vast majority of Catholics, which set it apart from the rest of the Church. In its ecumenical and interfaith dialogue, therefore, Focolare is not so much extending the work of the Catholic Church in these areas as enlarging its own boundaries. The *focolarini* may be guilty of no deceit when they state that they do not intend to recruit for the Catholic Church. But what is undeniable is that, as is their wont, they have every intention of recruiting for themselves. At Focolare's ecumenical meetings in the UK, where the majority of members are Anglican, little is heard about the Catholic Church and even less about the Anglican Church, but a great deal about the Ideal of Focolare and the thoughts of Chiara Lubich. The tone of these gatherings is intensely missionary. They follow the Roman line and therefore differ little from meetings held concurrently by the movement all over the world.

[1]Chiara Lubich, 'L'unità e Gesù Abbandonato', *Città nuova*, 1984, p. 118.

In the thirty years since Focolare came to Britain, it has only achieved a handful of conversions to Catholicism; but, far more important, all its non-Catholic members have accepted its key ideas – Unity, Jesus in the midst, Jesus forsaken, devotion to Mary – all within the context of the movement's methods, structures, culture. Above all – and this is considered of prime importance by the members of the movement – Chiara Lubich and her 'charism' are recognized. Internal non-Catholic members accept the movement's structures and methods as wholeheartedly as the Catholics. A video produced by the movement's St Clare Media Centre, *Many but One: The Story of Focolare in the Catholic Church*, is a series of testimonies by Anglicans of their discovery of the wonders of Focolare.

Genuine dialogue is a two-way street. But there is no sense in any of the movement's reports on its ecumenical activities of reciprocity – that is, anything the Catholic *focolarini* might have learned from Anglicans, Lutherans or Orthodox. Indeed, the attitude I discovered within the movement towards the Anglican Church was at best patronizing, at worst – behind closed doors – one of contempt. Shortly after I met the movement I was told by the head of the men's Focolare, Jean-Marie Wallet, now a married *focolarino*, that, following her first visit to Lambeth Palace in 1966, Chiara Lubich declared that 'There is more "supernatural" in the slipper of a cardinal than in the whole Anglican Church' ('*C'e più soprannaturale nella pantofola di un Cardinale che in tutta la Chiesa Anglicana*').

Given their conviction of possession of the truth, it is unlikely that the *focolarini* would approach this activity with any more humility than they do any other; they have everything to teach and nothing to learn. Indeed, ecumenism is seen as an area not of discovery and enrichment but of loving 'Jesus forsaken' in those who are in error.

The statutes of the movement in use in the early seventies encouraged the *focolarini* to dedicate themselves to 'the portions of [Christ's] Mystical Body most undermined by errors; and to commit themselves, as much as they are able, to the healing and retrieval of those parts of the Church torn away by heresy and schism'. A new draft in 1974 softened this somewhat by removing the second section of this clause.

Chiara Lubich was awarded the Cross of St Augustine in 1981 by the Archbishop of Canterbury, Dr Robert Runcie, 'in recognition of all Focolare had done among Anglicans to help foster and deepen their spiritual lives'.[1] Yet it is hard to see what relevance Focolare's work of selling itself and its own ideas can possibly have for others working in the ecumenical field. It has expanded into other Christian churches – nothing more. Focolare's ecumenical successes have no more relevance for ecumenism as a whole than their towns have to the world economy, and for precisely the same reasons.

The Focolare 'dialogue' with other religions began in 1977 when Chiara Lubich was awarded the Templeton Prize for Progress in Religion at London's Guildhall. She describes how she felt a rapport with the members of other faiths she met there. But concrete developments were to come later. The winner of the Templeton Prize for 1979, Nikkyo Niwano, founder of the Japanese Buddhist Rissho Kosei-kai (RKk) movement which has 6 million members, visited Chiara Lubich in Rome on his return journey to Japan. In December 1981, he invited Chiara to address 12,000 members of his movement at its headquarters in Tokyo.

In an interview with Vatican Radio before she left for Japan, Chiara Lubich summed up the purpose of her visit: 'I deem it a true gift from God for me, a woman and a Catholic, to be able to communicate to thousands of Buddhists my Christian experience, to be able to proclaim Jesus to those who maybe only know him by name, to be able to speak of his Gospel and of how, living it, its promises are verified, one by one. To give, in other words, a testimony of Christ.'

These words hardly suggest dialogue. Commenting on them in a book of Chiara Lubich's journals entitled *Meetings with the Orient,* the *focolarino*-priest Enzo Fondi confirms that 'According to Chiara, therefore, this was a case of "evangelization", in line with a spiritual experience and a type of dialogue that draws its fruitfulness from the Gospel.'[2]

This form of interfaith 'dialogue', therefore, is evangelization, or announcement of the Christian message; but it is the Christian message according to Focolare, the 'spiritual experience and . . . type of dialogue' referred to by Fondi. Certainly the movement – at least, in the short term – shows no interest in mass conversions

[1]Frank Johnson, 'All that is ours is yours', *New City*, August/September 1993, p. 151.
[2]Chiara Lubich, *Incontri con l'Oriente*, Rome: Città Nuova Editrice, 1987, p. 9.

to Catholicism. But it does set great store by tributes paid to the movement and particularly the recognition of the 'charism' of Chiara Lubich.

Following this encounter, Niwano requested the involvement of the *focolarini* in an interfaith organization of which he was one of the original promoters: the World Conference of Religions for Peace. Focolare appears to have played an increasingly influential role in this organization. But the movement's internal news-bulletins show that its main concern is to sell the movement within the organization.

Chiara Lubich's 'companion', Natalia Dallapiccola, was present at the Fifth Assembly of the WCRP held in Melbourne from 22 to 27 January 1989. There were tensions among some of the delegates; but, according to the conference call of 23 February 1989:

> At the crucial point on January 26th, Chiara's message was read by Natalia. In a plenary meeting, a sacred atmosphere was created . . . The adherence to Chiara's proposal was full and enthusiastic. Bishop Fernandez from New Delhi, taking his turn as President, turned solemnly to those present, saying, 'This message has brought us to the essential.' The turning-point had come. An atmosphere of unity had been reached.

At an earlier meeting, in 1987, the news report was even more categorical about Focolare's proselytizing mission: 'Natalia tells us that in the final plenary meeting and also in the group meetings it was possible to announce in a clear and incisive way the spirituality and the light of the movement.' This concept is put across with even more force in this summary of the event: 'The strength and power of the charism is entering the organization which unites religions for peace, the World Conference of Religions for Peace.'

Focolare's extraordinary conviction of its own uniqueness is shown by the fact that, even among non-Christians, it invites the recognition of its 'charism'. In a message Chiara Lubich sent to a meeting of 130 Muslim 'friends [there are 4,400 altogether] of Focolare' at the Mariapolis Centre of Castelgandolfo in 1992, she says: 'The manifestation of the intervention of God today is the special gift or charism, as we say, which we have had the adventure of encountering, and that is our Ideal which came to us in the most varied ways.' The orientation of the meeting was set with the announcement by the *focolarini* organizers that 'Only from you can we learn what this Ideal, this charism means, seen in the light of your Islamic faith'.

A report of this event in *Città Nuova* is full of the standard 'impressions' to be found in all reports of the movement's events: 'The Ideal of the Focolare is for everyone, it is not a utopia'; 'Chiara's speech, despite the fact that she is a figure of Christian culture, swept me up into this family dedicated to building a new world'; 'When I heard Chiara for the first time, I had the impression of reawakening'; 'In our culture a man is not supposed to cry, but I confess that at the words of Chiara's message I wept with emotion'.[1]

It is hard to see how this enthusiasm for Focolare can possibly have any relevance to worldwide interfaith dialogue. Ultimately, however, Focolare is not searching for common ground but for conversions. In *The Adventure of Unity*, which is aimed at a broad public, Lubich describes dialogue with non-believers as 'collaborating with men of good will to encourage or consolidate and extend universal brotherhood'. Yet in her teachings to internal members she explains how Focolare is coming to the rescue of these miserable wretches, with whom non-Catholic Christians are lumped together – hardly the equal partners with their own dignity that the word *dialogue* suggests. The hidden agenda of the movements' attempts at dialogue, like every other aspect of their culture, is expansion. Their missionary ambitions are clearly limitless; but to achieve them, in addition to divine assistance, they need the all too material props of wealth and power.

[1] Annamaria Pericoli, 'The Moslem friends of the movement', *Città Nuova*, no. 13, 1992, pp. 32-6.

10

WEALTH AND POWER

DESPITE THE HARSH VIEWS OF THE MOVEMENTS ON THE MATERIALISM of the modern world, they have shown considerable flair in the fields of finance and politics, which are the foundations of the vast multinational empires they are building. It is enough to look at the enormous outlay – over £30 million – required to finance NC's involvement in the 1993 World Youth Day in Denver. Exactly where these funds come from is harder to say. As NC does not officially exist as an organization within the Church, it is not accountable for its finances. But, as with the classic sects, its wealth and that of the other new Catholic movements is based on the regular financial contributions or tithes they exact from members.

One of NC's major outgoings is the work of the itinerant catechists and missionary families. Officially it is claimed that these leave for their destinations without any means of support, but other witnesses insist that this is not the case.

The personal wealth of catechists has been cause for comment, too. Members of St Nicholas Parish in Bristol noted that Father José Guzman of the United Kingdom National Team of Neo-catechumenate turned up to a meeting in an expensive outfit which included what seemed like a £300 Burberry coat. When I visited the first NC community of Canadian Martyrs in Rome, I was similarly struck by the quality of the clothes of the two leading catechists, Gianpiero Donnini and Franco Voltaggio, in marked contrast to the ordinary or even shabby clothes of the congregation at the Saturday-evening NC Eucharist service.

The attitude of the new movements to money has much in common with the gospel of prosperity preached by televangelists in the United States. This is a repackaged version of the protestant work ethic. God, it says, wants you to be wealthy – financial success is a sign of His favour. It is an absurd, simplistic, distasteful message, and a travesty of a religion in which poverty has a positive value.

Before the first scrutiny, Kiko Arguello tells his adepts:

> You may think that Jesus wants us to be poor, that we suffer. But it's not true. This comes from a context of natural religion. In all religions, poverty is a sign of purity. And wealth is a sign of impurity. This is a natural sense we all have. So people who have millions basically don't feel right out of a religious feeling of impurity, because there are people in the world who go hungry. We find this in all religions: poverty as a sign of purity. In the Middle Ages, therefore, when Christianity was at the height of natural religiosity, if St Francis of Assisi had not appeared in sackcloth, not even his own Father would have listened to him.

But the true message of the gospel, Arguello insists, is that we must experience not poverty but wealth:

> This is not Christianity. Jesus Christ does not tell you to sell everything you have because if you sacrifice yourself in this life you will gain heaven. Let's go on reading: Whatever you leave for love of the gospel – your house, your car, your woman, your mother, the field or farm, I promise I will give you on this earth a hundred houses, if he gives me a car, a hundred cars and so forth. It's not a question of being poor . . . As a result of sin we are all slaves and we don't enjoy money. The Lord wants us to be free and enjoy money, for us to be kings of the world, not that we make use of things that have no value . . . Christian spirituality is not of this stoic dressing-in-rags variety . . . I, brothers, go to preach the gospel and they give me everything. I travel by plane. 'Listen, we're fed up,' say religious people. 'What a great time you have!' Oh, so you'd prefer me to have a hard time, would you? What, are you jealous? In other words you'd prefer me to have it tough before going to heaven.

Arguello follows up this tirade with examples of how Jesus spent time in the houses of the rich, drawing the conclusion that: 'Jesus does not want people who sacrifice themselves, even though we have passed through a very religious era when there was a very masochistic brand of Christianity of self-sacrifice.' On the contrary, Arguello insists, God wants us to be rich: 'It is not that God wants you to be poor, but God wants to make you an administrator of higher goods, including material wealth, of whatever He wants.'

A special onslaught is reserved for the religious orders, for whom poverty is an important virtue:

> A mania for economic poverty has entered the Church, concentrating exclusively on money . . . with the result that by seeking this wretched poverty they have given enormous importance to money and fallen in the opposite trap . . . And whoever gives great importance to money, it's because he loves it so much.

In his view, the stinginess of the religious orders leads them to make unreasonable demands on their members:

> So, for example, if they sent a religious to a far-off missionary post. . . . Oh dear, what an expense to bring him back! And if they give such importance to money, in the end, the money needed to bring him back is more important than that poor priest who is a missionary there for six years: and someone who spends six years in Africa, by the end of it, is ready to go into a psychiatric clinic!

Even in the objects they need for devotional purposes, Arguello accuses, the orders are niggardly: 'For example, they bring out an edition of the psalms printed on rice-paper – really cheap – and they don't give it a leather binding because we Christians must be poor. This sort of thing.'

Of course, the attitude Arguello describes is in net contrast with that found within Neocatechumenate. Take the question of travel, for example:

> One of the things that surprises the religious orders is the mobility of the Neocatechumenal Way . . . Whatever has to be done, if it comes from God, we do it, cost what it may. God pulls the

money out from wherever He wants. For example, now [he is talking in 1981] in Italy we have a *convivence* to which itinerants from all over the world will come . . . (because they are leaving for two years and they will have many problems to deal with): just think how many thousands it will cost to bring 300 itinerants from America, from Japan, etc.!

The huge sums spent by the movement on flowers, vestments and lavish Church furnishings show how different their outlook is from the penny-pinching orders with their rice-paper books as described by Arguello.

The founder's views on money are riven with contradictions. Certainly, the frequency with which he and his followers address the subject of wealth and how to make people part with it suggests that they are as obsessed with the subject as those they accuse. Arguello uses the strongest possible terms to demonstrate that money is the root of all evil:

When a community is not listening to you, when the catechesis bounces off them, you already know what the trouble is: the community is attached to its money and does not want to convert . . . The point is that money can be idolatry and you have the power to cast out these demons . . . until you cast out the devil and you tell them there is a deep idolatry, they will not listen to you.

Some of the movement's most questionable practices are those used to divide members from their wealth. Principal among these is the black bin-bag, NC's version of the collecting-plate. Whether this was chosen as an apt or simply an ample vehicle for the gathering up of filthy lucre remains unclear. *Convivences,* NC's residential meetings, tend to be held not in cheap accommodation such as retreat-houses but in reasonably good hotels. For newcomers, the moment of financial reckoning comes as a shock.

A lay member of one of the committees of the Bishops' Conference of England and Wales, not himself a member of NC, but concerned about its impact on his parish, described such an event:

The last weekend [of the introductory catechesis] was spent in a motel. The location and all other details were kept a complete secret even to those attending. The notice said: 'Don't worry about costs . . . The beds are made . . . There is food in the larder; JUST COME.' Apparently the meals were very ample, and the weekend was, I think, found generally enjoyable, until towards the end when the question of money was raised. *They were asked for £4,000.* A bag was passed round to collect cash, cheques and IOUs. At the first go, so I've been told, only about a quarter of this sum was contributed. There then followed two more enforced collections, with what I can only describe as public harassment of certain individuals whose contributions were examined and declared to be insufficient. Eventually the full sum demanded was raised . . . One of the catechumens was there with his Catholic wife. They were absolutely shattered by this episode, and the wife was in tears. They must have parted with something in the region of £160, which they can ill afford . . . I only hope this does not drive this man away from the Church.

This scenario has been confirmed by other reports from Britain and elsewhere. An intriguing variation comes from a woman member in Rome, whose first *convivence* took place at a retreat centre run by Poor Clare nuns:

I was struck by the fact that at the end of the third day, when we had to pay the sisters' bill, a black bin-bag was passed among us while we were recollected in prayer in which everyone was to put 'what he could afford, with generosity and thinking of the brothers who were unable to pay'. The first time round, they did not collect the required amount. The sack was passed round again; and our catechist, sounding deeply moved, gave us to understand that something extraordinary had happened – not only had we reached the required sum, but it had been surpassed. There was a touch of magic about it. I was really impressed that those among us could have been so generous.

But this story had a postscript. Some years later, when she was already becoming disillusioned with NC, during a liturgy the responsible called her and some others apart and asked them

to collect some money as soon as possible because there was a community – at Mentana, I think – who were approaching a 'passage' and therefore, and I quote, 'we must do as we normally do and have a generous sum at their disposal, just in case the money collected first time round isn't enough'. I felt as though I had been stabbed! I realized that it had been the same the first time for us, that there had also been other people who had helped us in some way. It was still the help of Providence, but why not say so openly – why give that sense of mystery and magic, to make an impression on us. I spoke with the priest responsible, and he told me I should not judge!

According to this account, financial 'miracles' are deliberately manipulated to aid in the conversion of new recruits.

In addition to collections at *convivences,* when they have reached a certain level, all NC members are required to give a tenth of their income. Bearing in mind that the majority of members are middle-class professionals, the 'tithes' collected from thousands of members can be staggering. Members are not allowed to ask about what is done with the money.

For the leaders of the movement, the moment of truth for all those who join the Way comes during the first scrutiny when they are required to sell all their possessions and dispose of their savings. Members are put under extreme pressure to carry out this require-ment of the Way. In Britain members have been known to sell all their furniture – even their beds. Serious marital disputes have been triggered in cases where only one spouse belongs to the movement and either sells part of the furniture or gives away funds belonging to the family. When the bishop of the northern Italian town of Brescia called a halt to NC catechesis in his diocese, he made special reference to 'Family arguments between husband and wife, between parents and children over the unilateral renunciation of money'.

The pressure to give money and goods is incessant. According to Father Enrico Zoffoli, the bin-bag collection at the end of a *convivence* at the NC retreat centre of Arcinazzo near Rome reached the dizzying heights of over £2 million.[1]

Perhaps the most controversial use of these immense funds is the generous donations made to parish priests and bishops. An article in an Italian Catholic magazine suggests that these sums are buying

[1] Zoffoli, *Eresie del Movimento Neocatecumenale*, Udine: Edizione Segno, 1991, p. 89.

silence from many priests: '*Is there a material incentive to keep quiet?*
A parish priest told me, in this regard, how his Neocatechumenal
communities – the majority of whose members work in banks and
building societies – *had given him millions* [of lire] *for the church* [his
emphasis].'[1]

'It would be absurd', writes Father Alfredo Nesi in an open letter
to the bishops of Tuscany and bishops and cardinals of his
acquaintance in Brazil, 'if the fact that you receive 25 per cent of
the huge sums that circulate within the Neocatechumenal Way
could in any way be read as tacit consent or passive tolerance.'

Many opponents of the movement in Italy, including influential
theologians and members of the clergy, believe that these sums –
and the large amounts which allegedly go directly to the Vatican –
play a part in the lack of ecclesiastical interference which NC
appears to enjoy. Huge sums of money were spent by the movement
on the meeting for European bishops held in Vienna in April 1993
and the similar event in Rome in January 1994 for the bishops of
Africa. NC paid all the hotel and travel bills for the bishops and
cardinals who participated. To the suggestion that NC paid for
Bishop Cordes' holidays in Val Gardena in the Dolomites, an Italian
archbishop replied: 'And the rest! There's a lot more than just
holidays.'

It is even alleged that NC has told its followers: 'You must learn
how to buy bishops.'

Shortly after I arrived at Loppiano, one of the administrative staff
paid a hurried visit to our various workplaces. Visibly embarrassed,
he urged us to sign a form in which we renounced all the material
goods which we had brought with us to Loppiano. We were too
naïve to realize just how unreasonable the demand really was. After
all, we were at the stage of novitate and had not yet made a
permanent commitment to the movement.

There was a very practical reason for this requirement, as I later
discovered. Some Italian members brought substantial assets with
them to the town – such as cars. These automatically became
common property on arrival. It had happened that those who had
not stayed the course wanted their vehicles back. But, as far as the
movement was concerned, they were non-returnable.

[1] Luciano Bartoli, *Palestra del Clero*, May 1990, p. 375.

The alarming possessiveness of Focolare towards material goods was well illustrated by a story recounted by Dr Marcelo Claria, the superior of the Focolare community in Liverpool while I was there, who now runs the movement's psychiatric centre near Rome. He told us with unfeigned abhorrence of the sudden departure from the movement of a Brazilian *focolarino* I had known at Loppiano. Claria was at pains to point out, however, that it was not the defection that bothered him. He objected, rather, to the fact that the *focolarino* had been bought a new suit immediately before his departure, which, naturally, he had taken with him. The financial loss represented by the new suit, almost amounting to robbery, Claria made plain, was a far more painful loss than that of the person.

The concept of private property is vehemently rejected by Focolare, in flat contradiction of the social teachings of the Catholic Church. Instead, it promotes the 'communion of goods' – the renunciation of all money and possessions to the collectivity.

In a speech to the International Gen Congress in 1968, Chiara Lubich impressed this concept on the young people of the movement in inflammatory language. 'The preceding generation, I feel,' she confided, 'haven't got the strength: today, only a few, those totally given to God, follow this line.' The youth of the movement, she suggests, have the flexibility to build 'a movement which considers possessions as the patrimony of God to be administered for the good of all'. This 'patrimony' is dubbed 'God's capital'. The conviction that what belongs to the movement belongs to God is the inspiration behind the attitude of members to material goods. While individuals may sincerely espouse personal poverty, this does not conflict with their unlimited acquisitiveness on behalf of the movement. As an institution it is guilty of collective greed.

The foundation of Focolare's wealth, therefore, is the guaranteed income of the 'communion of goods'. For the full-time *focolarini,* this means handing over their salary at the end of each month. For other internal members, such as the married *focolarini*, volunteers, Gen, priests and religious, a financial commitment is required representing their 'superfluous', or what is left when the necessities of life have been covered. Each of these branches within the movement has its own economy, with a contribution going to the Centre of the movement in Rome. As with Neocatechumenate, the apparently limitless financial resources of Focolare are based on these contributions from members. But in addition to this normal

economy there are regular fund-raising drives for local and international objectives such as charitable projects or simply for the
acquisition of land or property. Huge sums are spent on travel and
accommodation expenses for national or international gatherings,
but the bulk of these are paid for by individuals on top of their
regular contributions.

The other pillar of the Focolare economy is known as 'Providence'. Again based on the Gospel idea of the 'hundredfold', this
is Focolare's version of the gospel of prosperity. Recently, Chiara
Lubich has spoken of the 'culture of giving' which the movement
should foster. Looking back to my days as a *focolarino*, I should rather
say that a 'culture of taking' was dominant. A constant flow of gifts
was expected; windfalls were the order of the day. Adherents and
sympathizers needed to be constantly nudged and reminded of their
duty to give goods and cash to the movement.

When we attended the Mariapolis we *focolarini* would never
have dreamed of putting our hands in our pockets to buy drinks;
others would and should pay. Holiday accommodation was always
provided free to the *focolarini* by members of the community.
Gratitude, though a gospel virtue, was not part of the Focolare
spirituality. Why should we feel grateful for what, according to the
Gospel, was our due?

The 'culture of taking' was so much a part of the Focolare way
of life that what would appear to be shameless scrounging in any
other context was perfectly acceptable. When we opened the first
men's Focolare in Liverpool at the beginning of 1973, we intended
to furnish our flat for nothing; but we were not prepared to accept
any old rubbish. We held a housewarming party, at which little
pictures were displayed around the flat in order to give people an
idea of what we needed. We may have been begging, but it was
begging with panache.

Much of the 'Providence' received by the movement is on a far
larger scale – legacies, land, properties. 'Providence' is not something that is simply awaited passively. It can also be claimed.
Convinced that 'Providence' was something that was our due, the
'culture of taking', in my experience, sanctioned some pretty shady
actions. The *focolarini*, for example, would photocopy whole books
at work. The mother of one of the young Italians, who was
attending Loppiano at the same time as me, was a switchboard
operator in Naples. Between them, they cooked up an ingenious

scheme which must have saved Loppiano hundreds of thousands of lire. Late at night, the young man would assemble *focolarini* from the most far-flung locations round the world. He would call his mother on the switchboard, and one by one she would put his friends in touch with their families – absolutely free, of course.

The authorities at Loppiano were constantly on the lookout for ways in which we could earn extra cash. One of the most extraordinary odd jobs I was asked to do was on behalf of a volunteer of the movement in Florence who was studying English at university. He was required to write a thesis on the novels of E. M. Forster – in English. As his grasp of English was poor and his knowledge of Forster even weaker, I was asked to write the thesis for him. I was seized by scruples momentarily, but then reasoned that if I had been asked to perform this task by my superiors it must be the Will of God.

They, of course, showed no scruples. The Will of God seemed to justify behaviour which in other contexts would have appeared deceitful. I and a fellow-student, whom I recruited to the movement while at university, managed to secure a research bursary to pay for our trips to a Focolare junket in Rome on the pretext that it was a cultural event. We successfully negotiated an interview with a panel of lecturers and wrote a follow-up report without ever letting slip the religious nature of our travels. This was done in the full knowledge of our superiors in the movement, who encouraged and praised our cunning.

As 'Providence' becomes the property of the movement itself, it is the full-time *focolarini* who benefit the most from it. Certainly they are assured of lifelong economic security. They will never experience true poverty or even the financial worries that are one of the greatest pressures of modern life.

The philosophy of the 'hundredfold' is taken very literally – the *focolarini* firmly believe that all they have left in joining the movement they will be given back a hundred times over. So, though they pride themselves on their poverty, they adjust easily to a life of relative comfort and lack of financial care. The *focolarini* are constantly travelling abroad, for instance. The Europeans attend their own meetings twice a year in Rome, sometimes more often if they accompany other branches of the movement for their meetings. In addition all the *focolarini* have at least a fortnight's holiday in the summer after the Mariapolis, usually in an attractive location by the sea or in the mountains – the favourite alternatives of Italian holidaymakers.

Among the upper echelons, such as the leaders of 'zones' or those at the Centre of the movement, there are ample funds available. Every new electronic gadget is purchased hot off the production line to facilitate the obsessive circulation of news within the movement: faxes, portable phones, laptops, portable printers are available in abundance – and always in the latest model.

Leaders of the 'zones' or at the Centre of the movement drive the finest cars with the pretext of heavy workloads and busy schedules. In fact they work for the movement full-time and their commitments hardly compare with those of overworked professional people. Despite the fact that the *focolarini* make much of the fact that they work for a living, this is not always the case. As with Opus Dei, those *focolarini* who become priests give up their professions – and these are often among the most highly qualified, including many doctors of medicine. In addition to the leaders of the 'zones', many other *focolarini* are 'unhooked' (*sganciati*) or released from the obligation of full-time work in order to dedicate themselves more fully to internal tasks. There are *focolarini* who have not earned their living for years, yet they are fully maintained by the movement. Despite much high-flown talk about the dignity of work, the full-time *focolarini* regard an ordinary job as an unfortunate necessity on which as little time as possible should be spent – hence the attraction of a profession such as teaching with its short hours and long holidays. Dedication to a job for its own sake would be considered an attachment, and there is certainly no imperative to accept overtime or obtain advancement as there might be for those with genuine financial pressures.

The FAIR marks of cults refer to groups which 'exploit members through unpaid employment and poor working conditions'. While at Loppiano, I was frequently employed, without pay, as an interpreter at the many international meetings held at the Mariapolis Centre in Rome and at Loppiano. Trade associations or codes regulating working conditions had no relevance in the context of Focolare; and if talks dragged on, as they invariably did, simultaneous translation sessions could last for up to three hours.[1] We

---

[1] Interpreting sessions should last no more than 20 minutes to half an hour.

would be stuck in unventilated booths in raging temperatures, so mentally exhausted that we switched to automatic pilot, oblivious of what we were translating. Stories circulated of *focolarini* who suffered nervous breakdowns under these conditions, and ran weeping from the translation-booths.

Chiara Lubich herself lives the life of a wealthy woman. She has her own large house set in landscaped gardens at Rocca di Papa in the Roman Hills, another at Loppiano, and still others in major centres of the movement – all for her personal use. Like many celebrities in the secular world, she has a penchant for Switzerland, whose climate especially suits her, and for the past few decades she has spent two months each summer in a rented villa situated in one of its most fashionable areas. She has a large and stylish wardrobe, with her clothes specially made for her by the Lilies of the Field fashion centre at Loppiano, and she travels in a large chauffeur-driven vehicle. She and the movement would claim that she is not personally wealthy and that these material trappings are merely the 'hundredfold', an expression of the affection its members feel towards her. The fact remains that hers is not the most credible of positions from which to rail at materialism and prophesy the imminent collapse of the Western world.

As in the case of Neocatechumenate, the bulk of Focolare's cash goes towards its expansion, including its many building projects and missionary activities. Massive amounts are spent on travel and communications. The bill for Chiara Lubich's fornightly conference calls alone is tens of thousands of pounds. Of course the movement's real wealth, which is constantly increasing, lies in its buildings and lands, often donated through bequests or by the Church – disused convents and seminaries, for example – or purchased through donations of members.

Many of the Focolare houses round the world are owned by the movement, but the most substantial properties are the Mariapolis centres, large enough to accommodate the various meetings of the branches of an individual zone and therefore with sleeping accommodation for a hundred or more people, a meeting-hall, a restaurant and a chapel. Figures from 1988 show that there were thirty-six of these centres around the world. In addition there were forty-three 'Houses of Loreto' (Case Lauretane) belonging to the full-time women *focolarine* and forty-two belonging to the men. These are substantial properties which form the headquarters for the male or female branches of each 'zone', with rooms assigned for various purposes including a chapel.

Even a relatively small 'zone' like Britain has the equivalent of a Mariapolis Centre – the Focolare Centre for Unity in Welwyn Garden City, just north of London. This large building, a former convent, was bought outright by the movement in 1986. The necessary sum was raised through an intensive fund-raising drive involving the entire community of the movement in the country. Focolare secured the property for considerably less than its market value as the order of nuns it had belonged to preferred that it should continue to be used by a Catholic organization. In addition Focolare owns nine substantial private houses around the country.

But by far the largest financial project of Focolare is the 'Economy of Communion'. When she launched this project in 1991, Chiara Lubich gave a new impetus to the founding of the movement's own towns. As we have seen, there are now twenty of these, and more in development; they could double or treble within the next five years. In Europe, towns are established in Italy, Switzerland, Spain, Germany and Croatia; while other towns may be found in the United States, Mexico, Brazil, Argentina, the Philippines, Australia and Africa. Even the United Kingdom and the Netherlands are planning their own towns. The financial worth of these settlements must be immense, and constantly increasing as new buildings are erected and factories with valuable plant are opened. But Lubich's project that these 'towns' should form the backbone of a new economy will ensure that they are not simply dead assets but an investment which will be fully exploited, providing a handsome new income for the movement.

Despite its wealth and size, Neocatechumenate is essentially an apolitical organization. Like extreme world-rejecting sects such as the Plymouth Brethren or the Jehovah's Witnesses, it is pre-millenarian in outlook, seeing the world on a relentless downward spiral of decline and decadence as it awaits Christ's Second Coming. Political and social activity is a waste of time; the only worthwhile effort is to save as many souls as possible. To date, therefore, while anxious to win power within the Church in any way it can, NC has shown itself hostile to any form of secular ambition.

Focolare and CL, on the other hand, while to some extent taking the same pessimistic view of the world, see themselves in an active role of preparation for the millennium. They will be instrumental, if not actually the principal agents, in bringing about a new world order, partly through their own organization but also by becoming 'guides and counsellors to kings and presidents'.[1]

Despite Chiara Lubich's claim that her motto has always been 'humility and concealment, not showing off, not making a noise', the movement she created has assiduously cultivated powerful figures in the Church, giving it a high profile in the Vatican from the earliest days. Yet they were not content just to woo the ecclesiastically powerful; their ambitions go much further. Their fundamentalist interpretation of Christ's phrase 'May they all be one', and the unique role of the movement in fulfilling it, is clearly outlined in a speech Chiara Lubich made to 920 Gen boys and girls at the Mariapolis Centre of Castelgandolfo on 18 January 1987 to mark the twentieth anniversary of the foundation of Gen:

> Take the charism in its entirety without watering it down, so that it can be passed on to the other generations just as it is. You will see miracles from a life like this – people who convert, the goal of 'that all may be one' will get closer, the world united will not be a utopian dream. In fact, God who is almighty, is with us. He is with you.

With this grandiose mission in mind, from its earliest days the movement has aimed at influencing powerful figures and bodies in the secular field. It is not surprising, then, that one of the first appointments Chiara Lubich made on bringing the movement to Rome in 1948 was at Montecitorio, the Italian parliament, with the eminent Catholic MP, Igino Giordani, one of the co-founders of the Italian Christian Democrat Party. At this time Giordani, who had been a leading figure in Italian political life for three decades, was becoming bitterly disenchanted with politics and politicians. He was an ardent admirer of the thirteenth-century mystic Catherine of Siena. A member of the Third Order of St Dominic, Catherine was celibate yet technically not a nun but a laywoman; nevertheless in her short but intense existence she had wielded authority over the popes and princes of her day. Almost immediately, Giordani was drawn to Chiara Lubich, who was also,

[1]Roy Wallis, *The Elementary Forms of the New Religious Life*, London: Routledge & Kegan Paul, 1983, p. 9.

technically, a laywoman, in whom he discerned a second Catherine and one who might also exert a spiritual authority over the great and the powerful. His desire for total commitment to the movement and its youthful foundress led to the creation of the category of married *focolarini*. The highly spiritual demands of Focolare provoked a fierce internal battle for this cultured, intellectual man, lasting for the next two decades. His swing to spiritual idealism following his meeting with Chiara led to the loss of his seat in the elections of 1953. Disillusioned with politics, he dedicated himself to writing and work for the movement, such as editing *Città Nuova*.

Through this initial contact, the *focolarini* became acquainted with other members of parliament such as the Honourable Palmiro Foresi, father of Pasquale Foresi, the first *focolarino* to become a priest. Acide de Gasperi, founder of the Christian Democrats and for many years Prime Minister of Italy, was cultivated by the nascent movement. When he attended the summer Mariapolis at Fiera di Primiero in the Dolomites, Chiara spotted him approaching from the balcony of her chalet and sang to him a verse from one of the Focolare songs current at that time: 'Tram drivers, students, doctors . . . and MPs are all equal once they get to the Mariapolis!'

To those members of parliament who, along with Giordani, were captivated by Focolare, Lubich offered a list of nineteen points they were to follow in their political lives. These were mainly of a highly spiritual nature – to help each other to become saints, to keep 'Jesus in the midst', to be aware that their political work would only be effective inasmuch as they were in unity.

Two decades later, the movement's methods of hooking celebrities had grown in efficiency: they would be packed off to Loppiano where they would be given the works. These visits were stage-managed from first to last. They would begin with an escorted tour round the town's various districts. Then they would be regaled with the kind of show that was to become the movement's characteristic public face at events such as the Genfest or the Familyfest – an extravaganza of songs, dances, mimes and 'experiences', carefully prepared to suit the tastes or background of the guest of honour. This phenomenon was especially marked when Chiara Lubich accompanied them on the visit.

This was the case when Cardinal Suenens, primate of Belgium, visited Loppiano in 1971. One of the most influential cardinals of the Church, a protagonist of the Council and at that time considered *papabile*, to win him as a close ally of the movement would be a major coup. Chiara Lubich had apparently been cultivating him for months. The preparations for this visit were even more painstaking than usual. Considered a left-winger at the time – at least in Focolare terms – he needed the full treatment. We were given regular updates on the background to this association. Suenens was a protector of the traditional international Catholic lay movement, the Legion of Mary, which began in Ireland but had spread within the Church worldwide. One of the movement's leaders, Veronica O'Brien, a close associate of Suenens, had decided to dispose of a large property owned by the Legion in rue Boileau in Paris. The declining numbers of the Legion of Mary meant that the building's upkeep was no long justifiable, and Veronica O'Brien was seeking a worthy successor among the newer lay movements in the Church. She was so impressed with Focolare that she felt that Suenens should know about it, too.

It is interesting to see how this episode is dealt with in a book of Cardinal Suenens' letters recently published in French. Although the encounter with the movement, the gift of the house (which is still Focolare's main centre in Paris) and Chiara's speech at the opening ceremony are all described, his links are played down and nothing is mentioned about his visit to Loppiano, his many personal encounters with Chiara Lubich and his introduction of the movement to his influential friends. In his book, for example, he mentions the fact that, according to Focolare custom, Lubich gave Veronica O'Brien the new name of Grace, but he omits to mention the fact that, so we were told, Chiara gave him the name of John. Suenens had been a close friend of Archbishop Montini of Milan prior to his election as Pope Paul VI. Together they had been considered radicals and, according to the account we received, there had been a pact between them that whoever became Pope would implement their ideals.

Once Montini ascended the papal throne, however, he modified his views to accommodate the right wing of the Church. This, Suenens believed, was a betrayal, and relations between them had become strained. One of Chiara Lubich's main goals was to bring about Suenens' submission to Paul VI. This mission, we are told, was accomplished. This was the significance of the new name. Suenens the old friend was now John the beloved disciple.

But frantic rumours were circulating on the gossip circuit known as Radio Loppiano. Chiara was spending a lot of time in Belgium engaged in secret meetings at the highest level. Speculation was rife on the identity of the high-powered new recruits. Then preparations were begun for a VIP visit to the town on an unprecedented scale, but no-one knew who the *pezzo grosso*, the 'big shot', was. There was a complete news-blackout on the event. We were not even allowed to refer to it in letters home.

La Signora, as she was referred to throughout her one-day visit to the town, was never named. Most of us, however, recognized her as Queen Fabiola of Belgium. It is well known that she and her husband King Baudouin were devout Catholics. Indeed, in the Low Countries it was long rumoured that the king, who died in 1993, was a member of the highly secretive and traditionalist Spanish movement Opus Dei. For a time in the early seventies, at least, he and his consort fell under the spell of Focolare. After the visit, the smokescreen of secrecy was dispelled and we were given detailed updates on the events which had led to the visit, of weekends spent at the Royal Palace in Brussels by Chiara Lubich, Don Foresi and Doriana Zamboni, one of Chiara's first companions, of new names flying hither and thither. According to these accounts, the palace was the scene of the dramatic and hoped-for 'conversion' of Cardinal Suenens when he fell to his knees before Chiara and pledged his obedience.

The Belgium connection came to a rather abrupt end. We were told that Suenens had suggested to Chiara Lubich that he should take on the role of the movement's protector. But that would have undermined Don Foresi's position as official 'ecclesiastical assistant', or Focolare's official representative to Church authorities. Suenens' offer was turned down, and relations cooled. News from Belgium petered out – of Suenens, his associate Veronica 'Grace' O'Brien, of the king and queen. Suenens, however, indicated his respect for Chiara by nominating her for the Templeton Prize for Progress in Religion, of which he himself had been a recipient in 1976.

Meanwhile, Suenens and O'Brien turned their attention to the Catholic Charismatic Movement. As this movement has no founder, Suenens was eagerly welcomed as protector; he had found what he had sought to occupy him in his retirement. Curiously this intense episode, of which I along with my colleagues at Loppiano was at least a partial witness, does not rate a mention in the cardinal's biography. In fact there is a passing mention of Chiara Lubich and

Focolare, but no indication of any kind of contact. It is unlikely that any of the protagonists of this incident will break their silence and give the definitive account.

The movement's early influence in the field of Italian politics was followed up in 1959 with the foundation of the St Catherine Centre for dialogue 'with people at the top' (the name was chosen by Igino Giordani). It was made up of members of parliament who had joined the movement. At the beginning of 1960, two members of the Centre were despatched to Cologne, Munster, East Berlin, Luxembourg, Brussels, Louvain and Paris to establish contacts in the fields of politics, education, economy, trade unions and health. At the Mariapolis which was held that year in Freiburg, the International St Catherine Bureau was formed. Following the foundation and consolidation of the New Humanity Movement, the Italian Bureau of Politics was launched in 1987 as Focolare's political wing, the result of years of effort to make inroads into the political arena.

New Humanity established one of its 'environmental cells' in the Italian parliament with three representatives of different parties, a senator and two deputies. While its presence at this level is modest, New Humanity is seeking to encourage a political influence and presence wherever the movement is firmly established. As well as members of parliament, it has produced many local government officials throughout the world.

Whilst favouring parties of Christian inspiration like the Christian Democrats and their current successors in Italy, the Popular Party, Focolare claims to allow its members political freedom. Nevertheless, the New Humanity Movement has formulated the 'Elected-Electors Pact', one of whose points is 'the defence and support of civil liberties (education, health, cultural and family concerns) against interference from the public sphere'. This is, of course, Focolare code for opposition to moral views which differ from their own.

Although Focolare has always aspired to influence the rich and powerful, for many years this process was piecemeal and haphazard, relying on chance meetings and introductions. In recent years, as its sphere of influence has expanded, a more concerted strategy can be discerned. Two of the 'mass movements' – New Humanity and Youth for a United World – spawned numerous activities in key areas of public life: politics, the arts and media, health, economy and science – thus beginning to fulfil Chiara Lubich's long-term plans for the 'clarification' of society.

It is by means of these offshoots or 'front organizations', with their bland names and soft-pedalling of the religious message, that Focolare seeks to influence powerful figures and infiltrate secular organizations. Prominent guests from the political world are invited to take part in the gatherings of these bodies, lending them credibility. At a one-day Action for a United World (AMU) meeting at Castelgandolfo in 1987, the 400 delegates included 'many personalities who are experts in the field of international co-operation', including Dr Civelli, a representative from the Italian Ministry of Foreign Affairs.

International organizations like the European Union and the United Nations are seen as prime targets for infiltration by Focolare members. In *The Adventure of Unity*, Chiara Lubich mentions 'a group [of members] which carries out its activities in the UN'. Focolare's International Bureau of Economy – another misleadingly bland title – appoints representatives for official contacts with the UN in Geneva and Vienna. In 1987, New Humanity joined the UN officially, becoming part of its Ecosoc commission. The New Families movement is represented among the UN's non-governmental bodies for the family. This rapport with the UN is also cultivated by the young people of the movement. In January 1987, according to a Focolare internal news-bulletin, a 'message from the Boys and Girls for a United World was brought to the UN'. Later the same year, a report on a Gen 3 meeting at Castelgandolfo in June tells us that Dr Farina of UNICEF was present. On 23 November 1988, thirteen Gen 3 (children) presented a document entitled 'Message on Television for a United World', together with 141,000 signatures, 'to people in influential positions', as the Focolare news-report relates – twenty-two ministers of the European Council gathered in Stockholm for two days in plenary session 'to conclude the work of the European Year for Cinema and Television'.

The report goes on to say that, through contacts of the movement, the children were introduced to 'VIPs from the European Parliament and from the European Council – to whom they were able to introduce the movement of Boys and Girls for a United World and the whole of the work of Mary, besides the message itself'. The VIPs included Marcelino Oreja, Secretary General of the European Council, who signed the petition which he described as 'profoundly stimulating'. Simone Veil, the President of the Commission for the European Year for Cinema and Television, gave it her signature, too, and 'said that she was happy to add this document to the others that were being given to the governments'.

While these activities in politics and international organizations may appear harmless enough, they show Focolare's determination to achieve a powerful presence in the secular field. Even the children with their petitions are succeeding in penetrating and carrying the message where adults would be scorned. What is Focolare's ultimate purpose in penetrating international organizations like the UN and the EU? Undoubtedly they see them as a medium through which they can work towards their goal of world unity. Focolare's success in this field is alarming. It must not be forgotten that underlying their lofty ideals of world unity are sect-like recruitment methods, esoteric beliefs, extreme right-wing moral views and a narrow, repressive cultural outlook.

One day in November 1993 the staff of Communion and Liberation's Italian magazine of Church affairs *30 Giorni* were nonplussed to see a black limousine with smoked windows, the kind used by Italian politicians, draw up outside their offices in Piazza Cavour, close to Vatican City. They were even more astonished when, amidst a flurry of black-suited bodyguards, they were summoned to an unscheduled editorial meeting and introduced to their new director, none other than the disgraced ex-supremo of the Christian Democrat Party, Giulio Andreotti.

By that time, the country's most prominent postwar politician, seven times prime minister, who had allegedly hobnobbed with top Mafia bosses – and it was claimed there were the souvenir snaps to prove it – was regarded with deep suspicion by the Italian in the street. Andreotti goes back a long way with CL, having been a regular visitor to their summer jamborees in Rimini in his glory days. Apparently, the top brass of CL were prepared to give him the benefit of the doubt when the rest of the country was baying for his blood. Nevertheless, it was widely believed that CL's traditionalist cronies in the Roman Curia, who regularly graced *30 Giorni*'s pages, regarded him as an unsuitable bedfellow. It could have been the reason why Cardinal Ratzinger, a long-time friend of CL, who had granted *30 Giorni* many exclusives in the past, turned down a request for an interview at this time, either out of disapproval or out of embarrassment. CL has never balked at controversy. Neither were they fazed by notoriety. In contrast with Focolare's low-key but single-minded progress in the secular field, Communion and Liberation's style has been high-profile and clamorous.

Since they were launched by CL members in 1980, the Meetings for Friendship between Peoples, instantly identified in Italy just by the English word Meeting, have been the ideal platform for encounters between the movement and major figures from the national and world stage. The 14th Meeting, held in 1993, as always in the last week of August at the Rimini Fiera, was no exception, in spite of the country's political upheavals. Celebrities present included Germany's Chancellor Kohl, who shared the stage with Mino Martinazzoli, secretary of the Italian Christian Democrats, and Andreotti himself. The climax of the event was the visit of the President of the Republic, who used the occasion – as many others have in the past – as a platform to launch an appeal for responsibility to all citizens, and especially the youth of the nation. But CL's political ambitions have certainly not been limited to a passive role of rubbing shoulders with the great and the powerful. For CL the political order is a prerequisite of evangelism, and therefore it has pursued power with an authentically religious zeal. 'The Christian has no fear of power,' Don Giussani declares; 'futhermore, in my opinion he should desire it, to make easier the way man must travel to achieve his destiny.'

CL's theory of a visible, united Catholic 'presence' in society, which later proved so consistent with that of Pope John Paul II, laid the foundations for its active political role. This had been attempted on a small scale, but with great pretensions, within the confines of the movement. Just as Focolare has its small towns, outside the mainstream of society, as concrete examples of the Economy of Communion, CL applied the same theory with its nurseries, schools, bookshops and consumer co-operatives, 'so as to create what we call units of transition, entities, in other words where an analysis and a political and social project in the wider environment are run on the basis of the new experience of Christian life inserted within the wider social context'.

The implication of the concept of 'transition' seems to be a quasi-Marxist one that CL's self-contained activities are forerunners of an eventual transformation of society. These business and social activities are, for CL members, 'pieces of new society'.

A decisive move in the direction of a formal political commitment came in 1972, shortly after the movement was reborn under the Communion and Liberation banner, with the formation of the Centre of Political Studies, run by Andrea Borruso and Alberto Garrochio. But CL's political début came with the Referendum on Divorce in 1974. Divorce had passed into Italian law on 1 December 1970 and was regarded by the establishment of the Church as a major defeat, a watershed in the battle against secularization. CL was approached by the secretary of the Italian Bishops' Conference, Monsignor Bartoletti, to assist in the fight for the anti-divorce line of the Christian Democrats and the Vatican. Relations between CL/GS and the Italian Bishops' Conference had always been strained, but the bishops' appeal was less a sign of rapprochement than an indication that other church organizations, such as Catholic Action, were far from convinced of the Church's line. Certainly CL did not need convincing on conservative moral positions.

CL's anti-divorce manifesto was an eight-page leaflet entitled *On Divorce*, of which hundreds of thousands of copies were circulated. It was in line with most of CL's ideological statements – reformulating a rigidly traditionalist position in ideological terms with a liberal ring to them. The document described the pro-divorce position as a 'bourgeois reform' and set out to prove that the pro-divorce line was not synonymous with progress and the anti-divorce lobby with reaction. It claimed the right of Christians 'to bring into society, freely and in secular form, judgements stemming from their involvement in the event which is Christianity'. No mention is made of the freedom of the non-Christians who might be obliged by law to follow these 'judgements'. CL attempts to undercut such objections, asserting that 'the sacrament of marriage as it is lived by Christians, is not an ideological point of reference, but a profound experience of humanity . . . which leads us to point out the harm that divorce does to men and to society'. CL clearly states its underlying political programme in this early document when it demands the right to 'demonstrate the fruitfulness of the Christian experience in building a tolerant, pluralist society on a human scale'.

In the same document, however, CL gave a hint of future clashes when it accused the Christian Democrat Party of having let things go too far, of having 'supported and defended a model of neo-capitalist development, and now . . . [bucking against] its inevitable consequences'.

Despite their best efforts to comply with the request of the bishops, there were those within the CL camp who doubted the wisdom of this last-ditch attempt to overthrow the offending law. The movement's leaders believed the referendum was too little too late and that Christian Democrats were delivering an inevitable victory into the hands of the enemies of the Church, a victory on which the opposing forces could capitalize for future assaults on moral issues.

CL's worst fears were confirmed when the Catholic faction was defeated, winning only 41 per cent of the votes. But in its post-mortem on this rout, a document entitled *After the Referendum*, the true extent of CL's Catholic traditionalism and its bizarre concept of democracy is shown in the comment: 'For many, faith did not suggest the certain and substantial gesture of obedience to the indications of authority.' Setting the event within the context of secular capitalism, the document stated its belief that 'The origin of capitalism was precisely the exclusion of the living fact of the Church as the Body of Christ'. CL's own political model is a kind of Christian society which has been extinct since the Middle Ages, a restored version of the Holy Roman Empire.

Shockwaves passed through the Church in Italy when, in 1975, the Christian Democrat vote dropped to 34 per cent and the PCI (communist) vote rose to an all-time high of 32 per cent. I recall how Focolare were preparing to move their headquarters to Switzerland in the event of a communist victory. No doubt similar plans were afoot in the Vatican. These dramatic measures appear a little ridiculous in retrospect – the Italian Communist Party was hardly that of the Soviet Union, and Enrico Berlinguer, its urbane leader whose wife was a practising Catholic, was no Brezhnev. Many Catholics were well aware of this, and had no scruples in switching their vote to the PCI. A group of Catholic intellectuals under the leadership of Raniero La Valle, an ex-editor of *L'Avvenire d'Italia*, the bishops' daily newspaper, became party candidates.

The basis of CL's ideology is a visible and united Catholic presence. In the face of this break-up of the Catholic vote, they set about rebuilding a united Catholic front. Their determined opposition to a secularized society was expressed in the fighting words of a young lecturer in philosophy of politics, Rocco Buttiglione: 'The Unity of Catholics constitutes the decisive instrument to resist this offensive.'

In an article of May 1975, a leading priest of CL, Luigi Negri, served notice on the Christian Democrats and Catholic Action:

> The grassroots of the People of God, that is the Christian community, no longer intends to delegate to the so-called Catholic 'associationism' [Catholic Action], irreversibly in crisis, the development of its cultural presence and it no longer intends to delegate to [the Christian Democrats] the development of its political initiative.

At about this time, the movement's political achievements began to show real muscle. In the local government elections of 1975, CL put up its own candidates for Christian Democrat seats. Although Don Giussani later claimed that candidates were acting on their own behalf, CL's internal magazine at the time made no attempt at subtlety. These are 'the candidates proposed by CL', it said. A number of CL candidates won places on the Milan municipal council, including Andrea Borruso, leader of the CL group on the council, who was later carried to victory as a parliamentary deputy on the CL vote. In the local government elections of 15 June 1976, a hundred CL candidates were successful. CLU, CL's movement of university students, had launched Popular Catholics, to unite Catholic students under one banner in the elections to student bodies held in universities throughout the country. This group rapidly established itself as a powerful force, often commanding more votes than the coalition of the left.

Against this background, CL launched its political arm, Movimento Popolare, to date the major political achievement of the new movements and sure proof of what their vast and tightly knit structures can achieve in the secular field. Movimento Popolare was launched on 21 December 1975 by the CL leadership as a movement within the Christian Democrats rather than a political party, with its aim to unite the 'popular Catholic base that has shown a broad will to rediscover its own Christian identity' – in other words, the 41 per cent who voted against divorce. Don Giussani preferred the name Movimento Cattolico, but it was hoped that the new organization could embrace not just Catholics but also others who subscribed to its traditional values. The aim was to ensure that the 'Christian fact' was no longer sidelined, but restored to its rightful place. The idea of starting a second party was rejected as 'intellectualistic'. The vehicle for Movimento Popolare's plans was to be the Christian Democrat Party, deemed to be 'the most suitable instrument at the present'. But this was to be a Christian Democrat Party according to the vision of CL, not made up of moderates but a Catholic and 'popular' party. At the helm of the new movement was a young CL activist, Roberto Formigoni, who was to become a Euro MP in 1984 and a member of the Italian parliament in 1987.

Almost immediately Movimento Popolare was branded a political party by the Italian media, and so, by association, was CL. The movement's growing notoriety was signalled by a story run in two papers – *Manifesto* and *La stampa* – on 14 February 1976 in which it was alleged that the movement was financed by the CIA. The suggestion was that it was serving the imperialist cause. Outraged, CL launched and won a libel action in June 1979. They published their accounts, which showed that the mysterious source of their funds was the monthly contributions of members.

CL's militants found themselves faced with a genuine war. In February 1975, two CL students of the University of Rome were ambushed by a fascist group while putting up posters by night, and severely beaten with hammers and baseball bats. In 1977 their various opponents were responsible for 120 attacks on individuals and centres of the movement. A document of the extreme left-wing Red Brigades ordered that 'The men and the bases of CL must be targeted, struck and dispersed. In schools, in districts and wherever CL takes root it must find no room to manoeuvre either politically or physically.'

CL was certainly seen as a serious threat by its enemies. The movement's leaders believed that the attacks against them were of an anti-Christian nature. But they were not the only Christians in Italy at the time, nor even the only Christians active in the political sphere. It was CL's particular brand of aggressive, rowdy, sectarian and, it must be said, effective politico-religious proselytizing that provoked such violent reactions. They were the one Catholic organization able to combat the advance of the Left.

In a sense the Italian media were accurate in identifying

Movimento Popolare as a 'party'. It acted through the Christian Democrat Party in its role as the rallying-point for Catholic political unity; its candidates stood as members of that party. But it did not identify with the party, which it saw as having sold the Christian message down the river.

For CL, the Christian Democrats were tarred with the same brush as the 'enemy' – the liberals. CL was a party within the party, with its own very clear conservative programme. They expressed this separate identity by describing themselves as a 'grassroots' group rather than one which is linked to the hierarchy (i.e. the Italian Bishops' Conference) as the Christian Democrats were. Movimento Popolare's platform was much more explicitly Catholic than that of the Christian Democrats – so much so that it earned itself the accusation of being fundamentalist and integrist. One of the most controversial factions in Italian politics, Movimento Popolare rapidly became one of the most powerful. At its height, it is claimed that it commanded 1-2 million votes out of a total of 40 million, which amounted to between 7 and 14 per cent of Christian Democrat support. It is said, however, that the influence of this pressure group was so strong that it could deliver anything from a quarter to a third of the total Christian Democrat vote.

Although the Movimento Popolare had an identity and a mind of its own, and had often been a thorn in the side of the Christian Democrat Party, ultimately the relationship between the two organizations was symbiotic. When the Christian Democrat Party collapsed ignominiously in the Tangentopoli, or Bribesville, scandals of 1992–3, inevitably the Movimento Popolare came crashing down with it. Officially it was said to have been dissolved; but this graceful retreat from the political stage did not imply that MP was merely guilty by association – it had had its own fair share of scandals, too.

MP and the CL militants who ran it had not been too choosy about the company they kept. They had their own long-term programme and were prepared to resort to virtually any short-term strategies which could bring them closer to their goal. Ideological compromises with liberalism or 'laicism' were anathema, but brief dalliances were acceptable: useful one-night stands could be countenanced as long as they did not lead to permanent relationships. Not surprisingly, this led to charges of prostitution and opportunism.

When Rémy Montaigne decided to stop publishing *30 Jours* in France, he also pulled out of the holding company, IEI. With him went his substantial investment. Eyebrows were raised at CL's chosen replacement on the board of directors. Vittorio Sbardella, Christian Democrat member of parliament for Rome, was regarded as Giulio Andreotti's right-hand man in the city. Sbardella was a man of the people. He had no pretensions to intellectualism but he was close to the ground and could guarantee votes. His pedigree was not of the most impeccable. As a tough, streetwise Roman youth in the fifties, he had been a member of the fascist Movimento Sociale Italiana. By the sixties he had joined the Christian Democrats as the bodyguard of Rome's leading politician, becoming his heir apparent. By the seventies he had succeeded him and was, in his own right, a powerful figure in the politics of the capital. It was at this time that he was co-opted by Andreotti as his lieutenant for Rome. And in this capacity the friendship with CL had blossomed. MP had proved that it could deliver at the polling-booths. Some of its most spectacular successes had been achieved in Rome itself.

In May 1990, CL's candidate, a university professor popularly known as Mr Nobody (Signor Nessuno) won the first round of votes in the city's mayoral elections, proving that CL had real clout. If CL had something to offer to Sbardella, it was clear with his appointment to the IEI board that he had something to offer the movement. Those working on the magazine at the time were aware that Sbardella had brought money with him. Later it was alleged that he had millions at his disposal, funds earmarked for Rome subways that were never built. In return, the magazine would do what it could to help the Christian Democrat faction he represented. Until his death from cancer in late 1994, Vittorio Sbardella was under investigation on a number of corruption charges. It is now unlikely that the truth about these allegations will ever come to light.

A number of leading figures in Movimento Popolare were named in the Bribesville scandals which continue to traumatize the country – Erba of Monza, Arioso and Intiglietta of Milan, and Gaviraghi of Concorrezzo. But perhaps the most spectacular case was that of Marco Bucarelli, president of IEI and vice-president of MP, who had clashed so violently with Ignatius Press, the original publishers of *30 Days* in the United States. Bucarelli represented that element of CL's political cocktail which had started its journey on the far right of Italian politics – like Vittorio Sbardella, in his teens, he had belonged to the fascist Movimento Sociale Italiana. At the age of thirty-five his dedication to CL's objectives was indisputable. But, as his altercations with Ignatius Press had shown, his methods were open to the charge of unscrupulousness. 'He was the most ideological of them all,' says Robert Moynihan, formerly a journalist on the English edition of *30 Days*. 'You could never reason with a man like that.'

While at a business meeting on 5 March 1993, Bucarelli received a telephone call from a major of the Italian Customs informing him that his home was being searched and that he should turn himself in at one of their offices. Bucarelli followed these instructions, and was arrested and imprisoned in Rome's Regina Coeli gaol.

A charge had been brought against him by a shareholder of Edit, the publishing company of *Il Sabato*. Until 1989, Bucarelli had been a member of the Administrative Council of Rome's second University, 'Tor Vergata'. The accuser, whose building company had won a major construction contract from the university, alleged that Bucarelli had threatened to 'cause problems' over the contract unless he agreed to become a shareholder of *Il Sabato*, then passing through serious financial difficulties. Bucarelli rejected the charges and, in a later interview with *30 Giorni,* suggested that his accuser had been pressured into making the charges by a third party. He suggested that the charges could have been engineered to scupper a deal on the point of being concluded at the time of his arrest which would safeguard the magazine's future and free it, in Bucarelli's words from 'any relationship with policitians'.

Clearly the editorial board was concerned, during this period when Bribesville was at its height, about such links.

Bucarelli's second, rather more daring suggestion was that his enemies might be within the Church: 'Giulio Andreotti, who I had spoken with just a few hours before my arrest, had advised me to be careful in view of the irritation of some ecclesiastical circles for an editorial initiative of *Il Sabato*.'

Could these 'ecclesiastical circles' be within the Vatican itself? What is clear is that Bucarelli's ties with political figures who had been accused in the Bribesville scandals were as strong as ever.

On 8 March, Bucarelli was interrogated for four hours by Judge Antonio Vinci, who was naturally interested in the fact that the supposedly unconnected organizations of CL, MP, *Il Sabato* and CL's various business enterprises seemed to find a point of contact in the person of Marco Bucarelli. But the judge emerged from the encounter none the wiser. Bucarelli denied any link between MP and the Compagnia delle Opere, the organization which embraces the businesses run by CL members. This, in spite of the fact that CdO was so closely affiliated to MP that, following its collapse, the movement's internal magazine, *Traccie*, was to describe the CdO as 'orphaned'. A link between MP and *Il Sabato* was also denied. In his eagerness to disclaim any connection between the two, Bucarelli went so far as to state: 'I take very little interest in the Movimento Popolare.'

'But aren't you its vice-president?' the judge retorted.

Bucarelli's extraordinarily evasive reply was: 'But in fact, as I said earlier, when it came down to it I was not absolutely sure whether I was.'

Bucarelli spent three weeks in prison and was interrogated on a number of occasions. His home and the offices of *Il Sabato* were searched. But it is one thing to accuse, another to make the charges stick. Bucarelli was released on the grounds of insufficient evidence.

In a skilful PR move, Bucarelli was presented in CL's publications as a victim, almost a martyr. The interview he gave in the May 1993 edition of *30 giorni* refers to an orchestrated campaign of 4,000 telegrams sent to Bucarelli at Regina Coeli from as far afield as Japan and Singapore, all containing the same message: 'We love you, Marco. Pray for us.' At the basilica of St Ambrose in Milan, 3,000 university students gathered at mass to pray for him, while CL members in Rome packed out the venerable basilica of Santa Maria Maggiore, the movement's traditional stamping-ground.

But the Bribesville scandal had stirred up emotions of outrage and anger in the populace. '*Ce l'hanno messo per il culo!*' ('We've been fucked!') roared the graffiti from the venerable walls of the Eternal City. Daily, new revelations of corruption, any of which could have made the headlines, filled twelve pages of each national paper. The atmosphere was one of condemnation rather than of understanding; to be suspected was to be guilty.

On the other hand, Marco Bucarelli did not help his case much with his *30 Giorni* interview. He propounded CL's political policy of 'realism' which had been practised since the early eighties. This is CL's euphemistic term for pragmatism – or opportunism as their opponents would have it. 'Realism' is CL's interpretation of Cardinal Ratzinger's definition of political morality as 'the art of possible compromise'.

'A fundamental criterion of political realism is recognizing "stepping-stones",' Bucarelli explained to *30 Giorni*, 'immediate props which can be used to defend areas of freedom.' He gives an example. When Bucarelli launched a public attack on President Cossiga at the Meeting of 1989, a scandal ensued which provoked the Vatican newspaper *Osservatore Romano* to retaliate against Bucarelli. *Il Sabato*'s solution to the problem was to appoint a friend of Cossiga's, Paolo Liguori, as director of the magazine. 'He was a very useful stepping-stone for two years of *Il Sabato*'s life,' Bucarelli observes. Another, he adds, was Sbardella. This official explanation for CL's dubious alliances that had been noted over the years serves to enhance rather than allay suspicions.

The other fact that remained indisputable was that the finances of various activities of the movement were closely linked to their political affiliations. One of the most notorious examples is that of the co-operative La Cascina di Roma. It was one of the most successful of a number of co-operatives run by CL members which provide meals to school canteens. Contracts are awarded by regional councils, and it is widely recognized that – at least prior to the recent political upheavals – companies were selected according to political criteria: a Christian Democrat council would favour a Catholic group, for example. CL's affiliations were to the conservative wing of the Christian Democrat Party but, in the spirit of 'realism', they had also fostered links with the Socialist Party. The work of La Cascina relied on these contacts. The political landscape was beginning to shift, however, and La Cascina lost a contract to a communist company. This was accompanied by charges made against the movement's co-operatives to the civil authorities and, as far as the movement was concerned, a press campaign aimed at discrediting the activities of these firms.

CL struck back in no uncertain terms at the Meeting in Rimini in August 1989. There, *Il Sabato* distributed a dossier entitled 'The Giant and the Cascina' in which it named its enemies as 'the powerful coalition linking communists, Christian Democrats linked to the President of the Party, neo-liberals led by the editor of the

Repubblica'. The dossier did not mince its words in attacking the 'Catholics for dialogue' – those who did not believe, like CL, in the Catholic block vote.

The strongest reaction came from the Vatican. The *Osservatore Romano* published an article accusing CL of fostering 'a climate of division and factionalism which, besides not being to the benefit of society, has assumed the grave responsibility of giving a disrespectful and irreverent impression which is certainly no help to the Catholic world'.

But more serious than this was an announcement appearing on the same page which declared that the Holy See wished to make clear that the two bishops who had attended the Meeting at Rimini – the presidents of the Pontifical Commission for the Family and of the Council for the Laity – 'had done so in a strictly personal capacity'. This represented a significant move on behalf of the Vatican to distance itself from the movement.

The official organs of CL were faced with a dilemma. They could hardly turn their fury on the body to which they had always declared fervent loyalty. But neither were they prepared meekly to submit. In a gesture which could be interpreted as dumb insolence, *Il Sabato* printed its now legendary 'white number' all of whose pages were blank. Every issue was accompanied by a copy of the Rimini dossier. *30 Days,* for its part, announced that it had 'decided to suspend publication of the various editions of the magazine'. This was quite a turnaround for *Il Sabato*, which had started life in the late seventies as the unofficial mouthpiece of the Vatican.

The leadership of Communion and Liberation in Milan, however, was alarmed at this unprecedented rebuff from Rome and decided to distance itself in its turn from *Il Sabato*. An interview to this effect with Don Giussani appeared in the Italian daily *La stampa* on 20 September 1989, and this was rapidly followed up by the announcement that CL would be withdrawing from the editorship of *Il Sabato* and disposing of its interest in the publication. The Italian bishops were united in their applause for this move; but this only showed that they were easily hoodwinked, because, in spite of the posturing, any changes were purely cosmetic and *Il Sabato* remained as closely bound to the movement as it had ever been.

At the end of 1993, *Il Sabato* was closed down in mysterious circumstances. It was a totally unexpected turn of events given that the journal had just managed to overcome serious financial problems and had moved into new premises, from which not even a single issue was produced. There appear to be two possible explanations, both of which are plausible. The first is that the magazine had become too much of an embarrassment to the leadership of CL in Milan, who were no longer prepared to allow the situation to continue unchecked. The editorial board of the publication was given an ultimatum to accept Rocco Buttiglione as editor – presumably to restore CL's official line – or be closed down. The hard-headed directors felt that extinction was preferable to Buttiglione.

Another explanation highlights the magazine's financial links with the Christian Democrat Party. The three television channels of the State-run Italian broadcasting network RAI, up until the Bribesville earthquake, were affiliated to the three main political parties – RAI 1 to the Christian Democrats, RAI 2 to the socialists and RAI 3 to the communists. In order to ensure that television did not deprive the press of its share of revenue, television advertisers were obliged by law to take a fixed quota of space in the printed media. This quota was assigned by each channel on a political basis. When the law was abolished in 1993, it was significant that *Il Sabato*'s advertising revenue instantly dried up and the magazine began to founder. The fact that this was not the case with other magazines suggests a particularly heavy dependence on this political source on the part of CL's magazine.

With the dissolution of Movimento Popolare and closure of *Il Sabato*, only *30 Giorni* remains as the last vestige of CL's powerful political apparatus. Which brings us back to the conundrum of Andreotti's appointment as its director. An outsider might have judged this move in the climate of late 1993 as inopportune. But, in the light of an incident described by former *30 Days* journalist Robert Moynihan, it appears stranger still. The Rome-based American journalist and Vatican expert was, and to some extent still is, an admirer of CL's basic ideas and wrote an appreciative article on the movement for the British Catholic weekly *The Tablet* in 1988. Today, however, he is puzzled and disillusioned by their bizarre political manoeuvring and opportunism. He recalls how, at the time of a highly publicized attack on a public figure, a debate was raging in the country about the choice of a new president. Andreotti was nudging into the position of favourite. Then came the attack, and the tide turned.

The day after the incident, Moynihan chanced to lunch in the same restaurant as a group of *Il Sabato* journalists together with the *éminence grise* of the movement in Rome, Don Giacomo Tantardini. Moynihan approached them and asked them how they interpreted this terrible event.

Tantardini's immediate response was to link Andreotti with the atrocity.

Moynihan turned to the others. 'Do you all agree with this?'

They nodded eagerly.

Later the same afternoon, Moynihan visited his former colleagues at *30 Giorni*. When he asked them their opinion on the Falcone affair their replies were identical to that of Tantardini.

'They repeated exactly the same phrases, as though they were brainwashed,' Moynihan recalls.

He confesses that he is at a loss to explain the leap from that position to Andreotti's appointment as director of the movement's flagship magazine. The most fair-minded explanation is that they made a mistake of which they have now repented. In his interview with *30 Giorni* following his release from prison, Marco Bucarelli hints at this, admitting that 'by mistake, in a certain period of '92 we misunderstood his realism, taking it for opportunism, and we unjustly attacked him'. But, even accepting this to be the case, it suggests a dangerous tendency of jumping to drastic conclusions. This is perhaps the supreme example of CL's political inscrutability and suggests that nothing the movement does or says can be taken at face value. Indeed, any speculation on its U-turns and apparent continuous changing of sides – even its apparently turbulent internal wrangles – may be fruitless. Perhaps it is all designed to confuse.

With the collapse of Movimento Popolare in 1993, CL's political presence was far from over. The defunct political wing left behind it a valuable legacy in the Compagnia delle Opere, or Company of Works. CdO was created to encourage networking among CL's vast agglomeration of manufacturing and service industries, and privately run social services. The scale is colossal: 200,000 partners, an annual turnover of nearly £2,000 million. In order to service its host of member companies, CdO has offices in twenty Italian cities. Just one of these companies, the notorious La Cascina of Rome, having weathered the storms of 1989, forms part of a group of forty firms with an annual turnover of £6½ million and offices in Rome,

New York, Cairo and Paris. But the CdO also has a political programme. Its slogan, for many years, has been 'more society, less State'. Although CL is a bitter enemy of international capitalism, it appears to have espoused some of its most fundamental tenets – and a happy and fruitful union it has proved to be. In its tendency to create a parallel society which serves all its members' needs, CdO's policy is privatization of the most extreme kind. The most radical aspect of the organization is its aim of providing a completely private system of social services – schools, hospitals, crèches, a high-profile network of employment agencies – the Centres of Solidarity.

Politically, the aim is that fees paid for these private services should be tax-deductible. CL shares Focolare's political goal of a Christian society which maintains its purity by minimizing outside interference. This conception of society is the source of their hostility towards the State. Although the CdO is not represented on the National Council of CL, and would claim to be a separate, though affiliated, entity, it is bound to the central organization through its leaders and membership.

It is ironic, in view of the movement's condemnation of international capitalism and the 'power' that manipulates it, that this is precisely the area of its own greatest success. As CL is poised to expand worldwide, CdO is sure to follow. It is the sleeping giant at the heart of the movement. If CdO represents the staggering wealth of CL, it also holds the key to its political future.

In their quest for wealth and political influence the movements appear to be comprehensible, even accessible. This veneer of normality is an illusion. The parallel societies they are creating are merely a side-effect or a manifestation of the strange, hermetic spiritual universes they have constructed which are the natural habitat of their members. For all the apparent gusto with which the financial and political activities are conducted, they are tolerated as a necessary evil. It is in their secret, invisible aspect, when the movements are at their most outlandish, that they are most themselves.

11

The Mysteries of the Movements

WHEN I WAS A MEMBER OF FOCOLARE WE WERE TOLD THAT, UNLIKE other mystical traditions, ours was not a gradual ascent to the heights of spiritual experience; instead we shot instantly to an elevated plane of enlightenment, progressing, as though along a mountain range, from one revelatory peak to the next. On close acquaintance, the markedly spiritual nature of the new movements becomes evident. It has earned them the tag, usually intended critically, of 'neo-mystics'. Focolare and NC are often accused of 'angelism', of an 'otherworldly' unreality which ultimately renders them irrelevant. According to some, it is a 'mysticism on the cheap', pre-packaged and pre-digested, requiring nothing from the individual but his or her assent. The spiritual lives of Focolare's internal members have always been based on imbibing the doctrine of the foundress, constantly reiterated and embellished through her speeches and diaries. This is the true sense of what is described as the 'collective spirituality' of Focolare.

In 1980, this collective dimension was crystallized into its most rigid and structured format when Chiara Lubich launched the concept of the 'Holy Journey' in a lecture to members of the Gen movement. The term was taken from a verse of Psalm 84: 'Blessed are those . . . whose hearts are set on pilgrimage [= Holy Journey].' Since then the spiritual lives of all internal members have been subsumed in that of the foundress through the fortnightly conference calls. The tone of these confirms the 'angelist' jibe with their unremitting emphasis on the movement's spiritual slogans like

331

'Jesus in the midst', 'Jesus in one's neighbour' and 'Jesus forsaken'. But the underlying idea of the Holy Journey shows it up as an exercise in communal navel-gazing; the aim is to become saints, to achieve 'perfection': 'If we love in this way, we will work toward our perfection. We will take new steps toward sanctity, because sanctity means virtue, heroic virtue.' This tendency to spiritual self-indulgence is taken to extremes with the declaration that 'Our ideal shows us the way to adorn our souls with virtue'.[1]

A form of Christianity whose main concern is that its followers should 'adorn their souls' is surely at the opposite end of the spectrum from those who are motivated by the urgency of human need.

This strong spiritual orientation is expressed in the movement's fascination with death. Its internal members are walking obituaries; when they meet with adherents or fringe members, the first news to be shared will be the latest deaths, or 'departures for the Heavenly Mariapolis'. While it is impressive to see a genuine Christian faith in the afterlife, death is stressed to such an extent that life is made to seem insignificant, unreal, marking time, merely the antechamber of the Other World. News of deceased members, including detailed accounts of their final days, conversations with, or letters to Chiara Lubich, and their last words, forms a substantial part of the internal 'updates'.

The cult of the dead is an important aspect of the spiritual life of members. Each of the movement's towns has its cemetery, the Holy Ground (Campo Santo), which is visited frequently, sometimes on a daily basis. When I was a member, communing with the dead of the movement – not necessarily people we had known in life – was second nature to us, as spontaneous as chatting to friends.

At Focolare funerals the pain and suffering of death is denied and replaced with an enforced jollity. The fact that loss and separation are not acknowledged suggests a dislocation from reality. Focolare funerals are celebrations. Even in the case of children who died within the movement – and I witnessed several such funerals – I never saw a tear shed. The obsession with death and its dominance over life is a vivid expression of the deep human-divine, world-spirit dualism espoused by the movement.

[1]Chiara Lubich, conference call, 28 April 1988.

CL expresses its spiritual line in an even more evident way. In the early seventies CLL, the movement's branch for workers, launched the 'liturgical way to liberation'. A CL group working in a factory would conduct a short service on site before work. The movement also encouraged the celebration of mass in the workplace. The only reaction this bullish attitude could possibly have aroused in the Italy of that time was outrage and aggression.

NC's disdain for wordly matters marks it out as the most angelistic of the three movements. Its intention, in fact, is to create 'celestial men': 'Every man who is our contemporary can receive, freely, a new Spirit, a new life, he can be a celestial man.'[1]

The atmosphere of the communities, as Kiko Arguello assures aspirant members at the first *convivence*, is a rarefied spiritual one. Everyone has 'experienced the sterility of good works' which are 'fruits of their own efforts', he reminds them, but the communities eschew activities aimed at society's improvement, realizing that 'no-one robs God of His glory'. Instead the ultimate goal is that 'this community will live in praise; every time it gathers, there will be a constant action of grace, with the Eucharist as the culmination . . . then you will experience some marvellous Eucharists'.

According to CL, today's liberal theologians deny grace because they do not acknowledge the Catholic Church's unique role as the channel of all grace. But CL and the other movements share a mechanistic view of salvation. Crucial to the process is the initial encounter with the group; its effect is almost magical, as long as the potential recruit has the correct disposition. Grace does not play a large part in the theology of the movements. They *are* grace. As Don Giussani says of those who meet CL, 'Bumping into a new human reality is a grace, *it is always a grace*'.[2]

Similarly, for the *focolarini* an event such as a speech of Chiara is 'a grace'. This faith in the movement, which leaves little room for the action of the Holy Spirit, justifies fanatical proselytizing. Once inside the movement, salvation consists of following its incredibly detailed precepts, jumping through a series of spiritual hoops. The *focolarini* actually use the term 'gymnastics' to describe the internal somersaults that members are required to turn in order to practise its many spiritual regulations. The language is one of effort: the word 'overcome' (*superare*) is an important one in the Focolare

[1] Letter from Kiko Arguello to NC communities, Rome, 8 December 1988.
[2] Don Luigi Giussani, 'E, se opera', supplement to *30 giorni*, February 1994, p. 45.

vocabulary. The starting-point of its spirituality is not so much an action of grace on God's part as an act of will on the part of the new recruit – the so-called 'choice of God'. Frenetic activity is promoted by the movements, activity within and on behalf of the organization. There is an emphasis on 'practicality', on 'facts', on a sense that, by implementing the movement's precepts in the minutiae of members' lives, their existence as a whole will be transformed. Despite its neo-mystical nature, words like 'facts', 'practical' and 'concrete' are in constant use within Focolare.

In the preparations for the scrutinies, NC members are asked to review aspects of their lives, such as their attitude to money, to their emotional life and to their work. In the notes they are given to guide their group sharing on these themes, the same words are repeated like a litany: 'Give concrete examples.' For it is only by reviewing the practical details of everyday life that the changes the movement wishes to achieve will be carried out.

The sloganeering and repetition practised by the movements are devices borrowed from secular totalitarianism designed to effect changes in members' lives. The relentlessness of this indoctrination can be seen in Chiara Lubich's conference calls:

> For these next two weeks I would advise that we make the effort to love in truth and in particular to see Jesus in everyone. Therefore to supernaturalize our way of seeing. To rise in the morning aware and convinced that we can and we must live in this way. We can love Jesus in the members of our family as we say our 'good morning' . . . We can love Jesus in our neighbours throughout the day . . . We can love our neighbours by seeing Jesus in them also when we use the vacuum cleaner or the broom, when we wash the dishes or leave the house to do some shopping . . . We can love Jesus when we dedicate ourselves to the activities of our movement, when we write a letter, or make a telephone call, or hold a meeting, or participate at a congress. . . . We can love Jesus in our neighbours when we pray. We always have this wonderful possibility and we can imagine that in each moment He tells us: you have done it to me.

NC's twenty-year course is proposed as a veritable sausage machine for Christians. Specific spiritual changes take place at designated moments of the Way, neither before nor after. The action of grace does not get a look in. Faith arrives at the final stage of the renewal of the baptismal vows, and not a moment sooner.

Shortly after its birth, Christianity encountered the mystery religions of Greece and Asia. These promised salvation through secret knowledge and arcane rites, which were, in fact, kept so secret that no record of them has been passed down to us. The fusion between Christianity and mystery religions produced Gnosticism, a mystical form of the infant faith which promised its adepts access to secret knowledge which would explain its mysteries. The attraction of Gnosticism is, of course, that it is 'mysticism on the cheap'. Salvation through knowledge is far less of an effort than that which requires sweat and struggle – and faith. Because all mysteries are explained, faith is no longer necessary.

Each of the movements possesses a gnostic element, a claim to 'secret knowledge'. It is paradoxical that the movements promote themselves as a return to Scripture, to the Word of God, and yet the vast bulk of the many words they purvey are the thoughts and sayings of the founders: these constitute the body of secret and exclusive knowledge offered by each movement. They offer something that the Church, of itself, cannot offer.

The Gnosis begins, therefore, with the revelation of the movement itself – the encounter. It is presented as something beyond reason, beyond words, something that can only be *experienced*. Words like 'illumination', 'light', 'fire', 'understanding' are used to convey what we are assured is indescribable. The encounter with the movement is portrayed as the most momentous event since the coming of Christ.

Kiko Arguello's version of salvation history, as recounted in the introductory catechesis, begins with Abraham and culminates in Neocatecumenate.

Don Giussani uses a very tangible phrase to describe the revelation experienced by those who meet CL and its members: they 'bump into' Christ. CL is the continuation of the historical event of the Incarnation: 'The event of Christ becomes present "now" in a phenomenon of a different humanity.' What this 'difference' is cannot be expressed in words. One thing is certain, however – that it is unique. It is something 'we could never have expected, we could never have dreamt of, it was impossible, it was not available anywhere else'.

This same sense of wonder is found in descriptions of the encounter with Focolare. In a recent internally produced video on the movement's expansion in the Anglican Church, a long-term member recounts how, when she first heard Chiara Lubich lecture in Canterbury, 'The whole of that room was filled with great joy'. Another recalls the first meetings she attended: 'We would arrive to a room that was full of music and full of light and full of joy. It seemed to me that there were certain secrets being shared in this room about the love of Christ and his presence amidst us.'

Chiara Lubich has always described her ideas as 'a Light from on high' – in other words, a direct revelation from God. In order to distinguish the uniqueness of this revelation, from the earliest days it was given a name: 'the Ideal'. It is significant that members do not talk about meeting the movement but of their encounter with 'the Ideal' – the reception of a doctrine, a moment of illumination.

We have seen how Chiara Lubich decided to 'put her books in the attic', making a conscious choice to reject human wisdom, relying only on the Light within her. In a speech of 1963, she described the very moment at which she first became aware of this Light while crossing a bridge in Trento with one of her pupils, Doriana Zamboni, later to become one of her 'first companions'. 'What I am telling you', Chiara said on that occasion, 'does not come from reason; it is a light that comes from somewhere else.' It was a moment of illumination: 'There and then I had the impression that it [the Light] came from on high. This is truly *the Ideal*. It was then. This is our Ideal therefore.'

Chiara explains this Light as the presence of 'Jesus in the midst':

> I have the impression that it was Jesus in the midst, that Light, it was Jesus, that Light. It was neither my reasoning nor hers; but she making unity allowed me to express and to say things that were so high and so beautiful (I say this because they are things of God) that we said: this is the Ideal.

This description leaves us in no doubt that the words of Chiara and the words of God are totally identified. The authority that is being ascribed to these words appears at least to equal the authority of Scripture, which is considered by contemporary Scripture scholars to be tempered by the cultural conditioning of its authors.

As the 'understanding' of recruits increases, they attain access to new levels of the 'Light' or revelations received by Chiara Lubich over the years. The basic doctrine, such as the so-called twelve points of the spirituality, is available to all in published form. Similarly, there are videotapes which are played publicly at open Meetings and summer Mariapolis gatherings. But there are tapes and videotapes which can only be viewed by certain levels of the hierarchy – say, the leaders of the Focolare centres or the 'zones' – or by the *focolarini* or other internal members only with the express permission of the higher authorities. Less easily controlled are the thousands of unpublished 'writings' (*scritti*) of Chiara Lubich which circulate on a semi-clandestine basis (they do, of course, contribute to the cult of the foundress) and are avidly collected by each of the *focolarini* and become their most treasured possessions.

Such material is restricted, because, in the movement's parlance, it is too 'strong'. This could be because it exposes more fully the demands made on members, or because it makes claims for the movement that outsiders might find shocking, or because it touches on a subject considered most 'delicate' of all: the foundress's visions.

In the summer of 1949, following a period of intense missionary activity during which Focolare had spread throughout Italy, Chiara Lubich and her 'companions' retreated into the Dolomites near Trento, to the village of Fiera di Primiero. During the two months they spent there, Chiara experienced a series of what she terms 'intellectual visions' on a daily basis. The trigger was her rapport with the Christian Democrat politician Igino Giordani, who visited the foundress frequently in her mountain retreat. The married Giordani sought a way to commit himself to Chiara with the same fervour as her celibate followers. She was uneasy about the idea of a vow of obedience, which Catholic tradition restricted to the unmarried. They decided to make a 'pact of unity' at the moment they received communion together at the daily mass, hoping for illumination on Giordani's problem. Instead a spiritual experience began, known in Focolare as the 'Paradise of '49'. At the moment of communion, in a vision, Chiara entered 'Paradise'. Immediately after mass, she recounted the vision to Giordani and her 'companions'. The same phenomenon recurred each day that summer.

In 1963, Chiara described the event:

We had the impression that God opened the eyes of the soul to the Kingdom of God that was among us and we saw Him who is in our midst, the Paradise that was among us, and in a scenario that was so divine, such an expression of the Trinity, we understood, all those years ago, what the role of this movement was as a whole and its role in each one of us in the Church.

The hierarchy of the Catholic Church has traditionally been reticent on private revelations. Certainly the faithful are under no obligation to give credence even to those most widely upheld such as those of Lourdes. Pope John Paul II is known to be personally sympathetic to visionaries and mystics, but even he was reserved in his welcome of members of a CL conference dedicated to the works of Adrienne von Speyr, a visionary closely associated with Hans Urs von Balthasar. 'I know that you do not expect from me in this friendly meeting', he told them, 'an authoritative judgement.'

The private revelations of Chiara Lubich, however, possess a supreme authority over the members of the movement. Belief in them, as in every aspect of the movement, is certainly not optional. It is said that, when Focolare was under investigation by the Holy Office of Cardinal Ottaviani in the fifties, Chiara was ordered to destroy written records of her 'visions' and she complied. Nevertheless, passages still survive and circulate clandestinely among the *focolarini*. Lubich has also recounted her experiences on tape over the years to various gatherings, mainly the top echelons of the leadership. Even within these revelations there are various grades of knowledge, and there are probably secrets known only to a very restricted group indeed.

Of course, in Focolare terms, Chiara Lubich's revelations are not private at all: they are, as aspects of the 'Ideal', part of the movement's collective spirituality, the product of 'Jesus in the midst', and therefore have binding authority. When the foundress shares her experiences with her followers, she is not merely sharing personal reflections; they are relived by the collective. Yet, although all internal members know of the 'Paradise', the details revealed, even to the *focolarini*, are tantalizingly few. This creates a powerful need to know, especially among the full-time members. Like the famous 'third secret' revealed by the Virgin Mary to the shepherd children at Fatima, the withholding of information is so frustrating that the merest crumb of knowledge would appear to be of earth-shattering import.

The details of the 'Paradise' are rather simple and banal – as, indeed, is the case with much mystical language – and yet with the build-up they are given, and in the 'atmosphere of unity', they are regarded with awe.

This secret knowledge has a number of powerful effects. It enhances the sense of belonging, welding members together. It discourages them from leaving – 'to whom should they go', for who else can tell them of these wonders? The sense that, even within the movement, this knowledge is restricted has a heightening effect. Inevitably, access to momentous revelations carries with it a sense of being numbered among the elect.

But the revelations vouchsafed to the foundress were not only on the great themes of Catholicism, but also on the movement itself, its role in the Church and even the role of individual members in the Church. The foundress 'saw' special plans of God, known as the 'designs' (*disegni*) for particular individuals – herself, Don Foresi, Igino Giordani and a number of her first companions who represented the 'aspects', or colours.

According to Chiara Lubich's visions, the movement as a whole is a unique and specific spiritual presence in the Church and in the world. Just as the Church is the body of Christ, Focolare is none other than the 'mystical body' of the Virgin Mary in the Church. This is vaguely hinted at as a presence of Mary in articles and writings for public consumption; but, talking internally in 1963, Chiara had no such scruples: 'We understood that this Work was nothing less than a mystical presence of Mary in the Church . . . Our task in the Church is the task that Mary would have today if she lived in the Church.'

Undoubtedly there are more detailed versions of this particular subject known only to a select few. An internal news-bulletin of 8 June 1989 hinted at this in an account of a visit Chiara Lubich and fifty members of the Co-ordinating Council of the movement made on 18 May to the Marian Shrine of the Holy House at Loreto on the Adriatic coast of Italy. The visit commemorated the occasion fifty years previously when Chiara, then a leader of Catholic Action, had foreseen the foundation of her movement. After a mass had been celebrated at the shrine by *focolarini* priests, Chiara read a prayer in which she said: 'Mary of the *focolarini*, Mother of unity, help us to be here on earth and then in heaven, your crown, your glory.'

This confirmed what we had been told at Loppiano: that Chiara and the first *focolarini*, those of the 'designs', would form the crown of twelve stars round the Virgin's head referred to in the Book of Revelation. The doctrines relating to the foundation of the movement are even more dangerous than the accounts of generic visions because they suggest – and this is the firm belief of members – that the movement was founded by divine intervention, giving it a status and authority akin to that of the Church itself.

Towards the end of my stay at Loppiano, we were taken on a 'pilgrimage' of the 'holy places' of the movement. In the city of Trento, this hagiographic tour encompassed not only the first Focolare, and 'the place where Chiara felt God call her to consecrate herself to Him' but even 'the spot where she met the first of her companions'. A sense of the movement's providential role in history was suggested when we were shown the church where Chiara Lubich was baptized – the very same which had housed the sessions of the Council of Trent: here, we were told, where the disunity had begun, five centuries later Chiara was baptized and the dawn of unity commenced.

At Loppiano we were force-fed on a heavy spiritual diet, and we could not get enough of it. We longed to hear mystical anecdotes. We begged our leaders to tell us about the 'Paradise of '49'. As there was no photocopier available, we would type Chiara Lubich's 'writings' with six carbon copies and distribute them among us. We were encouraged to feel a heightened spiritual sense among us in which the details of reality, of the 'human', faded and spiritual things seemed even more real, so that we could almost see them. It was as though we could touch God. We were made to feel that we of the movement were at the centre of the spiritual universe.

Some of the fledgling *focolarini* became so caught up in this atmosphere that they would become wild-eyed mystics in their own right, whispering private revelations in corners to anyone who would listen. But we were all encouraged to live in a wholly spiritual dimension. Every moment of our lives was coloured by the certainty that we could see God's hand in even the most banal particulars. This is part of the Focolare culture but it was especially strong at Loppiano. Meanings were read into every event.

The obsessive doctrine of 'Jesus forsaken' encourages members to find hidden significance in the smallest annoyances and inconveniences, all of which are regarded as 'suffering'. Difficulties of all kinds are spiritualized and seen as 'trials' or 'tests' sent by God, to be accepted rather than analysed and solved. The 'night of the senses' and 'night of the spirit' described by the great mystics were regarded as everyday events, especially among the full-time *focolarini*. Thus psychological problems, depression and breakdowns could go unnoticed and untreated. But 'suffering', especially illness and even death, was considered above all as 'payment' for the movement's successes. A death which coincided with an important advance of the movement was believed to have 'paid' for the 'grace'. Suffering was referred to as the 'coin' which purchased divine favours.

The doctrine of Communion and Liberation is based solely on the works of the founder Don Giussani. The principal 'revelation' of the movement is the charism. According to Giussani, without the 'charism' peculiar to a movement, and especially his movement, the Church is a house without life: 'The Charisms give life to the institution.'[1] This means that 'an individual on approaching the sacraments feels penetrated by a new will or listening to the word of God feels animated by a new image of his life . . . hearing the addresses of the infallible magisterium he becomes aware of the path on which he must travel, sacrificing himself completely'.[2]

As with Focolare, the core of CL's message is the uniqueness of the movement itself – it *is* the 'event', the Incarnation repeated today. Members discover a new plane of existence: 'The Christian event is the beginning of a new way of living this world; it sets in motion a new conception and a new manipulation of reality.'

Membership is described in visionary terms:

> The community, *the company*, where the meeting with Christ occurs, *is the place where our ego belongs*, the place where it acquires the ultimate manner of perceiving and feeling things, of grasping them intellectually and judging them, of imagining, of planning [*progettare*], of deciding, of doing.[3]

---

[1] Laity i.e. Christians, Interview with Don Luigi Giussani by Angelo Scola, Coop. Ed. Nuovo Mondo, Milan, p.22.
[2] op. cit., p. 23.
[3] Don Luigi Giussani, *The Christian Event*, Milan: Rizzoli, 1993, p. 49.

What all this apparently boils down to, as we discover a few sentences later, however, is the conformity of the individual who realizes that '*our point of view* does not follow its own path, but *submits to comparison and in comparison obeys the community*'.

Evocative synonyms for God, such as Mystery and Destiny, are used to add a sense of wonder to the movement/Event: 'Now the unexpected has happened. God, destiny, mystery has become an event in our daily existence: this is Christianity. And it is in this event that the ego comes into focus.'

More mystifying still is the declaration that 'The community, spread without limits, is the Mystery of this identity through which and in which I can say with fear, trembling and love to Christ: "You" '.

The resonant and poetic term 'memory' is used to denote a tired concept of traditional Catholicism – that of 'offering up'. Again a 'mystifying' element is added: 'The memory of Christ is the memory of a past which becomes so present as to determine the present more than any other present. Memory has become the key word of our community: *the community is the place where memory is lived.*' The various branches of the movement are defined in similarly exalted terms. Even the most practical, the Company of Works, which brings together the movement's various business activities and services, is described as 'the company among us [which] is not born as a social project or image of the future, but a miracle of change'.

The event of the movement, like the 'knowledge' offered by the other movements, is a divine illumination: 'We have been given a *light* that enlightens from the intangible depths of the heart to the final horizon *of the eyes*, the basis of an *experience* that *we can* have, that we are called to have, in which the final resurrection is reflected.'

Apart from the central doctrine of the movement as revelation, the internal knowledge of CL offers few surprises. While sharing the strong spiritual orientation of the other two movements, CL's language to a large extent avoids traditional religious terminology. It also appears to argue its case rather than simply make assertions as the others do. But this is an illusion. Behind secular-sounding catchphrases lie *a priori* arguments and assumptions within a closed-circuit thought-process. Nevertheless, through the skilful use of this jargon and an obscure, round-about approach to his subjects

Giussani suggests new insights, which he never quite delivers. His writings are not so much mystical as mystifying.

The Religious Sense, one of his key texts, is an arid, tedious collection of pseudo-intellectual musings on the fundamental problems of existence. Giussani has tailored his jargon to his target audience – university students (especially Italians) of the final decades of the twentieth century. His message, holding out as it does an existential solution to youthful *Angst*, clearly weaves its spell, judging by the numbers drawn by it. For all their semblance of rationality, Giussani's arguments are circular and self-contained. They all lead to the same point, the one 'answer' which is ultimately irrational and must be the object of faith: the movement, the 'event' which cannot be understood, 'as that which is unexpected is also incomprehensible'.

The gnostic element of Neocatechumenate is its *raison d'être*; it is a Way, or process of initiation, by strictly ordered stages, a feature it shares with the mystery religions of the ancients and modern secret societies such as the Masons.

The Way consists of two main elements: catecheses, originally given by Kiko Arguello and Carmen Hernandez and repeated verbatim by local catechists, and rites which are presented to members as being those of the Church, but which are in fact peculiar to the movement and unknown to other Catholics.

Like the adepts of the mystery religions which enjoyed such popularity in ancient Greece and Rome, NC members are sworn to the strictest secrecy. They may not divulge details of teachings received or rites undergone even to members of other NC communities in the same parish, let alone to outsiders. Like Freemasons, they are kept in complete ignorance of forthcoming steps or 'passages' of the mysterious Way. The only preparation will have been repeated reminders that this latest stage is even more crucially important than all the earlier crucially important stages. Indeed, it is vital that recruits should be ambushed with these demands in the disorientating context of an environment totally manipulated by the movement.

To outside enquiries on whether the catechesis is available in written form, the standard response is: 'The movement has only been in existence for thirty years; it is too early for anything to be written down.' A parallel is being drawn with the first Christian communities, in which teachings were passed on orally for several decades before they were set down in written form.

The comparison is hardly valid. NC are not refounding the Christian Church but taking their place within a large existing community which has a right to know the content of NC teachings. That is, of course, not how NC leaders see it. Besides, it is convenient to play down the existence of official texts because that way no-one – especially those with special rights, like bishops – can ask to see them.

But texts do in fact exist, transcribed from taped lectures by Kiko Arguello and Carmen Hernandez and circulated in photocopied form, though access to them is restricted to the top echelons of the movement.

It is, of course, essential to the monolithic structure of the movement that the teachings are passed on precisely as received from the founder. Very few members, even among the catechists, are in possession of the teachings in their complete form. The practice is to issue each talk to catechists when it is needed for a community. In this way, even the catechists are unable to form an overview of the teachings or examine recurring themes.

I have had sight of these secret writings covering the early stages of the Way, including the first two 'passages', amounting to several weighty tomes. Of course the secrecy of the teachings enhances their impact. As the initiates of ancient times discovered when they were led blindfold to the scene of the sacred mysteries, anticipation adds wonder.

Amidst the *longueurs*, the written catecheses do provide a number of surprises and even shocks. But these lie less in spiritual matters than in NC's methods and in the bizarre and extreme views of the founders on the world in general and on how members should conduct their lives. Judged simply by the standards of common sense, many of these appear sinister and dangerous.

When it comes to matters theological, the teachings have been condemned by some experts as heretical. This is a further and very practical reason for the wall of silence which surrounds NC doctrines. In their talks, Arguello and Hernandez constantly urge the imperative of silence on catechists because they are aware of the hostility their ideas and practices may provoke.

In the third talk of the introductory catechesis, Kiko Arguello strongly criticizes groups within the Church who espouse social causes and become involved in politics. He reserves especial venom for priests who have 'studied a lot of psychology and read a lot'.

At this point, Carmen interrupts with a warning: 'You must not tell people this; otherwise you will cause a terrible mess.'

Later in the same talk, Kiko refers to the fact that members – at a later stage – are required to sell all their goods. 'Don't tell people this,' he adds hastily, 'otherwise they'll run away immediately.'

In the very first talk, Kiko refers to the NC practice of raising their hands during the Lord's Prayer. This gesture is not restricted to NC; it was used by the early Christians and is now widespread amongst Catholics, especially those of the Charismatic tradition. Nevertheless, anxious not to cause alarm, Arguello instructs the catechists that 'only the one who leads should raise his hands, because people are not used to it and until they are catechized it could go against the grain . . . Experience has shown us this. If you all raise your hands, people will think you are fanatics.'

In his detailed instructions for the penitential celebration which takes place on the tenth evening of the introductory catechesis, Arguello points out the need for several priests to hear individual confessions. As some of these may not be acquainted with NC methods, he advises the catechists first to brief the parish priest so that he can pass the instructions on to his colleagues, 'because maybe the priests will disagree with you. But, if you have instructed the parish priest well, you will have prepared the ground so that he can explain how things must be done and why.' The dangers of rejection are skilfully negotiated in this case by utilizing the authority of the parish priest.

The written guidelines give a mass of detailed teachings and descriptions of rites and ceremonies. In the text, Kiko and Carmen constantly emphasize the importance of following these to the letter, despite the fact that they have claimed to Church authorities, as emphasized on a number of occasions by Cardinal Ratzinger and Bishop Cordes, that their transcribed talks merely provide a general outline to be used in conjunction with other Church-approved sources.

The talks which communicate NC teachings are, like those of the other movements, long, lacking in structure, abstract and obscure, using unexplained technical terms and the movement's own jargon.

Those who have attended the introductory talks and even the

first residential *convivence* without succumbing to NC's charms have remarked on the tediousness of these addresses, allowing no opportunity for questions or discussion. The mind-numbing quality of the instruction is part of the indoctrination process.

A detailed analysis of the NC Way might well prove equally stupefying. An overview of the early stages of the catechesis, however, highlighting some of its most troubling teachings, reveals why many ex-members have been so disturbed by this troubling 'gnosis' of our times.

The first volume of catechesis, *Guidelines to the teams of catechists for the phase of conversion*, runs to 373 typewritten pages and covers the fifteen talks of the introductory catechesis and the first *convivence* in which new recruits are required to commit themselves to following the Way. According to the title page, it is based on 'notes taken from tape-recordings of meetings with Kiko and Carmen in February 1972 for the guidance of the teams of catechists from Madrid'. The publishers are given as the Neo-catechumenal Centre 'Servo di Jahve' in San Salvatore, Rome, March 1982.

This volume of 'Guidelines' has been a source of controversy on the few occasions when it has fallen into the hands of outsiders. In a brief history of the movement's progress towards official approval, Kiko Arguello refers to an incident when some Canadian priests who, according to him, 'were against the renewal of the Council' obtained this document and 'saw heresies everywhere and maintained that it contained secret directives'.[1] Father Enrico Zoffoli used it as the basis of his two studies *The Heresies of the Neocatechumenate Movement* and *Magisterium of the Pope and the Catechesis of Kiko: A Comparison*. And yet the movement claims to have submitted these and other writings to the Vatican and received its blessing. The Holy Office of Cardinal Ratzinger, therefore, which has condemned distinguished theologians like Hans Kung, Edward Schillebeeckx, Charles Curran and Leonardo Boff, has approved these secret documents. This lends them a further fascination.

As the initial fifteen catecheses, which are given annually in NC parishes, are designed for complete newcomers, their first objective is to establish the uniqueness of the movement's mission. This is achieved in a very practical way as early as the second catechesis,

[1] *Il Cammino Neocatechumenale*, ed. Ezechiele Pasotti, Milan: Edizioni Paoline, 1993, p. 9.

by establishing the teaching credentials and absolute authority of the catechist. He (occasionally she) is an 'apostle' with powers that far outstrip those that any parish priest or even a bishop would wish to exercise. The catechist, for example, is qualified to recognize 'the signs of faith' in members – or, rather, to confirm their absence, because, as Kiko points out:

> During the catechumenate, you cannot yet show the signs of adult faith. It is the apostle, the catechist, who leads you in the catechesis, he who must watch over the Way, like a big brother, given that the bishop has recognized this charism in him to lead you to faith. He is certainly the brother who knows [if the Spirit of Jesus is present].

Some pretty bold claims are being made here. The first is that no 'signs of faith' can be shown during the catechumenate. Seventeen years is a long time to persevere without faith. The other startling assertion is that the catechist possesses a supreme power to judge who is a true believer and who is not. It will surely come as a surprise to many bishops that they have delegated such powers, perhaps even that they possess them themselves. Within the movement, however, this authority is accepted unquestioningly and exercised freely.

In the third catechesis, the uniqueness of NC is definitively expressed through the movement's partisan view of salvation history. A diagram is used to illustrate how it begins with Abraham, continues through the Old Testament with Moses, David, the Exile in Babylon, the prophets, leading up to Jesus Christ and then his followers in the early Church. Up to this point, the movement is in line with scholars of all mainstream Christian denominations.

But suddenly, in AD 314, after the reign of the Emperor Constantine, a pair of brackets appear on the NC timeline and the next event is the Second Vatican Council in 1962. 'With Constantine,' Kiko explains, 'a parenthesis opens going right up to our own times.'

During the intervening 1,700 years, we are told, the catechumenate of the early days of Christianity was no longer practised and the Church, therefore, entered a state of 'natural religion'. Although Kiko says this 'parenthesis' was 'not a bad thing', he then goes on to explain how the Church of that period was not really the Church at all. 'The amazing thing', Arguello observes, 'is that in the course of the centuries the Church did not die out altogether.'

The saints, the doctors of the Church, the religious orders are swept aside as we speed forward to Vatican II, a Vatican II which proclaims liturgical renewal, a new theology based not on the dogma of the Redemption but on the Easter Mystery, and finally Ecumenism – which Kiko Arguello equates with mission: oddly enough, all key elements in the NC package. We can guess what is coming next. 'But now', the founder announces portentously, 'comes the most important thing. How can all this work of the Council be brought to the parish? How can the renewal of the Council be applied to the concrete parish?' The answer is as simple as it is predictable: 'Through a catechumenal Christian community, opening a catechumenal Way.' Thus 4,000 years of salvation history is revealed to culminate in Neocatechumenate. And Neo-catechumenate is not one of the ways in which the Council is fulfilled – it is the *only* way.

Even at this early stage of catechumenate, a glimpse is given of the parish structure envisaged by NC:

> The community has the mission of opening a catechumenal Way in the parish. When other brothers want to enter it, as the community cannot be too large, they will join another community. Thus we will open new communities and form a new parish structure. Each community will have its presbyter [priest], its deacon, and the different charisms will appear in the community . . . so there will be a college of deacons, a college of priests, etc. A local church, in which the parish priest will be a kind of bishop, with its presbyteral college. This local Church is the discovery of the Council.

Or the discovery of Kiko Arguello, to be more precise. At a time when even a country like France cannot provide a single priest for each parish, it could be asked where all these priests are going to come from. Each stage of the NC Way requires a different Eucharistic liturgy. Some NC parishes in Rome already call on twenty-five priests on Saturday evenings to say separate masses for all the communities. This fact throws light on to the twenty-five

NC seminaries around the world and the huge numbers of vocations claimed by the movement. A large part of them will be needed to feed NC's own insatiable requirements for clergy.

The next stage of the catechesis cultivates further feelings of élitism in those about to join the NC community. A diagram illustrates the fact that only a third of the world's population is Christian, of which slightly more than half is Catholic. Of these, only 10 per cent go to mass regularly and only 1.5 per cent are 'adult Christians, that is, conscious Christians'.

Now the founder proceeds to strip off further layers in his search for true Christians, who are by now synonymous with NC members. He hints for the first time at the idea of the 'elect', God's chosen few: '. . . we do not sufficiently understand this idea of election.'

The parish is described as consisting of three concentric circles.

The inner circle is formed, naturally, by NC members, 'those called to form new communitites, called to be the Sacrament "Church". Not that they wanted to be the Church, but rather they have been elected by God to carry out this mission, this service.'

The next circle is formed by people who, according to Arguello, 'will not juridically enter the Church'. This group, apparently, includes those who believe themselves to be Catholics but do not belong to the comunities as, in practice, the majority of parishioners in NC parishes are not community members.

The most sinister aspect of this analysis of the parish, however, is found in the third circle: 'those who live in untruth, who have always lied to themselves. They are those in whom Satan acts with a real force. But not because they are bad and are to blame, but maybe because this is their role for some motive that we will not go into.'

This is dangerously close to the most extreme concept of predestination. Arguello's definition of the kind of people who fit into this category is particularly revealing of the movement's attitudes:

> They are maybe those who have the most to give humanly speaking, the most intelligent. (Judas was the most intelligent of the apostles, this is why he was the treasurer.) They are those who cannot stand the communities. This is a most important

mission, because without Judas, there is no Easter mystery of Jesus.

Several points are made here. The first is the condemnation of intellectuals, common to all the new movements – for intellectuals are the progressives, those who question. The second is a rationalization of the opposition the NC Way has always provoked; the movement's enemies are necessary to their reliving of the 'Easter mystery'. Paranoia is sanctioned as an essential element of NC culture. Kiko leaves no doubt about the role of the third circle and how they must be regarded by members:

> When that day arrives, they will have the mission to kill you, to destroy you. Basically, they live dominated by the devil because they have never been loved . . . They will not listen to your reasons, they do not recognize the Spirit, they say it is all angelism and a form of alienation to avoid lifting a finger.

Not much room is left for dissent or dialogue. Catholics who disapprove of some or all NC doctrines and methods are the main opponents of NC, as Kiko Arguello is only too well aware.

Again and again, the Guidelines claim divine authority for the movement. At each *convivence*, members are reminded that Jesus is acting through the catechists. It is a fact; there is no 'perhaps'. And the fact is couched in the form of a threat: 'Jesus is passing and maybe He will not pass again. . . . WITH US COMES JESUS. And who does Jesus heal? THOSE WHO RECOGNIZE THE FACT THAT THEY ARE BLIND. JESUS IS PASSING BE-CAUSE HE COMES WITH US' [his emphasis].

This categoric affirmation confirms once more the mechanistic nature of the Way; it is an infallible process which leads to salvation for those who follow it. Those who do not follow or who fall by the wayside not only will not be saved, but will not be part of the Church – even those who believe themselves to be devout Catholics.

The doctrinal aspect of the catechesis is singularly uninspiring: what distinguishes it from the current approach of the rest of the Catholic Church is the overwhelming emphasis on sin and death. From the very first catechesis, Kiko urges his listeners that 'God is the one who through your sins, your blindness, your pride, your sexuality, will give you light'. He invites them to pray: 'Can't you see I am fallen and impoverished? Can't you see that I was drunk, that I beat up my wife, can't you see that I masturbated? Don't you see what a wretch I am?'

One of the essential points of NC formula is the proclamation of the Kerygma, the key gospel message of the death and resurrection of Jesus. Two of the initial catecheses are devoted to recasting this concept in NC terms. The first step is to undermine the convictions of even those prospective members who are practising Catholics: 'Fundamentally, the point of this catechesis is to show the people that their Christianity is worthless and to look at their true reality.' The next stage is further to break down the resistance of potential recruits by building an overpowering sense of sin and death. A frequently repeated doctrine is that of sin as 'ontological death'. This phrase has no real meaning, for 'ontological' means to do with being and death is non-being. What Arguello is apparently trying to express here is an 'existential death' or an 'experience' of death – that is, the anguish, the isolation Man feels because he has sinned. This is fair enough as far as it goes, although it might be thought that Arguello is overstating his case when he says: 'Physical death and suffering are nothing compared to the death we experience in the separation from God when we sin. That is when we experience infinite terror, you lose your dimension completely. This is death.'

It soon becomes clear that the main function of the Way is to ensure that the adepts should plumb the abyss of their own corruption: 'Man', they are told, 'is dominated by the serpent, by the devil, by death, by sin.'

Arguello lists the evil forces Man is in thrall to as money and prestige, but also marriage, children and sexuality.

If the majority of Catholics of left and right would part company with Arguello at this point, he then plunges even further into apparent heresy:

Man cannot do good because he has separated himself from God, because he has sinned and he has been rendered radically powerless and useless, under the sway of the devil. He is slave to the devil. The devil is his Lord. (That is why neither advice nor sermons of encouragement are any use. Man cannot do good) . . . [You] are a servant of the devil that manipulates you as he wills, because he is much more powerful than you. You cannot fulfil the law, because the law tells you to love, not to resist evil, but you cannot: you do what the evil one wants.

This is dangerously close to the doctrine of total depravity, which was espoused by the Jansenists and which has always been condemned by the Catholic Church. The opposite view is taken by a great modern theologian, Karl Rahner, with his idea of 'anonymous Christians', or those who practise the virtues Christians aspire to without belonging to, or even knowing about, the Church.

Arguello underlines the active part played by the devil in this vision of depraved humanity. Of St Paul's phrase, 'It is no longer I who act, but sin that lives within me', Arguello's rather free interpretation is: 'By sin St Paul means the devil, the action of the devil in us.'

There is a strategy behind the idea of 'ontological death'. Members will be assaulted and ground into submission by the constant repetition of the message of sin and corruption over the many long years of the Way that lie ahead. Arguello leaves recruits in no doubt that a profound sense of one's personal sinfulness is the essential condition for understanding the Way. Grace does not enter the equation. Members are given such a strong sense of their own sinfulness that they become totally dependent on the movement for salvation. It is a mechanistic approach which leaves no place for God's grace acting directly on the soul. The extreme emphasis on man's sinfulness has the effect of absolving him from all responsibility for his evil actions: 'He is deeply flawed. He is carnal. All he can do is thieve, fight, be jealous, envious etc. He cannot do otherwise and he is not to blame.' It is vital that members should accept this reading of their situation if they are to progress on the Way. Testimonies of ex-members show just how effective this process is.

Much of the catechesis takes Scripture, particularly the Old Testament, as its starting-point, but with thousands of words of commentary from Kiko Arguello for every one of the Bible. The great and often difficult themes of the faith are reinterpreted using NC jargon as though the movement had unlocked their meaning.

The Exodus, which is the subject of the thirteenth evening of the initial catechesis, is interpreted as an archetype of the experience that every Christian must undergo. This is more than a useful parallel: it is a dogma for NC members. '*This story is your story. This is a primordial event which is an eternal Word of God for all ages and all nations,*' the founder declares emphatically. 'This is fulfilled literally. It has already been completely fulfilled in Jesus Christ and it must be fulfilled in you. If you are not in this Word, you are lost, because outside it there is only death' (his emphasis).

This is bad news for the mass of 'ordinary' Christians who know nothing of this 'catechesis'. Only in NC members, apparently, is this 'Word' fulfilled. Arguello prescribes in meticulous detail exactly how this should happen.

A common thread runs through these reinterpretations of Scripture. In each case, its authority is used to reinforce that of the movement, to canonize its structure and its hold over individual members. The movement itself is the subject of the catechesis; it is the gnosis or secret knowledge which brings salvation to candidates for initiation.

Having 'revealed' to each member the depths of his sinfulness and thus established his or her need for redemption, the next step is to prove that only the movement can provide it. The introductory catechesis is designed to show that Neocatechumenate is the only context within which the entire body of Scripture – Old and New Testament – makes sense. In a statement designed to shock devout Catholics, Carmen declares that, 'the book [i.e. the Bible] is not important, not even if we want it to be, in the Church.'

Arguello follows this remark by explaining the method for understanding Scripture: 'Let us see how these books were formed, how they reached us. In order to find out, we must begin at the end – in 1972, with us.' (He was talking in 1972.) He distinguishes between 'the Word of God', defined as divine intervention in history – in other words, an event – and 'Scripture', which is the written record of this event.

This would be an acceptable definition of the Catholic distinction between Scripture and the continuing life of the Church as a vital community. But Arguello's definition of 'the word of God' is much more specific, much narrower: it is the Neocatechumenal communities.

> This Word announces a promise to you. You will be completely freed from slavery in Egypt. Set out on the way with a

community, receive the Messiah that comes to free you, entrust yourself to him and he will lead you to the waters. In the waters do not be afraid, your enemies will be at hand to persecute you, but do not fear: I will destroy them.

There are warnings for those who decide not to accept 'the Word':

What happens is that many do not believe in this Word, and want to destroy their enemies by themselves. Therefore they leave the Way, they abandon Moses, and the advance guard of the Pharaoh, following close behind, descends on them and destroys them.

If there is a certain ambiguity in these statements, it becomes increasingly clear that Kiko's message is that the experience of the 'Word of God', which makes Scripture comprehensible, is only to be found in NC communities: 'The Church during this catechumenate will give you this Spirit so that you may understand these books with all wisdom, so that Scripture will become for you the Word of God.'

The practices peculiar to NC are portrayed as identical to the spiritual experiences which inspired the Scriptures. By themselves, these are merely 'a dead letter, a skeleton'.

In order that this skeleton should be covered with flesh, he who opens [the book] . . . must be a witness to the Scriptures because they are fulfilled in his own life. Only he who has written this book has the power to open it, because this book is sealed. A pagan understands nothing of it. BECAUSE CHRISTIANITY IS NOT A LETTER, IT IS AN EVENT, IT IS LIVING EXPERIENCES. Try and tell your cousin about the Easter you celebrated: he'll die laughing [his emphasis].

If anyone does not experience this direct affinity with Scripture, he is in trouble, Kiko warns the catechists:

. . . if you go into the community and the Scriptures are opened and proclaimed and they tell you nothing, then tremble! Because you are outside them. If when they are proclaimed you find yourself within them and you see that they say something to you because they are fulfilled in you, rejoice and sing . . . Rejoice because you are in the Way . . .

Just in case anyone is under the illusion that this experience can be found outside NC communities, Carmen dismisses attempts by other groups to understand Scripture: 'The biblical courses that are in fashion are of short duration, because, as the Spirit is not there that is present in the community that meets to pray and proclaim the Word, they end in boredom.'

To seal this proprietorial attitude to Scripture, the final evening of the initial catechesis is a solemn ceremony, aimed at evoking a feeling of radical commitment in the initiates. This is the consignment of the Bibles. It is a ceremony at which the presence of the local bishop is especially desirable. 'Inviting the bishop to the consignment of the Bibles', Carmen protests, 'is not a trick or a technique, as many people think, to conquer the bishop, but a catechesis given to the people: that in itself this book is nothing, but it is the apostles, the bishops, who transmit the book, because they have the power of opening the Scriptures.' It is not the bishops, of course, who will 'open the Scriptures' over the next seventeen years or so, but the catechists of Neocatechumenate, following the detailed guide- lines of Kiko Arguello and Carmen Hernandez. In this way the bishop's presence is exploited to give the movement a cloak of authority.

The first *convivence* is the most vital stage in the recruitment process. It is the moment when those who have followed the introductory catechesis are asked to make an initial commitment which will lead to the total submission of mind and will to the Way. Nothing therefore is left to chance. The opportunity is seized for an all-out assault on the minds and hearts of these unsuspecting newcomers. Every moment of the day from rising to sleeping is taken up with catechesis lasting for hours on end, interspersed with services planned to encourage personal commitment to the movement. This is no ordinary retreat, new recruits are repeatedly told; they are about to experience the direct action of God – the 'Lord is passing by'.

The 'Guidelines' give detailed descriptions of the rituals, designed for maximum psychological impact. The opening ceremony of light and darkness, held late on the evening of arrival, is an attempt to dramatize the movement's dualistic view of the human condition. Now that they have a truly captive audience, Kiko and Carmen do not mince their words:

> The darkness is a symbol of our blindness, of the sin in which we all find ourselves. Do not imagine that we are putting on a theatrical performance; the darkness expresses a reality that is within us. It is true that the darkness exists just as envy, hatred, adultery, selfishness and death exist. The darkness makes present here what happens every day in our lives . . . You are in the deep darkness of yourself, incapable of loving anyone but yourself.

Kiko is insistent that everyone should feel their sinfulness: 'If anyone here is healthy, if anyone can successfully love others, really love others, that is to give of himself to any other person, he must not stay here, he must go away.'

As the already cowed recruits are hardly likely to walk out at this stage, their continued presence is an admission of guilt. Arguello hammers this point home:

> We were not Christians, we knew nothing of Christianity, we are pre-Christians. We had never placed ourselves before the Word of Christ, we had never received a new Spirit from heaven and because of this we did not give fruit and our Christianity was enough to make you sick.'

Fortunately the *convivence* will provide the answer to this frightful realization: the NC Way. Still, according to the founder, things will have to get worse before they get better:

> We are beginning a Way that will bring us to the deep understanding of our reality. Of your own reality – of which as yet you know nothing. You do not know yourself and deep down you believe yourself to be good. If we walk along this way with Jesus, He will teach you what you are, what your true reality is, what sin means for the world . . . Discovering your deep reality of sin, you will know the immense love of God.

Arguello explains exactly what he means by 'our deep reality of sin':

> . . . the news we give you is that God loves you despite the fact that you are what you are, a sinner, a sexual hedonist, bourgeois, a couch potato, selfish, always looking after your own interests; that you accept others only when they build you up or help you; that you believe you are the king of the world. God loves like this: He loves you despite the fact that you are a sinner, despite the fact that you are an enemy.

At this stage, Arguello tells the catechists, they must throw caution to the winds, hitting candidates with the full force of NC teachings.

His introduction to the first main talk on the Eucharist, given on the morning of the second day, spells out the gnostic aim of NC teachings very clearly. Using words like 'enlightenment' and 'initiation', he explains that:

> Mystery is something that can be known, an illumination of the mind, something you can be initiated into . . . It is not, in other words, something incomprehensible to our reason, to be believed out of faith, as we are used to thinking with our rationalistic mentality. 'Mystery', on the contrary, means to understand better; to be enlightened on a reality that was hidden before.

Like the Gnostics of old, the new movements purport to *explain* the mysteries of Christianity to their initiates by revealing secrets that are hidden and that must remain hidden. For the elect, however, they will be mysteries no longer and therefore, as Arguello points out here, faith will be redundant.

Certainly, the unsuspecting new recruits are in for some shocks. Amidst hours of rambling catechesis, they are warned, for example, that they will be asked to sell everything:

> You must accept, in fact, that you will love God more than money. In the first Baptismal scrutiny in a few years' time, you will be told to sell your goods. And you will have to sell them all, because if you do not sell them you will not be able to enter the Kingdom, you will not even be able to enter the

catechumenate. Now you do not have the strength, but then you will, because you will be given the Holy Spirit so that you can do it.

They are also informed of the true extent of the submission the movement requires: '. . . in the catechumenal way . . . there is a perfect obedience. Because if there is no obedience to the catechist there is no Neocatechumenal Way.' This total dependence on the movement is pounded into recruits throughout the weekend.

Two wearying catecheses on the Eucharist take up most of the second day. They are given mainly by Carmen Hernandez, but with some key interjections by Kiko. Certain comments made in these talks are particularly disorientating for Catholics, for they appear to contradict fundamental articles of faith. Traditional Catholic beliefs on the Eucharist are undermined. Carmen derides the practice of con- serving the Sacrament in the tabernacle: 'I always tell the Blessed Sacrament Fathers, who have built an immense tabernacle: If Jesus Christ had intended the Eucharist to be put there, he would have made himself present in a stone which does not go bad.'

Although the Council restored primacy to the Eucharist in the context of the mass, playing down the often excessive Eucharistic celebrations of the past, such as processions and exposition of the Sacrament, belief in the Real Presence has not diminished. The practice of the Neocatechumenals, however, appears to suggest that, for them, the presence of the body of Christ in the consecrated bread and wine ceases with the end of the celebration.

Participants at NC masses celebrated in the prestigious basilica of San Giovanni Laterano in Rome were horrified to witness that priests dancing round the altar at the end of mass were trampling on large portions of consecrated unleavened bread that had fallen to the ground. Some members of the congregation took it on themselves to collect these portions and take them to a non-NC priest after the celebration.

If aspects of the teachings of the catechesis on the Eucharist have been condemned as heretical by some Catholic theologians, no expertise is needed to realize the disturbing implications of the doctrines expounded in the grand finale of the *convivence*. Here the claim that the NC Way is the true Church becomes explicit, and the potential followers are led to believe that they are the chosen few, the enlightened, the elect, predestined. At the same time one of the key features of NC philosophy is revealed for the first time, the source of its fatalistic attitudes and lack of commitment to social and political problems: the doctrine of 'the servant of Yaweh', which gives its name to this final catechesis.

Making the identification between Church and Way quite plain, Kiko begins with the declaration: 'Now I will tell you why we are travelling this Way, what the MISSION OF THIS WAY IS, WHAT THE MISSION OF THE CHURCH IS' [his emphasis]. After a long preamble, he comes to the point: 'THE CHURCH SAVES THE WORLD.' Significantly, he immediately defines what he means by 'the Church', not with a description that any bishop, priest or Catholic might recognize, but with a description of the structure exclusive to an NC parish: 'The local Church, a community of communities planned in a specific territory, in a city, is born because there an apostle brings the Word which is the sperm of the Spirit.'

All the key terms used here – 'community', 'apostle', 'the Word' – have been clearly defined earlier in terms of NC structure. But Kiko goes on to claim even more for these newly formed communities, suggesting that they supersede anything which has gone before:

> Those who accept and guard this Word [the announcement of the NC Way] begin a catechumenal way in community to form the Church, so that on them the Holy Spirit will descend. So they are born as sons of God . . . This is an amazing mystery: a group of men are deified and they form the Body of the Risen Jesus Christ, the son of God . . . And this saves the world.

Having made these extravagant claims, Arguello is anxious that his audience should realize that Neocatechumenate alone can 'save the world': 'For us it is very important that this should happen, that the world should see this and not something similar or a surrogate.'

Having asserted that NC alone constitutes the true Church, Arguello goes on, more alarmingly, to demonstrate that this 'Church' grants admission only to the 'elect', only to those 'who have the Holy Spirit. He who does not have it, will not go ahead.' The founder employs Christ's image of the Church as the 'salt of the Earth' to demonstrate that 'the Church' is composed of a tiny élite within the mass, just as a pinch of salt gives flavour to soup:

Nothing will happen to the person who does not go ahead: he will be a salted potato. Because it is not important to be salt, but that the salt exists which saves the world, that the Kingdom of God reaches all men, that everyone receives the announcement of the Good News. For this mission, God elects his Church. And God elects whoever he wants however he wants. . . .

The process of election does not depend on our efforts, Arguello suggests:

. . . if someone does not perform works of eternal life, he is not judged to be very bad. He simply is not elected to be the Church and that's that. We do not know if this has happened because he did not know how to respond to the Word; the only thing we know is that he does not have the Holy Spirit and therefore he is not elected. That's all. Because many are called and few are chosen. Many begin the catechumenate and few finish the last stage of the elect.

Perhaps the worst news of all is that the Holy Spirit carries out this rigorous selection process exclusively through the officers of NC itself, the catechists:

You might believe yourself very Christian, but your catechist may come along in the name of the bishop and tell you that there is nothing Christian about you. You might still think yourself a Christian of the first rank. And if your catechist does not see that you show the signs of Christianity you will not pass, because he has, in the name of the bishop, the charism of discerning spirits.

Apparently, in this narrow NC definition of the Church and its mission, the bulk of Catholics are rejected. While the élitist mentality is evident, the main intention of the catechesis is not to limit numbers by putting people off but to scare them into the communities by playing on their fears of rejection. After all, they are still reeling from the shock of discovering that for so many years they have been labouring under the delusion that they were Christians and members of the Church. As a final encouragement, Arguello suggests that they are actually 'predestined' to form the

Church. His reasoning is blindingly simple: 'God has chosen from the beginning those whom He wanted . . . I spoke at all the masses and only you came . . . if you are here and not others, it's for a reason.'

The founder returns to the idea of the parish as three concentric circles. The first, central circle is formed by the elect and those they will attract 'to form *the Church* as sacrament'. The next circle is formed of those who 'will never join the Church structure juridically, but who must be *salted, enlightened and fermented* by you'. How this will happen is never explained. Then we get to the third circle: 'This other group of people cannot bear this announcement. They are the pharisees who feel the Church denounces them and want to destroy it because it really grates on them. They are those who kill the Christians.'

And now Kiko comes up with a new concept, the answer to his initial question on the mission of the Church, of the Way: it is 'the servant of Yaweh'. This describes an attitude of total resignation and subjection that NC members must adopt. Before its persecutors, 'the Church has no other mission than to let itself be killed, let itself be destroyed, take on the sins of others'. If initiates are required to see themselves as wretched sinners, this catechesis requires a further subjection – the acceptance of evil that is done to them.

Arguello admonishes members not to be concerned with the problems of the world, nor to commit themselves to causes: 'Many young people want to commit themselves in politics, or whatever, and maybe at home they do not accept their father. Here that doesn't happen. Here, the first person you will accept will be your fascist father.'

Any kind of action for justice is postponed to a distant future when in some vague and mysterious way true Christians will effortlessly transform society: 'The day that you are Christian, your actions will be, too, and you will not be committed in any way because it will be Jesus Christ who acts when you act.' In the mean time, 'The Church is Christ himself who continues throughout history to let himself be killed for the sins of men . . . This is the spirituality of the martyrs. Today we discover that there is no other spirituality but this.' To ram this point home, Arguello praises a member who was ridiculed in his factory – along with the community – because he would take on any work he was given.

Wives are told, 'If it is now thirteen years since your husband last took you to the cinema, you no longer need pull a long face to get him to take you – understand that if he does not take you it is because he doesn't like it and he doesn't want to; without doubt he is a sinner who neglects you, but you love him the way he is, precisely at that point where he kills you.'

This martyrdom is a victory over the opponents of the Way. If NC members are glorified by the realization that 'The blood of Christians continues to be shed in the twentieth century for the forgiveness of sins', at the same time their opponents are cast in the role of Judas: 'Judas has a very active part in the Paschal Mystery of Jesus: his task is to kill Jesus.'

For Neocatechumenate, therefore, the persecutors of the Way are the new Christ-killers.

The two-year period following the first *convivence* is known as the pre-catechumenate. This stage of the Way is said to be based on the 'tripod' of the 'Word, Liturgy and Community'. Demands on members are increased. They are required to meet two evenings a week, once for the liturgy of the Word and once for the Eucharist. In addition there are monthly day-long *convivences*. A rota of teams prepares the liturgy of the Word for the Eucharist, which means that from time to time there will be an extra weekday meeting.

A 'responsible', or leader, is appointed from within the community. It is stressed that the responsible must be a layman: 'The great danger of the communities is that the priests kill them off without meaning to. In this way, the communities will have a lay responsible. The priest presides over the assemblies. The lay responsible, with a team of helpers, is the community's link with the team of catechists.'

Once again, the compliance of the fledgling members is urged, but the community is left in no doubt about its status: '. . . during the catechumenal way it is not an ecclesial community, it is not yet the Church.' Its task, throughout the long years of waiting for the renewal of the baptismal vows, is to '[eat] the bread of its sins'.

What this might mean becomes clearer in Kiko Arguello's introduction to the first scrutiny, a four-day *convivence* which concludes the two years of pre-catechumenate: 'The function of this period has been . . . to experience your reality of sin, your lack of faith, a tangible experience of your reality.' The movement's two-pronged attack on individual members is to break down their own self-confidence and feelings of self-worth and to urge upon them the benefits that only the movement can give, thus achieving the goal of total dependence. They must first discover that they have no faith, for instance, so as to experience the relief of knowing that only the movement can give faith. The Founder is quite blatant about the movement's destructive mission when he greets participants with this wish: 'I hope that during this time of the pre-catechumenate God has sent you many difficulties, many disasters, because that is exactly what had to happen for you to realize you have no faith.'

The corollary is that faith comes through Neocatechumenate. But only after many, many years, through the slow, grinding, process of the Way – this is no road to Damascus.

The steps which constitute this first 'passage' are threefold: a test of faith by the decision to sell their goods; a detachment from their spouses and children, and from their careers; and the signing of their names in the Book of Life. The last takes place at the formal rite of the first 'scrutiny', which, as it is presided over by the bishop, does not probe deeply into the lives and commitment of candidates. The real process of delving into the lives of members, the sessions which have been branded 'group confessions', takes place during the 'questionnaires' in which members are required to answer questions on their personal and family lives 'with concrete details', often facing public cross-examination by the catechists on intimate matters. Even priest-members may be exposed to this treatment, facing public humiliation before their parishioners. These preparations for the scrutinies, which are in fact the real scrutinies, are said by ex-members to go on for weeks as each member of the community, before the others, is rigorously cross-examined by the catechists.

The three questions of the 'questionnaire' which prepares the 'scrutiny' are designed to lay bare the souls of initiates:

1. Do you believe that your work is according to the gospel or up to now have you accumulated for yourself and not for God?
2. Is your emotional life (wife, husband, children, girlfriend, boyfriend, father, mother, brothers, sisters, friends, sex) a treasure

that you accumulate for yourself or do you live it according to the gospel?

3. Are you aware of your true relationship with money? To what extent is it your Lord?

All of these questions are designed to make aspirants examine and deepen their commitment to the movement. As if this spiritual striptease were not sufficiently humiliating to pay for admission to the next step of the Way, a further gesture of self-exposure is demanded from adepts, one that has been a source of great controversy – the revelation of one's personal cross.

'. . . This evening the Church in the rite will ask questions, set an exam,' Arguello prepares his disciples. 'The bishop will ask that question we asked you in the questionnaire: "What is your cross and what is its meaning in your life?".'

The instructions for the ceremony advise the candidates to be brief in answering this question addressed by the bishop to each in turn. In practice, the answer in the bishop's presence tends to be euphemistic, while within the NC community candidates are subjected to detailed questioning by the catechists on the precise nature of their 'cross'. Probing questions are asked on matters which may well be of a sexual nature or concern relations between husband and wife.

Not surprisingly, this scrutiny comes as a shock, even after two years of the Neocatechumenal Way. This is why, in his catechesis, Arguello cautions the faint-hearted: 'And let me tell you: if the Church sees that you have not understood this mystery, that the mystery of the cross has not been revealed to you, the Church will not sign you with the cross and you will not be allowed to pass into the catechumenate.'

Having goaded with threats, Arguello entices with promises of new revelations: 'This night, the Church will give you its secret weapon: the glorious cross.' He impresses on his listeners that they must be ready to accept 'the glorious cross' in all misfortunes that befall them. Having rammed this point home a number of times, he then tells them that they are incapable of doing it:

> You do not understand why your son dies, you do not understand
> why many evils befall you, why you are so selfish: do not rebel,
> accept the cross because God knows why. Take hold of the cross

so that Christ can take hold of it for you. AT THE MOMENT
THAT YOU CANNOT EMBRACE THE CROSS CHRIST
COMES INTO YOUR HEART TO EMBRACE YOU TO
IT [his emphasis].

The group meetings preparing this part of the 'scrutiny' are
required to consider two questions:

1. Are you prepared to let yourself be invaded by the Spirit of God
or are you afraid your life will change too much?
2. The cross is the sign of everything which destroys you. In
this moment what is your cross and why do you think God permits it? In other words: what meaning does the cross have in
your life?

Theoretically, the bishop is supposed to discern whether candidates have understood the glorious cross. As it is a concept – at
least, in this formulation – exclusive to NC, it is unlikely he will
have much to say on the subject. Nevertheless, Kiko Arguello is at
pains to warn his listeners that if, and only if, 'the bishop sees that
you are enlightened, that you know the secret of the glorious cross,
if he sees that you are not scandalized by the cross and you want
to receive Christ in glory, he will invite you to step forward and
sign you on the forehead with the glorious cross of Christ, with
sweet perfume.'

This example shows up NC rites for the manipulative shams they
are. Demoralized by two years of pre-catechumenate, aspirants are
browbeaten into total submission to the movement. The mystery
of human suffering and centuries of Christian insight into this
mystery are reduced to a glib formula like the 'Jesus forsaken' of
the *focolarini*. The movement dispenses revelations as and when it
chooses, more 'mysticism on the cheap'. 'The glorious cross' is a
continuation of the same theme as 'the servant of Yahweh' –
submission, acceptance, resignation. But the most important effect
of this stage of the Way is that an insoluble bond is being established
between each member and the community. Once the group is
privy to his or her darkest fears and secrets how can he or she ever
leave?

Perhaps the most dramatic and disturbing aspect of the ceremony
known as the first scrutiny is the signing of the Book of Life, the

community's own copy of the Bible. Moral blackmail is employed once more, as members are advised that they are free not to sign, not to proceed with the Way; they will, after all, simply be renouncing salvation. The signing of the Book of Life is not simply regarded as a symbolic gesture within the movement: it is definitive, regarded with fundamentalist literalism. Those who doubt or waver in the future will be reminded that they cannot turn back because their name is written in the Book of Life. 'Now signing your name you will say your yes to the election God has made of you from all eternity. Rejoice in one thing only: that your names are written in Heaven.'

Between the first scrutiny and the second scrutiny comes the 'passage of the Catechumenate', lasting from eighteen months to two years. At the midpoint of this period a three-day *convivence* known as the Shema is celebrated. It is named after the Hebrew prayer which begins: 'Hear, O Israel . . .'

The purpose of the *convivence* is to reaffirm the message of the first scrutiny – that of selling goods and also of detachment from work and family. The exhortation to sell goods is repeated *ad infinitum* during the weekend, but other startling themes also emerge.

One is the true nature of the community. The purpose of renouncing 'idols' – money, work, children, family, husband, wife – is so that the community can become the most important thing in the life of adepts. Ex-members testify to the pressure that is brought to bear so that this does in fact occur. But the catechesis makes no bones about it:

> When you entered the community you, too, were a polytheist and for you the truth, life, was in work, the family, your self-affirmation, in your children, in society, your car . . . and amongst these many things you also had the community. At this point in the Way, after four years, things have changed a bit and because now you are convinced that these things give you no happiness at all, now the Lord can say to you: 'Listen, Israel, I am the only one, the others are not Gods.'

Arguello elaborates the concept he outlined in the first scrutiny that the role of the community is to destroy the individual. He uses a particularly revolting image to impress upon members their total corruption, citing, as the *focolarini* do, the Pauline concept of the old man, the corrupt side of human nature:

> We have to discover this old man. Because this old man is not just some defect you have which upsets you. The old man is something much deeper. The little defects are the drops of oil that rise to the surface of the water and show that underneath lies a putrefying corpse . . . there's a body down there and if we do not go to the roots, if we do not remove the corpse, we are wasting our time.

The revelation of our true nature is almost more than we can cope with, according to Arguello: 'To highlight to someone the leap from where he thinks he is to where he really is would kill him. If someone made us experience this Way alone without supporting him constantly with the Word of God they would drive us to suicide.'

But this does not mean that Arguello is presenting a rosy picture of the community as loving and supportive. Far from it. Instead, in a breathless rant, he impresses upon his disciples his own repellent definition of the community as a loveless hell: 'During this time of the catechumenate God permits problems, conflicts, messes in the community which denounce man, confronting him with his reality so that, if people thought they were very Christian, after two years in the Way, realizing that they can stand neither Tom, Dick, nor Harry, they become more aware of their limitations.' But this is only the beginning. 'Later, the situation gets even worse, because then the gossip starts and the back-stabbing.'

Can this possibly be regarded as behaviour that should be encouraged in a parish group? Arguello appears to give it his wholehearted endorsement: 'But God permits all this, better still, if you like, He commands it. And that's wonderful!'

In case members are put off by this unedifying picture of NC communities, Señor Arguello reminds them in unambiguous terms of their crucial importance: 'We have agreed, brothers, that the community must be the "sacrament of Jesus Christ" and that it is the future humanity.' Arguello is specific: he does not say 'the future of humanity', which would suggest that the wider population might participate in this promised Utopia, but simply 'the future humanity', suggesting that no outsiders will be involved. He further clarifies the concept of the chosen few: 'The most important thing is this: we are passing from a situation of the "Christianized church" where, in order to be saved, everyone had to enter the Church, to a situation in which what saves the world is light, the light that enlightens.'

While orthodox Catholicism would no longer insist that there is no salvation outside the Church, it would certainly reject the idea that the true Church is only a tiny élite and all others – even those who believe themselves to be Christian – do not in fact constitute the Church. Arguello continues: 'We start from the conviction that Jesus envisions His Church as a "remnant", as a catalyst, as a leaven, as a light.' Throughout the history of Christianity, élite groups have sprung up, declaring themselves to be the remnant, the handful of true believers left in the last days before the Second Coming. NC's leader gives a curious warning: 'Do not think that because one enters the Church he is saved and because another does not enter he is condemned.'

This is an apparent contradiction of the promise made at the time of the signing of the Book of Life. Arguello's intention is to keep members on their toes – no-one can be sure he is saved until he makes it to the bitter end of the catechumenate, to the stage immediately preceding the renewal of the Baptismal vows, the stage of election, ten years and more in the future. He warns that 'Many are called but few are chosen (elected)': 'I, in fact, do not know how many of you will be the elect of God. Don't worry because nothing happens to those God does not choose.'

This contradictory mix of veiled threats and reassurance is surely designed to confuse and disorientate – and make members more receptive to whatever they are told in the long haul ahead.

After the two years of the pre-catechumenate and the passage to the catechumenate comes the catechumenate itself. There are another six stages still to come, each lasting approximately two years – Prayer, *Traditio Symboli*, *Redditio Symboli*, the Our Father and Election – before the renewal of the Baptismal Promises. Although members at the stage of the 'Shema' are still a long way from that final goal and, according to NC orthodoxy, becoming Christian and receiving faith, nevertheless Arguello assures his followers that they have been singled out in some mysterious way: 'You have been marked with fire, and no-one can take this away from you.'

He is a self-styled visionary: 'I have seen the Lord . . . I have seen the Madonna . . . I have seen miracles,' he claims in a lecture of 1988.[1] He even recounts how, in his first private audience with John Paul II, 'With great suffering I told him how the Virgin Mary had told me to form little communities like the Holy Family of Nazareth'. The 'suffering' was caused by the fear that the Pope would think him 'a visionary, a hysteric'. On the contrary, the pontiff appears to have taken the revelations in his stride.

Although the early stages of the Way do not appear to draw on the contents of these or any other visions, Arguello's pronouncements do appear to grow bolder with the passage of time. By 1988, in a letter to the communities, he describes the Way in terms that are nothing less than visionary: 'Behold heaven's solicitude for our generation: a Way of growth which brings our faith to the stature of the head, to the stature of Christ.'

But there is bad news, too, apparently revealed exclusively to Señor Arguello: 'The Way that Our Lord Jesus Christ opened through his Exodus, destroying death and leading mankind to heaven, *is closed once again.*'

It seems that there have been changes in celestial regions that have escaped the notice of the rest of the Church, even of the Pope. This apocalyptic declaration appears to confirm that in our age there is only One Way.

There are strong parallels between the bodies of 'secret knowledge' the new movements present to their members: they concern mainly the unique status of the movement itself in God's plan for mankind, but they also involve the reprocessing of the entire body of Christian doctrine in a very particular manner. The result is that members experience the initiate's elation of illumination, of psychological redemption.

This aspect of secrecy, so characteristic of the new movements, contrasts sharply with the rest of the Catholic Church, which does not deal in arcane teachings. An Italian priest who has criticized NC wonders 'Why things which are good need to be kept secret'.

The practical consequence of the 'gnosis' of the movements is the formation in each of them of a sense of their own uniqueness

---

[1] Notes taken from the Catecheses of Kiko, Convivence at Arcinazzo, 22-5 September 1988, p. 5.

which is so distinct that there can be no meaningful communication between them or with other members of the Church. It is this sense of election that renders defections from the movements nothing short of catastrophic – both for the movements and for the defectors themselves.

12

NO EXIT

SECTS AND TOTALITARIAN SOCIETIES CONSIDER THOSE WHO LEAVE TO be traitors and apostates. The new Catholic movements are no exception. To those who believe they possess the fullness of truth, defection is the ultimate sin. It also represents a terrible threat to those who remain. As the movements communicate their doctrines by brainwashing rather than by promoting the use of reason or encouraging members to build up a personal conviction, beliefs are easily shaken. One person questioning the universal truth sends tremors through the entire edifice.

Addressing the Memores Domini, the religious communities of CL, Don Giussani declares: 'Whoever, even for a short time, has been touched by this announcement and then goes away *will go away sad for ever like the rich young man in the Gospel, because there is no truth but this one.*'

He follows this threat of personal *angst* with another warning. Apostasy affects not just the individual but the whole community: 'The truth of the way followed by my mother and father, by my friends who have children, *visibly* depends on the way of those who have been called to virginity.'

The emotional pull of one's own parents and the children of others, *others depend on you*, is unscrupulously invoked here in order to appeal to the altruism of recruits – a technique used by all the movements. The strong sense of group identity induces powerful guilt-feelings in those who wish to break free. An ex-member of

CL observes that 'Outside the community was the Devil . . . to leave was like 'immersing yourself in worldly things . . . giving yourself to the Devil.'[1]

NC makes no bones about it. If you leave the Way, you leave the Church, you turn away from God. Once again the family is invoked, the most intimate emotions of members are brought into play: renegades are guilty of the ultimate betrayal.

One of the problems for NC members is the scrutinies. How can they leave this group that knows their deepest and darkest secrets?

Leaving an NC community is particularly painful in that, because it is parish-based, you come face to face, week in week out, with those you have abandoned. Despite the fact that ex-members are still attending church services, they are made to feel like outcasts. NC's way of dealing with the criticism implicit in the presence of ex-members is to ostracize them completely. Morally you are 'in chains', says one Italian ex-member. 'I went back to being a "course Sunday Christian", one that, according to many of them, is worthless; those who go to church without understanding the "Word of God" have no merit.'

Another way to deal with deserters is to deny their existence. This was the Focolare way. In theory no-one ever left. In reality those who did would be pursued relentlessly to return. When such efforts proved fruitless, elaborate lies would be told of sudden departures for foreign parts or rest-cures for mysterious illnesses, until eventually the missing person was forgotten.

The experience of the movement is a strong one: the commitment demanded is so overwhelming that the individual is conditioned to see his entire existence solely in terms of membership, of belonging – of being 'in unity', to use the jargon. Some who leave never succeed in finding themselves and their independence again. The longing for the group is like a wound that refuses to heal. It is hardly surprising, then, that some ex-members return even after many years.

But the number of *focolarini* who leave is striking. In 1977, there were 1,600 *focolarini* (men) and 1,100 *focolarine* (women).[2] Each year, fifty or sixty *focolarini* men and a similar number of women enrol in the school which was based at Loppiano and is now in Montet,

[1]L'adoloscente sublimato, Piera Serra, Guaraldi, Florence, 1978.
[2]Figures given in *Chiara*, Edwin Robertson, Christian Journals, Ireland, 1978.

Switzerland. Most of those who complete the course enter Focolare. Only two members of my course (1971–2) 'failed'. According to this growth rate, numbers by the end of the eighties should have been in the region of 2,000 for each branch. In fact there were 1,086 men and 1,676 women in 1988.[1] Even allowing for half a dozen deaths a year (bearing in mind that the vast bulk of the *focolarini* are aged between 20 and 50), this suggests a dramatic drop-out rate, especially for the men.

If, according to the party line, the only reason for leaving the movement is a fall from grace, strenuous efforts must be made to bring former members back into the fold. Those who do not respond are viewed with consternation. I recall how we regarded ex-members, particularly ex-*focolarini,* as wretched failures and secretly shrank with horror from the possibility that the same fate might ever befall us. Whatever other sins they might be guilty of, one was certain. They had been offered and had rejected the greatest gift available to today's Christians: the charism of unity.

The very idea that a person should find happiness elsewhere was intolerable. Whereas there was no gossip within the movement about other members, bad news about ex-members spread like wildfire. I never remember hearing good news of an ex-member – that he or she was happily married and successful. But I recall morality tales aplenty. A *focolarino* from Switzerland who was destined for great things in the movement left to marry. It was whispered that he had written to Chiara telling her that now his 'ideal' – the buzzword for the Focolare doctrine – was his wife. This was a sacrilege that struck us as the depths of degradation. Even more shocking was the story that circulated at Loppiano of an ex-*focolarino* who was now a transvestite prostitute, frequently to be seen outside Florence station. Is that how we would end up if we left?

It was vital that ex-members should be discredited and that horror stories should circulate. A saying often darkly used of ex-members was 'He who was the best has become the worst', implying that apostates were similar to Lucifer, highest of the angels, who became the Devil himself: once they had fallen there was no limit to the depths they could plumb. If the movement were to retain its credibility with members as the sole source of salvation, it was

[1] According to an internal news bulletin.

essential that they should be convinced that, should they leave, they would be lost in outer darkness. Indeed, we were convinced that apostasy was the worst possible fate that could befall us. The movement and the Church are so fused in the minds of members that many of those who break loose do leave the Church. A *focolarino* who is now a leading figure in the movement once told me that if he left the movement he would leave the Church and cease to believe in God as Chiara Lubich and Focolare were the only convincing proofs of the existence of God and the truth of the Christian message.

Before I left for Loppiano at the beginning of 1971, I spent three months in the London men's community. I shared a bedroom with David, a handsome and charming African-American who always seemed to be in the best of spirits. I was surprised to learn, shortly after I arrived at Loppiano, that David had been transferred to the New York Focolare. There had certainly been no hint of such a move just two months earlier. David visited Loppiano for three weeks later that year, and I realized that he was not living in a community, although he still appeared to be very committed to the movement. What had gone wrong? After all, he had seemed quite content when we were together in the London community.

For several years I heard no more of David. Some time after I had returned to Britain, we were visited by Giuseppe Zanghi, one of the first *focolarini,* a philosopher and priest from the Centre of the movement. As he had just returned from the United States, one of us innocently asked after David. His answer was damning: 'David is lost in the homosexual underworld of New York.' I was shocked at his answer, in view of the fact that matters of a sexual nature were never mentioned in the movement and also we were bidden not to judge others.

Thirteen years later I tracked David down while I was on a business trip to New York. He had not disappeared into any underworld, but into the galley of a 747, where he worked as a steward for a leading American airline. We met in an Irish pub on Second Avenue, and I finally heard the true story behind those events in 1971.

A leading member of the movement, had visited the London Focolare for 'private interviews' (*colloqui privati),* also sometimes known as 'the exam' (*l'esame),* in February 1971. In the course of one of these, David had casually mentioned that, in his youth, before joining the movement, he had had homosexual experiences, even though, since joining the movement, he had lived a life of celibacy.

To David's astonishment, the 'interview' was abruptly terminated and he was sent to pack his bags ready to return home to New York without more ado. Thirteen years later, his anger over this summary dismissal had not abated. He had come to believe that racism had also played a part. Whatever the reasons, and in spite of the fact that David had been a prominent member of the high-profile Gen Rosso band for a number of years, once he had gone it was mandatory that his reputation should be destroyed. In such cases the ancient principle of the Catholic Church held good: 'Error has no rights.'

It should be added that all the ex-members of the movement I have encountered have been highly successful in their careers, in spite of the fact that they have had to overcome the initial disadvantage of the lost years. Doubtless, they have had to deal with problems in their personal and professional lives, but that is the human condition.

The *focolarini* avoid these problems by opting out from life altogether. On one level they achieve freedom from the problems of everyday life such as money worries and emotional strains, but they pay a high price.

At the beginning of this book I pointed out that, whenever the topic of my membership of Focolare comes up, the conversation quickly narrows down to two questions: why I joined and why I left. By now, the answer to the second question should be clear. But the vision of the movement I have given in this book is not the way things appeared at the time.

The years I spent in Focolare were probably the most unhappy and unfulfilling of my life, and yet we were taught that suffering was essential to our way of life; 'Jesus forsaken' was the key to unity, therefore we should expect to suffer. This was why I endured a state of inner turmoil for so many years. The decision to leave was not a considered and conscious one. The 'Holy Journey' of Focolare is one not of self-discovery but of self-destruction and self-forgetfulness. Alienated from one's deliberately suppressed emotions, personal decisions become impossible. And, besides, all choices are made for the individual by the community 'in unity'.

I left not because I wanted to but because I was impelled to at an unconscious level by an instinct for survival. It is impossible to analyse the movement or gain any objective view of it while you are still inside. Indeed, my leaving Focolare did not imply any loss of faith in its ideals. But it was the process of leaving that was to reveal the movement's true nature – its narrowness, its exclusivity, its hypocrisy. Six months before I left I could never have imagined that I could ever have made a definitive break with Focolare. Once I had made that break, looking back over the past nine years, I saw that it had become inevitable.

After the relentless assault on our minds and personalities endured for two years at Loppiano, life in a Focolare community seemed almost normal. At the beginning of 1973, I arrived in Liverpool, where I had been assigned to open a new men's community. At first, there was just myself and Marcelo Claria, the *capofocolare*, an Argentinian psychiatrist, who at first lived in the hospital where he was working while I lived in a bedsit. My only previous visit to Liverpool had not left me with a good impression. But, to my great surprise, I fell in love with the city and its inhabitants almost immediately. And perhaps this 'attachment' was the beginning of the end.

I was to find a job in teaching – a profession I had never been attracted to, but a preferred one for *focolarini*; in addition to the long holidays, the short working hours leave plenty of time for the vital missionary work. Then there is the further bonus of recruitment opportunities among young people: many Gen are drawn in by *focolarini* and other members of the movement who are teachers.

Despite my lack of teaching experience, the next day I found myself facing a screaming mob in a classroom of Edge Hill Secondary Modern. Although the six months I spent at the school proved a baptism of fire, I found teaching rewarding. On orders from the London headquarters, I enrolled for a one-year postgraduate diploma of education starting in September 1973. I was offered a job for the following academic year in the English Department of De La Salle College, the Catholic Grammar School where I had done my teaching practice. Prior to entering the movement at seventeen, I had never been short of ideas and schemes. Now I had the opportunity once more, within the narrow boundaries of my work situation, to develop projects of my own.

I started a school film society, alternating cinema classics with box-office hits, thus reviving my interest in film. In the classroom, I found creative writing classes particularly fulfilling. Having specialized in drama during my postgraduate teaching course, egged on by my colleagues, a small class project I directed became a succesful end-of-year school play.

In Focolare terms, these modest efforts were a show of uncommon initiative and independence – perhaps too much. Nevertheless, after the monotony and conformity of Loppiano – so contrary to my natural inclinations – I was facing challenges and stimulation again.

Even the fact of setting up a new community meant finding suitable accommodation, dreaming up our famous housewarming party in order to scrounge furniture, contacting adherents of the movement to let them know we had arrived. And this exercise did not just happen once. We moved three times in the two and a half years I was in Liverpool; the third time to a large detached house in Sinclair Drive, near Penny Lane, in a rather smart area of the city. It was purchased by the movement, and the Liverpool men's community is still based there.

Another important element in my life in this period was my work with the youth of the movement. I had been appointed the Gen 'assistant' (leader) first for the North of England and Scotland, which was our catchment area at that time, and later for the whole of the United Kingdom and the Republic of Ireland. I was twenty-three at the time, and the Gen in Liverpool were mainly in their late teens and early twenties. One was actually older than I was.

Having lived for five years in a cultural void, I began to hear the music they were listening to and became aware of the films they were discussing. As *focolarini* we were totally out of touch with the culture of the times, never watching television or reading newspapers and only very occasionally seeing a carefully chosen film. Once I had left the movement, I discovered a nine-year blank in my knowledge of films, books and theatre which has never really been filled. Still, I had now opened a peephole to the outside world.

A Gen band was launched, putting on occasional concerts in churches and halls throughout the north of England. Encouraged by my drama work in schools, I would hire lights and plan the lighting and the staging. I began to create little mimes as part of the shows. Later these would be expanded and performed by larger mixed groups at Mariapolis and Gen gatherings.

Bubbling under these events was a 'secret' that had tormented me almost from the moment I met Focolare. Although the movement was built on secrecy, in my innocence I believed that being 'in unity' meant concealing nothing from the authorities, whom we saw as 'the focus of unity'. I felt that I was holding something back and, therefore, my unity was incomplete. From about the age of twelve I had realized that I was attracted to other boys of my own age and older at my single-sex school. Such matters were not talked about in Catholic schools in those days, perhaps not even today, and so I had informed myself as best I could, mugging up on Freudian psychology in the library. For many years, even after I had left the movement, I saw these 'homosexual tendencies' as a temptation or a vice rather than as a part of my make-up. As my teenage years wore on, I began to realize that I was not just passing through a 'phase', but my devout Catholicism provided an effective means of shelving the problem and I managed to sublimate all sexual feelings totally.

At the time I met Focolare, I had become virtually asexual at seventeen. Nevertheless, as I became more involved with the movement, I felt under increasing pressure to reveal my 'secret'. It took me some time to pluck up the courage. Part of the problem was that everyone else seemed to be even more asexual than I was – sex just did not appear to have a place in the Focolare universe. It belonged in the marriage bed, behind closed doors, and, as celibates, that was no concern of ours, thank goodness.

There was the other problem that I was being groomed as a *focolarino*. Would this confession earn me instant dismissal? With hindsight, bearing in mind David's experience, this had been a definite possibility. Perhaps that would have been a blessed release. Unfortunately I was not to be so lucky.

After dithering for weeks, I blurted my story out to Dimitri Bregant, the Yugoslavian doctor, now a priest, who has been the *capozona* of the men's branch of the movement in the United Kingdom since 1969.

His reaction came as a surprise. My feelings were not wrong in themselves, as long as I did nothing about them. But I was especially puzzled at what appeared to be his main point. On no account, he warned, should I blame my feelings on the movement.

I was taken aback. It was the furthest thing from my mind – after all, I had felt this way since my early adolescence. What did the movement have to do with it? It was not until many years later that the sinister force of this idea hit me. The plight of the individual is of little consequence; what matters is that the institution should remain unblemished.

According to the teachings of Chiara Lubich, 'suffering', that catch-all term which is bandied about so much in the movement, must not be analysed, and therefore there was nothing more to be said about my 'problem'. No questions were asked, obviously there was no discussion of my emotional life. That would be 'human', something we were forbidden to be. The only advice I was given was Focolare's magical answer to all problems – to 'love Jesus forsaken'. This meant that in my case – as, I am sure, in many others – the real question was never confronted.

'Jesus forsaken' was a cosmic carpet under which all distasteful, difficult and painful matters must be swept. The concept encouraged Focolare's 'culture of secrecy'. We were forbidden even to talk about our doubts and difficulties with friends within the movement. We were not to share our 'wretchedness' with others. As far as Focolare was concerned, a problem shared was a problem doubled.

This approach reflected Focolare's deep distrust of human nature. Openness, even between close associates, could only lead to trouble, possibly sin. Feelings are ephemeral, without substance and there-fore not worth discussing. We were only to share 'the light' – the illuminations we received when we followed the doctrine of Chiara Lubich. Thus all 'experiences' had to be positive. The result was total repression of anything that troubled us. In my case, this was a fatal error that was to bring much pain in the years to come. Human nature will not be dealt with in such a summary manner. When I made this 'confession' in 1969, I had no desire for sexual experiment. Having been in the movement from the age of seventeen, I had the sketchiest ideas of physical love. No doubt the prospect of celibacy was attractive at least in part because any kind of sexual choice was postponed for good. Nevertheless I was constantly aware of my orientation. There was a tension between this attraction I felt and the supreme purity of the 'Ideal' with which we were constantly being bombarded.

The conflict became particularly strong when I arrived at Loppiano where we concentrated on our inner lives to the exclusion of almost everything else. While the others were proclaiming the joys of unity and experiencing Paradise on earth, I was struggling with emotions that were all too human – if they were even that. After months of lobbying, I managed to obtain an interview with the godlike Maras, only to be told what I already knew: 'Love Jesus forsaken.' By a huge effort of will I finally managed to suppress my inner struggle and yield to the general euphoria.

Suddenly, in my second year in Liverpool, while I was studying for my diploma of education, the feelings I had repressed for so long, without attempting any kind of conscious resolution, irrupted in a violent and apparently irrational fashion. In a desperate reaction to years of attempting to forget and repress, I found myself enacting a 'Death on the Mersey' scenario, although I had heard neither of Visconti's film nor of Mann's novella at the time. On an impulse, I skipped college and spent a day tracking a mysterious stranger, chosen at random, around the centre of Liverpool. As dusk fell, I abruptly came to my senses, awakening as though from a dream. I could find no explanation for my actions and feared I was losing my mind.

In fact, although what I had done was beyond my control, not dictated by conscious forces, it made perfect sense. In the terms of Jungian psychology, I had recognized in a total stranger the estranged and alienated part of my personality. What this incident indicated without doubt was a profound personal crisis that demanded resolution.

It was a cry for help. But it was not to be heeded by the movement, however. I slept little that night. The next morning I phoned the *capozona*, Dimitri Bregant, who was now a priest, from a callbox. 'I have to come and speak to you – immediately,' I urged.

I caught the train to London and arrived at the men's Focolare just before supper. A tiny card-table had been laid for two in one of the sitting-rooms. I was to dine there with Dimitri, separately from the others, who tiptoed around us with exaggerated discretion.

This was the same man to whom I had first 'confessed' five years earlier. I told him what had happened the previous day. Was this the onset of insanity, I wanted to know. Is this where my twisted desires had led me? Bregant did not answer my query or even refer to what I had told him. Instead he told me again how difficult he knew it was, and instructed me to love 'Jesus forsaken'.

It is extraordinary to me now that, as a doctor and a priest, Bregant could not have seen that as a young, very naïve man of twenty-four I was in a profoundly disturbed state, and that to do nothing more than mouth platitudes could have had disastrous consequences. But, for hard-liners of the movement, its doctrines are the only answer. Besides this, I was a *focolarino*. I belonged to the movement. The idea that I might feel less pressurized outside the community, which seems logical to me now, was not considered. On the contrary, I was encouraged to take temporary vows of poverty, chastity and obedience for the first time at the meeting of the *focolarini* in Rome the following Christmas. This was a very serious step, and was the cause of more sleepless nights.

Fortunately, my 'brainstorm' proved to be an isolated incident. I was entering the most rewarding period that I spent in the Liverpool community. But my inner tensions bubbled underneath. Such were my scruples that for months I would rise secretly at six thirty so that I could go to daily confession before work although guilty of nothing more than masturbation and 'bad thoughts'. Now, the fact that I had vows had to be mentioned each time to my confessor. It was as though my sins were doubled.

The crisis came when, after two and a half years in Liverpool, I was told I was to be transferred to the Focolare in London. The authorities had decided to develop the English-language magazine *New City* and the publishing house of the same name. I was to find a part-time teaching post and devote the rest of my time to editing the magazine. The long-term plan was that I should switch to a career in publishing, bringing that expertise to the movement's operation.

Leaving Liverpool was hard. I had grown to love the city and its people. My period as a teacher at De La Salle College had been happy and rewarding. The headmaster pleaded with me to stay on, promising me promotion and even the position of head of the English department within a few years. As our identities as *focolarini* had to be kept hidden, I was forced to pretend that I was leaving out of choice and invent some lie as an excuse.

I was also leaving a lively and youthful Focolare community, with a relatively relaxed atmosphere, for the cold and conventual atmosphere of the men's Focolare at 57 Twyford Avenue in Ealing. Its personnel changed constantly during the period I was there, and there was little sense of belonging. The only time we met was for an evening meal at which Dimitri Bregant would bring us up to date on the latest news from Rome – every day, he would spend hours on the phone to the Centre of the movement – or else he would expound on the dreadful state of mankind. After that, everyone would disappear behind closed doors into one of the many rooms of the house to deal with mysterious paperwork or translate a tape for visitors. Although the atmosphere was more institutional than at Liverpool, paradoxically there was more time to think, more freedom of action.

Almost as soon as I arrived in London, the crisis which was to propel me outside Focolare was set in motion. But it had been a long time coming. Often the most important decisions in life are taken not at a conscious level, but at a deeper level of instinct: it is only later that the logic behind them becomes clear. This was certainly the case in my flight from Focolare. It was not decided by me or by others – it was inevitable.

For the first time, *New City* magazine was to have an English editor. The aim was to extend its appeal beyond the circle of the movement's adherents. I set about my task with enthusiasm and, as a trusted party member, was given pretty much a free hand. Alongside the mandatory thoughts of Chiara, articles on secular subjects would now appear, although always seen through the filter of the Focolare ideology. Instead of the entire magazine being translated from its Italian namesake, the bulk of the articles were now written directly in English. This fact alone struck some as suspicious – especially the women's branch in their role as guardians of orthodoxy. With each new edition, howls of protest would emanate from Clapham, where they had their headquarters. Subjects like literature, cinema and dance were introduced into the magazine – always in a spiritual key – but to the women, who knew nothing of such 'human' matters, they were profoundly disturbing. Where were the simple and reassuring platitudes? What did all this intellectualism mean? As I have already recounted, the shockwaves even reached Rome – and Chiara Lubich.

As I was charged with making *New City* magazine more accessible, I decided to see what everyone else was doing and broke the Focolare ban on reading newspapers and magazines. Thus, the brief glimpses of the outside world that I had caught in my work with young people became lingering, even wistful, gazes.

I discovered that the world had changed radically since I had left it. Particularly in one important detail. Before I had met the movement in 1967, homosexuality was a crime; now, in 1975, I could read gay-positive articles in prominent publications like *The Guardian* and *Time Out*. I was even confronted with this issue by my pupils. Eleven-year-olds would ask me in religious education classes why it was wrong to be gay if people were made that way. This was a tough one.

Although it did not occur to me at the time, these powerful new influences must have played their part in the personal crisis I experienced a few months after arriving in London. I began to suffer from serious insomnia, an affliction I have never experienced at any other time of my life. I hoped this would pass, but it continued for months. Then another strange symptom manifested itself: panic attacks that would strike whenever I was forced to sit for long periods. Not surprisingly, these occurred mainly during meetings of the movement. I would struggle with an overpowering desire to run out of the room or the meeting-hall, and keep on running. At our six-monthly retreat in Rome, I could not even follow the speeches of Chiara Lubich, as I sweated and squirmed, battling the impulse to escape.

At the same time, the long-repressed issue of my sexuality refused to be ignored any longer. I now felt that I had to understand the true nature of my feelings. I knew that the answer to this and to the strange, distressing symptoms I was experiencing could only be found – or, at least, sought – outside the Focolare community.

Of course, after nine years, and with vows of poverty, chastity and obedience, it was not just a question of packing my bags and saying goodbye. For a start, I had no intention of severing contact with the movement. I still believed implicitly in its message and its claims. But at some deep instinctive level I knew that if I did not get out of the community, and fast, I would be irreparably damaged. My exit would therefore have to be negotiated through the official channels.

It was only later, once I was outside, that the edifice I had sustained loyally for nine years began to crumble for me. It was then that I would share the experience of all who leave sects, 'people who have put their friendship networks, jobs, financial security and all their interests in one basket – and lost the lot'.[1]

No-one was more surprised than I when I boldly announced to Dimitri Bregant that I felt I should leave the community. Of course,

[1] Dr Elizabeth Tylden, quoted in *The Times*, Wednesday, 21 April 1993.

I did not put it quite like that. In large as in small matters, we were required to 'see things in unity' with the authorities, which meant submitting our ideas to them and abiding by their decision. For the first time in nine years, however, I had taken a decision alone, and I knew that whatever obstacles were presented to me I would not waver in my resolve.

I realized immediately that the movement would make it as difficult as they could for me to go. Dimitri outlined to me the stages I would have to pass through. First there would be a meeting in Rome with a responsible person from the Centre for the *focolarini* men. I would be required to explain my case to him in detail. Then I would have to see a psychiatrist – one who was acceptable to the movement – who would have to confirm that leaving Focolare was necessary and would be of help. I believe it was at this point that it was first suggested to me that the alternative to life in community – indeed, the only apparent alternative – would be to become a married *focolarino*.

This initial conversation took place in early December 1975, little over three months after I had arrived in London. Events had moved fast. But the six months it would take to extricate myself from the community were to pass very slowly indeed. I braced myself, and at the Christmas retreat for the *focolarini* in Rome at the end of that month spoke with the appropriate official – Enzo Fondi, one of the first *focolarini* – who, coldly and clinically, with obvious distaste, questioned me on my 'case'.

Usually encounters of this kind were marked by a forced warmth and paternalism. This one was unfriendly and unsympathetic. I was guilty of a cardinal sin: instead of passively submitting, I was dictating the agenda. This was unacceptable. Already I was being made to feel a traitor. But I held my ground. With some relief, I did not renew my annual vows along with the other *focolarini* that Christmas.

The next stage – consultation with a psychiatrist – was more tricky. I knew that if I was packed off to Italy and delivered into the hands of some Focolare-approved quack, which would have been the customary procedure, I would be subjected to some crackpot cure and might never be heard of again. This was not what I had in mind at all. It was essential at this stage that I remained in control. The minute I left the country, I would be entirely at the movement's mercy.

With the excuse that I would be more comfortable discussing the 'problem' in my own language, I suggested, therefore, that a suitable English psychiatrist should be found. This was not strictly true as, if anything, I was more used to discussing personal matters in Italian. Fortunately, however, my proposal was reluctantly accepted. Focolare did not have any tame psychiatrists in England and were in no hurry to find one. If the matter was to progress, I would have to set about finding a candidate myself – and then get the movement's seal of approval.

I had recently read a letter in the English Catholic weekly *The Tablet* from a prominent Catholic psychiatrist. Dimitri Bregant told me that this doctor would be acceptable to the movement, and so I wrote to him, requesting an appointment. There was one more hurdle to be jumped. In his reply, the psychiatrist told me that, while he would be willing to take on my case, I would have to be recommended to him by my GP lest he should appear to be soliciting patients through letters to the press.

Ealing has a large Polish community, and my Polish – and Catholic – GP gave me short shrift. This was all a lot of nonsense, he suggested. Why did I need to complicate matters by consulting a shrink when all I really needed was to go down to the parish hall and meet a good Catholic girl? Perhaps, I replied, not revealing the full details of my affiliation with the movement (I still felt very protective towards it), but this was what I wanted to do. Reluctantly he agreed to make the required recommendation.

As the process dragged on, the routine of life in community continued. I still had to fill in my *schemetti* each night, accounting for every tiny detail of my day, although sometimes I would let it slide for weeks and then have to make it up. The movement's practices began to ring hollow. I translated tapes of Chiara Lubich for visitors nightly on automatic pilot, an ability I had acquired in long sessions at Loppiano and in Rome. I was still obliged to hold forth at meetings with the Gen and other members, but the words turned to dust in my mouth. Physically I was still in the community, but in my mind I had already left. In those months I experienced a disconcerting split between my life as a *focolarino* and a personal, even private, life which I no longer resisted, as though there was a dividing wall of glass running through my brain. I did not know how long I could tolerate this split. My insomnia and panic attacks worsened.

Finally, on a balmy spring day in 1976, I caught a train from Paddington for my session on the couch. It was a revelatory encounter in a number of ways. I sat facing the doctor as he questioned me on my family, early childhood and adolescence. At last, I experienced the release of describing my feelings, thoughts and desires without fear of censure or condemnation. His apparent receptiveness encouraged me to dig deep into my memory, as incidents and feelings long buried came flooding back.

Now it was his turn to speak. Some of his observations were illuminating, and I learned things about myself that previously I had not been able or willing to grasp. Then he told me what I really wanted to hear: that I was under intolerable pressure living in the Focolare community and should leave as soon as possible. I was caught up in a vicious circle of guilt and the need for release in order to assuage it. My mission was accomplished.

But the doctor had just started. The really good bit was his prognosis.

'What sort of men attract you?' he asked. 'What age-group?'

'My own age, I suppose,' I replied, although, again, it was not a thought I had ever consciously addressed.

'And what is it about a man that attracts you, physically; what part of his body do you think of first?'

'The face,' I replied out loud. Obviously I had given the right answer.

'You know,' he mused, 'sexuality is a sliding scale, and there is really very little difference between a young man of your age and a slim young girl of nineteen or twenty. I am confident that we can re-educate your fantasy life. Through your parish youth club you could meet a nice Catholic girl with whom you will be able to have a perfectly normal relationship and eventually marry.'

Marriage is a powerful antidote to homosexual tendencies, he informed me; in particular, the rewards and responsibilities of children. This sounded encouraging. Perhaps my case was not hopeless after all.

'I will take your case on,' he agreed at the end of this pep-talk, 'but there could be problems.' Other clients leaving Catholic movements – Opus Dei was mentioned – had experienced terrible traumas, he warned darkly.

I consoled myself with the thought that he really did not understand my situation or Focolare. After all, my intention was not to abandon the movement completely – just community life. At this point I was convinced that I would find my place in one of its many other mansions. My heart sank, however, when I realized that this was not quite the end of the line. I should return with my superior, the good doctor insisted, so that he could explain the gravity of my situation, but, more important, to assure himself that the movement would pick up the tab for my treatment, which was going to be very expensive.

Although I had no yardstick by which to judge the psychiatrist's views at the time, they now appear self-evident nonsense. Even then, however, I was uncertain about whether I wanted my fantasy life 're-educated'. But I would worry about that later. In the mean time, I agreed to discuss the matter with my superior and fix another appointment for us both, knowing that this was the necessary condition for my freedom.

A few weeks later, Dimitri and I returned by car for this vital session. But my presence turned out to be superfluous. Dimitri was invited into the consulting-room for a cosy chat with the doctor; while I sat in the waiting-room leafing impatiently through magazines, wondering whether the doctor was making a good case for my release. When they emerged some considerable time later, I stood up expectantly, ready to join them for a three-way discussion. Instead, the doctor shook my hand and we left. A deal had been struck in my absence. I caught a whiff of conspiracy which unnerved me. Was this ethical? Did my views not figure in all this?

On the drive back to London, Dimitri was evasive about what had been discussed in his conference with the psychiatrist. I suspected from his brooding silence that what I had revealed in confidence had at least been hinted at – possibly to strengthen the case for my exit from the community and the need to finance the treatment.

'Well, we can try this,' Dimitri commented sombrely, 'and if it doesn't work there are always drugs that can be used.'

The idea of having something slipped in my tea appealed even less than the re-education of my fantasy life promised by the psychiatrist. I did not want my mind and feelings more completely – and skilfully – manipulated than they had been for the past nine years. Now I was free to leave Focolare I wasted no time and immediately began to take the necessary practical steps. But I also secretly resolved that none of the proposed cures would ever take place. Down the toilet went the valium that had been prescribed by my GP. My friend in Oxford would not be getting that fat fee after all, I decided.

Although, at last, the door to freedom had been unlocked, as far as Focolare was concerned it was not only left ajar, but wide open. Dimitri Bregant stressed that this was a trial period and need not necessarily be permanent.

As far as I was concerned, however, the step I was taking was irrevocable.

Then came the suggestion I had been expecting. I had witnessed a number of arranged marriages in the movement – in Loppiano, for example, it would suddenly be announced that a *focolarina* and *focolarino* who would not normally even have the chance to meet except with special permission were to wed. Nor did such an arrangement strike us as odd. Now it was my turn. I was offered the pick of the Focolare meat-rack. The women community members were not eligible, of course, being celibate, but I was asked if any of the Gen girls appealed to me? I named one, and Dimitri told me he would discuss the matter with his female counterpart. That was the last I heard of the matter. Once I moved out the territory began to shift more rapidly than I had foreseen.

Focolare had always used family loyalty as a lever, just as the other movements do: if you are faithful to the movement, you will draw your family after you; if not, you will betray them, too. This had always been a profound concern of mine, but when I told my family of my decision they accepted it so readily that further explanations were unnecessary. My mother, who, with all her doubts and queries, had made a noble effort to understand my membership of the movement, was delighted. Having completed her nursing training in Scotland, my sister, who is four years younger than me, was about to start on a midwifery course in London, so we decided to rent a flat together.

The first problems I encountered were financial. After six years of religious poverty in which my earnings would go straight into the coffers of the movement, I had no savings of any kind. As I was continuing to edit *New City* (unpaid, obviously), I would be earning a part-time salary from teaching until the end of the academic year. It was now May. I had a further disadvantage in that I had not handled my own finances since I left university in 1970. I had never paid rent or a fuel bill in my life. Although I managed to secure a full-time teaching post for the following September, the months ahead would be hard.

I found a pleasant two-bedroom flat which would swallow up half my monthly income, leaving me £60 a month to live on – desperately little even in 1976. Religious orders give financial help to ex-members, sometimes supporting them for up to a year until they adjust to normal society. But the *focolarini* offered no financial assistance, in spite of the fact that I was still to devote a considerable amount of my time to the magazine and other work for the movement.

While they were prepared to underwrite costly psychiatric treatment to 'reform' me, the practicalities of my survival did not have the same urgency. Presumably I was to trust to the Providence that they welcomed so eagerly. I needed a lump sum to pay my share of the deposit on the flat and on services like the telephone and fuel. The bulk of this was given to me by my mother. The *capofocolare* of the London men's community, Bruno Carrera, reluctantly agreed to lend, not give, me an additional £100.

This meanness was in striking contrast with what the movement had received, from myself and my family, over the previous nine years. Apart from all my earnings – which had been not insubstantial during my teaching years – it had also had my full-time services for six of those years as interpreter, translator, missionary and now editor. I had even donated a small legacy of £300 I had received at my grandmother's death in 1968 towards the purchase of the house at 57 Twyford Avenue, still the headquarters of the *focolarini* in London. My family had also lent £1,500, interest-free, towards the £9,000 purchase-price of the five-bedroom house, which today is worth in the region of £200,000. That £1,500 was a substantial sum at that time, and it was not paid back in full until several years after I had left the movement. To have borrowed money interest-free and spread the repayment over a number of years, at their own convenience, made the purchase of this house a spectacular financial coup for the movement. These offerings had been received eagerly, without even a thank-you; Providence was the right of the *focolarini*. For my part, I had become so accustomed to the philosophy of 'taking' practised by the *focolarini* – I had blithely been a party to it for so long myself – that I did not question the lack of financial assistance. Three years later they were still hounding me for the return of 'their' one hundred pounds.

As well as having no financial resources, I came out of the community with less, in terms of clothes and possessions, than I had gone in with. Fortunately our new flat was furnished, but some utensils had to be purchased.

Having become accustomed to agonizing over the purchase of a Mars bar, every expenditure was a major moral dilemma. I had always loved music – my classical record collection had been left behind me in Focolare – and I debated for days over whether to buy a bottom-of-the-range Soviet-made stereo for £20, which even then was dirt cheap. Eventually, racked with guilt, I took the plunge. But the model I acquired was faulty. I took it back. The replacement was no better. I returned to the shop four times that day. On the final occasion, the assistant ducked behind the counter when she saw me coming. I was distraught, interpreting these events, as I had been taught, as a sign of divine disfavour.

None of these material concerns, however, could dampen my enthusiasm for the new adventure on which I was about to embark. It had taken me six months to negotiate my release from Focolare, and it had been a nightmarish period of battling against the movement's resistance and coping with my health problems. Now it was over, and I moved into my new flat. Then an extraordinary thing happened. The symptoms of panic and insomnia that I had endured for almost a year disappeared literally overnight. They were replaced by a simple, even banal, emotion which none the less came with the force of a revelation. For the first time in six years, since I had entered the Focolare community, I experienced not supernatural or divine, but human, natural happiness – that emotion, which, according to the doctrine of Focolare, does not exist.

For the first time since I had met the movement I began to forge friendships outside its boundaries – or, at least, without the ulterior motive of conversion. I realized it was possible to enjoy other people for their own sake. Despite my lack of money, I made up for ten years in the cultural wilderness, devouring all the capital had to offer in the way of theatre, music, dance and film. As my sister and I share an appreciation for ballet and modern dance, we were often to be found indoors during the sweltering summer of 1976, in London's theatres, watching some of the world's top companies, always from the gods or standing at the back of the circle. At twenty-six, I was an adolescent discovering the world for the first time.

But I was not cultivating a social life as an alternative to the movement. Even at this stage, I had no intention of making a definitive break with it. Most of my friends were to be found within it, and I was genuinely fond of them. Nevertheless, the ties that had bound me so strongly for the past nine years were unravelling alarmingly fast. Of one thing I was instinctively sure: while I still believed implicitly in the Focolare doctrines, I no longer wished to be subject to its suffocating structures. I needed the freedom to build an identity of my own. For the first time in nine years I felt good about myself. Doors that had been closed were opening again, and I intended to explore them. Naïvely, I believed that I would be granted the space I required. I was mistaken. It rapidly became clear that my relationship had to continue on the movement's terms or not at all.

While my work with the Gen ceased upon my exit, I went on editing *New City* until I started full-time work again in September 1976. But now the amount of time I could devote to the movement was partly dictated by financial imperatives. My funds were so low by the end of the summer term, for example, that I was forced to take a post teaching English as a foreign language to tide me over the holiday period. This meant that, for the first time in a decade, I was only able to attend the five-day Mariapolis meeting over the two days of a weekend.

This was viewed with chagrin by the *focolarini*, who could not see why it was necessary, probably interpreting it as a gesture of defiance. They were undoubtedly concerned at my new in-dependence. It was becoming plain that I was no longer as biddable as they had always known me. Sometimes I would agree to invitations to meetings or to dine in Focolare, at others I would have prior engagements. The refusals began to outweigh the acceptances.

I was committed to one activity in particular, however. In 1975, the first large-scale international Genfest had taken place in the Palaeur in Rome before an audience of 60,000. Now the 'zones' of the movement were expected to follow suit, staging their own large-scale local events. The United Kingdom Genfest was to take place in 1977 and, as the only person in the movement in the United Kingdom with experience of directing theatrical productions, I was invited to attend the initial workshops. The subject was not open to discussion – it was the Gen/Focolare doctrine of Unity, Jesus in the midst, Jesus forsaken, and so on.

I brought to the project the reformist zeal with which I had approached *New City*. Fired by the new theatrical influences to which I had been exposed, I felt we could go beyond the usual formula of songs, experiences and mimes with a show that would be more integrated and theatrical. *A Chorus Line,* which went on to be Broadway's longest-running musical, had just opened at the Theatre Royal, Drury Lane. It had made a huge impact on me, partly because of its seamless staging, integrating dance, song and story in a single continuous arc, and partly because of its realistic adult subject-matter. It was also the first time I had seen positive gay characters presented without special pleading. It was an ensemble piece, using a confessional format to interweave the personal stories of its multiple characters. I felt this show could be a useful model for our production. Instead of recounting 'experiences', we could fictionalize our 'stories' so that they could function as drama while still conveying the underlying message. Deftly put together, the show could avoid the impression of sweetening the pill, the thinly disguised didacticism which usually characterized Gen meetings.

During the autumn, I attended two workshop weekends in Walsingham and Surrey, and the broad lines of the piece were drawn in. The key device would be striking transitions from personal stories simply told on a darkened stage to full-scale re-creations of these accounts, teaming with action, characters, with full scenery, costumes and high-key lighting. Ours was the classic 'school-play situation' where parts had to be found for numerous performers, so this approach fitted the bill. There was a gifted group of singer-songwriters among the English Gen at that time – it was the heyday of Don Maclean, Cat Stevens and Joni Mitchell – and they set to work on the musical score.

In the meantime, my other links with the movement had dwindled so that these rehearsals were the last tenuous connection. Although I did not want to lose contact, neither did I want to be under the control of the *focolarini*. Suddenly I was bombarded with calls, sometimes several times a day, summoning me to the Focolare centre in Twyford Avenue. I invariably declined. Sometimes my sister would tell callers I was out.

On one occasion a *focolarino* phoned to say I was to come to the Focolare immediately for a meeting with Dimitri Bregant. It was not convenient at such short notice, I replied. Minutes later, the doorbell rang. It was Dimitri and a couple of the *focolarini*. The mountain, most inopportunely, had come to Muhammad. As my sister was watching television in our living-room and I had no intention of ejecting her, we trooped into my tiny bedroom and, perched on the edge of my single bed, conducted an uncomfortable 'meeting'.

On another occasion, I pleaded a migraine attack – an affliction from which I do suffer occasionally – to a *focolarino* who rang to invite me over. He, too, turned up at the flat, and I had to leap hastily into bed fully clothed, with the blankets pulled up to my nose; the *focolarino* was duly ushered into the bedroom.

A short time later I received a peremptory phone call informing me that, as I was no longer involved with the Gen and the Genfest was their event, my contribution to the production was no longer required. I had turned down an offer to direct a school play because of my commitment to the Genfest. I now informed the school that I would be available after all.

In January 1977, I received a call from the new headquarters of the men's branch of Focolare in the United Kingdom, located behind Marble Arch in London's West End, a highly desirable flat which had been provided for the movement at a peppercorn rent by one of its wealthy supporters. I was imperiously informed that Dimitri Bregant wished to see me. Although all formal relations with the movement had now been suspended for some months, somehow the right buttons were pressed, and with a knee-jerk reaction I agreed.

The purpose of the encounter was not to find out how I was, nor even to discover how I saw my future relationship with the movement. Instead I was informed that I had to find a 'place' in the movement. It did not matter what it was – it could even be in New Humanity, one of the 'mass movements' and less structured than the internal branches. They felt that I was slipping through the net of the movement's structures.

They were right. Increasingly the idea of 'fitting in' with these structures was distasteful to me. For too long I had been crushed by them. I agreed that I would think the matter over and left, realizing deep down and with some sadness that I would not. Coercion of members came so naturally to them that they were unable to see that I had passed beyond the point where such tactics could be effective. In fact, they pushed me the other way. If I had to make a choice, then it was against membership of any kind.

Some weeks later I received a telephone call asking me to reassume the direction of the Genfest. Whether they were really in trouble or whether this was a last desperate bid to hold me, I am not sure. By that point, I did not care. I told them the truth: I had already taken on other commitments. The Genfest was staged later that year, at the Roundhouse in London, an unusual and popular performing-space.

The show had remained remarkably faithful to the original concept. The personal stories we had selected to feature in it were still the same – including, to my surprise and consternation, my own. The idea of moving between stark narrative sequences and full staging provided the form of the piece, as we had originally discussed. But, apart from a lack of stagecraft, the show's weakness lay in its heavy-handed delivery of the message, the very pitfall I had hoped to avoid. It was disturbing to see my contribution still recognizably there and yet not what I had intended at all. The friends I had brought with me cringed throughout the performance.

Foolishly, I had thought that some kind of loose relationship could continue; that maybe, after I had found my own path, I would return to the movement on my terms, with a stronger sense of my own identity. My pipe-dreams were dispelled by the ceremony at London's Guildhall in 1977 at which Chiara Lubich was presented with the Templeton Prize for Progress in Religion. I received an invitation and felt it would be ungracious to refuse. Besides, the lure of Chiara Lubich was still strong. All the first *focolarini* men and women would be there, including a number I knew personally, like the mercurial Maras from my Loppiano days.

Those internal members who were aware that I had left the Focolare community and, apparently, the movement, acknowledged me with nervousness and embarrassment. I later discovered, from a Gen who left the movement, that, in order to explain my sudden departure, the Gen and other internal members had been told that I was 'ill'. It must have puzzled them, therefore, when I turned up to this event in better health than they had ever known me.

It was even trickier handling those who seemed to have no idea that my position had changed at all and congratulated me on the latest edition of *New City* – which I had ceased to edit over six months earlier.

But the most disturbing moment came when I saw one of Chiara Lubich's first companions, Doriana Zamboni. I spotted her through the crowd at the reception which followed the presentation of the award by the Duke of Edinburgh. This was the woman from whom, as the female superior in England during the sixties, I had first heard the Focolare message of Love and Unity proclaimed.

'Ciao, Dori,' I saluted as I reached her.

She did not reply, but rather looked through me as though I were a pane of glass at someone else's feast.

I was reduced to a ghost. I left hurriedly. Goodbyes would have been superfluous. When I arrived home, my sister and a friend were waiting. They were alarmed to see me pale and visibly shaken.

Now that I no longer distinguished between 'natural' and 'supernatural' thoughts and emotions, I realized that I was sincerely (that word so foreign to the *focolarini*) fond of many of those I had known in the movement. But I had to face the fact that such merely human feelings had no place in Focolare. Despite my health problems at the time of my leaving, coupled with the difficult financial situation, not once did they ask how I was or if I needed help of any kind. I was never approached on a simple basis of friendship to go out for a meal or a drink. For all their talk of 'making yourself one', the *focolarini* were so out of touch with normal life that they were unable to see that some kind of rapport could have been maintained on this basis. But such a suggestion is purely hypothetical. For them the concept of no-strings friendship or simple socializing is quite meaningless. Over the coming years, I came to realize that the substance of relationships within Focolare, and therefore the basis of their attitude towards me, was the movement itself, its structure and doctrines.

Once the 'human' element has been banished from the lives of single members, what else is left? This was why all their overtures in that period were crude attempts to maintain a hold over me. Even years later, when, practically speaking, this hold had long since been eluded, they still saw me as an element in their power structure. Once they realized that I would not yield to pressure, the harassment ceased abruptly. I was relegated to the category of the Focolare files labelled 'M' – the Dead.

Over the next twenty years I was invited to a handful of large open meetings with this category of person especially in mind. Focolare does not ostracize members like NC. Prodigals who return to meetings are fêted. But, if they do not demonstrate remorse or rediscovery, interest rapidly wanes. Focolare has no need to shun ex-members: they are divided by a yawning, unbridgeable gulf from those within. Newcomers have potential; obdurate deserters have none and are therefore lost.

But though my contact with Focolare was at an end, and I had rejected its external authority over me, the beliefs internalized over the previous nine years still held me in thrall and would have an effect on my life, in some cases disastrously, for many years to come.

The most pernicious effect of indoctrination is its lingering influence, which can only be fully understood by those who have experienced it. This manifests itself partly in a great need to talk about past experiences in the movement, to try to make sense of what no longer makes sense, in order to externalize it and place it in perspective. It is almost unbearable to lose years, maybe decades, of one's personal history; and, far from being healed by time, the loss can get worse. Despite my enthusiastic entry into the brave new world of 1976, I remained fundamentally what Focolare had made me in the most formative years of my adult life. While I no longer consciously imposed its integrist, explicitly religious view-point on all the circumstances of my life, the side-effects were still strong.

Early adulthood is a time in which values are formed based on the most important components of life: friends, family, work, relationships. We had been indoctrinated with the view that none of these mattered. Now that I was no longer guided by the myriad obsessive axioms of Focolare, the 'nail in my head', I would often be overwhelmed with the despairing feeling that any efforts I might make were pointless because, as Chiara Lubich says, 'Everything is vanity of vanities and everything passes'. Death is the only reality.

Then there was the ego-destruction the movement sought to effect in members, the constant injunctions to 'die to ourselves', 'annihilate' and 'nullify' ourselves, the crushing insistence on our 'smallness' and 'nothingness'. The self-confidence of my adolescent years had been undermined and replaced by profound self-doubt and apprehension which often prevented me from achieving my goals. This was to last for many years, until I had proved to myself that I was capable of fulfilling at least some of my aspirations.

After a nine-year hiatus, I decided to pursue a career as a film-maker, the only ambition I had ever seriously entertained. After working for five years as a publicist on feature films, television and theatre, I eventually realized this aim and have earned my living as a director ever since. But, in addition to the negative thinking I had inherited from Focolare, I also had to throw off the ideological mindset that perceives the world through a rigid belief-system. I have described how the movements inculcate not just religious ideas into their adepts but an angle on every aspect of life and society. Such an approach is totally inimical to the kind of experimental, freewheeling attitude required for any kind of creative work. It was years before I could struggle free of the movement's mental straitjacket. The stultifying fatalism and acceptance encouraged by Focolare doctrines, together with a submissive attitude to authority, were also serious handicaps which took years to outgrow.

Although I had got rid of the bathwater, I believed I had hung on to the baby: I did not lose my belief in God and the Catholic Church, nor even the teachings of the movement, although I could no longer accept its practices. As for many others who leave the movements, however, life in an ordinary parish paled in comparison with the zeal and commitment, the noise and triumphalism, the twenty-four-hours-a-day Catholicism I had experienced. I, too, desired the 'strong' experience of God which, according to Chiara Lubich, ex-members cannot find anywhere else. The myth of Sunday Christians, half-hearted hypocrites with their 'watered-down Christianity which was not lived', appeared to be true. This 'normal' Christianity held no appeal for me. In addition to this, I could not shake off the conviction that in abandoning the movement I had abandoned God. For the next ten years I ceased to practise as a Catholic altogether.

But there was another area in which I was still strongly influenced by the movement. Although, for a while, I made a few sorties onto the fringes of London's gay scene, my experiments in this area left me weighed down with guilt and self-loathing. I was haunted by the moral question which appeared to face me at the time I left the community. The choice presented to me then by the movement and its agents was still very clear: I could either follow my gay nature and live a life of sin or I could marry. It was that simple.

It was hardly surprising, therefore, that just a year and half after leaving the movement, when the possibility of marriage presented itself, I seized it. I was convinced it was the *moral* thing to do. Ironically, Dimitri Bregant, the superior of the movement who had encouraged this course of action, did not even write to me when he heard that I was to marry, although one of the Gen I had known well, who was of course unacquainted with my reasons for leaving, did send a kind letter of congratulation. One of the rank-and-file *focolarini* was sent to the wedding to represent Focolare.

I do not want to lay the blame for my actions at the movement's feet; indeed, I and others had to pay the price for them, seven years and two children later, in the form of a messy and acrimonious divorce. By then, no doubt, the Focolare authorities had long forgotten the advice so easily dispensed and, when they heard the news, shook their heads in sad disapproval. Nevertheless, in making decisions – or not making them – the only raw material one has to work with is one's self. And, when I married, after nine crucial years of indoctrination, I was what the movement had made me.

Several episodes which occurred some years after my exit illustrate how apostates are viewed by those who remain.

In the early eighties I was invited to some anniversary bash of the movement, an excuse to wheel out the 'Dead'. I was reluctant to attend, but my wife insisted that we should go. We were greeted by the female *capozona*, who sat with us as we looked after our two small girls – one still a baby. I saw Dimitri a few yards away, but, astonishingly, this man who is a priest and superior of a movement whose platform is Love would not cross the floor to greet me.

After a while, I decided I should make the first move – it seemed the only human thing to do. He asked me about my work. I told him that I was running my own PR company in the entertainment business, but hoped eventually to direct films myself. He responded with a remark that in any other context would seem breathtakingly insulting.

'But surely, if you haven't made it yet, you never will.'

I was thirty-one at the time. Of course, he had no knowledge of my world, and he was later proved to be wrong. I now believe that it was not his intention to give offence. Extraordinary as this may sound, it was simply that he still 'saw' me, in that mystical higher reality of the *focolarini*, within the movement's structure. I was therefore under his authority, and he thus possessed the 'grace' to make sweeping pronouncements on my life and future.

News of my divorce spread through the movement like a bush fire. This was to be expected, as it was triumphant proof that my life was in ruins as a result of being 'out of Unity'. What they did not know, of course, was the role Focolare had played in persuading me that marriage was the course of action I should take. I made sure I informed all the *focolarini* I met after that time of this fact and also that I was now living in a rewarding, long-term relationship with another man. While I felt it was important to be truthful, I also felt strangely sorry for some of them, protective even. In one or two cases of members whose own sexuality was dubious, I actually refrained from discussing my own situation, fearing it could cause them too much pain.

One of those to whom I recounted my post-Focolare life in some detail was 'Sarah', now a full-time *focolarina*, whom I myself had recruited to the movement while at university. When I met her at a university reunion in May 1993, she appeared to be unfazed by what I had to tell her. But it provoked an extraordinary response, a classic example of 'making yourself one' in all things but 'sin': that is, showing love by listening, but 'going against the current' by making it clear you do not approve.

This lady, who is in her forties, teaches personal relationships in a higher education institute; and yet, later the same evening, she approached me and said in a measured fashion: 'I have never met a gay man or a lesbian, so I have no opinions on them one way or the other.'

I did not conclude from this observation that the *focolarini* were trying to snatch the crown of casuistry from the Jesuits; merely that nothing has changed – the modern world has passed them by.

It was many years, perhaps ten or fifteen, before I could stand back from the movement and view it with a degree of objectivity. Many ex-members I have met have been unable to do this, consistently viewing themselves as failures. This is one of the dangerous effects of sects which are approved by the Catholic Church. The lucky ones feel anger.

Looking back, I feel that the mental violence I experienced was a kind of rape of the soul by spiritual heavies, leaving deep and lasting scars. In a conversation I once had on the movement, my interlocutor, playing Devil's Advocate, suggested that my negative view of the years I had spent in Focolare was simply a rationalization for the fact that I now felt it was time wasted. I could not have remained in the movement for nine years if they had been years of misery.

This, of course, does not reckon with the doctrine of 'Jesus forsaken', which taught us to love – indeed, to choose – suffering. I answered with the dreams. The conscious mind can lie, but the unconscious mind cannot. For years after I left the movement, I had almost daily nightmares in which I was back at Loppiano, with no means of returning to England. 'But I'm married,' I would protest to my dream companions. 'I have children.' They would smile at me pityingly. I would be gripped by panic and horror. These emotions were a reflection of those years of trauma which still haunted me. I was not alone in this experience. At least one other ex-*focolarino* of my acquaintance was haunted for years by nightmares of being 'out of unity'. Such dreams express wounds at the deepest levels of the spirit.

Focolare cast a long shadow over my life, as it has over the lives of many. Like the other movements, it has been remarkably successful in convincing ex-members of its monopoly on God. In 1985, ten years after leaving the Focolare community, I divorced, which allowed me finally to discover a genuine resolution for my life. A short time later, I encountered Quest, the organization for gay Catholics which enjoys the support of Cardinal Hume and many other bishops. In the simple friendship and humility I found among its members, I realized God is not the exclusive property of any movement.

In the almost twenty years since I left Focolare, I have had sporadic encounters with members I thought I knew well. Sometimes we met by chance, but I also attended a handful of gatherings to which I was invited, accepting partly out of nostalgia and partly out of a lingering curiosity. Although I felt genuine affection for my former colleagues, I was acutely aware that in our conversations there was no feedback, no communication. The spark of mutual recognition, interest and affection that I experienced when meeting other old friends was absent.

Attending the 'Many but One . . .' event at London's Wembley Conference Centre in September 1993, I met a number of my contemporaries in the movement. With one, who left Loppiano to marry and whose ties with the *focolarini* have loosened over the years, I felt this spark, as we shared, with genuine delight, the successes and difficulties of the years since we last met. Part of the joy of reacquaintance was the realization that we had developed and changed and that therefore we had something new to share.

With those who had remained in the movement, however, conversations were stilted; their lack of real interest in anything I – or anyone – had to say was palpable. But what was extraordinary was that the same conversations could have taken place twenty-five years earlier. It was as though no process of personal learning or maturing had taken place and they had slipped into a premature and resigned middle-age. All they could do was perform the pre-packaged formula of 'loving' or 'making themselves one' in the Focolare sense.

There is a yawning divide between those within the movements and those outside, especially those who have left. Across this divide, there is no communication. I could find no point of contact with my old friends because members of the movement do not have experiences of their own, but live according to a prescribed formula. Their existence is second-hand, vicarious. They are not living their own lives but that of Chiara Lubich. Just as the movement is static, repeating the same ideas and phrases of fifty years ago, so are the members fixed and undeveloping.

It is this immensely high toll upon the individual that I most deplore within the movements. They have been robbed of their vital spark of individuality, and with it has gone the unique contribution they could have given to the Church and to society. Both are the less for the impoverishment of individuals. The rejection of what is human is the greatest heresy of the new movements, for it is impossible to be Christian unless one is fully human first.

13

THE GREAT DIVIDE

AT THE BEGINNING OF 1994, NEOCATECHUMENATE LAUNCHED AN aggressive new method of evangelization in the city of Rome, accosting passers-by in streets, in marketplaces, in shops, inviting them to attend the introductory catechesis. If this caused consternation among the public, most of whom assumed that these fanatical evangelists belonged to some extreme non-Catholic sect, it drew even stronger reactions from the diocesan bishops and parish priests, who felt that their territory was being invaded without prior consultation. But Camillo Ruini, cardinal-vicar of Rome, and his auxiliary bishops had little to say on the matter. When the NC leaders suggested these missionary tactics to Bishop Cordes of the Vatican's Pontifical Council for the Laity, he exclaimed: 'Not only *can* you do it, you *must* do it!' The fact that such methods were more associated with Hare Krishna and the Children of God was of no concern.

But the strongest encouragement of all came from the Pope himself. In fact, the idea had been presented to him as a response to his own invitation. Given the perception of the World Youth Days as somehow 'theirs', the NC founders decided that the hordes of NC participants should arrive early for the August 1993 event in Denver to persuade the public on the streets of the city, which has only a 15 per cent Catholic population, to turn out for the pontiff. When John Paul proclaimed to the crowds at the event itself that 'This is no time to be ashamed of the Gospel. It is the time to preach it from the rooftops,' the NC contingent felt that their new preaching techniques had received the papal blessing.

They were not far wrong. Learning of the movement's initiative to extend this mission to the city of Rome and other territories where the movement was established, Pope John Paul reacted with delight:

> You are preparing yourselves for large popular missions addressed in particular to all those who have fallen away from the Church or who as yet do not know her. I hope that the initiative of going out on the streets to proclaim the Gospel, in complete agreement with the local bishops, may yield an abundant harvest everywhere.[1]

With such enthusiastic support from the top, the fact that this 'complete agreement with the local bishops' did not exist hardly seemed to matter. So strong are the ties, real or perceived, between the movement and the papacy that Kiko Arguello has appointed himself as the Pope's personal 'John the Baptist', preceding him on his official visits in order to 'prepare the way'. Despite widespread opposition and criticism at all levels, the movement appears un-stoppable.

The same is true of Focolare. In 1994 it launched a worldwide programme of national and regional Familyfests as a follow-up to the 1993 satellite jamboree in which, to use its own apocalyptic description, 'the whole planet was caught up'. Events on the largest possible scale, usually with audiences in the thousands, would be held in 180 countries. In Italy alone there would be ten mass events, which were launched on Sunday, 6 March 1994 in the Vatican's Paul VI Audience Hall with the Familyfest for the Rome region; 7,000 attended. The slick *mise en scène,* incorporating multimedia presentations, full stage lighting and musical performances, along with the mandatory 'experiences', showed the movement's growing expertise and professionalism; this was closer to a rock concert or an American political rally than to a religious gathering.

But Focolare has every reason to be confident. It is currently regarded as the most powerful of the new movements within the

---

[1]'Holy Father's Encouragement to Ne-Catechumenal (sic) Way', given Monday, 17 January 1994 in the Sala Clementina of the Vatican, *Osservatore Romano,* English edition, no. 5, 2 February 1994.

Vatican power structures. The architects of the important synod for the world's bishops on the religious life scheduled for October 1994 were Focolare members. The author of the working documents of the synod – the *Lineamenta* and *Instrumentum laboris* – was the prominent *focolarino* religious Jesus Castellano Cervera, OCD, who co-opted other religious members of the movement to assist him – Fabio Ciardi, OMI, and Marcello Zago, OMI, secretary of the Vatican Secretariat for Inter-religious Dialogue – and the *focolarino* theologian Piero Coda, a secular priest of the diocese of Frascati. This prestigious assignment reflects the massive influence Focolare has acquired within the religious orders: over 60,000 religious internal members of the movement. It also shows how much the movement is trusted within Vatican circles.

The movement's success at grassroots level has been due in large part to the fact that, at a time of general uncertainty and, for Catholics, the additional uncertainty of the Council, they were able to offer firm answers. As a result, what would probably have remained limited local phenomena have expanded to fill a vacuum in the Church.

Their narrow, idiosyncratic formulas have expanded on an international scale. Although each, in its way, firmly rejects modern culture, they have become adept at seizing the *Zeitgeist* and making it work for them. In the late sixties, they countered political unrest with a traditional message, reinterpreted in radical terms. In the eighties, they concentrated on packaging and introduced the 'spiritual marketplace'. In the nineties, they are a model of privatization, offering the central government of the Church, for the first time ever, the opportunity to carry out large operations on a worldwide scale without it costing a penny. They are also cashing in on a spiritual rebirth of a markedly fundamentalist kind. To those shopping around for a brand of religion which repudiates the materialism of the eighties without giving up its advantages, the movements offer a range of suitable spiritual designer labels.

The future of the movements looks rosy. They are established in most countries of the world; each has a powerful and efficient centralized organization; as with other sects, their doctrine is designed for, and therefore appears to work best with, those who have no religious background. They have been able to respond on a massive scale to challenges facing the Catholic Church in recent years such as secularization, the shortage of vocations and the opening of the new territories of eastern Europe. There is no reason to suppose that this impetus should slow down – at least, not for many decades to come. Orders like the Franciscans or the Jesuits continued to expand vigorously for several centuries after the death of their founders.

Some observers of the new movements believe that they will be split by power struggles following the founders' deaths. This is to misunderstand the nature of these monolithic organizations. Like the communist regimes of Russia and China in their heyday, the internal manoeuvrings of these organizations are inscrutable. If there is discussion within the oligarchies governing the movements, no outsiders will ever know about it.

The founder of Opus Dei, Josémaria Escriva de Balaguer, died before lunchtime on 26 June 1975; by teatime that day, the crown prince, Father Alvaro del Portillo, had taken his place. The Father is dead; long live the Father.

Chiara Lubich at seventy-five has not played an active part in the running of Focolare for over three years. It is said that she has already named her successor, who will be accepted wholeheartedly by the compliant membership.

Kiko Arguello is still a relatively young man; but, when the time comes, no doubt his anointed will be waiting in the wings.

Rumours of a split in Communion and Liberation between the more spiritual circle around Don Giussani in Milan and the politically orientated Rome chapter led by Don Giacomo Tantardini may well be true, but Don Giussani always appears to have the last word, and his successor will be appointed in Milan – the man designated by the founder to continue his work unaltered.

The influence of the founders is unlikely to be reduced after their death. The ethos of the movements is profoundly conservative, with a constant return to the original ideas and a complete ban on change or development. Unlike the founders of the religious orders, they will still exercise a ghostly sway over their future followers through sound recordings and videotapes. One cannot help wondering if St Francis would be such a universally loved legend if the sermon to the birds had been videotaped for posterity. If anything, the personality cults will be even more uninhibited once the founders have departed in the odour of sanctity.

The beatification of Josémaria Escriva was one of the swiftest in recent church history, just fifteen years after his death. This was in the teeth of unprecedented opposition from clergy and laity, provoking the Vatican's Opus-run press office to declare a news blackout fifteen days before the event. Sanctification of the founder or members is the highest form of approval an association in the Church can receive. It is an infallible declaration that the saint enjoys the beatific vision in heaven.

Chiara Lubich's presence was more pervasive than ever at two large-scale Focolare gatherings I attended following her withdrawal from the movement's activities in 1992. The highlight of the Familyfest in Rome on 6 June 1993 was the sound-only message from the foundress, even though she was unable to attend. Similarly, the Familyfests planned for 1994 were designed to showcase that message.

The great institutions of the past, following the death of their founders, far from languishing, would experience a new expansion. Lacking the spiritual lead of the founder, they would focus on building temporal power. In the case of the new movements, they have a head start.

Focolare and NC are already firmly established in every major territory of the world. All three movements have highly placed members or allies within the Vatican and the episcopate throughout the world. They have become highly skilled in the field of church politics and will use their power bases to increase their influence and numbers within the hierarchy. Each of them nurses the hope that one day it will capture the supreme prize: the papacy. Perhaps a future pope could come from the 700 bishops affiliated to Focolare, or those close to NC or CL. Following the example of Pope John Paul II, who has favoured several new movements, a pope who singled out one for special support could help it achieve the ultimate goal of making its message the Catholic mainstream.

The most substantial hope for future influence within the hierarchy of the Church lies in the vocations to the priesthood produced by the movements. As the attraction to a male celibate priesthood declines among the majority of Catholics, it is increasing dramatically within the movements, in addition to their powerful influence over those who were already priests and religious. Not only parish priests, but also the bishops and cardinals of the future will come from these ranks. Appointments of conservative Opus

Dei bishops have caused deep rifts in a number of European dioceses. This phenomenon could be repeated on a far larger scale once appointments from the movements start in earnest.

How will the Church of the future, the Church of the movements, appear, as these rapidly growing organizations take on an increasingly important role?

Bishop Cordes observed to me in March 1994: 'Of course you must remember that each of these movements sees itself as having a message for the whole Church.'

This is an understatement. Each sees itself as having *the* message for the Church which will reform it from top to bottom. Focolare are convinced that their spirituality is the new gospel that must be carried to the whole world. In practice, the spirituality is always accompanied by the movement's structures.

But NC feel they have a similar mission. An Italian youth who joined a scout troop in an NC parish was told: 'The charismatics, the *focolarini*, the Scouts, Catholic Action etc., etc., are all good initiatives, but, if you want to be Christian, you have to follow the Neocatechumenal Way.' When he turned down the offer, he was told he had 'renounced God' and was an 'atheist'.

When pressed on relations with other movements in the book-length interview *The Adventure of Unity*, Chiara Lubich replies: 'For all their similarities, the charisms are more strongly differentiated than one might think.'[1]

Here, Chiara appears to be contradicting the address she gave to the Synod on the Laity in 1987, in which she presented the Focolare spirituality as *representative* or in some way embracing all the spiritualities of the new movements. In fact Focolare only collaborates with other movements – indeed, other Catholics – on the specific invitation of the hierarchy, such as at the World Youth Days. The *focolarini* take a stoical attitude to these collaborations; a *focolarina* told me that they do not think about the differing ideas of the other movements – they 'just get on with the job' they have been asked to do.

Chiara Lubich has stated categorically that her movement must concentrate on its own charism and goals:

It would be betraying its own vocation and the reason why God

[1] *L'avventura dell'unità*, p. 103.

inspired it, were it not to do this; because every gift of the Father to his Church is also a medicine for the mystical Body, that it cannot do without.[1]

While this dictum may apply to Focolare, it is apparently not relevant for others – such as the members of religious orders who are expected to dedicate a large part of their time to the charism of Focolare. This unenthusiastic attitude to collaboration falls well short of the hopes expressed by Pope John Paul II in a speech made to lay groups in France in 1980; while acknowledging the specific task of each group or movement, his emphasis seemed to fall more on the fact that they should work together:

> It is important to become aware of how the movements complement one another and to establish bonds between them: not just a mutual esteem, a dialogue, but a certain co-ordination and also a genuine collaboration.[2]

The fact is that true collaboration, mutual esteem, or dialogue between the new movements is impossible. For each movement its message is the ultimate. The *focolarini*, for example, see other spiritualities as falling short of their spirituality of unity. A *focolarina* of my acquaintance criticized a former member of the Gen movement because she had joined the sisters of Mother Teresa. The same woman attacked the French mystic Charles de Foucauld, one of the towering spiritual figures of the twentieth century, as 'too individualistic', despite the fact that his ideas inspired a number of modern religious orders and lay associations.

The divisions which stem from the very nature of the movements are one of the greatest dangers they present for the Church of the future, a danger which can be deduced from the words of Bishop Cordes quoted above and yet one to which he, the Pope and other advocates of the movements in the hierarchy seem to be oblivious.

In the same interview, Cordes assured me that the movements do collaborate, consult and even imitate each other. Yet each offers an essentially all-embracing experience, representing to its followers not just an aspect of the Church but the Church in its entirety. To

---

[1]op. cit. p. 102.
[2]Speech to local leaders of the lay Apostolate, Paris, 31 May 1980.

use their own terms, they are a 'totalizing' or even a 'totalitarian' experience. Their chosen objectives are mutually exclusive – they cannot *all* be called to save the Church and the whole world.

In addition, they offer a total and quite distinct experience to members: a language, a culture, an ideology or mindset through which the entire world is perceived. It is impossible for members of the movements to have dialogue with one another, for they exist in parallel universes, parallel churches.

Meaningful communication with 'ordinary' Catholics is even more unthinkable. When I left Focolare, I frequented an 'ordinary' parish for a while, but the faith it practised was not recognizably the same as that which I had followed within the movement. It was not a difference of degree but of substance. As the CL theologian Eugenio Correco has observed, the 'dynamics' of the movements are that of 'following'. The gap between devotion to a founder who nurtures you daily with spiritual bonbons and the anonymity of church pews is vast.

The fundamentalist Church of Christ sect has been criticized because it 'identifies itself so closely with God that people fear they must forsake God in order to leave it'.[1] This is exactly the kind of hold that the new Catholic movements have over members, which is why leaving is always so traumatic.

A Church in which the movements predominate will no longer be recognizably Catholic. Even in the pre-conciliar period, the sense of a common faith was strong. In the Church of the future this sense of belonging, of identity could be fragmented into groups which have virtually nothing in common with one another.

The movements described here, though powerful and representative, are not the end of the story. They are indicators of a new and growing brand of Catholicism. There are others of the same kind, and new ones are sprouting continually. There will certainly be a war among them as they jockey for power inside the Church, carving it up between them, and staking their claim on recruits both among Catholics and outside the boundaries of Catholicism.

Could this *de facto* schism develop into the real thing? It is certainly a possibility in certain cases. The kinds of dispute growing throughout the world between 'ordinary' Catholics and Neocatechumenate could develop in that direction. Some observers,

[1] Richard N. Ostling, 'Keepers of the flock', *Time*, 18 May 1992.

however, believe that the position of the movements within the Church is more subtle than that. It is a kind of co-existence.

One theologian in Rome who is closely linked with the Vatican told me: 'They pay lip-service to obedience but in reality they do their own thing.'

A prominent Italian Catholic journalist, Gianni Baget Bozzo, however, believes that 'The "movements" do not challenge the authority of the Church. They appropriate it. It is therefore not enough to reaffirm the Church's authority over them; it will never be opposed.'[1]

Pope John Paul II has been the point of contact which has held the movements together until now. If his successor is less sympathetic, the rifts between the movements and with the hierarchy and other Catholics could easily become wider. John Paul's 'Octopus Church' could become a mass of dissociated 'floating dioceses' on the model of Opus Dei.

The meetings between the movements spearheaded by CL in the eighties have not led to a genuine collaboration or co-ordination. At the time they were launched, CL's relationship with the Italian Bishops' Conference was very strained indeed. It desperately needed credibility and theological justification. Through an alliance on a massive scale with other movements, it succeeded in formulating and proposing ideas on the role of the movements that would not have been accepted had it tried to promote them single-handedly. Now it has full official approval, CL no longer needs this kind of credibility, and Focolare and NC make no bones about the fact that they do not need and never have needed anyone else. Each believes itself destined for maximum power and is possessed of a drive and an energy not to be found in mainstream Catholicism.

From the start of his papacy, John Paul II has looked to the future rather than to the present. His first encyclical, Redemptor hominis, proclaimed his vision of a united world for the new millennium. The slogans of his reign – New Evangelization, 'civilization of love' versus 'the culture of death', Christian Europe on the medieval model – and his encyclicals have filled in the details of this vision. It is conservative in both its theology and its view of church structure. And in the new movements he detected an outlook and

[1]G. Baget Bozzo, 'I consumatori di religione', La repubblica, Saturday, 21 October 1989, p. 10.

a can-do philosophy strikingly similar to his own. Not only were they responsive to his message, but they also represented a formidable base from which to launch the new Christendom.

Practically speaking, they offered two further advantages. First, they were streamlined and efficient, acting fast and producing instant results. The new evangelization would not remain a pious wish like so many pious wishes of past pontiffs; Pope John Paul has seen the first powerful waves of his mission sweeping across the world.

But, most important, the new movements have guaranteed that mission a future. No matter what direction the Church takes, John Paul II knows that his beloved movements are unstoppable. Even if he does not see in the new millennium himself, the new movements are his enduring legacy to the Church and to the world.

These groups represent the jarring change of gear in the Catholic Church that occurred with this papacy – from rapid advance to equally rapid reverse. If the Second Vatican Council introduced a new openness to the world, the new movements display a deep mistrust, even hatred, of the world. They are profoundly anti-progress. Like fundamentalist groups in other religions, the movements' attitude to contemporary society is parasitic: they make full use of the advantages it offers – such as the media and communications technology – while rejecting the culture which produced them.

They contribute nothing to the progress of society. Whereas the Council marked the coming of age of a Catholic laity which was intelligent, able to think for itself, with its own special expertise to bring to church teachings, the movements are a sad return to a brainwashed, submissive flock whose only duty is to heed and obey. Trends within the Catholic Church towards changing the traditional clerical male-dominated power structure by modifying the compulsory celibacy rule, ordaining women priests or allowing the laity to participate in decision-making are violently repudiated by the new movements. Any suggestions that the signs of the times, the indications of the Holy Spirit, might be pointing to these new forms are flatly rejected.

And yet Focolare, Neocatechumenate, and Communion and Liberation present themselves as the embodiment of conciliar values. The Pope has hailed them as 'among the most beautiful fruits of the Council'. Cardinal Ratzinger has declared, even more categorically, that they are the Council's *only* positive results. Perhaps, as the architect of Restoration in the Catholic Church, he esteems them for other reasons. In fact, for all their pretence of 'conciliar values', the new movements could be the wooden horse through which pre-conciliar practices are being restored on a vast scale.

They claim to be lay; in fact, they are run by priests or celibates and count large numbers of clergy, religious and 'plain-clothes' celibates among their members. They are producing vocations to the male celibate priesthood from among core members in large numbers, bucking the trend of the rest of the Church where numbers are dwindling. Their members are encouraged to retreat from the world – the opposite of the Council's desire.

They claim to be unstructured and spontaneous; in fact, they are organized into rigid but secret hierarchies on a multinational scale, exacting blind obedience from members, with a personality cult surrounding the charismatic founder who wields supreme authority.

They claim to have dialogue with other Christians, those of other faiths and non-Christians; in fact, dialogue is a synonym for mission. They are totally closed to the ideas of others but are willing to seize every opportunity to spread their own creed and structures.

They claim to embrace the post-conciliar concept of conversion as a continuous turning towards God; in fact, they exact a conversion to the movement, even from those who are already devout Christians and Catholics.

They claim an innovatory approach to faith; in fact, they have clothed arch-traditionalist theology in a new and unfamiliar jargon.

They claim that their 'existential' approach to faith and their emphasis on 'experience' make them especially suited to the mentality of our times; in fact, these terms disguise an anti-intellectual encouragement to a leap-in-the-dark acceptance of the movement's package.

They claim to emphasize community; in fact, they achieve exaltation of the institution through the systematic destruction of the individual.

They claim to espouse the Council's predilection for justice and peace issues; in fact, their main concern is recruitment with a token nod in the direction of social action. Their neo-mystic tone encourages an attitude of fatalism, and they condemn those who are fired primarily by the pressing need of the poor and marginalized.

They claim to break down the artificial distinction between faith and life, sacred and secular; in fact, they nourish a profound hatred for 'the world' and retreat from it by creating separate societies of their own.

They claim to be open to collaboration in all aspects of secular life; in fact, they believe they possess the fullness of truth, not only in spiritual matters but also in fields well beyond their competence.

They claim to renew the local Church in close collaboration with the diocesan bishops; in fact, they owe allegiance only to their central government, from which they receive all directives, and are creating dioceses within each diocese.

Additionally, they incorporate some of the worst aspects of the twentieth century: an assault on the individual, and an undermining of reason in the name of ideology. They will reinforce the image the Pope has built for the Catholic Church as the new world leader of the far right. But what is most dangerous and extraordinary is that in their fight for supremacy they have adopted the worst characteristics of their main opponents: first the communists, now replaced by the new official nemesis, the sects.

It is ironic that the most pernicious and inhuman idea of the twentieth century, the deification of the collective, has found its last refuge and most passionate proponents in the very Catholics who fought communism so fiercely.

But neither the movements nor Pope John Paul appear to balk at the idea of a Church using totalitarian or sect-like methods if they achieve results. Surely a Catholic Church – or, at least, its extreme right wing – which resorts to these methods is in desperate straits. And the contribution of such a Church to the world at large – despite its past reputation as a moral leader – is highly questionable.

The movements have spread far too widely for any attempt to suppress them to be feasible or even advisable. Besides, the Pope and many bishops have given them official approval, and major policy-changes simply do not happen in the Catholic Church. It must also be borne in mind that any attempt to reverse their progress could be catastrophic for their millions of fervent believers.

Damage limitation is the most that one can hope for at this stage in the development of these vast organizations. The only authorities in the Church which can effectively accomplish this are those who have given the movements so much licence: the local bishops. The majority of members of the movements themselves are in good faith. The Pope is probably too remote to judge what is happening on the ground. The local bishops, however, are in a position to know and have a duty to be informed on what is being done in their dioceses and in their names.

Ultimately the blame for the aberrations of the movements must be laid at the door of a timorous and indecisive episcopate. Respect for the Pope or fear for their careers does not absolve them from their responsibility to the faithful.

In his campaign to save his marriage from the ravages of NC, Augusto Faustini lobbied many bishops in the diocese of Rome, as well as the Pope and Vatican officials. A dramatic confrontation with one of these, Bishop Giuseppe Mani, auxiliary for Rome East, occurred in March 1993. Bishop Mani, who Faustini knew harboured doubts about NC, held a conference on the problems of marriage in Signor Faustini's district. When the bishop asked for one of the participants, preferably a man, to come to the microphone, Faustini volunteered. He began by praising the Church's, and especially Mani's, initiatives for the defence of the family, but then he posed a question to the bishop: 'What suggestions does the Church make in the case of the abandonment of the marriage by a spouse in order to follow a non-Christian, or non-Catholic sect, or even one which claims to be Catholic?'

In a letter he wrote to the bishop after the incident, Signor Faustini recalls how: 'Trembling, I don't know whether out of fear or embarrassment, you tried to grab the microphone from my hand! Then you did not reply to the question.'

He goes on to consider the motives behind this indecorous display of episcopal panic:

> Your Lordship, I understand that it is uncomfortable to take responsibility for something, but a bishop is compelled to take responsibility for matters regarding the Faith! If the bishops won't do this, who will? . . . Is it possible that the Neocatechumenals have become so powerful that you are afraid of them?

If one were to take a leaf out of Chiara Lubich's book and assign a 'Word of Life' or scriptural text to the Catholic hierarchy, it would have to be Christ's admonition to the Pharisees: 'You lay heavy burdens on men's shoulders and do not lift a finger to help them.'

Pope John Paul II has followed his predecessors in high style with fierce reiterations of traditional teaching on birth control, divorce and homosexuality; but neither Pope nor hierarchy has ever shown the slightest flicker of acknowledging any *responsibility* for the agony these heavy burdens cause. For a time, following the Council, 'co-responsibility' was one of Catholicism's buzzwords until it slipped quietly from the agenda around the time John Paul II acceded to the papal throne.

For once, Church officials must shoulder their burdens. In this case, the bishops are the only authorities in a position to study the new movements and take appropriate action. If they will not take on their responsibility willingly, then they must be forced into action by the laity. Controlling the activities of the new movements and bringing them into line with the needs of the diocese is a lost cause. The time that could be done has long since passed. Instead, the bishops must do what little is still possible. They must renounce their *laissez-faire* attitudes which may guarantee them a quiet life but which allow the lives of others to be destroyed.

The problem is that the movements, like the importunate widow of the gospels, lobby the bishops harder than any other groups, and their lordships are inclined to yield to the pressure, granting blessings, encouragement, visits and apparent approval. This must stop.

Then bishops must inform themselves, as is their duty before God, on the movements as they really are. At present only the movements' leaders are consulted. As skilled diplomats, they naturally feed church officials a line which they know will be accepted. The unwritten code, or culture, that governs the movements in practice is never disclosed. In order to avoid this concealment, a wide cross-section of ordinary members should also be questioned on teachings they have received and practices they have experienced.

Most important, the testimony of ex-members must be taken into consideration. Currently, church policy appears to advance a circular argument that the views of ex-members are untrustworthy on the grounds that they are ex-members.

During the controversial beatification process of Josémaria

Escriva, the postulator of the cause, Father Flavio Capucci, who is a priest-member of Opus Dei, was worried that the loud protests of former members would jeopardize Escriva's cause. He was delighted to be told by an official of the Vatican Congregation for the Causes of Saints that ex-members of orders and associations always produced negative evidence in such cases but that the policy of the Congregation was to ignore it. This is a dangerously one-sided principle.

Once the bishops have gathered accurate and objective information, the faithful have a right to be authoritatively informed of the dangers inherent in the various groups. Details of their working methods and doctrinal excesses must be pointed out, and official approval should be withdrawn or qualified. In this way a response will be given to thousands of ex-members or relatives of members who ask: 'How can the bishops allow this to happen?'

Most important, support groups and helplines must be set up – at least on a national basis – for those leaving the movements, providing exit-counselling and reassurance. Like ex-members of any other sect, defectors from the new Catholic movements are losing an enormous emotional, spiritual and possibly financial investment. But currently there is no safety-net in the form of organized support. The appalling truth is that those currently leaving the movements are made to feel spiritual failures, outcasts, apostates. In many cases, this feeling of having abandoned the Church and even God in leaving the movement leads to a loss of faith in those who were previously devout. The bishops must act to remedy this situation. They must be held responsible and not be allowed to shirk their sacred duty through fear of censure or worse.

There are other, more drastic courses of action, which would result in much greater harm to the Church. One is recourse to the ecclesiastical courts. Although canon law provides for certain grievances to be aired at a diocesan level, the sight of Catholic factions battling it out all over the world would be an unseemly one. The other, even more dramatic alternative is civil action.

At least one such case has been mounted in Trento, northern Italy. Gabriella Manizza, a forty-five-year-old housewife, has brought charges of coercion against four catechists of Neo-catechumenate who allegedly subjected her husband Fabrizio to unreasonable pressure.

In the official deposition, Signora Manizza alleges that they have 'deliberately induced [my husband] to extremely damaging behaviour both in regard to himself, the undersigned and the daughter of the union, Lisa'.

The document pulls no punches in its description of the charges: 'They have inculcated (in a sectarian, obsessive, relentless fashion) Fabrizio Manizza with the teachings and rules of behaviour of the insane doctrine of Kiko; leading him to lose his sense of discernment and, in practice, manipulating him according to their demented ideas'.

The first accusation is that of the general disruption of family life: 'The command to read the Old Testament for hours, to pray continually and the obsessive incitement to live, as he says, the Bible to the letter (otherwise no eternal life) has caused grave tensions and irreparable divisions within the family'.

As in other cases, this situation seems to confirm that those families NC cannot convert in their entirety it destroys: 'The undersigned is separating from her husband; the eldest son has left home; the younger daughter is obsessed with her father's incessant preaching.'

A more serious allegation is that, in response to the conditioning of the catechists, Signor Manizza has been driven to beating up both wife and daughter 'in order to make himself obeyed'. Of greatest concern to Signora Manizza is the alleged drain on the family's financial resources: 'The husband draws money from the family budget to give it to the community and, finally, the undersigned is concerned that her husband (well indoctrinated!) will sell the matrimonial home (which is in his sole name . . .) to transfer the proceeds to the movement (others have already done it).'

A successful outcome of such an action would alert the public to the dangers of the movement and could encourage similar actions. The long-term effectiveness of such legal battles in halting the progress of the movements is less certain. Other NRMs, such as the Moonies and the Scientologists, have proved resilient in such situations, adopting new techniques to improve their public image.

For most of those opposed to the new movements, the ultimate remedy is action from the Pope. So many ex-members and critics of Neocatechumenate, perhaps the most extreme of the three, have told me: 'If only the Pope knew the truth.'

While the pontiff may not be aware of the full details of the accusations against the new movements, he certainly knows that accusations have been made. Father Enrico Zoffoli personally presented John Paul with a copy of his book *The Heresies of the Neocatechumenal Movement*. CL has waged high-profile battles against the Italian episcopate and within the Italian political arena for decades.

The problem is that, given his admiration for the new movements and his investment in them – they are his hope for the future of the Church – he does not want to hear or give credence to these criticisms. Leading members of the hierarchy have testified how the Pope will change the subject when objections to NC are raised in private audience. Though the Pope's knowledge of the movements may be limited to what they and their supporters, such as Bishop Cordes, want him to know, it certainly appears that NC writings, filled as we have seen with strange and dangerous ideas, have been scrutinized by the appropriate authorities at the Vatican – although it could well be that, mindful of the Pope's approval of NC, they were looking over their shoulders as they filed their reports. It must also be borne in mind that the Vatican is now thoroughly infiltrated with sympathizers of the new movements.

It is impossible to say for certain exactly how much the Pope knows about the new movements and therefore to what extent he approves of their fanatical and sect-like nature. It is, however, a crucial question. If he has been deceived, it would be a very serious matter indeed. If not, the implications are even more dire. A remark allegedly made by the Pope, reported to me while visiting the United States for the World Youth Day in 1993, gives a very strong clue. It came from an unexpected source – nothing less than NC's internal grapevine, via members of the movement in Washington, DC.

As I had to pass through Washington on my return journey, I had decided to visit one of the parish groups whose banner I had spotted in Denver – the parish of St Thomas More, in one of the toughest districts in the south of the American capital. In the course of a long conversation with the parish priest and two Italian catechists, an extraordinary example of the Pope's approval was quoted with obvious pride.

Fortunately I was recording our talk, otherwise I would have been tempted not to believe my own ears; I have listened incredulously to the words in question many times since. Knowing from my own experience with Focolare how efficient and reliable the oral transmission of positive news can be within the movements, always avid for praise and approval, I am inclined to take this story at face value. Besides, the remark has a ring of truth about it; and, given its double-edged nature, one cannot see why members of the movement would have invented it. In the course of the Washington conversation, the parish priest suddenly recalled the example of 'the bishop of Puerto Rico' who told the Pope of the terrible troubles he was experiencing with protestant sects who were preying on his flock.

'But didn't you know', the Pope replied, according to the NC account, 'we have a sect of our own – Neocatechumenate.'

BIBLIOGRAPHY

Abbott, Walter M., S. J. (Ed.), *Documents of Vatican II, The,* Geoffrey Chapman, London 1966.

Arbuckle, Gerald A., Arbuckle, S. M., 'Is the Neo-catechumenate Way Compatible with Religous Life?' *Religious Life Review*, Vol. 33, Jan–Feb 1994, no. 164.

Arguello, Kiko and Hernandez, Carmen, *Orientamenti alle equipes di catechisti per la convivenza della rinnovazione del primo scrutinio battesimale,* 1972/86.

Arguello, Kiko and Carmen, Hernandez, *Orientamenti alle equipes di catechisti per la fase di conversione,* Centro Neocatecumenale 'Servo di Jahwe', Rome, 1982.

Arguello, Kiko and Hernandez, Carmen, *Orientamenti alle equipes di catechisti per lo Shema,* Rome, 1974.

Baresta, Luc, 'Le rendez-vous de Vienne', *France Catholique*, 7 May 1993.

Barker, Eileen, *New Religious Movements*, HMSO, London, 1992.

Bezier, Aude-C., 'Les Familles en Mission', in *L'Homme Nouveau*, 2/16 August 1992.

'Bishop checks Neocatechumenate', in *The Tablet*, London, 1/9 April 1994.

Blasquez, Ricardo, *Neo-catechumenal Communities – a theological discernment,* St Paul Publications, England, 1988.

Buckley, Joseph C., 'The Neo-catechumenate', in Priest and People, London, June 1988.

Cammino neocatechumenale – 'Il risonoscimento del Papa', in 'Avvenire', 20 September 1990.

Catechismo della Chiesa Cattolica, Libreria Editrice Vaticana, Vatican City, 1993.

'Cento famiglie in missione: alcune andranno in Siberia', in Avvenire, 4 January 1991.

Christifideles Laici, 'Post-synodal Apostolic Exhortation of Pope John Paul II on the vocation and the mission of the lay faithful', in *In the Church and in the World*, Catholic Truth Society, London, 1988.

'Conseguenze dell 'approfondimento del senso del Battesimo e la necessaria scoperta della vita come vocazione', in *Osservatore Romana*, Vatican City, 29–30 March 1993.

Cordes, Paul-Josef, ' "communio" nella Chiesa, La', in *I movimenti nella Chiesa* – Atti del 2 colloquio internazionale, Nuovo Mondo, Milano, 1987.

Cordes, Paul-Josef, *Charisms and the New Evangelisation*, St Paul Publications, England, 1991.

Comunita Neocatecumenali, Le, Edizioni Paoline, Milan, 1993.

'Dalla fede il metodo', in *Tracce*, Milan, February 1994.

Del Bello, Mario, 'Beyond the Wall', in *New City*, London, April 1991.

Dominian, Jack, *Sexual Integrity*, Darton Longman and Todd, London, 1987.

'Famille en Mondovision, La', ed. Alain Boudre, in *Nouvelle Cite*, Paris, July–August 1993.

'Family must rediscover daily prayer together – address of John Paul II to Neocatechumenal communities, in *Osservatore Romano* – English Edition', Vatican City, 2 February 1994.

Farina, Renato, 'La novita CdO', in *Tracce*, Milan, February 1994.

Gennarini, Giuseppe, 'Seimila dighe contro le sette', in *Avvenire*, December 1991.

Gennarini, Stefano, 'Una testimonianza di evangelizzazione nei Paesi dell'Est', in *Osservatore Romano*, Rome, 8 December 1991.

Giordani, Igino, *Diary of Fire*, New City, London, 1981.

Giussani, Luigi, 'In Cammino', supplement to *30 Giorni* November 1992.

Giussani, Luigi, *The Religious Sense*, Ignatius Press, San Francisco, 1990.

Granfield, Patrick, *The Limits of the Papacy*, Darton, Longman and Todd, London, 1987.

Hawkes, Nigel, 'Therapists will use sympathy to help survivors', in *The Times*, London, 21 April 1993.

Hebblethwaite, Peter, 'Mission of the Laity, The', in *The Tablet*, London, 13 February 1988.

Hebblethwaite, Peter, 'Movements and ministeries', in *The Tablet*, London, 6 February 1988.

Hounam, Peter and Hogg, Andrew, *Secret Cult*, Lion, England 1985.

'Idea of Movement, The', – Three speeches of John Paul II to Communion and Liberation with commentary by Mgr Luigi Giussani, supplement to *30 Days*, September 1989.

'Invest – or else', in *Catholic World Report*, San Francisco, April 1993.

Johnson, Frank, 'All that is ours is yours', in *New City*, London, August/September 1993.

John Paul II, *Discorso, in I movimenti nella Chiesa*: Atti del 2 colloquio internazionale, Nuovo Mondo, Milan, 1987.

'Laity at the Synod', in *The Tablet*, London, 24 October 1987.

'Laity in the light of the Synod, The', *The Tablet*, London, 13 February 1988.

Lifton Dr Robert Jay, *Thought Reform and the Psychology of Totalism: a study of 'brainwashing' in China*. W. W. Norton and Company, New York.

Lubich Chiara, *Cercando le Cose di Lassu*, Città Nuova Editrice, Rome, 1992.

Lubich, Chiara, *Colloqui con i Gen*, Città Nuova Editrice, Rome, 1974.

Lubich, Chiara, *Famiglia per Rinnovare La Societa, Una*, Città Nuova Editrice, Rome, 1993.

Lubich, Chiara, *Meditations*, New City, London, 1971.

Lubich, Chiara, *L'Unita e Gesu Abbandonato*, Città Nuova Editrice, Rome, 1984.

MacReamoinn, Sean, *The Synod on the Laity – An Outsider's Diary*, Blackrock Press, Dublin, 1987.

Moynihan, Robert, 'Valient for God', in *The Tablet*, London, 20 February 1988.

Murphy, Francis, X., *The Papacy Today*, Weidenfeld and Nicolson, London, 1981.

Ottaviano, Franco, *Gli estremisti bianchi*, Datanews, Rome, 1986.

Paliotti, Oreste, 'Da questo vi riconosceranno', in *Città Nuova*, Rome, 10 July 1993.

Paliotti, Oreste, 'Pace attraverso l'unita', in *Città Nuova*, Rome, 10 February 1993.

Paliotti, Oreste, 'Porte aperte alla Santita', in *Città Nuova*, Rome, 10/25 August 1993.

Peguy, 'The Freedom of Laymen', in *30 Days*, San Francisco, February 1991.

Pericoli, Annamaria, 'I musulmani amici del movemento', in *Città Nuova*, Rome, 10 July 1992.

Pochet, Michel, *Stars and Tears – A Conversation with Chiara Lubich*, New City, London, 1985.

'Pontefice Saluta in Vaticano: i nuovi missionari per Est-Europe a Sudemenica', in *Il Messagero*, Rome, 4 January 1991.

'Providence for Today' – speech of Chiara Lubich to Synod on the Laity, in *New City*, London, January 1988.

Robertson, Edwin, *Catching Fire – the spiritual ideal of the Focolare Movement*, Eagle, Guildford (England), 1993.

Rondoni, Davide, 'Il Nulla Gaio', in *Tracce*, Milan, February 1994.

Redemptor Hominis, Encyclical of John Paul II, Catholic Truth Society, London, 1979.

Rocca, Giancarlo, 'Il Lungo "Cammino" di Kiko e Carmen', in *Jesus*, Milan, January 1992.

Rocca, Gino, *Matrimonio, Amore, Vita*, Città Nuova Editrice, Rome, 1992.

Rocca, Gino, *Coscienza, Liberta e Morale*, Città Nuova Editrice, Rome, 1990.

Secondin, Bruno, *I Nuovi Protagonisti – Movimenti, associazioni, gruppi nella Chiesa*, Edizioni Paoline, Milan, 1991.

Serra, Piera, *L'adolescente sublimato*, Guaraldi, Firenze, 1978.

'Siate messageri della riconciliazione e apostoli della fraternita e del servizio', in *Osservatore Romano*, Vatican City, 4 January 1991.

Socci, Antonio, 'Yesterday's Heretic, Today's Pastor?', in *30 Days*, San Francisco, February 1991.

Sorgi, Tommaso, 'La Politica – un amore piu grande', in *Città Nuova*, Rome, 25 December 1993.

'Spunti di Metodo per la Scuola di Communita', in *Litterae Communionis*, Milan, December 1992.

'Theatres into Churches', in *New City*, London, May 1991.

Valente, Gianni, 'Un realismo insopportabile', in *30 Giorni*.

INDEX

Foucauld, Charles de, 408
Fox, Matthew, 115
France, 75, 109, 191 n
France-Catholique, 123
Francis, St, 51, 255, 298, 405
Franciscans, 66, 69, 86, 115, 116,
  170, 186–7, 278, 405
Frascati, 150, 404
fraternal correction, 55–6
Frediani, Eugenio, 247, 248
Freemasonry, 124, 125–6, 127–8,
  213
Freiburg, 314
Fribourg, 78, 200
FUCI, *see* Catholic Action
fundamentalism, 13, 14, 114

Garrochio, Alberto, 318
Gasperi, Acide de, 311
Gaviraghi, 323
Gen, *see* Focolare
Geneva, 200, 315
Gennarini, Giuseppe, 131–2, 136–7,
  183, 213
Georgia, 216
Germany, 67, 79, 167, 178–9, 191
  n, 201, 215, 216, 309
GIAC, see Catholic Action
Giannettone, Umberto, 48, 285
GIE 3F MEDIA, 123, 124
Gilder, Margaret, 84–8
Giordani, Igino, 30, 31, 230, 310,
  314, 337, 339
Gioventu Studentesca, see
  Communion and Liberation: GS
Giussani, Don Luigi, 6, 22, 29, 58,
  146; appearance, 27; bishops,
  139; 'bumping into Christ',
  335–6; 'centredness', 147;
  Christian Event, 24; 'Christian
  has no fear of power', 317;
  conformity and obedience, 278,
  279–80; cultural tastes, 213,
  287–8; defections, 371;
  doctrine, 126, 289–90, 341–3;
  expansion, 201; founds CL,
  118; Fraternities, 148; 'grace',

333; incomprehensible, 279;
International Convention
(1981), 78; International
Convention (1987), 80; John
Paul II, 173; modern world,
265–7; *Morality*, 24;
'Movementism', 185; political
involvement, 269–70, 320;
rebuff from Rome, 327;
Religious Awareness, 24; *Religious
Sense*, 24, 343; Synod on the
Laity (1987), 67, 71–2, 77;
Tantardini and, 405; theology,
279
Glemp, Cardinal, 129
Gloucester, 83
Gnosticism, 335, 357, 369
Graham, Billy, 128
Grazie, 51
Gregorian University, Rome, 24
Gregory VII, 186–7
Grottaferrata, 150
GS, *see* CL
Guardian Angels, London, 136
Guardian, The, 382–3
Guardini, Romano, 287
Guazzelli, Bishop Victor, 134, 136
Guevara, Mgr Abelardo Mata, 167
Gulf War, 126–8
Guzman, Fr José, 184, 297

Haarlem, 110
Haas, Bishop Wolfgang, 142–3
Hagemann, Fr Wilfred, 179
Hamburg, 62, 108–9
Hamer, Cardinal Jerome, 143
Hanselmann, Bishop, 179
Haynes, Ronald, 88–95
Haza, Ofra, 210
Hemmerle, Bishop Klaus, 141, 179
Henry IV, Emperor, 187
Hernandez, Carmen: bishops, 137;
  doctrine, 343–70; founding of
  NC, 156–7; heckles Pope,
  184–5; Italy (1968), 181; John
  Paul II, 7; joins Arguello, 7;
  recognition for NC, 159;